"Sometimes My People Get Mad when the Blackfeet Kill Us"

A Documentary History of the Salish and Pend d'Oreille Indians, 1845-1874

"Sometimes My People Get Mad
when the Blackfeet Kill Us"

— Pend d'Oreille Chief Big Canoe
July 10, 1855

"Sometimes My People Get Mad when the Blackfeet Kill Us"

A Documentary History of the Salish
and Pend d'Oreille Indians,
1845-1874

edited by
Robert Bigart
and
Joseph McDonald

published by
Salish Kootenai College Press
Pablo, Montana

distributed by
University of Nebraska Press
Lincoln, Nebraska

Publication of this book was made possible through the generosity of the Oleta "Pete" Smith Endowment Fund of the Montana Community Foundation.

Cover design: Corky Clairmont, artist/graphic designer, Pablo, Montana.
Cover illustrations:

Library of Congress Cataloging-in-Publication Data:

Names: Bigart, Robert, editor. | McDonald, Joseph, 1933- editor.
Title: Sometimes my people get made when the Blackfeet kill us : a documentary history of the Salish and Pend d'Oreille Indians, 1845-1874 / edited by Robert Bigart and Joseph McDonald.
Description: Pablo, Montana : Salish Kootenai College Press, [2019] | Includes bibliographical references and index.
Identifiers: LCCN 2019011264 | ISBN 9781934594254 (paperback)
Subjects: LCSH: Salish Indians--History--19th century--Sources. | Kalispel Indians--History--19th century--Sources.
Classification: LCC E99.S2 S66 2019 | DDC 978.6004/979435--dc23
LC record available at https://lccn.loc.gov/2019011264

Published by Salish Kootenai College Press, PO Box 70, Pablo, MT 59855.

Distributed by University of Nebraska Press, 1111 Lincoln Mall, Lincoln, NE 68588-0630, order 1-800-755-1105, www.nebraskapress.unl.edu.

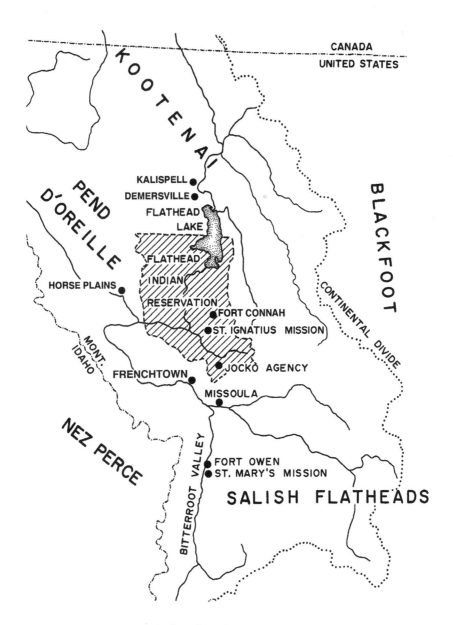

**Flathead Indian Reservation
Showing Tribal Territories
and Surrounding Towns**

Table of Contents

Detailed Table of Contents

Introduction

The written sources on the history of the Salish and Pend d'Oreille people in the nineteenth century offer important insights into the challenges and experiences of the tribal people during a dramatic and dangerous period. The sources reproduced in this collection give glimpses of tribal experiences during this period, but they must be used with caution.

Most important is to remember that almost all of these sources were written by white people who saw the tribes through the distortions of western European values and white bigotry. Virtually all of the writers believed that white American values, social norms, and "civilization" were superior to the traditional culture, norms, and values of the Salish and Pend d'Oreille people.

Some of the sources used language which was culturally loaded and offensive to twenty-first century readers. Documents using offensive language have been included where they describe specific incidents or actions by Indian people. Where documents used an offensive term for Indian women, the editors have represented it with "s...." It is important for the reader to look behind the language and bigotry of the authors to the concrete events. The events related by the writers may be accurate, despite the bigotry which shows up in the documents.

Selection Criteria

The editors have gone through the primary historical sources to find either statements of Indian leaders that express their concerns or descriptions of dealings of white people and other Indians with Salish and Pend d'Oreille people. The statements of tribal leaders in the form of letters from them or quotes from their speeches are valuable, but they also need to be used carefully. These sources might relate the concerns and views of the Indian leaders, but, in almost all cases, they were written down by white people who could have colored the documents.

The white eyewitness descriptions of the condition of the Salish and Pend d'Oreille people and their actions must also be used with discretion. Many of these accounts are fully dressed with the bigotry of the writer, but the specific events or concrete observations could still be accurate.

The editors have had a bias in selecting accounts that are readable and interesting. Many historical sources consist of small isolated references in diaries or short newspaper notes that are valuable but would make less interesting reading. The full source citation for each document is given in the introduction to the document, and the reader is encouraged to look up the sources and read more about the context behind the letter or article reproduced in this collection. Hopefully these documents will whet the appetite of the reader to do further research about the history of the tribes. They are starting points, not end points.

The Salish–Pend d'Oreille World in 1845-1874
Intertribal Warfare

The thirty years between 1845 and 1874 were an intensive period of danger, change, and crisis for the Salish and Pend d'Oreille tribes. After having lost population from disease in the century before 1845, the tribes were threatened with extinction from the war losses resulting from battles with much larger Plains Indian tribes. One way the Salish and Pend d'Oreille countered the military threat from the Plains tribes was by allying with other tribes from west of the Continental Divide and later the new white invaders who fought the same enemies.

Intertribal warfare dominated the sources we found describing the tribes in the early part of this period. The conflicts were bloody and nearly decimated the relatively small Salish and Pend d'Oreille tribes. There were some battles that resulted in especially heavy losses for the tribes. For example, in July 1871, Sioux Chief Sitting Bull led a decoy party of Sioux warriors who attacked a Salish camp in the Musselshell and lured the pursuing Salish into an ambush which resulted in the death of eighteen warriors (document 61). In December 1860, Pend d'Oreille Chief Alexander's camp of buffalo hunters was attacked by a large war party of Assiniboine and Cree Indians on the Milk River (documents 35 & 36). Twenty Pend d'Oreille were killed, twenty-five were wounded, and they lost 290 horses.

Most of the intertribal battles were smaller, less costly affairs. According to Father Pierre DeSmet's September 6, 1846, letter, an 1845 battle between the Salish and Pend d'Oreille against the Blackfeet on the plains resulted in the death of three Pend d'Oreille and one Salish (document 3). Twenty-three Blackfeet were also killed, but the Blackfeet tribe had a far larger population. Camille Williams, a Nez Perce historian, related an account of a skirmish near Fort Benton between the Salish and Nez Perce and the Crow Indians which occurred about 1850 (document 9). Two Salish women were scalped and one was killed. Other examples of Salish and Pend d'Oreille losses in Plains battles can be found in the documents reproduced here.

Some of these battles may not have been as devastating as the 1860 and 1871 encounters mentioned above, but their cumulative cost to the Salish and Pend d'Oreille threatened the survival of the tribes. Governor Isaac Stevens wrote in his 1855 report on the Indians along the proposed northern railroad route that, "The Flatheads [Salish] number about sixty lodges, but many of them are only inhabited by old women and their daughters. The tribe has been almost exterminated by the Blackfeet, and the mass of the nation consist of Pend d'Oreilles, Spokanes, Nez Perces, and Iroquois. I estimated their number at 350." (Isaac I. Stevens, "Report of Explorations for a Route for the Pacific Railroad," in *Reports of Explorations and Surveys, to Ascertain the Most Practicable and Economical Route for a Railroad from the Mississippi River to the Pacific Ocean, 1853-4* [Washington, D.C.: Beverley Tucker, Printer, 1855], vol. 1, page 150.) In August 1871, Frank Wilkeson, a Northern Pacific Railroad surveyor, witnessed a battle between the Pend d'Oreille and the Blackfeet in southern Alberta (document 63). His account did not give an exact casualty number, but he did give a highly colored account of the brave Pend d'Oreille negotiating peace with the cowed Blackfeet.

Spiritual Powers of Christianity

Missionaries and spiritual powers were also important for the Salish and Pend d'Oreille. St. Mary's Mission in the Bitterroot Valley was closed in 1850, but St. Ignatius Mission was moved to its present location in the Flathead Valley in 1854. John Mullan noted in his January 20, 1854, letter that while in camp in 1853 he was awakened in the morning by the singing and praying of the Salish (document 13). Mullan described his Salish guides as "pious, aged, firm, upright, and reliable men; in addition thereto, they entertained a religious belief which they never violated. They partook not of a meal without asking a blessing of God; they never rose in the morning or retired at night without offering a prayer to God."

According to several sources, the Salish and Pend d'Oreille and their enemy tribes credited Christianity as a powerful war medicine. In his September 6, 1846, letter Father Pierre DeSmet wrote that the enemies of the Salish acknowledged that, "The medicine of the Black-gowns. . . is . . .the strongest of all" (document 3). DeSmet went on to relate examples of the Salish praying before battle and winning victory against great odds. One example was an 1846 battle between the Salish and Pend d'Oreille and a Blackfeet party four times their size.

Government Relations

The 1850s were also a time of challenging relations between the Salish and Pend d'Oreille and the United States government. The 1855 Hellgate Treaty is still important in the twenty-first century. At the negotiations on July 10, 1855, Pend d'Oreille Chief Big Canoe gave a long speech which asked why a treaty was needed when the tribes and the white men were not at war (document 18). He also dramatically complained that "the Blackfeet, your own powder and ball shooting at us and you white man. . . .both die with your own powder and ball," and "Sometimes my people get mad when the Blackfeet kill us." On July 13, 1855, the treaty negotiations took a dramatic turn (document 19). Governor Isaac I. Stevens showed his haughtiness and lack of diplomacy. Alexander thought that Stevens talked "sharp; you talk like a Blackfoot." Later Stevens derided Salish Chief Victor as "an old woman? dumb as a dog?" The main point of contention was the location of the Flathead Reservation. Stevens finally got Victor to sign the treaty by promising to have the President survey the Bitterroot and Flathead Valleys and choose the best place for the Salish — Article 11 of the Hellgate Treaty (document 20). Victor almost immediately regretted the provision and on April 25, 1857, Owen reported Victor and the other Salish "now say they will never leave this valley" (document 27). This controversy continued until 1891.

Two months later, in October 1855, the Salish, Pend d'Oreille, Nez Perce, and other tribes negotiated a treaty with the United States government where the Blackfeet made new promises to live in peace with the western tribes and allow a common hunting ground where the western tribes could hunt buffalo on the plains (document 21). Alexander played an important part in the negotiations. Relations continued to be hostile, as the Blackfeet did not honor their pledges. As John Mullan wrote on November 18, 1853, the Blackfeet "have kept their promise most faithlessly" (document 25).

A particular irritant from the Hellgate Treaty for the tribes was the erratic delivery and poor quality of the annuities the government shipped to the tribes. Agent John Owen was disgusted when he learned that the first annuity shipment after the treaty was ratified in 1859 was mainly consumables such as coffee, rice, and hardbread (document 33). Owen wrote on May 25, 1860, that, "The Flatheads are not a barbarous people. They know very well that the lands they sold were not to be paid for in hardbread & the likes." That November 29, when the annuities finally arrived at the Flathead Agency, Owen complained that the products shipped were of poor quality and the coffee was moldy. Reportedly the coffee had been on a steamship that sank in the Missouri River, retrieved from the water, and then sold to the Indian Department.

On April 25, 1865, Victor and five other Salish chiefs complained to the Governor of Montana Territory that white settlers were moving into the Bitterroot Valley in violation of the Hellgate Treaty provision that the valley was to be closed to white settlement until the President had surveyed the Bitterroot and Flathead Valleys (document 44). Flathead Agent Aug. H. Chapman on October 28, 1866, tried to calculate the amount the Hellgate Treaty tribes had been shorted in their annuities (document 46). Chapman concluded that in 1866 the government owed the tribes more than $30,793.50 for annuities that had been misappropriated or charged twice. In a speech by Salish Chief Ambrose enclosed in the August 22, 1868, report by Special Indian Agent W. J. Cullen, Ambrose stated that "Not one half of what was promised us has ever been received by us" (document 50).

A copy of a contract with James Fullerton, a Washington, D.C., lawyer was signed by Salish Chief Charlo, Pend d'Oreille Chief Michelle, and Kootenai Chief Eneas on July 1, 1872 (document 66). Fullerton was to represent the tribes in a legal effort to get the annuities and other goods and services promised in the Hellgate Treaty and not delivered. Unfortunately, no record has been located to indicate any suits or other actions resulting from this attorney contract. Presumably this was the first legal representation hired by the Flathead Reservation tribes.

Relations with the White Men

The Salish and Pend d'Oreille Indians had a long history of good relations with and alliance with the white men who invaded Montana in the nineteenth century. William T. Hamilton left a remarkably detailed and perceptive account of his travels with a Salish buffalo hunting camp on the plains between October 12 and 19, 1858 (document 30). His account detailed the rich social life, singing, and dancing that made camp life so pleasant. The Salish hunters showered him with generosity and hospitality. Another example, which is included in this collection, is John D. Brown's account of traveling with a Salish and Pend d'Oreille camp on the plains between the fall of 1862 and January 1863 (document 38). Brown was a white prospector. The camp was led by Salish Chief Moise. Brown was an honored visitor and treated with great respect. He joined the Salish and Pend d'Oreille in a fight with the Piegan Indians. He was also Moise's guest during the Christmas 1863 celebration.

The Salish and Pend d'Oreille had to work hard to keep the peace with the white men, despite cultural and language differences which could have led to conflict. An October 22, 1873, article in the *Weekly Rocky Mountain Gazette* documented cultural communication problems that rarely left historical evidence (document 76). When the Pend d'Oreille buffalo hunters visited

Helena, they made it a point to check the white people's garbage for discarded clothing, material, metal objects, and other things that were valuable to the Pend d'Oreille. This time, some white people complained that good clothing was missing after the Pend d'Oreille went through town. The Pend d'Oreille women brought out the rags, clothing, and other gleanings to show the Deputy Sheriff they had not taken anything that was of value to the whites.

On May 7, 1871, Charlo and six other chiefs complained about the problem of white settlers in the Bitterroot Valley "and the results of the contact and association are, the drunkenness of our young men, to whom the whites will sell whiskey, as well as the demoralization of our women, which it seems impossible, with the greatest watchfulness on our part, to prevent"(document 60).

Some sources show how successful the Salish were in fostering good relations between the white settlers and Salish Indians living in the Bitterroot Valley. Carrie May Warren's reminiscences of life in the Bitterroot Valley between 1874 and 1890, are an example of friendship despite cultural difficulties (document 82). Warren remembered cordial relations between the Salish and whites in the valley. The whites did not even lock their doors. On New Year's Day the Salish went to all the white men's houses to shake hands in greeting and respect.

Farming and Cattle Replace the Buffalo

The documents in this collection spell out the willingness of the Salish and Pend d'Oreille tribes to develop farms as the buffalo herds declined, their problems in getting plows and other farming equipment, and their success in growing their farms and cattle herds between 1855 and 1874. In his report on the 1855 treaty negotiations for Congressman James A. Garfield, Henry Crosby, Stevens' secretary, noted that in 1855 the Salish and Pend d'Oreille cultivated small patches of ground where they raised potatoes and other vegetables (document 17). The tribes also had a few cows in 1855 and some excellent horses.

In his September 20, 1858, letter, Owen reported that when he asked Victor how to spend a $1,000 gift from the government (document 29), Victor asked for half of the money to be spent on ammunition and tobacco and the other half to be used for a plow and to prepare a field to plant wheat so they would have flour as the buffalo were growing scarce. In the April 25, 1865, letter from Victor and five other Salish chiefs to the Governor of Montana, Victor noted that they had received some plows from the government that spring and "we are all busy, and in great earnest to make ourselves fields" (document 44).

According to Chapman, on October 28, 1866, Big Canoe said "We are now willing to work; get us seed, stock, harness, Oxen, wagons, and farming and other tools, and see what we can do" (document 46). On June 14, 1867, Flathead Agent John W. Wells wrote that when he tried to call a council with the Bitterroot Salish Indians he had to wait several days because the Salish were busy plowing and sowing their fields (document 49). Special Agent Cullen on August 22, 1868, recorded the story of an elderly Bitterroot Salish Indian who lacked farming tools: "Look at these; they are my tools; I scratch the ground with my nails" (document 50).

On January 23, 1871, Agent C. S. Jones found the Bitterroot Salish had 90 heads of families, and some 54 of them were well-to-do farmers who produced 500 to 600 bushels of wheat annually (document 59). In his September 1, 1871, annual report, Jones reported that the reservation Pend d'Oreille had 70 farms ranging from 5 to 60 acres, averaging 15 acres each (document 64). In 1870 the Pend d'Oreille produced over 3,000 bushels of wheat, 900 bushels of oats, 1,000 bushels of potatoes, and 50 bushels of corn. The Pend d'Oreille had 800 head of cattle, 100 head of hogs, and 2,000 horses. The reservation Salish had 35 farms averaging 12 acres each which in 1870 produced 2,000 bushels of wheat, 5,000 bushels of oats, 650 bushels of potatoes, and 60 bushels of corn. The reservation Salish had 600 head of cattle, 100 hogs, and 1,100 horses.

The critical shortage of farming tools among the Bitterroot Salish was demonstrated in a November 23, 1872, article in a Deer Lodge newspaper (document 71). The author found Indian women in the Bitterroot threshing wheat by hand on a large cloth. Another Indian farmer was able to hire a thresher to harvest his grain.

One of the most important accounts of Salish Indian farming was given by Martin Charlo to Verne Dusenberry, a Montana State University English professor (document 57). Charlo described how the Salish farmers had worked hard over the years to develop farms in the Bitterroot Valley and later on the Flathead Reservation only to suffer repeated setbacks when the government intervened to force them out of the Bitterroot Valley or to construct an irrigation system in the Jocko Valley.

Conclusion

Between 1845 and 1874 the Salish and Pend d'Oreille people suffered greatly from intertribal war losses against much more powerful Plains Indian tribes. They struggled to get the United States government to honor its promises of educational and economic aid in exchange for ceding western Montana for white settlement. New powers from the missionaries gave some spiritual assistance and comfort. Keeping the peace with the white settlers was always a challenge and took constant work. One of the most significant changes, however, was expanding the farming and cattle herds to take up the slack from the declining buffalo and other game resources. The Salish and Pend d'Oreille people found capable leaders who made it possible to survive these traumas. The tribes persisted and worked hard to maintain their economic and political independence.

Robert Bigart
Joseph McDonald

Chapter 1

Documents of Salish and Pend d'Oreille History Between 1845 and 1849

Document 1

Snapshots of Salish Battles
Against the Blackfeet and Bannack Tribes
ca. 1845-1846

Source: Nicholas Point, S.J., Image IX C 9.062-081, Oversize Drawer 1, Rocky Mountain Sketches by Nicolas Point, De Smetiana Collection, Jesuit Archives and Research Center, St. Louis, Missouri. Accessed October 22, 2018, https://jesuitarchives.omeka.net/items/show/164.

Editors' note: These drawings of the war experiences of Salish Chiefs Victor, Ambrose, Teltella Fidele, and others and the Pend d'Oreille woman warrior Quilix are tantalizing. They may have been drawn to illustrate a manuscript describing the war experiences of Salish leaders in the 1840s, but no manuscript has been located. As it is, the drawings and their captions can only offer snapshots of the remarkable bravery of the Salish leaders of the time. A few of the drawings refer to events mentioned in an undated letter by Father Point in P. J. De Smet, S. J., *Oregon Missions and Travels Over the Rocky Mountains, in 1845-46* (New York: Edward Dunigan, 1847), pages 400-404. The French captions on the drawings, presumably written by Point, have been translated by Elizabeth A. Hubble.

The Blackfeet referred to in the captions who were friendly with the Salish were probably the Little Robes band who were on good terms with the Salish until they were wiped out in a battle with the Crow Indians in 1845. For more about the drawings and their historical context see John C. Ewers, "The Nicholas Point Drawings: A Pictorial Record of Plains and Rocky Mountain Indian Life 150 Years Ago," *Columbia: The Magazine of Northwest History*, vol. 10, no. 3 (Fall 1996), pages 24-30.

The first arrivals. Teltella (the Faithful), Ambroise, Isaac, Ferdinand, Manuel.
Drawing by Nicholas Point, S.J., IX C 9.062, Jesuit Archives and Research
Center, St. Louis, Missouri.

The conquerors of the Blackfeet take them to the Black Robe with whom
they offer to shake hands. Drawing by Nicholas Point, S.J., IX C 9.063,
Jesuit Archives and Research Center, St. Louis, Missouri.

The principal Blackfeet smoke with Victor in the Black Robe's lodge and promise that from this point forward the Flathead's prayer will be theirs. Drawing by Nicholas Point, S.J., IX C 9.064, Jesuit Archives and Research Center, St. Louis, Missouri.

The Blackfeet and the Flatheads make mutual exchanges amicably. Drawing by Nicholas Point, S.J., IX C 9.065, Jesuit Archives and Research Center, St. Louis, Missouri.

Insurrection averted [or calmed down]. Drawing by Nicholas Point, S.J., IX C 9.066, Jesuit Archives and Research Center, St. Louis, Missouri.

A Blackfoot chief, after having seen the Catholic ladder that Ambrose, chief of the Flatheads, explains to him, asks to become part of the Flatheads, him and his twenty-eight lodges. Drawing by Nicholas Point, S.J., IX C 9.067, Jesuit Archives and Research Center, St. Louis, Missouri.

Hunters descend on the Blackfeet. Drawing by Nicholas Point, S.J., IX C 9.068, Jesuit Archives and Research Center, St. Louis, Missouri.

Extermination of thirty Blackfeet by the Pend d'Oreilles at the head of whom is a woman named Quilix. Drawing by Nicholas Point, S.J., IX C 9.069, Jesuit Archives and Research Center, St. Louis, Missouri.

Victor, surrounded by an entire Blackfoot camp, saves himself from their hands after having broken his bow, his last resource. Drawing by Nicholas Point, S.J., IX C 9.070, Jesuit Archives and Research Center, St. Louis, Missouri.

The great chief Victor defends himself all alone against an entire Blackfoot village with a single arrow as his only arm. Drawing by Nicholas Point, S.J., IX C 9.071, Jesuit Archives and Research Center, St. Louis, Missouri.

Victor pursuing two [mountain] goats, is attacked by a considerable party that he had to put to flight. Drawing by Nicholas Point, S.J., IX C 9.072, Jesuit Archives and Research Center, St. Louis, Missouri.

Ambrose, on the same day, disarming a Blackfoot, breaking his bow at the moment when another Blackfoot takes flight, and chasing five runaways into the river. Drawing by Nicholas Point, S.J., IX C 9.073, Jesuit Archives and Research Center, St. Louis, Missouri.

Adolphe protects a sick man and kills a Blackfoot with his lance after having been wounded by two arrows that he pulled out himself on the battlefield. Drawing by Nicholas Point, S.J., IX C 9.074, Jesuit Archives and Research Center, St. Louis, Missouri.

Teltella (the Thunder) falls on a Blackfoot party with his hatchet in his hand. Drawing by Nicholas Point, S.J., IX C 9.075, Jesuit Archives and Research Center, St. Louis, Missouri.

Smoiré attacks a Blackfoot fort all alone. One of whom he starts to ride like a horse. He took part in sixty-five battles and was never wounded. Drawing by Nicholas Point, S.J., IX C 9.076, Jesuit Archives and Research Center, St. Louis, Missouri.

Having no more powder, Teltella wounds a Blackfoot with the barrel of his gun. Drawing by Nicholas Point, S.J., IX C 9.077, Jesuit Archives and Research Center, St. Louis, Missouri.

Isaac takes a Blackfoot's knife at the moment he was going to be stabbed.
Drawing by Nicholas Point, S.J., IX C 9.078, Jesuit Archives and Research
Center, St. Louis, Missouri.

Alone, Eugene follows a Blackfoot party who had just killed his sister.
Drawing by Nicholas Point, S.J., IX C 9.079, Jesuit Archives and Research
Center, St. Louis, Missouri.

Ignatius, Victor's son-in-law, puts to flight nine Blackfeet after receiving two serious wounds. Drawing by Nicholas Point, S.J., IX C 9.080, Jesuit Archives and Research Center, St. Louis, Missouri.

Isadore hits a Bannack with an arrow that will plant itself in the earth behind the dead man. Drawing by Nicholas Point, S.J., IX C 9.081, Jesuit Archives and Research Center, St. Louis, Missouri.

Document 2

The Sign of the Cross in a Battle Against the Crow Indians
August 1846

Source: Cornelius M. Buckley, S.J., *Nicolas Point, S.J.: His Life & Northwest Indian Chronicles* (Chicago: Loyola University Press, 1989), pages 277-285.

Editors' note: Father Point told of a battle on the plains between a combined party of Pend d'Oreilles, Flatheads, Coeur d'Alénes, Nez Percés, and Blackfeet against the Crows. The western tribes made the sign of the cross before the battle and defeated the Crows. Father Pierre De Smet wrote about the same events in his September 6, 1846, letter. Footnotes have been omitted.

Flathead and Blackfeet: Brothers-in-arms for the First Time.
by Nicolas Point, S.J.

Almost all of the Flatheads were hunting [in August 1846], and yet war between them and the Crow, a large nation we hoped to conquer for the Lord, was imminent. So, after offering the Holy Sacrifice in honor of the Queen of Heaven, the patroness of St. Mary's, we left this pious reduction on the day of Mary's great feast. This day, August 15, [the Assumption, 1846], was also the anniversary of our first meeting with those destined to become her children. On the following day, accompanied by four half-breeds of the Crow nation, three of whom were from the Red River, and by four Indians, two of whom were Blackfeet, we entered the famous pass called Hell's Gate. It goes without saying we experienced the horrors of that terrifying gorge, horrors which I have described in previous letters. But in this letter it is not my intent to describe scenery but rather to record historical facts. But I will say that what struck me most on this trip was the abundance of fruit we came across, in much greater profusion this year than usual. And near Three Forks I noticed a huge variety of flowers, due to the moisture of the soil, I should think. Another day's distance approaching Crow territory, we were struck by the diversity of bushes growing everywhere, and by many deep ravines as well. Such a country offers ideal haunts for wild beasts and for the Blackfeet as well, and indeed it is regarded as headquarters for both. For this reason it is better for a small group like ours to pass through this country under cover of darkness. But since we had more reason than most travelers to put trust in Divine Providence, we decided to make our way during only part of the night and all of the day. Still, we resolved to be particularly discrete, and to walk without making any noise. Such a resolution, however, was difficult for our young escorts to keep, and as soon as four bears appeared on our right our defenders took off recklessly, shouting and firing. "Oh, how rash; how rash!" cried Father [Pierre] De Smet in vain, but this did not bring them back at all. Far from it. They seemed to be charging harder than usual even for a hunt, and the result was an accident. Our youngest Blackfoot charged the bears with such abandon that his horse stumbled, causing horse and rider to tumble over one another. We thought that surely both had broken their necks, but both escaped with only stiff necks. By forcing us to halt, this event gave us the opportunity to say Mass on the following morning. This we did in the middle of the brush as quietly as thieves, making up for the previous day's imprudence. After breakfast our poor little Blackfoot climbed back on his horse, but his neck was still stiffer than we had expected it would be, forcing us to begin our day's journey at a slow pace. But it wasn't long before we picked up the same trot that had brought us this far. With the Indians sprains and many other kinds of ailments heal rapidly. Besides, pending danger makes one exert oneself more.

At last we came on the Flatheads' trail, and the remains of a recently built camp our Blackfeet found were most encouraging, for here were the long poles used exclusively by their tribesmen; the pickets set in position according to the methods peculiar to the Nez Percés and the indisputable signs that the Flatheads, too, had camped here. All of these remnants convinced our guides and ourselves that all three nations had become allies to show strength against the Crows, who were not merely mighty in numbers but also ready to pick a quarrel. At this point it seemed to us that we had all but reached our tribe, and so to be united with them we took off across the fields in the direction where we thought they were. But what happened? After pressing ahead without a stop until noon, we found nothing before us but a wilderness without water. We decided not to tire all our horses further, but that the best mounts would continue the search while the others rested. But where could the tribe be? Which way should we go? Fortunately at this juncture, and to our great relief, a herd of buffalo came charging in our direction, and as everyone knows, when these animals stampede in one direction, it is a sign that they are being chased from the other. And who besides our own hunters could be pursuing them? Although this argument was not altogether convincing to us, it seemed to be so to our guides, and so off they took without further adieu. As for us, we followed their example a few minutes later, but hoping to find a safe spot to await their return, we headed in the opposite direction. Six hours later the two groups were still separated from each other. Were our guides dead or alive? Were they fighting the Crow or were they enjoying the fellowship of the Flatheads? The answers to these questions we did not know, but what we knew only too well was this: we were lost even though we were back almost to our point of departure. A short distance ahead of us we could see a gorge or, rather, a wide crevice in the middle of the prairie, and it was toward this point that we directed our steps. The crevice was quite deep and honeycombed with Indian defenses and fortifications. Presently we came upon a little spring around which we discerned human tracks. This discovery caused our Blackfeet to rejoice for a second time, and they immediately took off for a reunion with our scouts. Then in a few minutes, pale and trembling, the Blackfeet returned. What was the matter? The tracks were not left by friends but by enemies, and if we continued in the direction we had chosen we would be done for, killed. We were headed straight toward a Nez Percé camp and it was true that the Nez Percés were anything but well disposed toward the Blackfeet. But we finally convinced our Blackfeet that they had nothing to fear if they came along with us. So, after more coaxing they agreed to continue, hiding themselves behind us as we proceeded. Finally, when we arrived among the Nez Percés, we learned that our trust in Providence had not been in vain, for this meeting became an occasion for rejoicing for everyone present. For me, because I recognized right off several catechumens I had instructed only a few months previously in the truths of our holy religion. For Father De Smet, because he was delighted to make their acquaintance. And for the Blackfeet, who received nothing but the warmest welcome from the hands of the Nez Percés. This was so because they were with us and also because of the awkward position in which the Nez Percés found themselves. Despite their small number, their ignorance of the country, and the fact that large war parties were scouting the territory in all directions, these Nez Percés had rashly come into Blackfeet land. Just the day before we arrived, the best of their horses had disappeared from the corral, a proof the enemy was not far distant. As long as we remained with them we tried to make the teachings of our holy religion penetrate their hearts, which were already well disposed, thanks to their dealings with the Flatheads and Coeur d'Aléne. Each evening our friends who had accompanied us — Flatheads, Pend d'Oreilles, Crees and Blackfeet — mingled with the camp's young people and then, converging from every corner of the camp, began singing, shouting, jumping up and down — in a word, Indian showing off, and in a manner I had never before seen or heard, since such demonstrations were out of character for the Flatheads, especially so since their conversion, and not according to the customs of the Oregon peace-loving Indians. But when the Blackfeet and Nez Percés have reason to believe enemies are stalking in the vicinity, they carry on like this. The fewer their numbers, the noisier their antics; the more they quake with fear, the more they strut and swagger. The reason is easy to understand.

The Nez Percés had designated August 27 [1846], three days since we and our scouts had parted, as the day for their big hunt. By this date we were a good distance from the Nez Percé and Blackfoot camps as well as from the spot designated as our rendezvous with our scouts, a fact which meant that these scouts would now have a considerable distance to cover in order to find us. These matters were on our minds when, accompanied by a Flathead named Peter John, one of the scouts appeared in camp. Peter John, incidentally, was the first of his people to pray in the Flathead language, and for this reason he was named after Father De Smet.

What news did he bring? We were about to go to war. Were the Crows numerous? Indeed they were; five times our size.

Leaving camp with Peter John, Father De Smet instructed me to remain behind to baptize some children on the morrow. Then, after placing nine souls on the road to heaven, I set out with all of our companions on the following day. As best we could we followed Father De Smet's tracks, for we had no other guide. We had traveled some distance when we spotted a camp on the horizon. Whether it was Flathead or Crow we could not yet determine. But there was one matter about which there was no question — we were in enemy territory. All about us series of trenches, battlements, earthworks, and buttresses told us plainly that war was the only purpose they served. Their presence was made all the more awesome by the fact that the countryside teemed with warriors. But as we progressed, the sharp eye of our Blackfeet served to lessen their anxiety. Finally, a knight of this wilderness came running toward us. His presence gave us assurance beyond doubt, for he was George, a dear friend of the Black Robes'. On one occasion he had saved a Black Robe's life, and now this same Black Robe stood before him! You can imagine our mutual delight. Yet, George's joy seemed flawed. He looked like a man who is uncertain whether he had conducted himself correctly. What had he done? On the day before he had fought the Crows alongside his brothers-in-arms with such valor that victory was theirs. But wouldn't this victory delay the conversion of the vanquished? That was his apprehension, the cause for his melancholic expression, an expression which was reflected on the faces of several others who had also participated so nobly in this same encounter. But we could only praise their behavior when that evening, we heard from their own modest lips, the most modest perhaps that have ever existed, an account of those incidents which had forced them to use means other than patience in dealing with the Crow. We then reassured them and watched the doubts dissolve. However, all of us still had reason for apprehension, for we expected a more infuriated enemy to return and clear the record of their shameful performance on the field of battle. But our fears were for naught; the Crows, no more ashamed than terrified, dared not to renew the combat.

Among the Crow, as among all Indians who frequently engage in warfare, there are some truly brave warriors, but if one listens to those who are the least brave, he will hear that there is no nation under the sun comparable to the Crow. In describing their daring and strength, they like to compare themselves to a raging buffalo — it never retreats; no barrier can hold it back; it tears down everything that gets in its way. On the other hand, they regard their enemies as mere women or even as young calves who can but tremble. So they described the Flatheads. But, as we have already seen, this rhetoric had not prevented the Flatheads from hunting in Crow territory nor had it prevented them from taking under their protection the remnant of that wretched tribe (the Little Robes), which two years previously had escaped the wrath of the Crow. It would never do, said the Flatheads, that the Crow imagine that because now we live in the fear of the Lord, we fear men more than before. It is our intention to teach the Crow with harsh lessons that the opposite is true. God knows we want peace, that we will never be the first to break it, and that we wish the Crow well, but if they attack us we will defend ourselves with vigor. Such was the attitude and such were the words employed by the Flatheads when the Crow set up camps near them and began to threaten them.

How did these Crow, once so full of pride, now behave toward their former friends? Instead of treating them as friends or even as sincere people, they insulted them beyond all limits. One Crow armed with a stick, they bragged, was all that it would take to chase off one hundred Flatheads. And despite their chiefs, who tried to moderate their folly, these brutes added insult to injury when they pretended to sack the Flathead camp by tearing down branches that formed the palisade, and even by going so far as to aim their rifles at Flathead chiefs, who remained as brave as they were patient. Matters had gone this far and Victor, the head chief, had felt the surge of exaltation that immediately precedes the war cry building up in himself when another cry was heard: "The Black Robes are coming! And the Nez Percés and Pend d'Oreilles!" This news was repeated over and over again until it re-echoed throughout the camp. When the Crow chiefs heard the cry which confounded their people's intent, they added to their counsels for prudence the cry *Amaraba! Amaraba!"* that is: "We must go! We must go!" The repetition of this word, accompanied by vigorous beating with poles, convinced even the most obstinate; so, they all decided whether they liked it or not to retreat without striking a blow.

The Flatheads spent the night thanking heaven for such a happy ending. But the next day in broad daylight the Crows stole thirty horses right from under their noses; and, because of a misunderstanding, one innocent Crow was forced to pay the price for the guilty. This mistake was all that it took to enrage all the other Crows. In spite of prompt atonement for this all too hasty injury, the fires of war flared. God allowed this evil but only because He wanted to see His own cause triumph.

Around ten o'clock in the morning the Crows came galloping in a cloud so thick it hid the hills from sight, and they pressed down on the allied camp under the illusion that nothing could stem their force. But the allies had expected a sudden attack, and so after safeguarding all who were not able to defend themselves behind a strong stockade, they ranged themselves in a line outside the camp to await the action. As soon as the attackers were within musket range, Titche Loutso — or Moses, as he was named at baptism — first prayed there with his little troops which formed the vanguard, then stood and addressed them. "My friends," he said, "if God wishes us to be victors, that we shall be. If He does not, may His will be done. Meanwhile, let us turn our thoughts to Him and be brave." Immediately one of his men fired at the enemy. The Crows ceased their attack and began making a series of turnings and caperings in a most swaggering fashion, all of which only served to tire their horses. Victor, seeing what was happening, shouted: "Now, brothers, mount! Forward!" Every warrior rushed the enemy with such force that the Crows' cavalry had to fall back two miles, retreating to their base of operations with the same speed they had used in charging. The head chief's two feathers were seen constantly on the road of honor just like the plume of Good King Henry in days of yore. The story was that on whatever flank Titiche Loutso directed his horse, whole rows of the enemy took flight. However, making up in numbers for what they lacked in courage, the Crows charged again and again, but each time they were made to see that God's children were invincible when they placed their trust in their heavenly Father. During these combats the youngest warriors displayed a fearlessness which astonished the elders who in turn attributed this mettle to their Christian faith. Even women proved to the Crows that if the weaker sex was to be found on the battlefield it was in their own ranks. At the very height of the melee a mother of seven threw herself with such frantic energy between her eldest and a Crow that the latter had to run off. Another younger woman went out onto the field of battle and picked up the arrows that rained down upon her and with these she replenished the depleting quivers of our warriors. A third woman, having advanced too far in pursuit of the enemy, wheeled her horse about with uncanny dexterity just as several enemy hands stretched out to pull her down and galloped back to our lines, leaving the enemy stupified by her retreat. Finally, the famous Huitix [Kuilix], mentioned above, accompanied by a few braves and armed with an axe, gave chase to a whole squadron of Crows. When they got back to camp, she said to her companions, "I thought that those big talkers were men, but I was wrong. Truly, they are not worth pursuing."

In all the fighting, nine Crows were killed and fourteen were wounded. One Flathead had fallen off his horse, but was none the worse for it, and never had the supporting Blackfeet shown such heroism. Nicolas and Gervais, the first baptized of the nation, had distinguished themselves in a special manner, and yet not one hair of their heads had been touched. Both they and the Flatheads attributed their good fortune to the fact that they had made the sign of the cross before engaging in combat. What confirmed them in this pious belief was the death of a young Nez Percé whose father, the tribe's chief, had not protected himself as they had with this sign of victory. So, with sentiments of faith and thanksgiving, they offered seventy-six of their children to be baptized. This was the greatest fruit of the whole day.

May this beautiful harvest of their Church be a continual proof of right over might, and even more of heaven over hell.

Document 3

Another View of an 1846 Battle with the Crow Indians September 6, 1846

Source: Pierre DeSmet, S.J. to "Reverend and Dear Father Provincial," Sept. 6, 1846, P. J. De Smet, S. J., *Oregon Missions and Travels Over the Rocky Mountains, in 1845-46* (New York: Edward Dunigan, 1847), pages 288-310.

Editors' note: Among other things, Father DeSmet related accounts of a number of battles between the Christianized Salish Indians and their enemies where the power of the cross gave the Salish victory. Father Nicholas Point wrote about the same journey east of the Continental Divide and the battle with the Crow Indians in 1846 as Father DeSmet described in some detail in this letter. The Blackfeet who fought with the Bitterroot Salish and Pend d'Oreilles, were survivors of the Little Robes band of Blackfeet who were friendly with the Salish and Pend d'Oreilles and had been decimated by the Crow in an 1845 battle.

A. M. D. G.

Flat-Head Camp, Yellowstone River,
September 6th, 1846.

Rev. and Dear Father Provincial, —

After an absence of about eighteen months, employed in visiting the various distant tribes, and extending among them the kingdom of Christ, I returned to the nursery, so to speak, of our Apostolic labors in the Rocky Mountains. Judge of the delight I experienced, when I found the little log church, we built five years ago, about to be replaced by another which will bear comparison with those in civilized countries, materials, everything ready to commence erecting it, the moment they can procure some ropes to place the heavy timbers on the foundation. Another agreeable surprise, however, yet awaited me; a mill had been constructed, destined to contribute largely to the increasing wants of the surrounding country. It is contrived to discharge the two-fold charitable object of feeding the hungry and sheltering the houseless. The flour mill grinds ten or twelve bushels in a day; and the saw mill furnishes an abundant supply of plank, posts, etc., for the public and private building of the nation settled here.

Indeed, the location stood much in need of so useful a concern. The soil yields abundant crops of wheat, oats and potatoes — the rich prairie here is capable of supporting thousands of cattle. Two large rivulets, now almost useless, can, with a little labor, be made to irrigate the fields, gardens, and orchards of the village. The stock at present on this farm, consists of about forty head of cattle, a fast-increasing herd of hogs and a prolific progeny of domestic fowl. In addition to the mill, twelve log houses, of regular construction, have been put up. Hence, you can form some ideas of the temporal advantages enjoyed by the Flat-heads of St. Mary's village.

St. Mary's, or Bitter-Root valley, is one of the finest in the mountains, presenting, throughout its whole extent of about two hundred miles, numerous grazing, but few arable tracts of land. Irrigation, either by natural or artificial means, is absolutely necessary to the cultivation of the soil, in consequence of the long summer drought that prevails in this region, commencing in April and ending only in October. This difficulty, however, if the country should be ever thickly settled, can be easily obviated, as the whole region is well supplied with numerous streams and rivulets. These remarks apply to the valleys contiguous to St. Mary's, the general aspect of them differing perhaps but slightly in regard to the heights of the mountains, the colossal dimensions of the rocks, or the vast extent of the plains.

After what has been said in my former letters in relation to religion, little now remains that has a direct reference to it; but you will learn with much pleasure, that the improvements made in the Flat-head village, afford the missionary stationed there great facilities for prosecuting successfully the grand object of his desires, viz., the eternal happiness of the poor benighted Indian tribes, placed beyond the reach of his immediate influence. The village is now the centre of attraction to all the neighboring, and many of the distant tribes. The missionary always avails himself of these occasional visits, to convey to them the glad tidings of salvation. Among the recent visitors were, the great chief of the Snake Indians with his band of warriors; the Banax and Nez-Percés, conducted by several of their chiefs, — even several bands of Black-Feet; besides these, there were also, on their return from the great hunt, almost the whole tribe of the Pends-d'Oreilles, belonging to the station of St. Francis Borgia. These last in particular, the greater part of whom I baptized last year, may be said to rival the zeal of the Flat-Heads in the practice of their religious duties.

After the festival of Easter, the abundant supply of provisions, in the granaries and cellars of the village, enabled the minister to invite all the visitors present to a feast, consisting of potatoes, parsnips, turnips, beets, beans, peas, and a great variety of meats, of which the greater portion of the guests had never before tasted. Among the industrial products which are mainly owing to the skill and assiduity of their present pastor, Father [Gregory] Mengarini, I must not forget to mention a kind of sugar, extracted from the potato.

Let us next turn to the improved condition of the people themselves. Polygamy — or rather a connection, if possible, still more loose — is now, thank God, entirely abolished among our newly-converted Indians; there is, consequently, an evident increase of population. The reckless abandonment of the helpless infant — the capricious discarding of wife and children — the wanton effusion of human blood — are no longer known amongst them. Our feelings are not outraged by the brutal practice, heretofore so commonly witnessed, of a father considering a horse a fair exchange for his daughter; the justice of allowing the young Indian maiden to choose her future partner for life is now universally allowed; — the requisite care of their offspring is regarded in its proper light, as a Christian duty; — attention is paid to the wants of the sick; — changes of treatment, with the remedies administered according to our advice, have probably been the means, under Providence, of rescuing many from premature death. The long-cherished vindictive feelings which so frequently led to depopulating wars, are now supplanted by a Christian sense of justice, which, if unfortunately compelled to take up arms, does so only to repel unjust aggression or defend their inherent rights, but always with the fullest confidence in the protecting arm of Heaven.

Indeed their unbounded confidence in the God of battle, is well rewarded; a truth which the enemies of the Flat-Heads invariably acknowledge. "The medicine of the Black-gowns," (an expression synonymous with the true religion,) "is," say they, "the strongest of all." Did time permit, I could adduce almost innumerable instances to confirm the belief universally entertained here, that Almighty God visibly protects them in the wars they are compelled to wage with the hostile tribes. A few of these, for the authenticity of which I can vouch, may suffice for the present.

In 1840, when threatened by a formidable band of Black-Feet, amounting to nearly eight hundred warriors, the Flat-Heads and Pends-d'Oreilles, scarcely numbering sixty, betook themselves to prayer, imploring the aid of Heaven, which alone could save them in the unequal contest. Confident of success, they rose from their knees in the presence of their enemies, and engaged the overwhelming odds against them. The battle lasted five days. The Black-Feet were defeated, leaving eighty warriors dead upon the field; while the Flat-Heads and Pends-d'Oreilles sustained a loss of only one man; who, however, survived the battle four months, and had the happiness of receiving the baptism the day before his death.

In 1842, four Pends-d'Oreilles and a Pointed Heart were met and immediately attacked by a party of Black-Feet. At the first onset, the Black-Feet had to deplore the loss of their chief. Aroused by the noise of the musketry, the camp of the Pends-d'Oreilles rushed to the assistance of their companions, and without losing a single man, completely routed the enemy. Their escape is the more remarkable, as rushing into the entrenchments of the Black-Feet, they received a volley of shot poured in upon them by the enemy.

The Flat-Heads were again attacked, during the winter hunt of 1845, by a party of the Banax, which, though outnumbering them nearly three times, they soon put to flight, with the loss of three of the Banax party. The Flat-Heads acknowledge that the Banax are the bravest of their enemies; yet this did not deter them, though but seven in number, from fighting a whole village of the latter, that had rashly violated the rights of hospitality.

During the summer hunt of the same year, the united camp of Flat-Heads and Pends-d'Oreilles, when threatened, hesitated not a moment to engage with a band of Black-Feet four times their number. The latter, fearing the "medicine of the Black-gowns," skulked around their enemies, avoiding an open fight. The former perceiving this, pretended flight, in order to draw the Black-Feet into the open plain: the snare succeeded; and the Flat-Heads and Pends-d'Oreilles suddenly wheeling, attacked and repulsed them with considerable loss, driving the enemy before them in hot pursuit, as they would a herd of buffaloes. Twenty-three Black-Feet warriors lay dead on the field, after the engagement, while the Pends-d'Oreilles lost but three, and the Flat-Heads only one.

I shall close these sketches of Indian warfare, so remarkably evincing, as they do, the special protection of Heaven, with an account of an engagement which, as it was the occasion of my first interview with the Black-Feet, and by its consequences contributed much towards my favorable reception among them, will not I trust, prove entirely devoid of interest, if given a little more in detail.

In 1846, while engaged in one of these hunting excursions, the camp of the Flat-Heads was reinforced by thirty lodges of the Nez-percés, and dozen lodges of the Black-Feet at their own solicitation. The Flat-Heads encamped in the neighbourhood of the Crows, purposely to renew the terms of peace, if the latter felt so disposed. The Crows, perceiving in the united camp, the Nez-percés and Black-Feet, with whom they were at war, and knowing their own superiority both in numbers and bodily strength, (they are the most robust of the Indian tribes) rushed into it like a torrent, evidently more anxious to provoke a contest than to make overtures of peace. The calm remonstrances of the Flat-Heads, and the wise admonitions of their own chief, were lost upon the now almost infuriated mutinous band of the Crows.

If the threatened outbreak had occurred at that moment, it is probable that the whole united camp would have been massacred in the hand-fight, for which evidently the Crows came prepared, with loaded guns and other destructive weapons, while the Flat-Heads and the others were totally unprovided. At this critical juncture, fortunately, indeed I may say providentially, my interpreter Gabriel, and a Pend-d'Oreille named Charles, forced their way breathless into the disordered camp, and announced the arrival of the *Black-gown* who had visited them four years ago. The alarming scene they witnessed was indeed what they had expected for as we travelled to overtake the Flat-Head camp at the place designed for their interview with the Crows, we perceived from the marks of their daily encampments, that some Black-Feet and Pends-d'Oreilles were with the Flat-Heads; we accordingly feared a collision would result from the interview. I therefore despatched with all possible speed, Gabriel and Charles, to announce my arrival. Well did they execute the commission — they rode almost at a full gallop during a whole day and night, performing in this short period a journey which occupied the camp fourteen days. This intelligence roused the Crow chiefs to an energetic exercise of their authority. They now seized the first missiles at hand, and enforced the weight of their arguments upon their mutinous subjects, as long as there was left in the united camp the back of a Crow on which to inflict punishment. This forced separation, though it may have checked the present ebullition, could not be of long duration. It needed but a spark to rekindle their hostile dispositions into open war. The next day, as if to provoke a rupture, the disaffected Crows stole thirty horses from the Flat-Heads. Two innocent persons were unfortunately charged with the

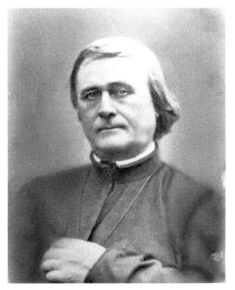

Father Pierre DeSmet, S.J.
Photograph 802.09a, Jesuits West Archives at Gonzaga University,
Spokane, Washington.

crime, and punished. The mistake was discovered, the *amende honorable* was made, but to no purpose. The Flat-Heads, aware of their dangerous position, employed the interval in fortifying their camp, stationing their women and children in a place of safety, and arming themselves for the contest. An immense cloud of dust in the neighborhood of the Crow camp at ten o'clock, announced the expected attack. On they came, with the impetuosity of an avalanche, until within musket shot of the advanced guard of the allied camp, who had just risen to their feet to listen to a few words addressed them by their chief, Stiettietlotso, and to meet the foe. "My friends," said Moses, (the name I gave him in baptism) "if it be the will of God, we shall conquer — if it be not his will, let us humbly submit to whatever it shall please his goodness to send us. Some of us must expect to fall in this contest: if there be any one here unprepared to die, let him retire; in the meanwhile let us constantly keep Him in mind." He had scarcely finished speaking, when the fire of the enemy was returned by his band, with such terrible effect as to make them shift their mode of attack into another, extremely fatiguing to their horses. After the battle had raged for some time in this way, Victor, the grand chief of the Flat-Heads, perceiving the embarrassed position of the enemy, cried out: "Now, my men, mount your best horses, and charge them." The manœuvre was successful. The Crows fled in great disorder, the Flat-Heads abandoning the pursuit only at sun-down, when they had driven the enemy two miles from their camp.

Fourteen warriors of the Crows fell in the engagement, and nine were severely wounded, as we subsequently learned from three Black-Feet prisoners, who availed themselves of their capturers' defeat to recover their liberty. On the part of the allied camp, only one was killed, the son of a Nez-Percé chief, who fell by the hand of a Crow chief, in so cowardly a manner, that the indignation of the allied camp was at once raised into immediate action — it was in fact, the first shot fired and the first blood drawn on either side; the boy was yet quite a child. Besides this loss, though the engagement lasted for several hours, only three were wounded, two of them so slightly that by application of the remedies I brought with me, they recovered in a short time; the third died a few days after my arrival in the camp.

This defeat was the more mortifying to the Crows, as they had been continually boasting of their superior prowess in war, and taunting their enemies with the most insulting, opprobrious epithets. They had besides, forcibly and most unjustly drawn on the engagement.

Indeed, I look upon the miraculous escape of our Christian warriors, in this fierce contest, as further evidence of the peculiar protection of Heaven; especially when I consider the numerous instances of individual bravery, perhaps I should say reckless daring, displayed on the part of the allied camp.

The son of a Flat-Head chief named Raphael, quite a youth, burning to engage in the contest, requested his father to let him have his best horse. To this the father reluctantly consented, as the boy had been rather weak from sickness. When mounted, off he bounded like an arrow from the bow, and the superior mettle of his steed soon brought him close upon the heels of a large Crow chief, who, turning his head round to notice his pursuer, pulled up his horse to punish the temerity of the boy, at the same time bending to escape the arrow then levelled at him. The boy must have shot the arrow with enormous force, for it entered under the lower left rib, the barb passing out under the right shoulder, leaving nothing but the feathers to be seen where it entered. The chief fell dead. In an instant a volley was poured in upon the boy — his horse fell perfectly riddled, with the rider under him. — He was stunned by the fall, and lay to all appearance dead. According to the custom of the Indians, of inflicting a heavy blow upon the dead body of their enemy, he received while in this position, a severe stroke from each individual of the several bands of Crows that passed him. — He was taken up half dead, by his own tribe, when they passed in pursuit of the enemy. The ardour and impetuosity of the young men belonging to the Flat-Head camp amazed the oldest warriors present, and formed the theme of universal admiration, as well as the dread of their enemies. Even the women of the Flat-Heads mingled in the fray. One, the mother of seven children, conducted her own sons into the battle-field. Having perceived that the horse of her eldest son was breaking down in a single combat with a Crow, she threw herself between the combatants, and with a knife put the Crow to flight. Another, a young woman perceiving that the quivers of her party were nearly exhausted, coolly collected, amidst a shower of arrows, those that lay scattered around her, and brought them to replenish the nearly exhausted store. The celebrated Mary Quille, already distinguished in numerous battles, pursued, with axe in hand, a Crow, and having failed to come up with him, returned, saying: "I thought that these great talkers were men. I was mistaken: it is not worth while even for women to attempt to chase them."

The little party of Black-Feet, animated by a spirit of revenge, for the loss of half their tribe, massacred the preceding year by the Crows, and probably influenced by a feeling of their safety while they fought in company with the Flat-Head Christians, did signal service in the combat.

In the meantime, Gabriel and Charles, fearing the threatened outbreak, immediately started back to meet me and hasten my arrival, my presence being considered necessary to prevent the effusion of blood. I arrived at the Flat-Head camp the day after the battle. I found everything ready to repel a second attack, should that be attempted. I immediately sent an express to the Crows, to announce my arrival, and at the same time, to convey to them the great desire I had to see them, especially for the purpose of effecting a reconciliation between the contending parties. But it appeared that after having buried their dead, they retreated precipitately; so that no account of their destination could be had. My express told me that there must have been excessive grief in the camp of the Crows, as the usual marks of it could be traced in every direction, such as the dissevered joints of fingers, and the numerous stains of blood, caused by the wounds which the parents of the deceased inflict upon themselves on such occasions.

Shortly after my arrival, the Black-Feet came in a body to my lodge, to express in a manner truly eloquent, their admiration of the Flat-Heads, with whom in future they desired to live on terms of the closest friendship. "To their prayers," said they, "must this extraordinary victory be attributed. While the battle lasted, we saw their old men, their women, and children, on their knees, imploring the aid of Heaven; the Flat-Heads did not lose a single man — one only fell, a young Nez-Percés, and another mortally wounded. But the Nez-Percés did not pray. We prayed morning and evening with the Flat-Heads, and heard the instructions of the chiefs." They then begged of me in their own affecting way, to take pity on them and be charitable to them: they now determined to hear the words of the Great Manitou of the whites, and to follow the course which the Redeemer had marked out on earth. Having addressed them on the nature of the life they had proposed to adopt, they all without exception presented their children for baptism, to the number of eighty.

The day after this sacred ceremony, they called on me, requesting to be allowed to express in their own way, the excess of joy which they felt on account of this two-fold victory. On returning from the late field of battle, the warriors, at the head of whom was a young chief, chanted songs of triumph, accompanied with the beating of drums; at each beat, they sent forth a wild and piercing shout; then followed the song, and so on alternately; — wild as the music was, it was not without harmony. It continued thus, during almost the whole of our route. We marched along the right bank of the Yellow-Stone River, having on our left a chain of mountains resembling those old portals to which history has given the name of "ancient chivalry." We had scarcely arrived at the encampment, when the Black-Feet commenced, under the shade of a beautiful cluster of pines, their arrangements for a dance, insisting, at the same time, upon showing the Black-gowns how highly they valued their presence among them, and how gratified they would be to have them witness this display. There was, indeed, nothing in it that could give occasion to offended modesty to turn aside and blush. I need not tell you it was not the polka, the waltz, or anything resembling the dances of modern civilized life. The women alone figure in it, old and young; from the youngest child capable of walking, to the oldest matron present. Among them I have seen several old women upwards of eighty years, whose feeble limbs required the aid of a staff in their movements through the dance. Almost all appeared in the best costume of the warriors, which, however, was worn over their own dress, a sort of tunic they always wear, and which contributed also not a little to the modesty of their appearance. Some carried the arms that had done most execution in battle, but the greater part held a green bough in the hand. In proportion as the dresses increase in singularity, the colors in variety, and the jingling of the bells in sound, in the same degree is the effect upon the rude spectator heightened. The whole figure is surmounted by a casket of plumes, which by the regular movements of the individual is made to harmonize with the song, and seems to add much gracefulness to the whole scene. To lose nothing of so grand a spectacle, the Indians mount their horses, or climb the neighboring trees. The dance itself consists of a little jump, more or less lively, according to the beat of the drum. This is beaten only by the men, and all unite in the song. To break the monotony, or lend some new interest to the scene, occasionally a sudden, piercing scream is added. If the dance languishes, haranguers and those most skillful in grimaces, come to its aid. As in jumping the dancers tend towards a common centre, it often happens that the ranks become too close, then they fall back in good order to form a large circle, and commence anew in better style.

After the dance, followed the presentation of the calumet. It is borne by the wife of the chief, accompanied by two other women, on the breast of one of whom rests the head of the pipe, and upon that of the other, the stem handsomely adorned with feathers. The most distinguished personage of the nation precedes the calumet bearers, and conducts them around the circle of dancers. The object, probably of the last part of the ceremony, the termination of the rejoicings, is to indicate, that the best fruit of the victory they celebrate is the peace which follows. To establish this peace upon a better foundation, is a thought constantly uppermost in my mind. May God grant that our efforts to plant the crop of peace among these wild children of the forest, be not unavailing; I earnestly recommend these souls to the prayers of the faithful.

Having thus, more fully perhaps than the limits of a single letter would seem to justify, redeemed the promise giving in my last, of recounting some of the advantages, spiritual and temporal, which the Flat-Heads enjoy, it may now be proper to resume the course of events up to the present date. On the 16th of August we left St. Mary's by a mountain gap, called the "Devil's gate," a name which it has probably received from the fact of its forming the principal entrance of the marauding parties of the Black-Feet. We encamped the first night, at the foot of the Black-Foot forks. Innumerable rivulets, and several beautiful lakes contribute largely to this river. Towards its head, to the north-east, there is an easy pass for cars and wagons. The valley we ascended, is watered by a beautiful stream called the Cart River. It was through this valley we wound our way in former days, with all our baggage, to the spot where St. Mary's now stands. We crossed the mountains in the vicinity of the Arrowstone fork, another easy pass, and descended a tributary of the Jefferson as far as its outlet, through rather a wild, broken, and mountainous country, with here and there an extensive, open plain, the ordinary resort of innumerable herds of buffalo. The seventh day found us encamped in the immense plain through which the forks of the Missouri diverge, ascending to the source at the very top of the main chain of the Rocky Mountains. In travelling through these wilds, great care is to be had in order to avoid the sudden attack of some of those straggling war-parties that infest this neighborhood purposely to search for scalps, plunder, and the fame of some daring exploit. We halted every evening for a few hours, to take a bite, as the trapper would say, and to give some food and rest to our animals. When it was quite dark, we would kindle a brisk fire as if to last until morning; then under cover of the night, proceed on our journey for about ten miles, to some unsuspected place, thus eluding our enemies, should any have followed in our track, or be lurking in the neighborhood, awaiting the midnight hour to execute their murderous designs. From the three forks we went easterly, crossing by an easy pass the mountain chain which separates the head waters of the Missouri from the Yellow-Stone river, a distance of about forty miles. We followed in the track of the Flat-Head camp for several days, when I sent Gabriel, my interpreter, with a Pend-d'Oreille Indian in advance to discover what direction the camp had taken, and to bring back speedy news regarding their movements; and also to learn the disposition of the Crows, whom I designed to visit. Four days later I was met by a few Flat-Heads on their way to find me, when I was apprised of the treachery of the Crows, and the severe chastisement they had so deservedly received. I travelled the whole of that night, and arrived next day in the allied camp, as I have already informed you. Having failed to obtain the desired interview with the Crows, our attention will be now turned towards the Black-Feet, with whose favorable disposition to receive the gospel you are already acquainted. The result of this determination will form the subject of my next letter. I recommend myself to God in your prayers.

    I remain, with sentiments of profound respect and esteem, reverend, dear father, your very humble servant and brother in Christ.

P. J. De Smet, S.J.

Document 4

A Pend d'Oreille Chief Visits
a Piegan Village
November 1846

Source: Cornelius M. Buckley, S.J., *Nicolas Point, S.J.: His Life & Northwest Indian Chronicles* (Chicago: Loyola University Press, 1989), pages 329-334.

Editors' note: Peter George was a Pend d'Oreille chief who visited a Piegan village in 1846. Father Point mentioned that the visit took courage and was surrounded by violence. Some footnotes have been omitted.

A Noteworthy Visit of a Pend d'Oreille Chief and of Two Mad Dog Braves
by Nicolas Point, S.J.

I have already reported that the visit of Peter George, the grand chief of the Pend d'Oreilles, far from pleasing the Piegans, had provoked them greatly. Indeed, several Piegans behaved shamelessly toward him, a fact I was not aware of at the time. Even though the two nations had only recently smoked the peace pipe together, the Piegans did not hesitate to attempt to steal at Peter George's camp. One of these thieves was caught red-handed, pardoned at the chief's request, only to turn around and steal from his own patron. This theft was all the more contemptible because Peter George had added a splendid mount to his gift of life to the pardoned offender, on condition that when he returned to his camp he would persuade his people to heed the words spoken by the Black Robes and live as brothers with the Pend d'Oreilles. Peter George had come to the Piegan camp, accompanied by his son Jules and his nephew Louis, to object to such an obvious violation of all rights. Even though born a Flathead, Peter George, because of his outstanding qualities, had been elected by unanimous vote great chief of the Larger Lake Pend d'Oreilles. He stayed in my lodge, where soon the most important warriors of the Piegans gathered. First, the noble visitor congratulated them for having a priest in their midst, an advantage which his children, even though baptized, did not enjoy. His speech was the essence of tact, not a word of blame or of self-interest escaped his lips. But the less he seemed to promote his own interests, the more incumbent it became upon the missionary to do so. I, therefore, emphasized the advantages of a peace based on justice, stressing the need for restitution in the present situation. The Piegans listened attentively and approvingly, but they declared that since the thief had left their camp with the booty, it was impossible that restitution be made, at least at the present. What gave credibility to this answer was the fact that other Indians in a similar situation had given the Piegans the same response. That evening there was a coming together for prayer at which time the missionary reiterated what he had said about justice and insisted on the obligation of making restitution. When the instruction was over, Peter George went out with his nephew, perhaps to see for himself what the results of this last recommendation would be. Suddenly we heard several rifle reports. I saw armed Indians running hither and thither, seemingly not knowing what they were doing. The whole camp took on the aspect of a fort surprised by the enemy. A cry: "The Pend d'Oreilles! The Pend d'Oreilles!" I could hear Sata delivering a forceful address. Big Lake stopped me: "Don't go in that direction," he said. More rifle reports made me dread what was happening to the Pend d'Oreilles. But like the end to a storm, the noise gradually diminished and deep calm ensued. Silent Piegans filled up my lodge and with total composure Peter George returned as if there had been no bullets fired at all.

But what had happened? Confident that they were safe among the Piegans, our visitors had gone out for a chat. As they were leaning against a tree, a Blackfoot stealthily drew near and fired almost point blank at Peter George's nephew. Fortunately he was not a member of this tribe, and moreover his attempt did not succeed. All of the racket came about in the effort to protect Peter George, on the one hand, and on the other, to hold up the assassin. How was it that in the course of such a brawl not a hair was harmed on a single person's head? I attribute this to Heaven's protection. Since this drama the Piegans understand better that something besides noise, something even more awesome that an attempted assassination is needed to intimidate a Pend d'Oreille chief.

In order to protect our guests from another treacherous act, the Piegans, who were well disposed toward them, placed them incognito in another lodge. But why was it that during the course of that evening Big Lake came to my lodge and took away the quiver with arrows that Peter George had left there? Did he fear the Pend d'Oreille would take on the whole camp at night all by himself? Not likely. The more probable reason is that some Piegans feared that had Peter George's people heard the rifle fire, they would hasten to the aid of their great chief.

Be that as it may, the next morning when they had finished their breakfast, Peter George and his two companions got up and left. But scarce had they traveled a hundred paces from the lodge when Peter George's eagle eye spotted the horses that had been stolen from him. It took our brave only a matter of seconds to run to them, grab them and lead them back. The thieves were not there, but their fences [the receivers of the stolen goods] were bound to make an attempt to repossess their stolen goods, and this is, indeed, what they attempted to do. But Peter George, intent on defending his rights, drew his sword so fast and with such force that the fences retreated, not converted, certainly, but profoundly abashed by the failure of their efforts. Now victorious over both injustice and violence, the chief bade farewell to the Piegan camp and returned to his own, where he was welcomed with new attestations of esteem and affection.

We then had a very different type of visit, one from two Mad Dogs. Among the Blackfeet the name 'Mad Dog' is given to members of a kind of superstitious brotherhood whose principal feature is a ridiculous sort of bravery. A Mad Dog never backs away from an enemy, no matter who he is, unless some brave among his confreres beats him back with a stick. As their peacetime rituals are all but interminable, almost always someone is overcome by exhaustion. Should someone take pity on the man and offer him some food to restore his strength, he has to throw it at him as one tosses a bone to a dog. Otherwise he will not touch it.

These rituals are contained in a dance resembling the minuet which builds up progressively, and includes every kind of bow imaginable and also a kind of humming. This humming is sometimes languid and slow and at other times fast and jerky. From time to time it is interrupted by whistles and the beat is measured by a kind of rattle called a *chichiquoi*. This instrument, which they regard as more precious than we would consider the field-marshal of France's baton, consists of three distinct parts. First, there is a round poppy-like head containing the small bones that make muffled sounds to harmonize with the singing; then there is the body, somewhat narrow and decorated with the richest material that can be found; finally, there is the buffalo tail, adorned with features, fringes and ribbons of all colors. Because this object is a symbol of great courage as well as a talisman which gives courage and many other precious virtues, it is not unusual for its owner to refuse to exchange it for four horses. So, like the stem of the calumet, it is also a lucrative object; it can make a man rich and the whites have not been above making their future from it. I have heard that a simple hollowed out tube of finger size thickness and two or three feet long, decorated with large headed yellow nails, brass wire, ribbons and other baubles, has been traded for as many as six horses. But in spite of the value a Mad Dog attaches to his *chichiquoi*, three men of this breed who had talked to the Black Robe about true prayer turned theirs over to him. A fourth threw his in the middle of a field. This man had just returned safely from a perilous adventure, attributing its success to the sign of the cross he made each time he found himself in danger. This same man told me that once he was traveling with a Gros Venture. When the Blackfoot made the sign of the cross his companion scoffed at this new medicine in a disrespectful manner; but, he added, "he soon had cause to repent, for he wandered off just a few steps looking for a deer to kill when he was riddled with bullets from the rifles of an enemy party. My few companions and I remained hidden at the very spot where we had prayed and were not seen. If they had indeed seen us, which is doubtful, they didn't dare attack us."

This same Mad Dog and one of those who had entrusted me with his *chichiquoi* were the two visitors who came to the Piegan camp while Peter George was there. The first Mad Dog offered to exchange weapons with the Chief. Among Indians this exchange is a token of friendship, particularly so when the weapons of the one who offers are of greater worth than those of the one who accepts. And such was the case on this occasion.

After having gone into some detail about the famous *chichiquoi* and about the stem of the calumet, it may not be out of order to say something now about the bear knife. This weapon, regarded as formidable by the Indians, is simply a dagger, the handle of which is fashioned from a bear's jaw bone. Like the man who possesses the *chichiquoi*, the one who carries this weapon never retreats in the presence of an enemy. Moreover, this is the only weapon he can use in attacking the enemy or in defending himself. I once heard a Frenchman brag more about capturing a bear knife then he would have had he captured the enemy's flag on a European battlefield. How is the right to carry the bear knife conferred? First of all, by buying it at a high price from its owner. Then the knife is thrown hard at the buyer who must catch it six inches from his chest. You can see that unless the brave's adroitness is on a par with his courage, it is all over for him. One bear knife I saw had the reputation of having reddened itself with the blood of three Piegans in this feat of agility and courage.

It is rare that there is more than one bear knife in each tribe. The present carrier of this knife among the Piegans was once the greatest coward known, but then he dreamt that another brave was killing him with the knife. The dream transformed his spirit, and when he awoke he found himself to be what he has since remained: the worthy carrier of the bear knife. This valiant knight has honored me by adopting me as his brother. This title is not preserved without risk if the adopter, just like the Piegan, does not join discretion with courage. This is the reason why traders, who understand their own interests better than anyone else, have one, but only one brother in each tribe.

Document 5

Sioux Chief Sitting Bull's Red Feather

1846

Source: One Bull, "Why Sitting Bull wears a red feather as a head ornament," Walter S. Campbell Collection, box 104, folder 21, Western History Collections, University Libraries, University of Oklahoma, Norman.

Editors' note: In 1846, a Salish war party or horse raiding party attacked a Sioux village on the plains. The young Sitting Bull was in the village and was injured in fighting off the Salish raid. No Salish account of this battle is known. The emblem of Sitting Bull's bravery in this battle against the Salish, a red head feather, can be seen in most later pictures of the Sioux chief. The 1846 date is given in Robert M. Utley, *The Lance and the Shield: The Life and Times of Sitting Bull* (New York: Henry Holt and Company, 1993), pages 15-16.

Why Sitting Bull wears a red feather as a head ornament.
By One Bull

When the Teton Sioux were camping round the Mussellshell River country, they were still at war with all other Tribes except the Cheyennes, Utes, & Arapahoes were their Allies, hence they were prepared to meet them at any time.

One day, the standing scouts reported that a war-party of some unknown Tribe had been seen sneaking round behind the high places near the camp. Several young warriors volunteered to look up this party. Sitting Bull was then fifteen years of age, 1845 [sic] — just a year after he was decorated as a hero in a battle with the Crows. He did not ask any one to join these volunteers, simply saddled up his pony, took what he really needed and started off without any fuss of any kind.

When the war-party, consisting of about fifteen warriors, was out some distance, they were suddenly attacked from a deep ravine. They were Flathead Indians — about twenty of them. The leader of the Sioux, Strikes the Kettle, immediately commanded their defense. They met the enemy. A bitter fight was on. The Flatheads, dismounted and behind their horses were shooting away at the Sioux. Young Sitting Bull told the leader he was going to make a dash on horse back along the enemy's line. They rather applauded him for his daring offer. He galloped up, then made his horse run on a full speed and dashed along the enemy's line in the thickest of bullets fired on him. He succeeded getting through. He was wounded in the right foot.

Both sides lost about half their number, though the Sioux were mostly wounded. The Flatheads were driven off toward North.

When the Sioux warrior got back to the Camp a big victory celebration was given and Sitting Bull was decorated again, but this time, with a red feather indicating wounded on battle-field. He was again declared a young hero.

This entitled Sitting Bull, the honor of wearing a red feather as head ornament.

Document 6

Cowardly Lolo Killed by a Grizzly Bear

ca. 1846

Source: "How Lolo Was Named," *The Daily Missoulian*, Nov. 26, 1916, ed. section, page 4, col. 3-4.

Editors' note: Duncan McDonald told this story about Laurent, the cowardly part-French husband of a Flathead woman. Laurent was killed by a grizzly bear in about 1846. The Blackfeet attack on the camp of Laurent and his family in the Salmon River area would then have been about 1837. The Indian pronunciation of Laurent — Lolo — was given to the mountain and creek near Missoula. McDonald's story illustrates the danger of attacks by enemy tribes and wild animals that were a part of everyday tribal life in the Northern Rocky Mountains in the early nineteenth century.

How Lolo Was Named

Duncan McDonald of Ravalli was in town the other day, and as oft-times happens, dropped into The Missoulian office for a visit with his friends. He was just returning from attending the federal court in Butte, where he had been called as a witness, and had been talking with his old time friend, General [Charles S.] Warren, regarding the pioneer days in Montana.

He was in a more communicative mood than is usual and during the course of his conversation to a Missoulian representative said: "I saw an article in The Missoulian some time ago, written by Judge [Frank] Woody, regarding the origin of the names of the various creeks in western Montana and to my surprise the judge fell into the usual error regarding the origin of the name Lolo.

"I have noticed that all the articles and books regarding the early Montana history have fallen into the same error regarding the name of the famous land mark of western Montana. Mount Lolo, which name, Lolo, was also given to the creek on this side of the mountain, which flows into the Bitter Root river as well as the creek of the western slope of Lolo peak which empties into the Clearwater river, in Idaho.

"These authorities all seem to agree that the origin of the name Lolo as it is now known, must have been some old Indian name as the original spelling

40 years ago was Lou Lou. That spelling was afterwards changed to its present form by the United States postal authorities when Lolo postoffice was first established 30 years ago."

Knowing from the tone of Duncan's voice and his communicative spirit that a good story was evidently forthcoming, The Missoulian representative expressed sympathy with Duncan's viewpoint and in response to his inquiry as to the real origin of the name Lolo, Mr. McDonald told him the following interesting story:

"My wife's mother, who died six years ago at the age of 84 years, has oft times told me the story regarding Lolo, which I will not [now] tell you:

"The original Lolo was a half-breed Frenchman by the name of Laurent, who lived with the Flathead Indians along in the early part of the last century. I do not know where he came from or who was his father, but he was evidently some Frenchman connected with the old Hudson Bay company's fur trading parties that explored this country in the early part of the 19th century.

The Indians could not pronounce the letter 'R' and, therefore in calling his name, 'Laurent,' they gave it a pronunciation of La La. You know that Laurent in French, is the equivalent in the English language to the name Lawrence, and is pronounced La-ra, so the Indians called it La La.

"The Indians have always told me that Laurent (or La La or Lo Lo) was a coward. During the latter part of his life they rather held him in contempt on account of his cowardice to his wife and child, when they were attacked by a party of hostile Blackfeet over in the Salmon river country, some time in the '30s. And their Flathead woman also told me this story about Lolo's cowardice — Mrs. Preaux, whose descendants on the Flathead reservation are now called Pelleu, died about seven years ago. She lived a neighbor to me, her house being situated between Ravalli and Dixon.

"She said that some years before his death, Laurent (Lolo) with his wife and child, in company with a French half-breed named Preaux, were hunting in the Wood river country, near the headwaters of Salmon river, about 50 miles south of where Salmon City, Idaho, now stands, trapping beaver.

"While in camp a party of Blackfeet surprised and attacked them. At first the Blackfeet pretended to be friendly and wanted to trade with them. Laurent and Preaux were inclined to believe Blackfeet were in good faith, but their Indian wives, knowing the Blackfeets' character, felt certain that treachery was contemplated.

"While the parley was going on, Laurent sneaked off into the brush, leaving the women and children at the mercy of the Blackfeet. Each woman had a child, and seeing that they were deserted followed Laurent into the brush. Mrs.

Preaux warned her husband that the Blackfeet were deceiving him, but Preaux remained. The women heard shooting and afterwards found that Preaux had been killed as well as two or three others of his companions.

"After some hours the two women found Laurent hidden in the brush. They wandered for some days in the wilderness and finally found a Flathead camp near where Salmon City now stands.

"My wife's mother has often related to me the story of Laurent's death, which I fix approximately about the year 1846. It seems that a party of Flatheads and Pend d'Oreilles were on their way to the 'Buffalo country,' over in central Montana and were encamped at the foothills of the Woody mountains, a few miles south of Fort Benton. Laurent, or Lolo, was with them, with his family.

"It was customary with the Indians, before breaking camp in the morning, for the men to hunt. Laurent went up one side of the gulch and an Indian named Hast-Ski-Lu (meaning Good Man), a Pend d'Oreille Indian on the other side of the gulch. Soon Hast-Ski-Lu noticed a grizzly bear following Lolo's tracks, and he shouted across the gulch to Lolo: 'Look out, there is a bear tracking you!'

"Lolo, like some other people in these later days, 'was too proud to fight,' and so hid behind a log, hoping the bear would not find him, but the bear jumped on him and killed him.

"Another Indian, named Tz-caugh (meaning Spark), noticed a few minutes later that a grizzly bear was following him. It was the same bear that had just killed Lolo. The bear was right close and the Indian saw that he was covered with blood, but this Indian, Tz-caugh, stood his ground and fought with the bear. He was a powerful man. While tussling on the steep mountain side, the bear on the upper side of him, the Indian in trying to get the upper side of the bear, started pulling the bear towards him.

"This started a log rolling down the mountain and the bear in his rage, his eyes being filled with blood, took after the rolling log, thinking it was Tz-caugh, who, in this way, escaped, returning to camp badly chewed up and bitten. After a long time he recovered from his wounds. My wife's mother, who was with the party, said that she was present at Lolo's funeral rites, which were held in the camp before the Indians again started on their journey to the 'Buffalo country.'

"The daughter of Hast-Ski-Lu, the Indian who saw the bear kill Lolo from the other side of the gulch, is now living at St. Ignatius Mission. She is the wife of Joseph Silipsto, who is a grandson of the old Flathead chief, Silipsto. He was the one who guided my father, Angus McDonald, to the location for the old Hudson Bay's trading post which he opened on Post creek in 1847. The location of the old post being about a mile up the creek from where the main road leading from St. Ignatius to Ronan crosses Post creek."

When Duncan had concluded his story of Lolo, and how the Indians had changed the letter "R" into "L," The Missoulian man wondered if that might not also explain the origin of the word "Missoula."

Father Pallidino [Lawrence Palladino], in his book, "The Indian and White in the Northwest," advances the theory that Missoula probably came from the Selish word, "Mis-ula" — "the place of meeting."

Is it not possible that the Indians, in trying to pronounce the word "Missouri," which was the general name applied to the early white trappers of the American Fur company, with headquarters at St. Louis, might have also stumbled over the letter "R" in Missouri and given it the more euphonious sound of Missoul-la, which afterwards attached itself to the present city at the mouth of Hell Gate canyon?

Document 7

Little Faro's Rebellion Against the
Priests' Teachings
1847

Source: Gregory Mengarini, S.J., *Recollections of the Flathead Mission: Containing Brief Observations both Ancient and Contemporary Concerning this Particular Nation*, trans. and ed. Gloria Ricci Lothrop (Glendale, Cal.: The Arthur H. Clark Company, 1977), pages 233-236.

Editors' note: This is Father Mengarini's cryptic report on the Little Faro Rebellion of 1847 when the Bitterroot Salish Indians rebelled against the teachings and influence of the missionaries. No record has been found giving the Salish side of the story, and Mengarini does not make the Indian motives clear. The 1847 rebellion foretold the 1850 closing of St. Mary's Mission.

Mengarini's Official Report for 1847 Containing an Account
of the Little Faro Rebellion

Lothrop note: The village rebellion led by the Flathead brave, Little Faro, was an echo of the Indian protest against whites in the Oregon Territory which flared intermittently throughout the region during 1847. In his official report to the Father General of the Society of Jesus, Mengarini details the events, the inability of the chiefs to quell them and the eventual reunion of the factions.

St. Mary's Mission
February 21, 1848

Father Gregory Mengarini to Father General
Paternity

Along with this letter is included for Your Paternity, the letter which I started to dispatch in September of last year, but which Father [Joseph] Joset was unable to mail for he received it in November after the mails had left. This overdue letter carries with it the pain you would have felt had you been able to witness the trials of St. Mary's Mission. It was but temporary as you will see from my second letter in which I shall explain the events and describe how I with the aid of Our Father *Facit nobilissi miserricordia suam*, which was, however, preceded by great tribulation.

The Flatheads who returned from the buffalo hunt somewhat after my return from the Coeur d'Alene, appeared somewhat more well-disposed. At the same time, the whites, not content with having usurped the lands of the savages, reintroduced the game of the hands, teaching it to the younger Flatheads who they cunningly succeeded in luring to the other side of the river. Two brothers then declared they were no longer Frenchmen but Americans and in lowered voices began to criticize their religion and the [illegible].

The youths then began to play in the village itself, near our house. Several of the chiefs murmured against the resumption of this vice, but they made little impression, and thus were satisfied simply to say, "*Tsalgatt*, it is not good."

All these things were reported to me, and foreseeing that things would get worse if the chiefs continued to behave as they did, I began instructing them in particular and exhorting them strongly to do their duty so that calm would reign over the community and it would not be seduced. But one approach or another accomplished nothing. Finally, when all the leaders as well as the subjects developed an antagonism toward the whites, and toward one of the Flatheads who had become good friends with them, then they wished the Father to cast them out. Now, this friend of the whites who until now [illegible] old things [illegible]. I will only say that this herald who announced the end of penance and declared himself leader, caused great injury to the missionary effort and for sometime greatly upset the relationship between missionary and savage.

He, I now believe, took offense at a correction that the missionary thought he had given with the best intention. On Sunday when all the savages gathered in church to recite the rosary, he interfered and began to harangue them publicly in the church, uttering the most insulting things against the missionaries, yet in such a manner that I understood nearly nothing. From that he went on to inveigh against and complain against the chiefs. And not one (with the exception of our interpreter Francis) shouted out any disapproval of this diatribe. No one attempted to still this tirade except this one poor blind man, nor did they demonstrate the slightest sign of disapproval.

When from several villagers I learned the extent of the scandal given and the negative attitude of the chiefs, I decided that it was necessary to give a little lesson to all, so as much to reveal to the scandalizer the great harm done, as to give to the others a lesson regarding the profanation of the house of God, I decided during the night that the church would remain closed and we would not give benediction, thinking that thus I would finally shock them.

During that same day an epidemic of Smallpox erupted. A young girl died that evening. Again I called the chiefs and openly spoke to them, reminding them that forty others were dying. In other words, the toll appeared to be three times that of other years. Perhaps, I suggested, this was a warning from God to shock them into at least controlling the scandalous talk in church, even if they wished to do nothing more. If they did this, tomorrow we would say Mass. If they did nothing, we would not say Mass, but instead dismiss the people. There was one who went to the scandalizer and pleaded with him not to again enter the church [to interrupt], but the next day no attention was given. The scandalizer not only entered the church with braggadocio, but placed himself as close as possible to the altar amidst the chiefs, and assumed the air of being on the pulpit. Father [Anthony] Ravalli who was the same opinion as I took the responsibility of saying Mass in order to prove to the savages that I was not alone in opposing them. Father Ravalli had already vested, the prayers had begun when we saw the scandalizer nearby. Ravalli interrupted the prayers, unvested, and dismissed the people. Then we announced that there would be no more prayer in church until one of the chiefs or someone else would come to the missionary with the assurance that scandalizer would not again enter or appear.

The scandalizer was greatly praised by the two whites who claimed to be American and encouraged by them, he continued his harangue throughout the day, running about the village like a man possessed. He shouted at the missionaries and urged them to leave. Then he turned upon the chiefs calling them puppets (and not without cause).

But who would have thought that instead of a day or two to ventilate their grievances, instead three weeks would pass before there would be relief from this harassment. Frequently, men came running to complain that there was no one to impede this rabble rouser. But all ended with that for the chiefs appeared to be sleeping.

But in the meantime the scandalizer was struck with the disease. The throat, mouth and tongue swelled, yet he continued his attacks each day. And he recovered. But on that same day the youngest of his children who out of affection he had given his own name of *Sioux Taren*, was attacked by a cancer [?] in the mouth which in three days spread across his face. It was accompanied by such a stench that all were obliged to leave the house. The fourth day he died. But instead of opening his father's eyes, this only served to harden him, and his invective became worse than ever, finally shouting that the prayers offered in the tent were as dry as buffalo sinew. Then the chiefs withdrew to deliberate. Four of these went to the house of the poor scanadlizer imploring him to present himself before the great chief. But they were received with the greeting of puppets, and following this atheist's refusal, they retired one by one. One of the first went to report to the missionary that some wished to take action while the others did not.

Things were reduced to this extreme state. The missionaries were exhausted of resources. They had offered Masses and Holy Communions, had sought the prayers of the congregation offered to the Immaculate Heart of Mary, and had worked for months using all human means to shake the Flatheads, especially since many were dying each day from Smallpox.

Finally, God moved the heart of one man of advanced age, who suffered to see the extreme weakness of the chiefs. The day following their announced disagreement, he remained in the tent with the chiefs after prayer and in a fine forceful manner requested permission to address the scandalizer himself. Without much ceremony he prepared to act. The scandalizer, now seeing his opportunity at an end, allowed himself to be conducted like a lamb before the chiefs who flogged him and subjected him to a scathing exhortation. In a matter of one day all took on a new aspect.

Chapter 2

Documents of
Salish and Pend d'Oreille History
Between 1850 and 1854

Document 8

Blackfeet Chief Cut Hand's War Story

ca. 1850

Source: "The Baker Campaigns," *The Benton Weekly Record* (Fort Benton, Mont.), Mar. 19, 1880, p. 2, c. 2-3; and "Historic Ground," *The New North-West* (Deer Lodge, Mont.) Jan. 5, 1877, p. 3, c. 1.

Editors' note: Piegan Chief Cut Hand obtained his name in a battle with the Salish Indians sometime around 1850. The Blackfeet war party fought the Salish in the Deer Lodge Valley. Cut Hand played dead while his finger was being chopped off, which would have required remarkable bravery and self-control.

The Baker Campaigns.
The Only Correct Account of the Piegan Massacre Ever Published.

Upon Little Dog's departure to the happy hunting grounds, there appeared several candidates for the Piegan chieftainship, the most noted of whom were Cut Hand, Mountain Chief, Bull's Head, Bear Chief, and Big Lake; and after the usual councils and ceremonies preceeding an Indian election, Cut Hand was chosen as the most fit leader, by the discontented and turbulent element, which at that time held the balance of power in the nation. He was renown as a man possessing all the qualities of a first-class brave, and had gained his appropriate name long before on a war expedition to the West side of the Rocky Mountains, at which time he was defeated by the Flatheads and several of his companions were slain. In that encounter he was so severely wounded as to cause his fainting upon the field of battle and to be regarded by the victors as a corpse. It was fortunate for him, that the Jesuit Missionaries had succeeded in convincing the western Indians, that it was a barbarous and unchristian-like practice to scalp a fallen foe, and the Flatheads contented themselves with stripping the bodies of the Piegans of artificial ornaments, especially the brass rings and bracelets, articles which were not only prized for their intrinsic worth among savages, but were also highly valued as trophies of war. Cut Hand had an unusual amount of metal about his person, and his left hand, while he lay there in stupor, was readily relieved of its adornments, — but his despoiler finding it a difficult matter to draw the rings from the swollen members of the right hand, and becoming impatient, he drew a knife and proceeded to unjoint the fingers from the apparently dead war[r]ior. The sharp touch of cold steel had the effect of recalling consciousness, but Cut Hand realized his position at once and understood perfectly well what was happening to him. Straining all his savage nerve to the utmost he more thoroughly simulated death and not a muscle of his body was allowed to quiver during the process of amputation and the stripping of his person. The victorious Flatheads were so completely deceived in this case that it was a difficult matter afterwards, to convince them of the truth. But the story of the marvelous escape from death is genuine in every particular, and the Piegan lived to return to his tribe, where the testimony of his right hand could not be doubted. Ever afterwards he was known as the Cut Hand, although "Cut-throat" would have been by far the most deserved designation. He became more deeply steeped in dirty villainy than any other chief of the northern tribes, and his camp was sought as an asylum by nearly all the desperadoes and horse thieves that infested Montana from 1864 to 1869. When troubles arose among the Bloods, Blackfeet, or Piegans, Cut Hand never refused protection to the criminals, and the murderer of Malcomb Clark, Jamas Quail, Charley Carson and others, could be found enjoying his hospitality. Being a splendid talker and possessed of engaging manners, he was enabled to cloak treacherous designs, with the mask of friendship towards the whites, and appear as an ally when he was the most inveterate enemy.

[The rest of this article was an extended screed defending Major James Baker's 1870 attack on Blackfoot Chief Heavy Runner's band of peaceful Blackfeet on the Marias River.]

****

Historic Ground

If when noted events occur and are recorded the scene is known as historic ground the locality where battle has raged and memory alone preserved the event may be transformed from the prospectively traditional to historic ground even by the record of a country newspaper. Henceforth then, Deer Lodge shall rank with Marathon and Manassas Gap, with Waterloo and Wyoming. Mr. Duncan McDonald, himself of Flathead maternity, came up from Missoula a short time since with Chief Arlee and others of that tribe, and informs us the space intervening between Deer Lodge and Missoula was, in the olden day, the scene of innumerable conflicts between the Pen d'Oreilles and Blackfeet, many notable fighting grounds being pointed out as they passed along. But the great battle that occurred between the two tribes took place where Deer Lodge stands, probably 40 or 50 years ago. The main fighting strength of the two tribes was engaged and the battle swayed furiously to and fro entirely across the valley and upon the bench lands. Large numbers of Indians and horses were killed. In the evening of the day of the battle, Standing Bear, the principal war chief of the Pen d'Oreilles, was shot in the head and killed in a charge on Tin Cup Joe Creek, near where Col. W. L. Irvine now lives. It is presumable from this event that the Blackfeet held the field and were victors.

The manner in which Cut Hand, the noted Piegan chief, who was killed a couple of years ago, received his war name is given on the same authority as follows: He was with a party of Piegans crossing the Deer Lodge and Boulder trail. They were met by a party of foes on the bald hill above Cariboo and overpowered. Cut Hand was shot and fell; others of his comrades fell on or near him. Their enemies rushed on them and supposing Cut Hand dead, beside subjecting him to the tonsorial twist cut off several of his fingers on which conspicuous and attractive brass rings were displayed. He endured this treatment while feigning death so perfectly that the enemy were deceived and while they were in pursuit of others he crept away and escaped. Henceforth he took the name of Cut Hand and was a terror on the war-path.

Document 9

Crow Indians Attack Flathead and Nez Perce Camp on the Plains ca. 1850

Source: Camille Williams, "Scalping the Flathead woman by the Crows," box 6, folder 34, Lucullus V. McWhorter Papers, Manuscripts, Archives, and Special Collections, Washington State University Libraries, Pullman, Washington.

Editors' note: Camille Williams was a noted Nez Perce historian. He sent this manuscript to Lucullus McWhorter when he was helping McWhorter with his Nez Perce books. The version here follows Williams' manuscript as closely as possible and keeps Williams' capitalization, punctuation, and spelling. Some periods have been added. According to the manuscript the battle was about 90 years earlier, which would make it about 1850. The Crow attack on the Flathead women and horses, illustrates how dangerous the plains buffalo hunting trips were.

[Scalping the Flathead woman by the Crows]
related by Camille Williams

the story of scalping the Flathead woman by the Crows happen several years before my father was wounded with Cloud Piler at Rose Bud Creek. in this fight I will mention Cloud Piler was not there, you got the story mixed up, here is the story.

Flat-Head and Nez Perces had a camp near Fort Benton although main Nez Perce camp was some where else. there must had been ¼ Nez Perces with the Flatheads, this was in spring time at the time all creek holes are filled with water. at that time Crows were enimies of Flat-head and Nez Perces so the Crows decided to attack Flathead camp. three bands started to look for Flathead camp and while on their way to attack one of the Crow chiefs dreamed that blood flowed only on the Crows side. he told the dream to other chiefs next morning, but they just laughed at him, so he started with his band back home. the two other chiefs kept on looking for the Flathead camp. the[y] finally found camp ground that was abandoned several days before. all warriors were ordered to surround the vacant camp of the Flatheads to find out whether the Crows were to be outnumbered. the Crows found out that they would outnumber the

Flathead about 3 to 1. the Crows followed to next camp ground but found it vacant but fresh. there the Crows decided to attack the enimey when the men go killing buffalo, so they can take all horses and women of the Flatheads. when the Flatheads were in new camp two young women remembered that they had forgotten two butcher knifes at the camp the[y] moved from. so following morning 3 young women started back to vacant camp to look for their knives. two of them rode on one horse one riding single. while the[y] were at the vacant camp early in morning before sun rise, the Crows noticed them. not looseing time the young Crows jumped on their horses to capture these women although the chiefs ordered them not to attack but disobeyed the order went right and others followed, but the sharp eyes of women saw them coming at full speed toward them. they got on their horses and started toward their camp which was about 7 or 8 miles away. one Crow caught up with them about 1 mile from camp or the two that rode one horse put past them wanted to capture the one on the lead riding single, but he failed overtake her as his horse was exhausted so he turned back about ¹/₂ mile from Camp to meet the two riding one horse. just as the sun rise, he met them and captured the two. then appeared hundreds of Crow warriors behind them. their guns and spears shined by the sun, they all stopped where the women were captured.

in a very short time the Crow warriors sang their war song, thrown in air two scalps of the two women, and just about that time a Crow warrior riding strawberry roan horse. horse wearing red flannal around its neck with small bell tied to flannal, drove a band of Flathead horses, away about 100 yards from camp. leaving lot of Flathead a foot. the Flatheads and Nez Perces were surprised. if the Crows were quick to drive all camp horses off Flatheads and Nez Perce would had been defeated, as there was no one ready for the emergency. so Flatheads and Nez Perces ran for their horses. it wasn't long the fight was on on the open praire. the Crows did out numbered Flatheads and Nez Perces. on the way to meet the enimey the[y] found one of the young women alive and naked and scalped. they helped her and took her to camp. the other was scalped with Tomyhawk, her head cut in two with hair on layed dead. the fight was fierce. the Crows thought that they would never be driven off as their chief, used to come out close to Flatheads with bow and arrow and shoot like if he was hunting chickens. he finally was shot on the leg down he went. it wasnt long when he was killed than the chase started, and that is where my father's hair bridle come off. the horse ran among the fleeing Crows in the thickest of the shooting, but the horse ran into a deep hole of water. he got off there and horse went right on with the Crows never expected to be seen again by his master. the Crow were chased long way off, when one Nez Perce warrior caugh up with several young Crows driving several horses. they at once abandant the horses the Nez Perce made a sign to them to leave the horses. so he wont harm them as they were boys. my father's horse was among the band. after the fight Flathead and Nez Perces looked over the dead Crows when coming back from the chase. they found one Crow alive played poosume. he fought them as he had his gun. this Crow was shot by Kao-kol-snee-ni Red Owl half breed Nez Perce half brother to my mother.

loosing no time all ran for the Crow when he fell wounded. my grandfather, Houl-lis Won-pon "War Singer," caught him on the head so he was entitled to the scalp. the Crow had fine long hair of aburn color. toward evening one Flathead warrior led a roan horse, red flannel and small bell around the horse's neck. the one that Crow rode when he drove off Flathead horses at the time of the attack in morning. the horse was taken away from in the fight or in a mix up fight and hand to hand. the scalp I still got but hair is short now as this happened about 90 years ago when father was young. the scalped woman lived till old age took her. this fight occured way before the Rose Bud Creek fight where my father was wounded, when Cloud Piler was the leader. Cloud Piler was killed 17 years before Nez Perce war of 1877. Piler knew that he was to be killed before he started from his own camp. his words were "I never made death" or he meant that Creator made death or that human should not live forever. those that heard him spoke the words knew that he meant that was his last day.

It was said that one old man a Flathead was killed in this fight. Crows unknown. the dream of the Crow chief that turned back with his band came true.

C. W. [Camille Williams]

Document 10

Nine Bulls and Walking Man on War Party Against the Blackfeet ca. 1850

Source: "Nine Bulls and Walking Man Looks for the Blackfoots," Vera Hanscen writings, SC 1204, Montana Historical Society Archives, Helena.

Editors' note: According to tribal records, Joseph Quequesah was born in 1877 and died in 1946 and his father was born in 1850. No information was found to date the horse stealing raid against the Blackfeet referred to in the story, but it could have been about 1850. There is no way to tell how accurately Hanscen recorded the story, but it is typical of many war stories told about warriors of the nineteenth century. Vera Hanscen was employed as secretary to the Confederated Salish and Kootenai Tribal Council for a short time during the middle 1940s when most tribal members were either in the military or working off the reservation. She wrote an account of her work in a manuscript, "The Indian Council — Yesterday and Today," which is also preserved in the small collection of her writings in the Montana Historical Society Archives.

Nine Bulls and Walking Man Looks for the Blackfoots
Story told by Joe Quequesah

My father told me this story when I was a boy, my father's name was Nine Bulls, he died here at Crow Creek, near Ronan at the age of 86.

One time during the early part of winter, there was no snow on the ground but it was cold. Nine Bulls and Wal[k]ing man took off for the plains on foot to hunt for the Blackfoots to steal their horses. One night Nine Bulls had a dream of what they call the medicine dream. In this dream he saw a Blackfoot brave sitting on the ground about twenty feet away. he was facing them with his big long pipe in his mouth smoking and singing his medicine song and on about the center of the pipe stem was tied on the ears of a grizzily [sic] bear, every time the enemy would puff on his pipe Nine Bulls noticed they were drawn closer to the pipe. This meant that the Blackfoot's medicine was going to devour them and they would be killed early that morning if they didn't see this. Nine Bulls was a great medicine man himself, which he knew of the buffalo. Nine Bulls medicine spirits spoke to him saying dont be frightened but do just as I tell you to do and if you do so, you will get back home safe. You have been spotted by that brave and at day break you will be charged by the enemy, just sing that same song he is singing and when you finish you and your friend get going. Nine Bulls started singing which wakened himself and his friend they both sat up. Walking Man so surprised started to question everything was explained to of what happened and what they should do. At this time light was beginning to show so they hurried on over a hill near by but before going over they looked back at their camping ground and seen a band of blackfoots running around there. Walking Man said to his friend that was a close one no fooling.

So they went on their journey. One day they spotted a large camp and getting much closer they hid in an old washout until dark. then they started for horses. Nine Bulls noticed Walking Man mounting on one when he heard a man yelling and shooting at them he noticed his friend taking off as fast as the horse could go, there was nothing else for him to do but run, looking back he saw that there was no chance to get away. he then threw himself in a patch of rose bushes and in the meantime he had lost his buffalo rapping (se-cum) and his bow string was shot in two. while he layed [sic] there he thought of his dream that he was to escape all danger and he did too. he remained there until his enemies disappeared when he took off to there [sic] hiding place there he stayed until the next night when he tried his luck again but this time he got to an old mare with a colt and managed to pick up another one then went on towards home on his way he got very cold fearing that he may not make it he kills the colt with his arrows and used the hide to wrap himself with which he found to be a life saver. then he went on for a long ways off before he stopped to rest when he wakened about daylight he had one hard time to get up. the raw hide had frozen so stiff on him he had to crawl out of it. the whole tribe thought that Nine Bulls got killed the night of the raid. In returning home he found his friend Walking Man. They were very glad to see there [sic] brave warrior back home again.

Document 11

Chief Victor's Story About a Blackfeet Attack at Hell Gate
ca. 1850

Source: Steve A. Anderson, *Angus McDonald of the Great Divide: The Uncommon Life of a Fur Trader, 1816-1889* (Coeur d'Alene, Id.: Museum of North Idaho Press, 2011), pages 83, 85-88.

Editors' note: This story, told by Chief Victor to Angus McDonald, was probably dressed up considerably by McDonald, who had a very florid writing style. It seems likely that the story had a factual event as its basis, or similar events had actually happened. There is no internal evidence to indicate the date of the events referred to, but it may have been about 1850. Blackfeet raiding parties were a deadly part of life in the middle nineteenth century deep into Salish territory in western Montana. Some footnotes have been omitted.

A Flathead Tradition: The Vision Before Battle
by Chief Victor/Many Horses via Angus McDonald

A small company of my people were camped years past on the plain of the cold springs — that plain which is on the left of "Hell's Gate" as it issues out from the defile of that name — that plain, whereon there gathered Red Men of past ages, [and who] held their annual races of both horse and foot in short or long heats to any distance they pleased. The Hell's Gate mountain towers east of and over that plain in solid red and grey granites, clad on its western slope with luxuriant grasses, and its summit covered with ever-talking pines. From its top readily can be scanned the three [river] valleys of the Bitter Root, the Hell's Gate and Missoula. On that pine-clad elevation, surrounded almost by the ethereal blue, the enemies of my people were wont to sit for days and weeks spying if perchance they might see any unprotected mortal that moved in either of those beautiful valleys below.

On that day of which I am to speak, a small camp of Flatheads was pitched by the cold spring of said plain and on the right bank of the Bitterroot River. Women and children were out digging that root on that plain. A little group of men were inside of one of the large tents telling, as they passed the pipe, the loving and dire incidents of their lives. Another group was on the outside lying on the fresh grass, scanning the green and bald mountain steeps in front of them, and anon looking back at Mount Lolo which rose remote and grey, looming like [the] coming night, while on its top the snow glistened in the sunlight like the Evening Star to the west.

The roving eye of one of this latter group observed grazing on the steep of the Hell's Gate mountain five buffalos. In a moment, the camp was aroused from its sluggishness and turned into wild excitement [as] the men were soon off on the best buffalo chargers in swift pursuit of the much coveted game, thoughtless of all save the chase.

When they reached the spot where the bulls or cows had been seen, they could find no trace of them. [However,] other signs were there and the terrible shape of the human foot in the mountain sand soon told them the meaning of it. Quickly and anxiously all turned their eyes to the camp, which in its oblique distance was far, yet clear below them. There, in the clear daylight, they saw the enemy [Blackfeet] as clearly at their work of slaughtering the camp.

Stung by the deception and the truth of it, they whipped their horses to their swiftest powers down the mountain side and over the plain towards their camp. But alas! Before they reached it, the enemies' work was finished and they were in flight, and all their own loved ones lay dead, slain before their eyes.

There was one there, the father of three little girls, and having no son his affections were much centered on them. He found them and their mother slaughtered and nude, lying in their own blood, and their little skin sacks of roots strewn around them as if to mock their humbling industry, and silently, and bitterly suggesting some of the terrors that wait on the generations of men and show how often our sweetest labors are overwhelmed by some dread unknown.

That father sat on the earth beside his loved ones, and before he had gathered the wrecks that had been made so remorselessly of the lives of those so much and so dear to him, and realizing that they were taken from him forever, and considering his own lonely condition, he wept in his [most] intense being. As his fierce, overflowing black eyes were turned to look at the steeps up which his enemies were already dimly disappearing, he said in his mind to the sun that was shining in full flame above him and which then seemed to him as careless as it was observant of the world: "You saw this. Were you not there to see it? Did you give light to the thief and murderer to slay the innocent? But you dry the sands, you harden the stones. Help me to avenge my children."

He arose and gathered the dead and quickly dug one shallow pit for the four and covered their rest forever. He then, to prolong his lament and commune with his woe, ascended the lofty round summit that overlooks the valley of the Missoula and that of the plains of the Kamas and the *Sit-kait-koo* or Flathead Lake. On that summit, he stalked and talked for days and nights. There, he accosted the forest below him, and the glens which held the winds. There, he spoke to the firmaments and to the moon and to the distant peaks that looked to him nearer the edge of space than where he was and to *Amot-Kaine*, the unknown cause of life and death, "head of what is," asking and imploring power to avenge his woe.

On the morning of his last day on that summit, a strong gale swept from the western mountains. From out of the heavy murmur that followed it, a voice from "*Alla-la-lee-meah*" (the old Virgin who controls the storms and hurricanes and tempests) said in front of him "Thou art here?"

"Yes," he said sadly, "yes, I am here."

And the voice again said "Yes, thou art here in earnest. Be my words to you what you will do and thy purpose will be heeded. Go to the hot spring that boils from the earth on the other side of the plain of the Kamas. Wash in that spring thy whole body and thy head. Be thy hairs and nails and joints and grooves of thy flesh thoroughly clean as thou wert never clean. On the morning of the fifth day, as the dawn beats up her first light, be on the top of the mountain that is east of and nearest the boiling spring — the mountain of the Rattle Snake's House. There, a friend will tell you more and tell you what thou shalt heed to prevail. But before he speaks to you, his voice will reach you four successive times from the sky in the way of the day. He will offer you a thing — refuse it. He will offer you a second thing — refuse it. He will offer you a third thing — take it [and] refuse it not. Go and forget not!"

The man therein descended from the mountain, and tying his bow and quiver upon his head swam the river that ran between him and the plains of the Kamas, and did as the voice directed him.

There was no sound on the plains. There was new mist in the mountains.

On the morning of the fifth day after being thoroughly cleansed, he was on the top of the mountain of the Rattle Snake's House. He was there as day and night, like the spirit and the flesh touch one another. The heaven was spotless without a cloud, without a gust to mar its beauty. The bird of the three songs and of the earliest morning lay had just finished her first address when the man immediately sat on a rock and felt as if tied to it. A pressure as of a whirlwind upon a feather was upon him, and he heard a prolonged and solemn voice in the sky afar toward the dawn. It was such a sound, as gives the cry of discovery. The rays of the yet hidden sun shone in redder lights on the tops of the higher mountains when the cry sounded the fourth time — as if it touched him, and he saw a shape like a naked man in his prime approach him, walking on the mountain. The shape was beautiful and powerful to look upon. His hair was twisted down his shoulders, dark as an Indian's; its points were of a brown crimson as if tinted in hot blood. His form was red and smooth as the blood covered quartz rock smoothed and polished by the rivers. His face glowed like a stream of Northern Lights. There was a wreath of flowers around his head and a long red feather in it stood erect. His height was like that of a little cloud that covers the sky before you think of its first shape. And thus the man spoke of the interview with this strange and dread Presence. He said in front of the man "My son, thou art here?"

And the man said "I am here."

And [the Presence] said "Thou art saved from man. I meet your life." He then took the feather from his wreath and offered it to the man. The man thereon turned his head, refusing it. The Strange Presence then flung it on the mountain and it grew as a pointed reed of the marsh.

Next, he took off and offered the man the wreath on his head. The man turned his head refusing it also and [the Presence] threw it on the mountain top and it grew a tall, red willow.

Lastly, he took a thing like a bar of burning yellow iron from his mouth, and hung it on the man's neck. Some long hairs as if of men were fixed to, and extended from, it and the Strange Presence said to the man "My son, fear not. These hairs are the lives of your enemies which I give into your hands. I have followed your grief, your steps and your watchings. Your weeping will be stayed and your woe will surely be avenged. I am a sun that will go with you to battle. Go to thy people and tell them when they see the foe that thou wilt be the foremost to enter the fight. Go, fear not. Be resolved and lead. My son, look at me!"

Hereupon, the dread and kind Presence walked and climbed the air backward bearing toward the morning. As the man looked, the Presence climbed his backward way. First, he seemed to obscure the light of the sun, then to become involved in, and mingled with its firs and disappeared. As he entered the sun, a tremor held the man's limbs and the earth for the length of a strong man's breath.

The man obeyed his words and came to his people and told them of the words and acts of that dread and Strange Presence. A few days after this, our enemy, the Blackfeet, were seen approaching us. The men were soon at the enemy in our arms — afoot and on horseback. The man led as he was told. The Blackfeet horses fell in the holes of the badger and the fox, breaking their limbs. Their bows, when bent, would break and their lances in unexpected ways were broken. They were confounded and smitten, and none of them lived there that day except one, to whom he gave his life that he might go tell how his people were all slain on the plains of *Ska-ka-how*. Here also, on this same plain and ridge, the Flathead tribe killed all the Snake men that came to fight us save one, to whom we also gave life to go and say how his friends who had come against us had fallen.

(Hereupon, the old chief [Victor] with a smile of sarcastic wonder playing around his manly nostrils said "Behold they thought he would never die, but he died." The old chief [then] ceased talking and, lighting his pipe, looked so solemnly and thoughtful out into the night that I could not but feel that this tale had probably been not altogether a [piece of] fiction to his people — whatever it might be to us.)

Document 12

A Pend d'Oreille Warrior's Fight for Survival

1851 or 1852

Source: "Nerve of a Savage," *The Benton Weekly Record* (Fort Benton, Mont.) Feb. 20, 1880, p. 2, c. 2.

Editors' note: This account of remarkable control and fortitude on the part of Pend d'Oreille warrior at the start of the 1850s, emphasized the dark side of tribal warfare in the nineteenth century. The battle where the Pend d'Oreille warrior was injured took place on the plains.

Nerve of a Savage.

In 1851 or '52 a party of Pend d'Oreille Indians, who had come across the range on one of their periodical summer hunts, were encamped on the Teton. They had succeeded in obtaining a large supply of meat, and were joyfully making preparations for an early return home, when one day their camp was assaulted by a party of Blackfeet. Several of the Pen d'Oreilles were killed and a number of them wounded. Among the latter was a young warrior who had been shot through the leg in such a manner that the attending to the wound, with the hope of saving the limb or even the life, seemed beyond the skill of his people. The prevailing hot weather was beginning to act upon his condition, and the Indian knew that his life would have to be forfeited by mortification unless the leg could be amputated. He desired very much to live long enough to reach his own country and be buried there with his fathers. A request to his companions to perform the surgical operation was denied, and in his despair he caused such necessary preparations, for cauterizing, etc., to be made as his savage knowledge of surgery seemed to warrant. Then he deliberately went to work and amputated his own leg. Having performed the operation successfully, the medicine men came to his assistance and aided in bandaging the stump.

The Indian was conveyed home by means of the lodge-pole vehicle and reached his country alive but terribly reduced in flesh. Kind assistance here attended him and through their efforts he was restored sufficiently to enjoy life on a peg leg for three or four years afterwards.

Y.

Document 13

A Trip from the Great Plains
to the Bitterroot Valley
September 14-30, 1853

Source: John Mullan, "Report of an Exploration from Fort Benton to the Flathead Camp...," Isaac Stevens, *Reports of Explorations and Surveys, to Ascertain the Most Practicable and Economical Route for a Railroad from the Mississippi River to the Pacific Ocean* (Washington, D.C.: Beverley Tucker, Printer, 1855), vol. 1, pages 301, 307-312, 315-318.

Editors' note: Lt. John Mullan relied on the geographic knowledge of the Salish during Gov. Isaac Stevens' 1853 explorations of the Rocky Mountains for a planned railroad route to the Pacific Ocean. His Salish Flathead guides took time off from their fall buffalo hunt to take Mullan and his party across the mountains to the Bitterroot Valley. Mullan was impressed with the religious devotion of the Salish Indians in the 1850s.

Report of an Exploration from Fort Benton to the Flathead Camp,
Beyond the Muscle Shell River, and Thence by the Southern
Little Blackfoot River to the St. Mary's Valley
by Lieutenant John Mullan, U.S.A.

Cantonment Stevens, Bitter Root Valley,
January 20, 1854.

Sir: I have the honor to report that, in conformity to your letter of instruction, dated at Fort Benton, September 8, 1853, directing me, with a "select party, to proceed to the camp of the Flathead Indians, then on the Muscle Shell river, one hundred and ten miles southeast of the Missouri, and there procuring the most intelligent and reliable Flathead guides, to make my way to the St. Mary's village, exploring the best pass to that point across the Rocky mountains from the headwaters of the Muscle Shell river," I left Fort Benton on the morning of the 9th of September, taking with me as a guide the "White Brave," a Blackfoot Indian, Mr. Rose, an employé of the American Fur Company, as interpreter, and Mr. [Frederick H.] Burr, to make a barometrical profile of the route travelled. In addition, there were three voyageurs and two Blackfeet Indians. My general course from Fort Benton to the Muscle Shell river lay in a direction south by east, by a very good road of four days' journey, passing between High Wood and Judith mountains — two of the principal spurs of the Belt mountains — crossing several prairie streams that empty their waters into the Missouri. . . . . .

September 14, 1853. — Commences very cold and cloudy. At half past 4 a.m. the thermometer stood at 38° Fah., the appearance of the clouds in the west giving indications of rain. The air from the Snow mountains this morning we found exceedingly chilly, making an overcoat quite comfortable. We resumed our march at 6.30 a.m. During the evening of the previous day we examined to see if the Flathead camp had passed the Muscle Shell below the point where we struck it. Our guide examined on both sides of the river, and finding no trail on either side, we concluded that their camp must be still up the river. We had heard they were on the river, above the forks; so we turned our horses' heads up the river in search of their camp, which course we pursued for four miles, when we found unmistakable evidence that they had gone down the river. Retracing our steps, we followed the river along the left bank for nineteen miles, to our noon halt. After journeying six miles below our camp of last night, we fell upon a camping ground of the Flatheads, which we supposed they had left about three days before. About the same distance farther down we fell upon a second camp they had left, where we had nooned.

The valley of the Muscle Shell river still continues to be well grassed and well wooded, the cotton-wood still abounding; the stream retaining its general width. When journeying down the river, we passed the mouth of the fork from the southwest that rises in the snow mountains. The northwestern fork takes its rise in the main chain of the Belt mountains. The southern fork is well wooded, by which means you can trace it far along in the distance, as it rounds through the valley to the base of the mountains.

At our nooning of the day, there was to our left, rising from the bluffs of the valley of the river, a high and wooded ridge, extending to the Highwood mountains, the wood being principally of pine.

Having found that the trail of the Flatheads crossed the Muscle Shell, we passed to the opposite bank, when we entered a very rough and rugged country, crossing a short prairie in the interval. About two or three miles after leaving the Muscle Shell we passed a high ridge of rocks, covered with pine. This ridge was about three hundred feet high above the valley. This was only the commencement of the bad lands that extended back from the river for a distance of many miles. Ascending a high peak in following the trail, we could see far into the distance, but no sign whatever of the Flatheads met our view. The appearance of the trail indicated that it was at least six days old. I here concluded that with my pack-animals it would be impossible for us to overtake them at our present rate of travelling, so we went into camp, which I placed in charge of Mr. Burr, and early the next morning started with the Piegan guide, mounted on two of our best horses, in search of their camp. This we followed for a distance of about eighty miles southeast of the Muscle Shell, when we found them encamped in a very beautiful valley, formed by the rocky bluffs of a deep ravine.

The first few miles of the journey lay over a very rough and rugged country, that led through a deep, wide valley, which was bounded on each side by high, steep, rocky hills. This rock was hard sandstone, the strata of which were horizontal. This formation I could trace by its exposure for many miles, which extended back into the prairie. About fifty miles from the Muscle Shell the country changes into a large and beautiful prairie, which is dotted by many large and beautiful lakes, in which we found the greatest abundance of ducks and geese. Much game of every kind was to be found through this portion of the country. No streams were to be seen — in fact no water, save that of the lakes, and the very many coulées to be found through the whole section of the country. About 7 o'clock of this day we neared the Indian camp. Their horses I could see at the distance of many miles, being so very numerous. I took them to be a large band of buffalo; but by a nearer approach, and with aid of my glass, I soon saw they were horses. When the guide and myself had reached their camp, three or four men met us at the entrance, and invited us to enter the lodge of the chief. They very kindly took care of our horses, unsaddling and watering them. As soon as the camp had heard of the arrival of a white man among them, the principal men of the tribe congregated in the lodge of the chief. When they had all assembled, by a signal from their chief they offered up a prayer. This astonished me; it was something for which I had not been prepared. Every one was upon his knees, and in the most solemn and reverential manner offered up a prayer to God. For a moment I asked myself, was I among Indians? Was I among those termed by every one savages? I could scarcely realize it. To think that these men should be thus imbued, and so deeply too, with the principles of religion, was to me overwhelming.

After the prayer, I asked if there was any one in the camp who could speak English. This question to them was like Hebrew; they understood me not. I then asked, in French, if there was any one who could speak French. At this, one spoke up that he could. Imagine my feelings of joy at this. It fully and amply repaid me for the many and frequent annoyances that I had met with in studying the language, for I had started without an interpreter, trusting to fortune to find some one who could understand me. I requested him to act as my interpreter for the remainder of his tribe. He was a full-blooded Flathead, and he told me he had learned to speak French on the prairie, among the French Canadians and the French half-breeds. I explained to him in detail the object of my visit to their camp; that I had come among them having a message from their father, which came from the Great Father, who requested them to send their principal chiefs and braves to meet their agent west of the Rocky mountains, and that I desired them to accompany me to the St. Mary's village, west of the mountains; that my sole purpose among them was for the good and welfare of their tribe, and I explained to them the benefit and necessity of some of them going with me. The chief told me that he would let me know in the morning what he thought of it, and had in the meanwhile prepared for me a supper of boiled buffalo-tongues, and a bed of buffalo-robes, upon which I slept soundly till morning, when I was aroused by the same men, who had assembled before I had arisen, singing and praying. The interpreter being present with the remainder, I asked him what the chief thought of my proposition that some of the chiefs should accompany me. He said he was opposed to it; but that *he*, with all of his lodges, would move off to see the Governor [Isaac Stevens], killing game on the road. He said that they had crossed the mountains to kill meat for the winter for themselves and family, and that they could not think of going singly. I explained to him the impossibility of his seeing the Governor at all by travelling with all his lodges, for he would necessarily be compelled to travel slowly, and that I desired to travel quickly in order to arrive west of the mountains in good season. I told him it was not absolutely necessary for him to go, but that he could send some of his principal men. Finally, after much persuasion, this he consented to do, and said he would give me five, who were accordingly ordered to accompany me; one, however, of the number, not placing so much reliance in what I had told them as the remainder, turned back, and the remainder of them followed me to my camp. When we arrived next day, having travelled about one hundred and fifty miles in the search for them, I remarked the great affection displayed in their parting; they bid their families and friends a most affectionate farewell — something that is not always to be seen amongst Indians. They had with them one hundred and twenty lodges, being Flatheads and Pend d'Oreilles; only fifty lodges, however being Flatheads. There were seven lodges, with Victor, their principal chief, on their way to St. Mary's village. The Flatheads are a fine-looking, noble race of Indians; they have conformed more to the customs of the whites than any Indians west of the mountains. But they show the Indian still; they are profuse in the use of paint, and are great lovers of beads, and are fond of trinkets, gewgaws, and ornaments of every kind. The women are kept in the same wretched state of drudgery as the women of all other tribes of Indians; they pack and unpack the horses, pitch and strike the lodges, cook, carry wood, water, and, in fact, do everything there but hunt. Their young men are fine-looking and athletic, and exceedingly intelligent. I asked them if they had any troubles to complain

Lt. John Mullan
John Mullan Papers (box 12, folder 5), Booth Family Center for Special
Collections, Georgetown University Library, Washington, D.C.

of, and, save with the Blackfeet, they said no. They say that were it not for this bad nation they could live happy and contented; but these, their enemies, make incursions into their country, carry off their horses, kill off their men, and all this without provocation. They represent that with the whites they are always at peace, and are always glad to see or meet with them, and look upon it as a bright spot in their history that they have never as yet shed white man's blood, and they could not see why their interests by the whites were so much neglected. They said they desired to have a general peace with all the Indians, both east and west of the mountains, and that they expected much, very much good, through the interposition of their agent; they spoke very sagely and very affectingly, and felt all they said. They have little or no gesture in speaking, but, as among all Indians, express themselves to a great extent in signs. Four of the five came with me, but the other, thinking it all a hoax, started back; but the four, arriving at my camp, partook of an excellent supper, and after their usual smoke were perfectly contented and happy, and appeared much more willing to accompany me than to return to their camp.

September 18, 1853. — Commences very cold and windy, the thermometer being 38°. The Snow mountains, which lay in full view this morning, are covered to near their bases with snow; the wind, blowing immediately from them, is cold and chilly. Having remained in camp three days and four nights, our animals recruited very much, and were well prepared to withstand a long day's march. Resuming our journey this morning, I noticed that our guide showed an evident disposition of unwillingness to accompany me farther. Through the interpreter he had asked me to release him from his engagement, and to allow him to return to his home. This I refused to do. I told him that he had engaged with Governor Stevens to conduct us to the Flathead camp, thence to the village of St. Mary's, west of the Rocky mountains, and that he must fulfill his engagement before leaving. He appeared very sullen, and promised to accompany us to the end of our journey. When everything was ready, I told him to mount his horse and come on; he said he wished to smoke, and that he would overtake us in a short time. Presuming that he had fully made up his mind to accompany us, I thought nothing of it, but rode on without him; we have not seen him since. I only regretted that he had not received a cudgelling before leaving. Our Flathead guides, however, proved this day invaluable, and gave promise to conduct us quickly and safely across the mountains. Our journey lay up the valley of the right bank of the Muscle Shell river. We struck one of its forks coming in from the south, upon which we nooned eight miles above its junction with the main stream. This fork, or tributary, flows through a beautiful and well-grassed valley of two and a half miles in width. The stream, with a rapid current, is at present only ten yards wide, with a gravelly bottom, well wooded to its source in the Snow mountains, the cotton-wood occurring in great abundance. Extending for a long distance on the right bank of this fork is a bed of lignite, of twenty-five feet in thickness. From this fork our trail led over a very excellent road for twelve miles, till we struck the main stream of the Muscle Shell, crossing in the mean while several prairie streamlets that empty their waters into the Muscle Shell. Travelling up the river four miles farther, we encamped on its right bank, finding an abundance of grass, wood, and water. Game, to-day, was very abundant. Buffalo in large bands, antelope, elk, geese, and ducks were seen during the day. The night of the day was mild and beautiful till towards daybreak, when it became cool and chilly from the Snow mountains.

September 19, 1853. — Commences clear and cold; the thermometer at sunrise 24$^{1}/_{2}$°. We resumed our journey at 6 a.m., following up the valley of the northwest fork of the Muscle Shell, which on this day we found much less wooded than that already travelled, still continuing, however, well grassed. The Belt mountains to-day approach quite close to the banks of the Muscle Shell on the north. We saw plainly to-day that the Snow mountains are not a separate and distinct range, but form a part of the Girdle or Belt mountains, and are called the Snow mountains when the range crosses the Muscle Shell, where they increase in elevation to such an extent that many of the higher peaks are always covered with snow; hence the name that has been applied to them of the Snow mountains. The range of the Belt mountains running along the Muscle Shell, taken in connection with the spur along the Missouri opposite Fort Benton, and the range running from the Missouri to the Muscle Shell, form the two parallel sides, and diagonal of a parallelogram, the diagonal having a general direction of northwest and southeast. The country south of the Muscle Shell, extending to the base of the Snow mountains, is very rugged and broken, while that to the north, towards the Belt mountains, is partially wooded, and rises gradually from the Muscle Shell river to the base of the mountains. We passed this morning the mouth of the southwest fork, coming from the Snow mountains, which was well wooded, and as large and rapid as the northwest fork, with which it made an angle of 38°. By following along the southwest fork you strike the Missouri at or near the gate of the mountains, and cross the main chain of the Rocky mountains by following up the Jefferson fork of the Missouri. On the left bank of the river we noticed this morning a rock formation, occurring in thin layers, similar to that about sixty miles south of the Muscle Shell. As a general thing, the banks of the Muscle Shell and those of its tributaries are of a clay formation mingled with much gravel, the bed of the stream being also gravelly and rocky. Having travelled a distance of twenty miles, we nooned on the right bank of the river, where we found excellent grass, but no wood; which latter seems to be more scarce the farther we travel up the river. At 2 p.m. we resumed our march continuing along the right bank of the river, over a very level and beautiful prairie that extended to the base of the Girdle mountains, which at this point cross the main stream or northwest fork of the Muscle Shell, and run towards the south for three or four miles, crossing the southwest fork, where, bending more to the east, making an angle of 30° with the main river, they become the Snow mountains. After travelling six miles farther, our trail lay through a pass in the Belt mountains, formed by the valley of the Muscle Shell river, which we followed to our night's camp, crossing the river at its head branches, several of which are unwooded, the grass of the valley being excellent. The mountains on each side of the valley of the northwest fork are about 1,000 feet high, well clad with the yellow and spruce pine, growing to a height of seventy-five feet, perfectly straight, and from twelve to twenty-four inches in diameter near the ground. The mountains are formed of a cream-colored, unstratified rock, exposures of which would be seen at times along the slopes. The willow, in great abundance, is found on the banks of the head branches of the stream growing to a height of six and eight feet. We camped to-night on the left bank of the stream, having marched thirty-five miles.

September 20, 1853. — Commences cool and clear, the thermometer at sunrise being 24°; frost last night was exceedingly heavy, covering the ground like a coating of snow. Our camp of last night being in the valley of one of the head branches of the Muscle Shell, with high mountains on each side, it is possible that we had frost much heavier than if we had been on the plains. We resumed our march this morning at 7 a.m., our trail being over a very excellent road along the left bank of the head branch of the Muscle Shell, on which we encamped, for about two miles, where, leaving it to our right, our course lay to the west over a prairie road at the base of the slope of the range of mountains to our left. After passing over this well-grassed prairie road, which formed the divide of the valley, we fell upon the headwaters of a stream flowing towards the west and emptying into the Missouri, which, from its general character, valley, bed, and direction, we took to be the Smith's river of Lewis and Clark; it is called by the Indians — — — —. It rises in the western slope of the mountains, receiving tributaries, small but rapid, from many points in the mountains on the north and south. The hills here, and along our whole journey, continued to be covered with the cedar, bush-willow, and spruce-pine, which grows small but exceedingly abundant. To-day hills and mountains assumed a more rugged appearance than we had noticed on any day previous; high rocky bluffs at times outcropping from the hills, of a dark black or brown color, commingled with a light cream-colored rock apparently of a hard texture. The hills on each side of the valley were from five to six hundred feet high. The brooks, streams, and rivulets passed and crossed to-day were very numerous. The grass along our whole route was exceedingly fine and luxuriant in the valley; along the slopes of the mountains, however, which were covered with rocks and pebbles, the grass was very spare and dry, contrasting well with the beautiful green meadows of the valley below. Game to-day was very scarce, only one elk and four antelope being seen during the day: the latter being exceedingly shy, precluded all possibility of approach; the former we succeeded in killing, but he proved unfortunately to be a six-year old buck, poor and good for nothing, which we sorely regretted, as we were now without meat. We nooned to-day on Smith's river, where we found good water, grass, and wood; the latter, however, was not abundant, the stream here having a width of forty feet. We continued down the valley of this river during the remainder of the day, which was from a mile to a mile and a half wide, and perfectly level. It is probably one of the prettiest valleys to be found in the mountains. For miles you see before you a level prairie bottom, bounded on each side by the gently sloping hills of the Belt mountains, which are covered with a thick and even growth of the pine, and through the middle of this prairie the Smith's river, with its banks bordered by the willow, birch, and cotton-wood, flows. The water of this stream is clear and cool, its bed pebbly, and current rapid. The weather to-day has been very warm, rendering a coat uncomfortable, contrasting greatly and agreeably with the weather of the two days previous. Some of the higher peaks of the mountains on the south side of the valley were covered with snow, while none was to be seen on the mountains towards the north. After a long day's march we camped on the left bank of Smith's river, where we found good wood, grass, and water. We had a luxury to-night in a string of mountain trout, brought into camp by one of our Flathead friends; these trout, which form a very excellent dish, were twelve inches long, of slightly yellow tinged color, and spotted on the upper half, and look not unlike the common mackeral of the East. Our Indians displayed on this occasion a trait worthy of notice. They were without meat, or anything to eat. We were without meat, but had a little flour left from our small stock of provisions. These being the first fish caught by any of the party, they insisted on our taking them, which we refused; but still insisting, we were compelled to accept them. This is certainly an example of boundless generosity. I cannot say too much in favor of these noble men who were with us; they were pious, aged, firm, upright, and reliable men; in addition thereto, they entertained a religious belief which they never violated. They partook not of a meal without asking a blessing of God; they never rose in the morning or retired at night without offering a prayer to God. They all knew the country well, and made excellent guides and good hunters; and when they could not find fresh meat they accepted of the remnants of our scanty table with the greatest humility and contentedness, contrasting well with our Blackfeet friends, who had just left us, who made free with anything belonging to us, and who looked upon our table as their own. These Flatheads have always been, as an Indian tribe, held in the highest estimation, and this I can fully confirm from actual observation. When one or two went out in the morning to hunt, they gave full details as to water, grass, wood, halts, meeting each other, &c., so fully did they appreciate their position. The night of this day was exceedingly mild and pleasant; the frost, however, being very heavy, which before morning coated the ground as with snow. . . . .

September 26, 1853. — Commences cool and cloudy; the rain ceased near morning, leaving everything wet and disagreeable. We resumed our march at 7.10 a.m. down the valley of the Hell Gate river, on its left bank, continuing at times in the valley over the prairie bluffs that bound it, in order to cut off the many bends of the stream. We crossed the stream several times during the day, finding the ford with water two feet deep, and the stream from eighty to one hundred yards wide. About 11 a.m., when on the left bank of the river, we struck the trail of a party going towards the east — the trail being but a few days old. We found a small pile of stones, and in it a small piece of paper with the following written on it: "F. W. Lander, engineer N. P. P. R. Ex., passed here with nine men September 23, 1853, towards St. Mary's. — Hugh Munroe, guide." His trail tended at that time due magnetic east, while ours was due magnetic west. I thought it possible that the guide of Mr. Lander's party had taken the Hell Gate river to be the St. Mary's or Bitter Root river, and in that case was following it up to strike the St. Mary's village, the point of junction of the several reconnoit[e]ring parties then in the field. Laboring under this impression, and knowing full well, from having four Flathead guides with us, that we were travelling on the proper trail and in the right direction, I deemed it expedient to despatch Mr. Burr and an Indian guide, with directions to follow their trail a reasonable length of time, and if he met with the party, to warn its chief of his error; and in case he could not overtake them, to retrace his steps, and follow on our trail to the village of St. Mary's. To this effect he and the Indian, mounted as well as the condition of our animals admitted, started at 12 m. on their trail. We passed to-day quite a large tributary to the Hell Gate river, coming in from the west-southwest, called the Flint creek, by following which, our Indians stated, led to a road of two or two and a half days' journey to the St. Mary's village, across the Bitter Root range of mountains, but by a much more rough and rugged trail than the one we were then travelling. They stated that the road was by the Gun Flint creek, and is the one travelled by the Blackfoot Indians in the spring, when visiting the Flathead country to steal horses. I thought it probable, therefore, that Mr. Lander's party had taken this road across the mountains, and in that case Mr. Burr could not overtake them before reaching the village of St. Mary's.

Continuing our journey over a series of prairie hills till 2.30 p.m., we encamped on the west bank of the Hell Gate. Here the stream was well wooded; channel-water two feet deep, clear, and the current quite rapid; bottom stony and gravelly.

The weather during this afternoon was cool and cloudy, which, towards the middle of the night, changed to a cold rain, rendering our overcoats very comfortable. Game during this day has been exceedingly scarce; one antelope was all that was seen during the day; at night, however, one elk came near the camp, when three of the party started, one on horseback, in pursuit of him. They succeeded in wounding him, but not so badly but that he escaped. The Indians were exceedingly anxious to capture him, since they had nothing to eat, but were dependent on our bounty, which was necessarily small and limited. Here I am forced to mention the patience and fortitude of these Indians. Here they were, brought from their tribes and homes, and in the midst of their hunting season, to guide and accompany the whites across the Rocky mountains, and when without anything to eat they displayed a degree of Christian fortitude rarely seen among any other class of people; but willingly did we share our scanty fare with them.

September 27, 1853. — Commences cool and cloudy, giving indication of rain; the thermometer at sunrise being 42°. We resumed our journey this morning at 6.30 a.m., continuing our course along the banks of the Hell Gate river, which we crossed five times during the day, finding a good ford at each crossing, with water about two feet deep; the current very rapid and bottom rocky. The stream continued to be well wooded; the valley in places being a pine forest, the trees growing to a great height, and perfectly straight. We found the valley to-day running nearly west, but the stream itself very tortuous, and making large bends. We saw no game to-day. We saw on the road in abundance what is called by some the mountain apple, a small red berry, growing in bunches from six to nine feet high. They looked very much like the apple seen on the rose-bush when the flower has been plucked or withered. The taste is somewhat similar to that of the apple of the States, and when touched severely by the frosts are said to be very good.

The mountains on each side of the valley are still clad with pine; the valley itself being to-day very level, affording a beautiful road; the grass being very good. After a march of twenty-five miles, we encamped on the right bank of the Hell Gate river, finding good grass, wood, and water.

About seven o'clock p.m. the Indian guide who had accompanied Mr. Burr returned, stating that Mr. Burr was back thirty or forty miles. I concluded, therefore, to remain in camp until he should return. The night of this day was mild and pleasant. We passed, about 10 o'clock a.m., a second trail leading to St. Mary's village, which was to our right, being the one followed during the high-water seasons.

September 28, 1853. — Commences cool and cloudy. At 8 o'clock a.m. it commenced raining, which continued during the day, though moderately. We remained in camp to-day; our Indians amusing themselves in fishing and arranging their trinkets, &c., as they were now approaching their village and wished to show to advantage, both among their own tribe and the whites. The men were engaged in attending to their animals, &c., making moccasins, or boots of dressed buffalo-hide, for those that were lame; this latter we were compelled to do some days back, as several of our horses were tender-footed; being unshod, and crossing the streams so often, the beds of all of which were rocky and pebbly, told upon the feet of our animals. This plan of making boots or moccasins for them we found to answer very well.

About 7 o'clock p.m. Mr. Burr returned. He reported, "that after leaving my trail on the morning of the 26th, he followed on the trail of the horse-tracks which we had seen, which tended north forty-five degrees east; he followed till he came to one of the camps; he dismounted and followed one of their camp-fires, and found the ashes still warm, thereby showing he was not many miles distant from them; that he followed the trail over a very rough, difficult, and rugged road to the top of a high hill, from which he could see far in the distance. Towards the north lay the valley of a large stream, the banks of which were well wooded, the valley well grassed." From his description, I took this to be the Big Blackfoot fork of the Hell Gate river. When gaining the top of this mountain, the Indian refused to follow him farther, but turned his horse's head westward.

Mr. Burr reports, that if his horse had been in good condition, he would have followed them alone; as it was, he was compelled to retrace his steps, and follow the trail of the Indian.

September 29, 1853. — Commences cloudy but warm, thermometer at sunrise being 39°. We resumed our journey at 6.30 a.m. down the Hell Gate river, following along its right bank by a very excellent road, which lay principally through a pine forest of the valley. At a distance of six or seven miles we struck the Big Blackfoot fork of the Hell Gate river, which we found to be a rapid stream, from fifty to sixty yards wide at its mouth, with a rocky bed, and channel-water twenty inches deep. We crossed it about twenty yards above its mouth.

Where the forks come together is a beautiful prairie bottom, well grassed. This place is called the Hell Gate, a name given it by the Flatheads and other Indians west of the mountains, from the fact that here the Blackfeet Indians have committed many murders and robberies; it being the debouch of the defiles of the mountains, and where Indians are generally found, and must pass in going to the buffalo hunt east of the Missouri.

It is a perfect gate in the mountains, forming a well known and noted landmark. From receiving the large volume of water brought down by the Big Blackfoot fork, the Hell Gave [sic] river has swollen to a large stream, with a rapid current, and eighty yards wide. At 11.30 a.m. we fell upon the trail of a large party from the Big Blackfoot fork; a short time after, upon the trail of two wheels with animals shod, which we concluded was the trail of the main portion of the expedition: they had passed this place only the day before, the trail of the wheels being that of the odometer wagon.

At 12 m. we halted on the right bank of the main stream of the Hell Gate river, having travelled fifteen miles, finding here good grass, wood, and water. Resuming our march at 1.30 p.m., we continued for two miles farther along the Hell Gate river; crossing it at a point where formed a gravelly island in the channel, we found the current here quite swift, water about two feet deep, and bottom as above, very pebbly and rocky.

We now entered upon a large and beautiful prairie lying between the Hell Gate and Bitter Root or St. Mary's river, which latter at a distance of three or four miles we struck, finding it a bold, rapid stream, and of the same size and character as the Hell Gate river. We struck the Bitter Root river where it makes a great bend, going to the west, and about eight or nine miles above its mouth.

This river rises in the main chain of the Rocky mountains, is about ninety miles long, and flows through a beautiful valley, where is the residence and home of the Flathead Indians. It is noted for its abundant and rich grass and for its exceedingly mild winters.

Travelling up the Bitter Root river for a distance of six miles, we crossed it, camping on its left bank, finding good grass, wood, and water; our camp being where the main party camped on the night previous. The night was cool, with a heavy frost.

September 30, 1853. — Commences misty and cool but towards ten o'clock becomes a beautiful bright day.

We resumed our journey, at 7.30 a.m., up the Bitter Root valley, but a very excellent road, crossing several small tributaries coming in from the west, making one crossing of the Bitter Root river about ten miles from our camp of last night. At a distance of six or seven miles farther we halted on a small stream from the east, about three miles below the St. Mary's village, the sight of which we all greeted with feelings of joy. We were visited by several Flathead Indians, who informed us that "Suryarpees" arrived yesterday, meaning thereby the expedition. Resuming our march, we reached the village at 3 p.m., on the twenty-second day from Fort Benton. Here we were met by the Governor and several members of the expedition, who had expected us in much sooner. Mr. Lander's party, whom we started in search of, arrived safely.

Our Indian delegation was presented to the Governor, who talked with them as the representatives from their tribe, setting forth the good intentions of the government, &c. We were glad to find ourselves at our journey's end.

. . . .

Truly and respectfully, your obedient servant,

John Mullan.

Governor I. I. Stevens,
In Command of the Northern Pacific Railroad Survey, &c.

Document 14

The Flatheads Ambush a Blackfeet War Party

November 4, 1853

Source: "The Upper Missouri," *New York Daily Times*, Nov. 11, 1853, page 1, c. 3.

Editors' note: This account of an 1853 Salish ambush of a Blackfeet war party might be exaggerated, but probably describes a real event. In the 1850s, the Salish had to be constantly vigilant for Blackfeet raiders.

The Upper Missouri.
From the Selkirk Settlement.
Correspondence of the New-York Daily Times.

St. Louis, Friday, Nov. 4, 1853.

I have not written for some weeks, because nothing of any interest had been received here by myself or others from the country westward. This morning, however, I am in receipt of letters from the Upper Missouri and Pembina, in the Selkirk Settlement. From the Upper Missouri I learn that the Blackfeet have been quite troublesome during the Summer. They have a hereditary feud with the Assinaboins, the Crows, and the Flatheads of the Columbia. With the latter they have had a number of skirmishes during the Summer. The last one was an event of some importance in the warlike annals of the red man. If you have ever read the letters of Father [Pierre] DeSmedt, a Jesuit Missionary, and a man of brilliant and lively genius, you will have formed some idea of the Rocky Mountain range north of the forty-seventh parallel. It forms a treble wall of rugged granite for many miles together, the only passes through which are fissures opened ages since by volcanic fires. The Blackfeet, in the early part of the Spring, made two irruptions into the Flathead country, passing each time through several of these fissures. In these irruptions they perpetrated a deal of mischief, and took some scalps. Instead of returning the visits, the Flatheads were cautious enough to concentrate a considerable force, and send out scouts to discover what route their enemies would pursue in a third expedition, for they well knew that their success would stimulate them to more hazardous undertakings. The scouts watched them from the pinnacles of the first range, and then again from those of the second. When they had passed both of these they hurried into camp, for they well knew where the only available pass in the third range was located. The whole body of Flatheads proceeded, by forced marches, to the pass. A few only encamped in the mouth of the gorge — just enough to produce the conviction that they were guarding it, and that their force was inadequate to the undertaking. A much larger body posted themselves behind cliffs at its outlet, and a number hurried to the heights overlooking it. When the Blackfeet arrived, a furious charge was made, and the wild and terrific war-whoop reëchoed. Enough resistance only was made to tempt them forward. After they had proceeded nearly two-thirds of the distance through, the signal yell was sounded from the cliffs, a shower of arrows whistled through the air, and these were followed by immense masses of rock, which seemed to leap wildly from the precipitous heights, to the comparatively dark chasm through which the Blackfeet were hurrying, in the hope of again surprising their foes. It was too late to retrace their steps. In that direction there was no hope of escape. Their only hope was in rushing through to the outlet, where they were sure they would be safe, and from whence they could move in what direction they pleased. They were mistaken: their wary enemies completely surrounded them the moment they debouched upon the arid plain, and a vindictive and bloody conflict ensued. The Blackfeet were utterly routed, and nearly all of them were slain and scalped. It is not known that more than three escaped; and they escaped only because they were overlooked in the heat of the conflict. It was from them that the rumor was derived by the Traders in the vicinity of the Great Falls of the Missouri. Their story is, of course, exaggerated, but they represent their own numbers as near six hundred, and the forces of the Flatheads as double as numerous. The exaggeration must be enormous. It is not at all probable that the Blackfeet or the Flatheads would or could muster such a force; and it is still less probable that nearly six hundred men were slain. The half of that number would be a larger loss than was ever known to have been sustained in a savage conflict. The truth, I imagine, is, that a conflict did take place, and that the Blackfeet were over-reached, and received a sound drubbing. Thirty, or even fifty, might have been killed, and a hundred or two hundred might have been engaged.

From Pembina, I learn that the Colonists have enjoyed good health, and that the crops are much better than was anticipated, after the great flood of May last, when so many houses and fences were swept off. There is little or no emigration to the Colony. It has furnished a considerable quantity of supplies to the voyagers and traders of the Hudson's Bay Company, and received in return goods suited to its wants. The half-breeds and some of the whites are now out upon their regular Fall hunt. On their return, I suppose a party will as usual, be dispatched into the Northwestern States, to traffic for hardware and other necessaries. My correspondent promises me a copy of the notes of a journey recently made by an employé of the Bay Company from Oregon *via* the Slave Lake to Pembina, and thence to York Factory. When I receive it, I will condense the contents for you, and also give you some idea of the present condition of the fur trade in British America. No local news of any note.

Yours,

L.

Document 15

Pend d'Oreille Chief Alexander Returns
Horses Stolen from the Whites
November 18, 1853

Source: John Mullan, "Report of Lieut. John Mullan, U.S.A., on the Indian Tribes of the Eastern Portion of Washington Territory," and James Doty, "Reports of Mr. James Doty of the Indian Tribes of the Blackfoot Nation," Isaac Stevens, *Reports of Explorations and Surveys, to Ascertain the Most Practicable and Economical Route for a Railroad from the Mississippi River to the Pacific Ocean* (Washington, D.C.: Beverley Tucker, Printer, 1855), vol. 1, pages 437-442.

Editors' note: Gov. Isaac Stevens had plans to negotiate a peace treaty between the Rocky Mountain Indians and the Blackfeet and other Plains Indians in 1854. Despite the perfidy of the Blackfeet promises to stop stealing Salish and Pend d'Oreille horses, Salish Chief Victor was committed to honoring his word to Stevens. John Mullan described how Victor insisted that the Pend d'Oreille traveling with the Salish return horses they had stolen from Fort Benton. Pend d'Oreille Chief Alexander personally led the party restoring the horses to the whites. James Doty also described the dangerous journey of Alexander and five other Pend d'Oreille to Fort Benton in November 1853 to return the stolen horses.

Report of Lieut. John Mullan, U.S.A., on the Indian Tribes
in the Eastern Portion of Washington Territory.

Camp Stevens, Bitter Root Valley,
Washington Territory, November 18, 1853.

Sir:

I have the honor to state that your instructions with reference to the council of Indians to be held at Fort Benton during the coming season have been duly carried out, and information has been given to all Indians visiting this place concerning the same. The objects and results to be obtained have been fully set before them and explained in detail, and now especially do the Flatheads await particularly for the expected change that will be wrought, through the agency of the government, in their relations with the Blackfeet Indians.

The Flatheads, as a nation, have more reason to complain of a want of attention and care, on the part of the government, than any other tribe of Indians, probably, in North America.

Their numbers have been so greatly diminished during the last few years, by being murdered by the Blackfeet, that at present there remains but a handful of the noblest of the Indian tribes of North American to tell the tale of woe, misery, and misfortune, that they have suffered at the hands of the Blackfeet, these hell-hounds of the mountains.

For years now has their country been the theatre where have been committed murders the most brutal, and robberies the most bold and daring, until there is not left a spot but that is pointed out to the traveller where some innocent and unsuspecting Flathead was put to the knife in cold blood, or where were shot down scores of friendly Indians, by these devils of the mountains. So long has this state of things existed, the word "Blackfoot" has become the by-word of terror and fear among all the tribes of Indians west of the Rocky mountains; and now it is that the young Flathead child is taught, as soon as it can comprehend the words of its father, to watch and guard his nation against the inroads of these devilish fiends.

Thus are the seeds of enmity and hate thus early sown; and when the child becomes the full-grown man, he deems it his duty, a duty he owes not only to his family but to his tribe, to ward off the encroachments of these their enemies. Thus it is deadly feuds have ever existed among these Indians, and so will they ever exist until our government shall take such measures as shall put an end to the same.

When you passed through the country of the Blackfoot nation, they promised to live on terms of friendship with their neighbors the Flatheads, and now I have to communicate that since that time they have kept their promise most faithlessly. News has just reached me, by the Pend d'Oreille Indians, that while the chief, Victor, was on his way to the buffalo hunt, east of the Missouri, he encamped on a prairie after having crossed the dividing ridge, and while there a part of his horses were stolen by a war party of Blackfeet. There were Pend d'Oreilles with him also at the time. The Flatheads started in pursuit of the Blackfeet, and succeeded in killing one and wounding a second. The dead body of the Blackfoot was seen by Mr. [Abiel W.] Tinkham's party on their route from Fort Benton to this place. The Pend d'Oreilles being highly incensed at this want of faith on the part of the Blackfeet, they having been told by Victor that they had promised you most faithfully to abstain from all further depredations, followed the Blackfeet into Fort Benton, and there seeing a band of horses and mules, they chose from this band a number of Indian horses. These they thought belonged to the American Fur Company. They reason thus:

Alexander (English name.)
Tum-cle-hot-cut-se (Indian name).

Pend d'Oreille Chief Alexander
Drawing by Gustavus Sohon, NAA INV 08501800, National
Anthropological Archives, Smithsonian Institution, Washington, D.C.

"Here are these whites, the employés of the American Fur Company, who have bought, and who do still buy, from the Blackfeet the horses that they steal from us, thus giving encouragement to their thieving propensities; and here are some of our horses; we will take them off;" and so they did. On arriving at the camp of Victor they narrated what had taken place, when the chief Victor told the Pend d'Oreille chief to take the horses back to Fort Benton, and turn them over to the chief at the fort; and this they did. The horses were turned over to Mr. Clark at Fort Benton. These same Pend d'Oreilles joined Mr. Tinkham on their return, on his fifth day out from Fort Benton, and accompanied him to the village of St. Mary's.

The chief Victor said that the Flatheads had promised to live in peace with the Blackfeet, and only to war when their lives were threatened, and that none of his men should steal horses from either the whites or Indians; that, since you had promised to protect them, the matter should be referred to you. Here, then, is an act of bravery, nobleness, and honesty, on the part of these Indians, that is but seldom, if ever, met with among any other tribe of Indians, either east or west of the Rocky mountains; and here, too, is a strong and evident example of the reputed faithlessness of the Blackfoot nation.

This last act of bad faith on the part of the Blackfeet has occurred at a most unpropitious period. Since here I have told the Pend d'Oreilles and Flatheads of the council to be held at Fort Benton, and the promises of the Blackfeet; but here the Blackfeet, by their acts, have given the lie to everything that I have told the Flatheads; and now I fear that the Flatheads will place all the promises made you by the Blackfeet in the same category that they have placed those made to them and others for the last half century. They have told me that the Blackfeet have made the same promises time and again, and as often have they been violated. And now I would most urgently recommend to you that the absolute and great necessity of the establishment of a military post, at or near Fort Benton, be set forth before the proper department, and that immediate action be taken on it. The necessity for this is becoming more and more apparent, and is being more and more felt every day. The presence of a military force only will restrain the Blackfeet from their incursions and depredations on their neighbors. The council, should it be held next summer, will probably do a great deal towards the settling of the feuds that exist among these northern tribes; but I fear that it alone will prove ineffectual. It, however, with the presence of a military force, will, I think, succeed in putting an end to the enmity that has existed among these tribes for centuries back.

They have never been made aware of the power and influence of the government, save in your council with them at Fort Benton; and what they now need is to have the fear of the government held over them. And a policy

I should recommend would be, should they continue to keep their pledges as faithlessly as they have before, that our military force should be sent among them, put every man, woman and child to the knife, burn down their villages, and thus teach the nation that since persuasion will not, force must and shall effect the ends that we have in view. This will be a forcible, and, I think, salutary example to them, and will, I think, be the only means of accomplishing the purposes of the government. They had better by far be totally exterminated than left to prowl the mountains, murdering, plundering, and carrying everything before them.

I have also found, myself, in this valley, a Nez Perce scalp taken by the Blackfeet quite recently, and but a few days have elapsed since twenty-five of them were taken at Hell Gate; and thus, I think, they will ever be through the land of the Flatheads, until they receive a prompt, thorough, and severe chastisement at the hands of the government.

Truly, your obedient servant,

J. Mullan,
Lieutenant United States Army.

Governor I. I. Stevens,
In Command of the N. P. Railroad Survey, &c.

Fort Hall, Oregon Territory,
December 14, 1853.

Sir:

I have the honor to report, that previous to leaving the country of the Flathead Indians, on the 28th of November last, I had assembled the chiefs and principal men of the tribe together, when I distributed among them such presents as you left with me, and at the same time communicated to them what you had done, and what you had intended and promised to do for them; and particularly setting before them the objects of the council to be held at Fort Benton during the next summer. They received the intelligence of the council with much joy and exultation, and they now look forward to the coming summer as a time from which they are to date a new and happy period in their nation's history. In reply to the many things told them, they said they were deeply and fully aware that they were a helpless and miserable race of beings; but now their hearts were glad to hear that the government had not neglected them, but that it intended to send an agent among them, who would superintend their interest and welfare; they said what they wanted the government to do for them now was, to send a man among them who would teach them how to till the soil, and to send them agricultural implements and seeds; and that they neither desired nor demanded more than this.

And now what I would recommend is the appointment of an intelligent, reliable man; one who, with a good moral character, combines a degree of firmness and resoluteness, and at the same time is an excellent practical farmer, and who is also a member of the Catholic church. This last I mention and recommend from the fact that the Jesuit priests have been among the Flatheads for ten or twelve years, and have laid among them a foundation upon a better and firmer basis than has ever been laid among any Indian tribe either east or west of the mountains, upon which a superstructure can now be built which will be an ornament not only to the district where it will be erected, but to our whole nation. This man, so appointed, could perform the duties of Indian sub-agent; could enclose a farm, and have the necessary buildings, in the Bitter Root valley, to whom the Indians could apply in need for information and help; who, by his high moral stand, could and would exert a powerful and salutary influence over the Indians; and who could, in case the mission is re-established at the St. Mary's village, fully cooperate with the priests there stationed, and cause the Bitter Root valley, at no distant day, to teem with life, business, and happiness. Such a man, no doubt, can be found in Oregon who would willingly accept of such a post; if not in Oregon, at least in the States. And another thing I would recommend would be, that the man should be a married man, with a family. He would thus have every inducement to comfortably settle himself for life, and be less disposed to become dissatisfied, and thus destroy the good intentions of those who have the supervision of our Indians affairs. While at this place, application has been made to me, by a man living at Fort Hall, for the post for his father, who at present is a farmer at Manayunk, Philadelphia county, Pennsylvania, and also a Catholic, with a family. His name is Hugh Damsy. I told him I would mention his case to you. As to who he is, his capacity, &c., I know nothing; only his son seems to be an upright, sober man, and who, from year to year, trades on the emigrant road.

I think myself some man should be appointed whom you well know, or who comes to you recommended by those who have had an opportunity of judging him. That there is a necessity, and that a great one, that some one should be among the Flatheads to teach them to till the soil, there can be no manner of doubt; and as it has been partially promised them, and as they fully expect it, I recommend to you that it be urgently set forth before the proper department, and that action should be had upon it during the session of the coming Congress. I shall be able to send you, by Lieutenant [Guvier] Grover, the present number of the Flatheads, their relations, power, intercourse with other tribes, &c. The report of the council at Fort Benton has spread throughout the whole Indian country as on the wings of lightning, and has been received as the harbinger of glad tidings to all. It is a matter that *must not* be let fall to the ground, but the sparks that have been struck by our expedition must be fanned into a flame until it shall envelope all the Indian tribes both east and west of the Rocky mountains. For myself, I feel a deep interest in it, and, for one, should regret to hear that our government has overlooked, either partially or completely, the interests of so many thousands of souls that it is in duty bound to protect. One great result obtained from this council, and of course the treaty, will be the settling of the whole of the eastern portions of Washington and Oregon Territories, and thus blot out forever from the map of our country what is now looked upon as the great desert, as it were, extending from the Missouri to a hundred miles west of the Rocky mountains, thus occupying a central position in the heart of our country, and replace it by one continued belt of thriving settlements and villages, where the stir and bustle of business shall resound, without cessation, as along our civilized and settled borders. Should the matter be let passed during the coming season, I doubt whether it can ever be undertaken again under as favorable auspices. Should you have received any intelligence from Washington in regard to the subject, you will oblige me by referring to it in your communication to me in the Bitter Root valley.

Truly, your obedient servant,
J. Mullan,
Lieutenant United States Army.

Governor I. I. Stevens,
In Command of N. P. Railroad Survey, &c.

* * * * * * * *

Report of Mr. James Doty of the Indian Tribes of the Blackfoot Nation.
Fort Benton, *December* 28, 1853.

Dear Sir:

Enclosed you have additional receipts, omitted to be sent by Mr. [Abiel W.] Tinkham, for quartermaster's property in my hands.

As requested in your letter of October 3, 1853, I send herewith a report upon those particulars concerning the Blackfoot nation which you directed me to examine. It includes the plan of a farm and list of agricultural instruments, and is accompanied by a rough draught of the agency buildings deemed necessary.

By the enclosed thermometrical register, since October 1st, you will perceive that we have had no cold weather, no snow, and indeed no winter. Can the same be said of the entrance to the South Pass?

We are passing the winter comfortably if not pleasantly. The men have conducted themselves in all respects in a praiseworthy manner.

Rations will hold out tolerably well, with the exception of flour and coffee. In case an express is sent to this point, I would suggest that a pack-horse or two be also sent, loaded with flour, coffee, and beans.

Early in this month I procured, without cost, about 1,000 pounds of fresh meat by sending out pack-horses with the Indian hunters, so there is no danger of starvation. The oxen, horses, and mules are in first-rate condition; many of them are fat.

I am happy to inform you that the three horses reported to you as stolen have been returned; so that up to date not an animal in my charge has been lost.

The recovery of these horses is worthy of notice, as indicating, in the Indians who returned them, an honesty, and moral as well as physical courage, seldom seen among white men, and never expected of Indians.

On the 1st of November, six Pend d'Oreille Indians came to this post and delivered up all the horses that were stolen. It appears that they were taken by two young Pend d'Oreilles, and run to the Pend d'Oreille camp, then hunting beyond the Muscle Shell, under the command of the chief of that nation, "Alexander." The horses were recognized by the stamps as belonging to the whites, and the young men confessed having stolen them at this post. A council was held, and it was determined that it was a great sin to steal horses from white men who were friendly to them; that the wishes of the "Great Soldier Chief," who had been at the St. Mary's, were known to them, and they had promised compliance with them; that stealing these horses would give the Pend d'Oreilles the name of liars and triflers; that they had always borne a good name, and were ashamed to have mean things said of them now: therefore, the horses must be taken back by their great chief and five principal men of the tribe; accordingly, they came boldly to the fort and delivered up the horses without asking any reward, but, on the contrary, expressing much sorrow and shame that they had been taken.

Thus these six Indians proved themselves not only honest, but brave in the highest degree, coming, as they did, five days' and nights' march into an enemy's country simply to do an act of justice to strangers. They remained here two days, and on departing were accompanied by Mr. Clarke and myself fifteen or twenty miles on their journey. During their stay here a number of

Piegan warriors about the fort became very troublesome to the strangers; so much so, that we were compelled to detail a strong guard for their protection.

Suitable presents were given them from the Indian goods left with me. No event of great importance has occurred among the Indians since your departure.

The "Little Dog's" camp was attacked not long since by a party of Crees and Assiniboins, and himself and another were wounded. He has, however, determined not to revenge it, but to wait until the council is held.

I am sorry to inform you that many of the Indians do not abide by their promises to remain at peace this winter. About five hundred, principally Piegans, have passed this post, on their way to war, since October 1st; about one hundred were induced to turn back. In the same time eight hundred or a thousand warriors must have passed above and below the fort, on their way to the Flatheads, Snakes, and Crows, as I have, from time to time, heard of large parties of Bloods, Blackfeet, and Gros Ventres, on the march; and parties are constantly going from the different bands.

Several of the chiefs have taken a very decided stand for peace, and keep the warriors of their own bands at home. Others say, "this is the last winter we can go to war; next summer the white soldiers will stop us; therefore, let us steal this winter all the horses we can."

It is becoming a serious question in my mind whether these Indians will desist from their predatory incursions until a sufficient military force is stationed in the country to check every attempt at sending out war parties. No military force, however, is needed to protect white men in this country.

Good interpreters for the government are very difficult to procure, because such can get higher wages from the traders than the government pays. The only man I can at present recommend is a Mr. [Jemmy Jock] Bird. He is a half-breed, English and Blackfoot; is an elderly man, respectable and intelligent, and the best interpreter in the country. He may not wish the situation of interpreter at the agency, but can no doubt be engaged for a council.

In my intercourse with these Indians I have been especially careful to have them understand that I made them no promises.

Trusting that we may see you at an early day in spring, I am, very respectfully and truly, yours,

James Doty.

Governor I. I. Stevens,
Washington Territory.

Document 16

A Trip by Canoe from St. Mary's Mission to St. Ignatius Mission November 1853

Source: George Suckley, "Navigability of the Columbia," Isaac Stevens, *Reports of Explorations and Surveys, to Ascertain the Most Practicable and Economical Route for a Railroad from the Mississippi River to the Pacific Ocean* (Washington, D.C.: Beverley Tucker, Printer, 1855), vol. 1, pages 291-298, 301.

Editors' note: According to George Suckley's report, the Bitterroot Salish had some farms in 1853, a small village of wooden houses, and cattle. Suckley made a brave attempt to canoe down the Clark's Fork River. Seven miles above the original St. Ignatius Mission, he met a camp of probably Lower Pend d'Oreille or Kalispel Indians led by All-ol-sturgh and benefited greatly from their generosity and hospitality. Suckley described the St. Ignatius Mission in what was to become Washington state and seemed to get most of his information about the Pend d'Oreille from Father Adrian Hoecken and some of the observations were probably colored by Hoecken's prejudices. The mission maintained a farm that was worked jointly by the missionaries and Pend d'Oreille farmers. Some derogatory terms were used by the author.

Navigability of the Columbia.
Report of Dr. Geo. Suckley, Assistant Surgeon, U.S.A., of His Trip
in a Canoe from Fort Owen, Down the Bitter Root, Clark's Fork,
and Columbia Rivers, to Vancouver.

Olympia, Washington Territory
December 19, 1853.

Sir:

I have the honor to submit the following report concerning my operations while at the Flathead village of St. Mary's, and my subsequent reconnaissance of the Bitter Root, St. Mary's, Flathead or Clark and Columbia rivers, agreeably to instructions received from you dated October 2. . . . . .

. . . . The St. Mary's valley, so called after the Roman Catholic mission which was here established, is situated between the Rocky and Bitter Root ranges of mountains. The valley at Fort Owen (on the site of the former mission) is about twelve miles wide. It is very fertile, watered by cool, sparkling brooks, and surrounded by lofty and picturesque mountains. It is inhabited by the Flathead or Selish Indians. How they obtained the name of Flatheads I am unable to say, as the custom of flattening children's heads is not practised by them. The men are rather below the average size, but they are well-knit, muscular, and good-looking. Although professedly Roman Catholics, they still keep up their aboriginal mode of dress, and many of their old customs. They are remarkably honest, good-natured, and amiable. On account of the depredations and constant aggression made upon them by the Blackfeet, and their own migratory habits, it was found inadvisable to keep up the mission among them. It was accordingly abandoned three years ago. They still remember the good teachings of the missionaries, as evinced by their honesty and chastity. Although few in number, they are very brave, and invariably attack the Blackfeet when they meet. The custom of scalping dead enemies is abandoned by them. Owing to the incursions of the Blackfeet, who steal their horses, they have but a few good animals left — so few, that some are prevented from buffalo hunting in consequence. They raise some wheat and potatoes, but depend principally on the chase for subsistence. They have quite a large number of cattle; these they corral at night to prevent them from being killed by the Blackfeet. The latter Indians do not steal cattle as they do horses, but kill them out of malice. The brothers Owen purchased the mission buildings of the priests, and established a private trading-post. This is called Fort Owen. It is surrounded by the Flathead village, numbering sixteen wooden houses. The soil of the valley is exceedingly fertile. Cattle do not generally require foddering in the winter, the snows are so light. All the numerous streams abound in fine trout. Grouse in the valleys and on the mountains, bear, deer, elk, beaver, and mountain sheep, are abundant. Buffalo were formerly in great numbers in this valley, as attested by the number of skulls seen and by the reports of the inhabitants. For a number of years past none had been seen west of the mountains; but, singular to relate, a buffalo bull was killed at the mouth of the Pend d'Oreille river on the day I passed it. The Indians were in great joy at this, supposing that the buffalo were coming back among them. In addition to the foregoing, I collected considerable information respecting the missions, and the past and present condition of the Indian tribes on my route. Much of this is contained in my journal, from which I take the following extracts. . . . .

November 7. — Made an early start. Paddled nine hours. At dusk we encamped with some Indians, on the left bank of the river, about half a mile above the outlet of Lake Debeoy. There are four lodges at this place, all built after the fashion of the Sioux lodges, with the single difference that they are covered by mats of reeds instead of skins. These mats are made of rushes laid parallel and fastened together at the ends. For convenience in travelling, the mats are rolled into cylindrical bundles, and are thus easily carried in canoes. Our breakfast and lunch to-day consisted of camas roots and dried berries, a little flour and hard bread crumbs (our last) being sprinkled in to thicken the compound, thus making a somewhat palatable compound or mush, or gruel. This fills up the stomach, but does not allay hunger. Our provisions are out, the ground is covered with snow, and the sky obscured with clouds. The weather is excessively cold. Our tent is wet, as indeed it has been for a week or more. Our robes and some of our blankets are in the same condition; and, on the whole, our situation is quite uncomfortable. Under these circumstances, I concluded to lodge all night with the Indians. Our hungry stomachs were quite willing to partake of any hospitality they might offer in the shape of food. With these feelings I entered the lodge of All-ol-sturgh, the head of the encampment. The other lodges are principally occupied by his children and grandchildren. They provided us with dried camas and berries, also a piece of raw tallow, which tasted very good. Shortly after our entrance, All-ol-sturgh rang a little bell; directly the lodge was filled with inhabitants of the camp, men, women, and children, who immediately got upon their knees, and repeated, or rather chanted, a long prayer, in their own language, to the Creator. The repetition of a few pious sentences, an invocation, and a hymn, closed the exercises. In these the s....s took as active a part as the men. The promptness, fervency, and earnestness all showed, was pleasing to contemplate. These prayers, &c., have been taught them by their kind missionary and friend, the much-loved Father [Adrian] Hoecken, (S.J.) He is stationed at the Mission of St. Ignatius, from which we are, I hope, but a few miles distant. The participation of the s....s in the exercises, and the apparent footing of equality between them and the men, so much unlike their condition in other savage tribes, appear remarkable.

November 8. — We ate some more dried berries and some dried fish for breakfast, and, after making our Indian friends some presents, pushed off in our canoe for the mission, which we reached after paddling seven miles. I walked up to the door of the mission-house, knocked and entered. I was met by the reverend superior of the mission, Father Hoecken, who, in a truly benevolent and pleasing manner, said, "Walk in, you are welcome; we are glad to see the face of a white man." I introduced myself and the men, and stated that I had come all the way from St. Mary's by water, after a journey, or rather voyage, of twenty-five days; that I was out of provisions and tired. He bade us welcome, had our things brought up from the boat, an excellent dinner prepared for us, and nice room to sleep in, and treated us with the cordiality and kindness of a Christian and a gentleman. In these kindnesses the Reverend Father Mennetree [Joseph Menetrey], and the lay brother, Mr. Mageau, cordially took part — all uniting in their endeavors to render us comfortable and make us feel at home. From the Reverend Mr. Hoecken I have the following particulars concerning the mission and the condition of the inhabitants in its vicinity: The mission was established nine years ago; the whole country at that time being a vast wilderness. Its inhabitants were the Kalispelms. They lived mostly from the Pend d'Oreille or Kalispelm lake, down the Clark river, to this point; they speak nearly the same language as the Flathead or Selish Indians. Another mission (St. Mary's) was at the same time opened among the last-mentioned tribe. Between these two, in the vicinity of the Horse and Camas plains, on the Clark river, another band, calling themselves Kalispelms, has since been formed, of which Ambrose is the chief; this band consists of a number of floating and wandering families, composed of Spokanes, Kalispelms proper, and Flatheads, who, having intermarried, have formed a habit of sojourning at this locality during their annual migrations to and from the buffalo hunting-grounds. In all, the two bands of Kalispelms number about one hundred lodges — say sixty of the Kalispelms proper, or those who recognize Victor as their chief — and have their headquarters at the mission, and about forty of the new band already alluded to, who look up to Ambrose and who live above Lake Pend d'Oreille. The Flatheads number about forty-five lodges. These are not all inhabited by Flatheads, there being but very few pure Flatheads left, the race having been almost exterminated by the Blackfeet. The mass of the nation now consists of Kalispelms, Spokanes, Nez Perces, and Iroquois, who have come among them, together with their descendants. Pierre Baptiste, the old Iroquois at Fort Owen, thinks that there are about sixty lodges among the Flatheads, but says that many of them are only inhabited by old women (widows) and their daughters. For the first two years the missionaries lived in skin lodges, accompanying the natives on their periodical hunts and visits to their fishing-grounds, &c. During this time they found it very hard to live. Their food consisted principally of camas roots and dried berries, which at best contain but very little real nourishment. They raised some wheat, which they boiled in the beard for fear of waste — parching some of the grains to make a substitute for coffee. After this, they slowly, but steadily, year by year increased in welfare. Each year added a small piece to their tillable ground. They then obtained pigs, poultry, cattle, horses, agricultural implements, and tools. Their supplies of tools, seeds, groceries, clothing &c., are shipped direct from Europe to the Columbia river. There are two lay brethren attached to the mission. One of these, Brother Francis, is a perfect jack of all trades. He is by turns a carpenter, blacksmith, gunsmith, and tinman — in each of which he is a good workman. The other, Brother Mageau, superintends the farming operations. They both worked hard in bringing the mission to its present state of perfection, building successively a windmill, blacksmith and carpenter's shops, barns, cow-sheds, &c., besides an excellent chapel, in addition to a large dwelling-house of hewn timber for the missionaries. The church is quite large, and is tastefully and even beautifully decorated. I was shown the handsomely-carved and gilded altar, the statue of "Our Mother," brazen crosses and rich bronzed fonts; work which, at sight, appears so well executed as to lead one to suppose that they all must have been imported. But no; they are the result of the patient labor and ingenuity of the devoted missionaries, and work which is at the same time rich, substantial, and beautiful. Works of ornament are not their only deeds. A grindstone, hewn out of the native rock, and moulded by the same hand which made the chisel which wrought it; tin-ware, a blacksmith's shop bellows, ploughshares, bricks for their chimneys, their own tobacco-pipes, turned with the lathe out of wood and lined with tin — all have been made by their industry. In household economy they are not excelled. They make their own soap, candles, vinegar, &c.; and it is both interesting and amusing to listen to the account of their plans, shifts, and turns, in overcoming obstacles at their first attempts, their repeated failures, and their final triumphs. The present condition of the mission is as follows: Buildings — the house, a good, substantial, comfortable edifice; the chapel, a building sufficiently large to accommodate the whole Kalispelm nation; a small building is attached to the dwelling-house — it contains a couple of sleeping-rooms and a workshop, a blacksmith's shop, and a store-room for the natives. These are all built of square or hewn timber. Besides these, there are a number of smaller outbuildings, built of logs, for the accommodation of their horses and cattle during the winter, and an excellent root-house. The mission farm consists of about one hundred and sixty acres of cleared land. Wheat, (spring,) barley, onions, cabbages, parsnips, peas, beets, potatoes, and carrots, are its principal products. The Indians are especially fond of carrots. Father Hoecken says that if the children see carrots growing they must eat some. Says he, "I must shut my eyes to the theft, because they *cannot, cannot* resist the temptation." Anything else than carrots the little creatures respect. The Indians are very fond of peas and cabbage, but beets, and particularly onions, they dislike. The other productions of the farm are cattle, hogs, poultry, butter, and cheese. Around the mission buildings are the houses of the natives. These are built of logs and hewn timber, and are sixteen in number. There are, also, quite a number of mat and skin lodges. Although the tribe is emphatically a wandering tribe, yet the mission and its vicinity is looked upon as headquarters. Until farms are cleared and properly cultivated by these Indians, their wandering habits must necessarily continue. Their migrations do not generally extend over a tract of country of more than one hundred miles square. The journeys are performed with horses and canoes. Many individuals of the nation prefer to use canoes entirely; they are made of the inner thin bark of the white pine, spread over red-cedar hoops, sewed with spruce roots, in the manner of the birch canoes of the Chippewas and other eastern Indians. The white-pine bark is a very good substitute for birch, but has the disadvantage of being more brittle in cold weather. These canoes are also shaped somewhat differently, not being turned up at the ends like those of the Chippewas.

Just above Lake Pend d'Oreille the Clark river divides into three streams, which again unite, thus forming two or three large islands. One of these streams is wide, shallow, and swift. Here the Indians annually construct a fence, which reaches across the stream, and guides the fish into a wier or rack, where they are caught in great numbers. To the natives this is a place of great resort. To Lake Rootham long celebrated for the superior quality and vast numbers of its beaver, they go to catch the latter animal and to hunt deer. To other places they go to hunt deer alone; to others to cut flag and rushes for mats, and still again to others to hunt bear. The old method of cooking fish in bowls of wicker or basket work, heating the water by hot stones, is still occasionally practised; although the operation is not very cleanly, it is still very rapid, and the fish thus cooked have an excellent flavor. In summer the Indians live principally on fish, which they catch not only by wiers and fish-traps, but by the hook and line and by spearing. They also collect camas and bitter roots, and a berry, called in some of the eastern States the sugar-berry or sugar-pear. These they dry separately, and also in cakes, with moss, for winter use. This food affords nourishment merely sufficient to sustain life. In the autumn, in addition to hunting venison and bear, they dry meat and fish for winter use. When the severe cold weather has fairly set in, the whole band moves to some noted venison hunting-ground, where during the heavy snows the deer cannot escape, and are readily pursued and killed with clubs.

They hunt over the whole section so thoroughly as entirely to exterminate these animals in that locality, leaving none to breed. In this way they have destroyed the deer entirely in all but two or three places. To each of them they will proceed during the coming and one or two subsequent winters; the deer will then all be destroyed, leaving the inhabitants no dependence, unless by that time they shall have sufficient land under cultivation to support them; otherwise, there will be a great deal of suffering among these people. Last winter they killed eight hundred deer; these were but just sufficient for their wants. The Indians say that in old times there were but very few deer; latterly they became much more plentiful. About six years ago there was a very severe winter and a very heavy fall of snow. The Indians wantonly slaughtered many thousands of these animals, most of which were so poor as almost to be reduced to skin and bone, and for the most part unfit for food. The same winter many deer died from cold and starvation. As the deer are easily killed during a heavy fall of snow, the Indians are in the habit of praying for the latter as a great blessing. The following is a short account of the operations of the missionaries: They came among these Indians about nine years ago, and found them to be a poor, miserable, half-starved race, with an insufficiency of food and nearly naked, living upon fish, camas and other roots, and, at the last extremity, upon the pine-tree moss. They (the Indians) were in utter misery and want — *in want of everything*. Their whole time was occupied in providing for their bellies, which were rarely full. They were of a peaceable disposition, brave, good-tempered, and willing to work. Of spiritual things they were utterly ignorant. Unlike the Indians east of the mountains, they had no idea of a future state or of a Great Spirit; neither had they any idea of a soul. In fact, they had not words in their language to express such ideas. They considered themselves to be animals nearly allied to the beaver, but greater — and why? Because, they said, "the beaver builds houses like us, and he is very cunning, too; but we can catch the beaver, and he cannot catch us — therefore we are greater than he." They thought when they died that was the last of them. While thus ignorant, it was not uncommon for them to bury the very old and very young alive, because, they said, "these cannot take care of themselves, and we cannot take care of them, and they had better die." The missionaries had an arduous labor before them. They commenced by gaining the good will of the inhabitants by means of small presents, and by the betrayal of great interest in their welfare in attendance upon the sick, and, as they prospered, by giving the poor creatures food, seeds, and instructions as to farming. The Indians could not help seeing that no hopes of temporal or personal benefit induced the missionaries thus to labor among them. The missionary told them that they had a Creator, and that he was good; he told them of their Saviour, and of the manner of addressing him by prayer. To this they listened and believed. The name they gave the Creator, in their own language, is "the One who made himself."

Of the soul they had no conception. In the beginning the priests were obliged to depend upon the imperfect translations of half-breed interpreters. The word "soul" was singularly translated to the Indians, by one of these telling them that they had a gut that never rotted, and that this was their living principle or soul. The chief of the tribe became converted, and was baptized Loyola; the mass of the tribe followed their leader. They now almost all pray, and have devotional exercises in their families, and seem in a fair way for further advancement. To show you the good sense, foresight, and benevolence of the priests, I will relate a short conversation I had with Father Hoecken, who is the Superior of the mission and has been among the people from the first. Says he: "Doctor, you will scarcely believe it; surrounded by water as we are, we often have difficulty in getting fish even for our Friday dinner." I replied, jokingly: "I suppose, father that the *Indians* find no difficulty in observing a fast on Friday." He answered immediately: "I never spoke to them about it; it would not do. Poor creatures! they fast too much as it is, and it is not necessary for them to fast more." The people look up to the father and love him. They say that if the father should go away they would die. Before the advent of the missionaries, the inhabitants, although totally destitute of religious ideas, still believed that evil and bad luck emanated from a fabulous old woman or sorceress. They were great believers in charms or medicine. Every man had his peculiar medicine or charm, which was his deity, so to speak; and of it they expected good or ill. With some it would be the mouse; with others the deer, buffalo, elk, salmon, bear, &c.; and whichever it was, the savage would carry a portion of it constantly by him. The tail of a mouse, or the fur, hoof, claw, feather, fin, or scale of whatever it might be, became the amulet. When a young man grew up, he was not yet considered a man until he had discovered his medicine. His father would send him to the top of a high mountain in the neighborhood of the present mission. Here he was obliged to remain without food until he had dreamed of an animal; the first one so dreamed about becoming his medicine for life. Of course, anxiety, fatigue, cold, and fasting would render his sleep troubled and replete with dreams. In a short time he would have dreamed of what he wanted, and return to his home a man.

During the winter all the large game killed is brought to the camp and distributed equally among all. One man is chosen as distributor for the winter. To his lodge the animal is brought. He immediately cuts it up into a number of pieces corresponding to the number and size of the various families. As soon as it is all cut up, the chief cries, "Come and fetch." Immediately a delegate from each lodge appears and carries off the piece assigned him. Singular to say, no grumbling or dissatisfaction is ever manifested at the division. This custom was in vogue before the missionaries came among them; it was first established by their late chief, Loyola. He appears to have been a remarkable man, and a good chieftain and Christian. Although of a very quiet and taciturn disposition, he was good disciplinarian and maintained his authority well. He was generally beloved, and had great influence over the tribe. Before his death, which occurred two years ago, he named the present chief (Victor) as the best man to be his successor. After his decease an election was held, at which all the members of the tribe voted, and by which Victor was almost unanimously elected. He is a small man, young, and of good countenance; but so good and amiable in his disposition, that he is scarcely able to maintain his authority over the tribe. One of his punishments is to whip the offender, but this he never does unless the culprit first consents to the infliction; after which, the latter will frequently laugh or run races, or play a game, or do something else in the way of fun to show how little he cares for the punishment.

At the mission they have a small mill, by which the Indians grind their wheat. The mill is turned by hand, and will grind but three bushels a day.

The missionaries say that these Indians are industrious and not lazy, as compared to other Indians; that they are willing to work, but that the land is so poor, and so little of it is susceptible of cultivation, that they cannot farm enough. The mission farm, as already stated, contains about one hundred and sixty acres. This is kept up for the natives, as but a few acres would be amply sufficient for the missionaries. Each Indian who wishes it is allowed a certain amount of land to cultivate for his own use, and is provided with tools and seed. The farm is for the most part on a terrace, raised some fifteen or twenty feet above the bottom of the river valley. The mould is rich and black, but very thin. Beneath this is a bed of bluish clay, very retentive of moisture and very barren. A small portion, (about two acres,) on the site of a former swamp now cleared and drained, is of deeper rich black muck, and yields excellent crops.

The land generally does not bear much cropping, and soon wears out. They cannot extend the farm higher on the mountain slope, on account of the poverty of the land and the abundance of springs. The large prairie of the valley-bottom, below this terrace, is about twenty feet above the present level of the river. This, although good rich land, is rendered unfit for agricultural purposes by the annual overflow, which subsides so late in the season as not to allow any ploughing or other work to be done upon it before the middle of July, too late for almost any crop.

The missionaries have long wanted the natives to move to the Cœur d'Alene valley, or to the Camas and Horse Plains, where the land is better. They have offered to transport the things necessary to build new houses, but the people are unwilling to go. They say: "This is our country; here are the graves of our forefathers; here we were born, and here we wish to die; we do not want to leave our country, poor as it is."

A few inches below the surface of the earth can be found the ashes and cineritious deposit of a volcano. The stratum is about one-third of an inch thick. As you proceed in a north-northeasterly direction, it becomes thicker and thicker. Hence we may infer that the crater was in that direction, and probably can now be found. The inhabitants have never seen it. They do not travel from curiosity, and the direction is among mountains from the very door of the mission. In the tribe there are men and women still living who remember the eruption. They say that it came on during the afternoon or night, during which it rained cinders and fire. The Indians supposed that the sun had burnt up, and that there was an end of all things. The next morning, when the sun arose, they were so delighted as to have a great dance and a feast.

In the neighborhood of the mission is a large grotto, said to be fifty feet square and very handsome. I was unable to visit it.

The Kalispelms are brave in battle, and are said to be feared and avoided by the Blackfeet. They are not quarrelsome, but are of good disposition. The missionaries have done great things for them — for their bodies as well as their souls. Theft is of rare occurrence. The people seem to be devoted to religion, so far as external forms go and to the extent that their present understanding will admit. It would take three hundred and fifty acres to supply them with sufficient food when the deer are destroyed. A little government aid could be well applied. Powder is dear with them, as also is everything else. Furs are scarce, and, in consequence, the people are very poor. While sojourning in these parts, I was told that there is an abundance of lead ore on the Kootenaie river. Black lead is found at St. Mary's, and gold on Hell Gate river. Copper and silver are said to exist in the mountains north. . . .

I am, sir, respectfully, your obedient servant,

George Suckley.

Governor Isaac I. Stevens,
In Charge of N. P. Railroad Exploration, &c.

Chapter 3

Documents of
Salish and Pend d'Oreille History
Between 1855 and 1859

Document 17

An Eyewitness to the Hellgate Treaty Negotiations
July 1855

Source: Henry R. Crosby to James A. Garfield, July 23, 1872, James A. Garfield Papers, Manuscript Division, Library of Congress, Washington, D.C., series 11, vol. 9, "Removal of Flathead Indians, 1871-1872," pages 77-93, reel 131.

Editors' note: Henry Crosby was the secretary for Isaac Stevens' 1855 treaty negotiations at Hellgate and Missouri River. This extended letter or briefing paper was written to give James Garfield background information before his 1872 trip to negotiate with the Bitterroot Salish. Crosby's letter represents a firsthand account of the negotiations for the Hellgate Treaty. He made some intriguing comments about publishing the story of a Pend d'Oreille woman warrior, but no Crosby manuscript giving her life story and experiences has been found. Some commas have been added.

Department of Justice
Washington, July 23d, 1872

Hon. James A. Garfield
Hiram, Ohio
General,

In compliance with your request to furnish you with what information I might possess with regard to the Flathead tribe of Indians I make the following statement, prefacing it with the remark that I accompanied Governor Isaac I. Stevens, of Washington Territory, in all of his Indian expeditions in the spring and summer of 1855 — drafted at his suggestion most of the treaties and took notes of the daily proceedings at the various meetings. What I state therefore, is derived either from my own personal observations, or obtained directly from the Indians themselves.

The treaty with the Flatheads Pend 'Oreilles and Kootenais was made in July 1855. The Council ground was on the Bitter Root river near the junction of the Hellgate and Blackfoot rivers. There is a small town now in the vicinity called Missoula. It was laid out and the settlement started by the packmaster of our expedition, a man named [Christopher P.] Higgins. He came across from

St. Paul, Minnesota, in Stevens exploration in 1853, of the Northern Pacific Railroad as Sergeant of the dragoon escort (1st U.S. Dragoons). He has been quite a successful trader with the Indians & whites, is a shrewd sharp man and always looks out well first for his own interests. He is perfectly reliable, but he is not exactly the man you will want to employ in any business arrangement with the Indians as they will be to him a secondary consideration to himself.

The three bands of the Indians at the treaty are all small. They then numbered not more than five or [missing word] hundred each. Since then I suppose they have slightly decreased. The Flatheads occupied the Bitter Root Valley, their present home and the place from which it is proposed to move them. The Pend 'Oreilles were near Flathead Lake and in the vicinity of the Catholic Mission, which was established on its present site, I think as early as 1845 or 6. The Kootenais had their lands farther to the north and partly in the British possessions.

The Flatheads and the Pend d'Oreilles are closely connected having much intermarried with each other. The Kootenais however are evidently a strayed off branch of the Blackfeet, though so remote that there exists no good feeling between them. Their language is very similar.

These Indians all cultivated small patches of ground. They raised potatoes and other vegetables; had a few cows and some excellent horses. The Flathead horses are considered by far the best Indian horses in the interior of the country; their stock having been much improved by the Hudson Bay Company, who had at their post some excellent Canadian stallions. The saying of the Blackfeet was "that a Flathead horse was always a good horse."

In the spring and fall of each year, these three bands went together over on the headwaters of the Missouri to hunt buffalo. The great range of these animals was struck about sixty or seventy miles east of Fort Benton. In these semi-annual hunts they had to pass immediately through the Blackfoot country. As these latter Indians were their deadly enemies and robbed and murdered their people whenever they could catch them at a disadvantage the bands had to ~~hunt~~ travel together for mutual protection. The great disparity in numbers ~~of their foes~~ rendered this necessary.

The Blackfeet were for years and up to the time of the treaty made with them by Gov. Stevens, in September 1855, on the Judith, below Fort Benton, the terror of all the north Missouri country. "Their hands were against every man and every man's hands against them." They were at perpetual war with the Crows and Snakes and every tribe in their vicinity. They were the most warlike Indians on the continent. All the books of adventures in the Rocky Mountains, speak of the dreaded Blackfeet, as the bloodthirsty savages who never took captives or spared life. You will find them described in Washington

Irving's account of the adventures of Captain [Benjamin] Bonneville, & also his Astoria. They were perpetually sending out war parties in all directions. These parties started on foot with their guns and bows and arrows. To each party of ten there was a moccasin boy of some twelve or fourteen years of age, he carried three or four pairs of moccasins for each man, so they were amply provided with foot covering should they stay away for several months which they frequently did, as they sometimes went hundred of miles before they succeeded in capturing horses, or taking scalps. The men carried on their backs their horse hair lariats. Horses were the great object of the expedition as an Indians importance and wealth was estimated by the number of horses he owned, but scalps, no matter how taken, were great prizes and made the man a brave who could bring one back with him. The Blackfeet were divided into four bands, the Piegans, Bloods, North Blackfeet, (the worst of all. They ranged into the British possessions and bought from the Hudson Bay Company posts ammunition and fire water) and the Gros Ventres. The latter are evidently a branch of the Arrapahoes, whose language they speak and whom they closely resemble in habits and customs.

The Blackfeet being thus numerous and the whole body of their young men seeking distinction in war parties, they scouted the country for hundreds of miles and in all directions. The small streams running into the Missouri near its head, were filled with beaver and were therefore much hunted by the white trappers. They did so, however, at the risk of their lives, as the Blackfeet in turn hunted them and there are, or were a few years ago, many white men's scalps in the Blackfeet lodges. When I was at Fort Benton in 1855, I frequently read from Bonneville or other books incidents in which ~~was~~ were related the death of white trappers, and the Indians themselves, who had participated in the murders, would say whether the story was correctly told and if not, describe the facts of that particular affair.

The white trappers were always great friends of the Flatheads. From the time of Lewis and Clark, to whom they gave great assistance, they had been on good terms. It is the boast of the Flatheads, that they have never shed a white man's blood. That he had always found a welcome, food and a home in their lodges.

Victor, the chief said at the council, "Why do you want to put us on a reservation by ourselves. There is room enough in the Bitter Root Valley. We want the whiteman to come and settle alongside of us; to take up a piece of land and help us keep off the Blackfeet. We have always been brothers. We have lived and fought together and across the mountains in the ~~Missouri~~ country of the big river. You will find the white man's bones and the bones of the Flatheads in the same grave. You ~~can~~ cannot tell them apart.

Victor pled so hard for his people to be left in their old home that Gov Stevens agreed to it, and that was the reason the article of the treaty was added to it, which permitted him to remain, subject however at any time to the ~~future~~ action of the President, should he deem it advisable, as he does now, to remove them over to the main reservation on the Jocko.

I have often heard the old trappers who I met in Oregon and in the mountains say "The Flatheads are not Indians. There is nothing Indian about them except their skins. They are white men and if all white men were as good it would be better for the world. They only fight when they have to, for their own lives. They do not steal and what white man ever heard a Flathead lie."

This was their character years ago. Not having been among them since the organization and rapid settlement of Montana, I cannot state whether it is such now. I only know, that at the time of the treaty, ~~we~~ all of us who belonged to the expedition, considered it the best field in which to test the experiment of bringing the Indian to the civilization of the whites. The Flatheads had a natural tendency that way and the manner in which they have been treated is a burning shame and disgrace to the government. No wonder that the Indian loses faith in the white man and says that he speaks with a forked tongue and there is no truth in him. If most of their Agents had been sent to the penitentiary for grand larceny, it would have been no more than justice. They have been robbed from the very day of the confirmation of the treaty till now.

They were promised school houses for their children Blacksmith and Carpenter's shops and mills to grind their grain. If the mills were ever built they were burnt down before they derived any benefit from them. There were other mills that must make the profit in the valley; and the schools and shops never had even a temporary existence. The twenty years in which annually they were to receive large supplies from the government has nearly passed away and the many thousands of dollars have only enriched those into whose hands it has gone as the Agents for its proper expenditure.

These ~~were~~ have been the rewards for the protection of our people years ago and to a tribe who as far back as 1837, sent ~~a deputation of~~ some of their young men to the white settlements in the state of Missouri, asking to have "a missionary come to them and bring them the word of the Great Spirit, the Good God." Their friends, the trappers, had told them of the preachers and the Bible.

Grey [William H. Gray], in his history of Oregon, narrates this Bible story, which is a well known fact. He says "That it is the only tribe on the continent which can truly claim that they have never shed the blood of a white man; yet they are far more brave as a tribe than any other Indians. They never fear a foe no matter how numerous."

Father [Pierre] de Smet gives in his book of the missions in the Rocky Mountains, an account of a battle in which 60 Flatheads defeated several hundred Blackfeet, who ~~had~~ attacked their camp.

There is a woman still living I believe amongst them, whose history has the romance almost of Joan d'Arc. She is now about 60 years of age, would never marry, always took care of the sick and wounded, and led the tribe in all of its battles. In hand to hand encounters she killed more Blackfeet than any half a dozen of the bravest warriors. She made so many narrow escapes that the Indians, both friends and foes, thought she bore a charmed life and her very appearance in the fight was encouragement on one side and dread on the other. She had an unwriteable Indian name but the Catholic fathers christened her Mary.

~~Had I have gone on this mission I intended to have written an account of her in my sketches of Montana for Harper's Magazine.~~

Though I have written this, as you will perceive hastily yet I have made it much longer than I intended and now to end with the practical part.

For your Interpreter take Francois Sark-sa, the latter signifies one eyed half-breed. He is a half breed Iroquis. That is his father was an Iroquis (Canadian) and his mother a Flathead. He is a farmer, speaks English tolerably well, French and several Indian languages. He is considered very reliable and trustworthy. He has a brother, whose name I forget, who is also a good interpreter. Of the Catholic priest Father [Adrian] Hoecken, a Hollander ~~was~~ is the best. He is not there now, unless I have been misinformed. If he is, you can place confidence in him. Father [Anthony] Ravalli, an Italian, is I think also trustworthy, but Father Menatré [Joseph Menetrey], a Frenchmen, is a perfect Jesuit. You cannot trust him in any matter which he might deem would be against the interest of his mission.

The distance you will have to move the Indians will be about forty or fifty miles, perhaps not so much. I should take the Chiefs with me first, and go over and pick out the place. All they want is a few waggons & they can move themselves. Some few of ~~them~~ their number will remain, take up, or keep their present farms and become citizens. The great body of them will stick together. If each family could have marked off for it, a twenty or forty acre lot, be assisted in building a small & comfortable log house and then have a cow and a calf, some little stock given them, it would be a great encouragement and do much to make them satisfied with the removal.

Stevens idea about the Jocko reservation, was to gather there in course of time, not only these three bands but also the Spokanes and Colville Indians who speak the Flathead language and the Coeur d'Alénes. The reservation was made large for this purpose and the selection was ~~made~~ also, because it was so well surrounded by ~~the~~ mountains that it could not very well be encroached upon by the whites.

In all of these treaties, one of the principal objects of Stevens, was to induce the different tribes of Indians through whose lands the route would lay, not to throw any obstacles in the way of the building of the North Pacific Railroad. He was the originator of the scheme and obtained the appointment of Governor of Washington Territory for the more effectually carrying out his plans.

He surveyed the route in 1853, and threw into the work all the remarkable energy and ability which he possessed. Aside from the benefit he thought it would be to a fast disappearing race, to place them on reservations and teach them the habits of the whites, he desired to get the Indians off the line of the Railroad. The speedy completion of the road was the avowed purpose to which he proposed to devote his life. This was unfortunately frustrated by his death at the battle of Chantilly in Virginia. He fell, a subordinate General in an army, of which all military men who knew him well, readily concede he would have been its greatest commander. To which position, had he survived the battle, it was the intention of President [Abraham] Lincoln to have appointed him.

With great respect
Yr Obt Svt
Henry R. Crosby

Document 18

Pend d'Oreille Chief Big Canoe: "Sometimes My People Get Mad When the Blackfeet Kill Us" July 10, 1855

Source: Excerpt from "Official Proceedings at the Council Held by Governor Isaac I. Stevens, Supt. Indian Affairs, W. T., with the Flathead, Pend Oreilles and Kootenay Tribes of Indians at Hell Gate in the Bitter Root Valley, Washington Territory, Commencing on the Seventh Day of July, 1855," Robert Bigart and Clarence Woodock, eds., *In the Name of the Salish & Kootenai Nation: The 1855 Hell Gate Treaty and the Origin of the Flathead Indian Reservation* (Pablo, Mont.: Salish Kootenai College Press, 1996), pages 30-38.

Editors' note: Pend d'Oreille Chief Big Canoe gave the longest speech at the 1855 Hellgate Treaty negotiations. The translation is sometimes hard to follow but his points are obvious even in the English translation. Big Canoe could not understand why a peace treaty was needed when the Pend d'Oreille and whites had never been at war with each other. He seemed to feel there was enough land in western Montana for both Indians and whites. His frustration with U.S. government policy towards the tribes was obvious: "You white man don't be afraid, you can see it — the Blackfeet, your own powder and ball shooting at us and you white man. Now I and you, you white man, both die with your own powder and ball. I think so when I think about it — stop that, quit giving them powder and ball. . . . Sometimes my people get mad when the Blackfeet kill us." Despite Big Canoe's unhappiness with the negotiations, he did sign the final document. Some footnotes have been omitted.

July 10th, Tuesday.

The Indians assembled at 2 p.m. and at 2½ p.m. the council opened.

Present the same as yesterday.

Governor Stevens said: "My children: I explained yesterday the kind of a treaty I wished to make with you; that I desired the four tribes — the Flatheads, The Upper and Lower Pend 'Oreilles and Kootenays to go on one tract of land. You went to your camp and have since been thinking and talking about it: you have come here; I wish to know what you think about it. Speak out your minds fully."

Big Canoe (Pend 'Oreille) said: "Listen I will speak. I spoke a while ago —
I heard — I talked, then I went away, now you see all these people. I will not
go away now. Some of them said 'It is good for you to go' that is the reason I
come here; that is the way I spoke — I am going to tell you what I heard when
I went away. I said to them perhaps you are mad; I am very glad of it — then
I left. I spoke to them in this way. It appears to me that you have two ways —
how is it? When you talk you tremble, ashamed of yourself, are you afraid of
him? (the Gov.) We are not talking bad — we are counseling — he is a very
smart chief. You do not know what to do? If you (Victor) had told me before,
I would have spoken long ago about this our land. Now I told him (Victor)
when I do talk I will tell you what we will do with this, our rights. It is our land
— when I first saw you, you white man, when you were travelling through, I
would not tell you take this piece it is our land — when you come to see me
I believe you will help me. If you make a farm I would not go there and pull
up your crops. I would not drive you away — farm it — it is our land both of
us. If I go to your place on your land — If I get there [and say] give me a little
piece. I wonder would you say here take it. I will wait till you give it. I will be
amongst you, very good, I am with you. It is just like my own country — then
I would come back to my own country. That is the way with you white man.
I expect that is the same way you want me to do here, this place. You want to
settle here me with you.

"Here you are going back and forth on our land: go back to your country
— we [are] all one — we [are] all one close together. We [are] all great friends
you white man. When my old people long ago first saw you we were friends
— we never spilt the blood of one of you. They my old people are gone, all of
them — it is the same now, I am the same, I never saw your blood. I want my
place. I always thought no one wanted ever to talk about my place. Now you
talk, you white man — now I have heard. I wish the whites to stop coming.
You know everything you white man — you come and talk about my country,
then you would say we are very poor. You just talk as you please to us; it is that
way. Now you tell me never to go to war. Then I sit [sat] down, I kept quiet
— I was listening to you and you wanted to talk — now [that] you are here I
think [it is] so, I wish it may be good — perhaps you will put me in a trap, if I
do not listen to you, you chiefs, white men — I will beg you, I told this when
you talk my chief (Victor) you tremble this way, I wouldn't speak, I wouldn't
tremble, he is a chief — we all are people — you are white — I am black. I
know you, you, you my chiefs. My heart is heavy because you could not make
it up yesterday. I am very poor, we heard you long ago. I hope it is so.

"When I lay [lie] down my heart is sad, now my chief you say now I am
blind if I want to talk. Here are my eyes, my heart, my brain, I study. You white

men; there are your eyes [papers] lying all over the table, that is the reason you are smart, you always look at your papers; now you talk, it is right when you talk straight. I from my heart and my brains speak. I told my chiefs that when I think I believe I am going to talk this way; the way I beg you — when we call for some of our things I expect you want it then your Indian children. When you see something you say give it to me, I like it. You speaking and I tell you no — I think yes, don't impose upon us. I think yes you like it. Let us alone now. You tell us give us your land; if we say no, I am very poor, that is all the small piece I have got. That is the reason I have come, I am not going to let it go I did not come to make trouble. Therefore I would say I am very poor.

"You Flatheads I think this is my country, I don't think I made a mistake, my grand father's country. I was raised up there across the mountains. I saw my aunt over there, she tells me I am pure Pend 'Oreille. I think I have two bodies; this is mine too, that is the reason I talk; we are talking bad [to] one another, I beg you. I told these people a while ago, now you give me a piece of your land. He is a chief, if we tell him we are very poor, he will keep us — no perhaps he thinks yes we are very poor, he likes my country, we are very poor, we do not like to impose upon each other, this is what I am talking about. When we ask further little things, then you will think we won't give you any land. You will stop anyhow both sides. Talk about treaty, where did I kill you? when did you kill me? What is the reason we are talking about treaties; that is what I said, we are friends, you are not my enemy. I said to them you do not know what to do. I expect you thought so when you tell the Governor. No, I expect you will stop powder and ball being given to us. Why would he stop it. When did I shoot you with your own powder and ball. Our old people when they saw you knew what powder and ball was and never tried to frighten a white man with it; here are the last of us — you see them all now sitting around, where have we made a difficulty with the whites. Here is my country, I think it is in a good place, not a dangerous place. You white man don't be afraid, you can see it — the Blackfeet, your own powder and ball shooting at us and you white man. Now I and you, you white man, both die with your own powder and ball. I think so when I think about it — stop that, quit giving them powder and ball.

"What will you do with us, we are very poor, you see us sitting around here, you know it yourself, we do not ramble about on war parties. There is a Frenchman (Indian name for all traders) coming. I will [not] hide where no one can see me and kill him. No; when I see a white man I go up to him, it makes me smile, I shake hands with him; that is the reason I ought to be let alone. You white people are smart and all the time teaching me. I don't want you to impose upon me. I want you to stop. I am that way you white man like yourself. I am glad to see you — I don't [want] you white man to be sorry for it and you my people. I did not think you white people would tell all over the country about me. You will never see in your papers that the Flatheads or the Pend 'Oreilles have killed any of you — perhaps you are glad of it — I am proud of my old people — I am very poor — they had only a bow and arrow when they saw their enemies; they fought them a long while and then left them — then they say [from] you white man, from you we got guns and powder, that is the reason my people have never spilt your blood. You see us, we are very few, our enemies are very afraid of us, we drove them before us. When my enemies charge upon you (trappers) here I am behind you with your powder and ball, that is the reason we are fast friends. When I travel over the mountains towards my enemies I always think of you white men. I always thought the white man would help me, load my gun for me. Look at me how poor I am — look yonder at our enemies, you see it yourself — you white men with your own eyes. There is the priest, he says he thinks they will listen, here is me, I think they will not. I think if my children die it is all the same as white men — that is the way my heart and brain thinks.

"These are dark Indians, the bad fire (hell) comes to them, fighting one another; it is growing; they are getting worse and worse, there he lays, the Indian he takes some little things and puts on him, he let it go out — here you I sell it there where he lost his things this Indian, there where he put it out, there where they all raise up from one; their dark skins were ahed [sic] of them all — that is what I said a while ago. There you are carrying your things about. I won't hide what I said. I said I will ask him — is that the thing you put the fire out with, I will take it, I will never ask for it; then he said he did not know what to do — I cannot step over your things. There are your goods — which way shall I go. If I go to war I will take my horses. I am alone that is the way I studied. Suppose the Blackfeet come along — when he gets along side that things he cannot cross over — from there it will be white ground — both sides — I think so —

"Sometimes my people get mad when the Blackfeet kill us. There are you white men — you are just listening if they are plenty, you stop our people right here and prevent them going on war parties. We listen to the white people here on our ground — we are not afraid of our enemies, no, we are not afraid of them — that is the way with my heart. I don't know what these sitting around think about it. I don't know how they studied when the white men taught me how to pray. I don't know anything about it, though I spoke about it. The priest told me not to be running around in the lodges in the night, the way I saw myself, I did not like it, we came very near all night — the Crows came to us, then the Blackfeet — there is where it was lost. When I meet you I feel glad, when I got the news the white man, the chief is coming, I was glad — Yonder are the Crows — then the Blackfeet, I don't want to see them.

"Look at these Kootenays, I don't understand them; when I see the sun very low I pray — look at the Kootenays, they are always praying. Look at the Blackfeet, I don't like them. That is the way I talk to you sitting there, I am begging now — I am not talking saucy. Here are your goods — I am on one side and Blackfeet on the other. If he steps over these goods and comes to me what would you think. I am only one side — I listen to you; he kills me, kills me all the time and drives my horses away, you know it, we are poor. We drove one band of horses from the Blackfeet — I talked about it to my Indians. I said give me the horses back, my children — don't you know their pasture, let me have them — my chief took them back. You talked about it strong my father — I am afraid of your arms, way yonder from the Crows they took me — we talked about it, my chief took them back, that is the way we act.

"If I beg you I want you to help me: now you have just come here, now you are going over there and going to talk again. I do not know your minds — you are taking a great many goods, I think so; that is the reason I am quiet and sit down on my land. I thought nobody would talk about land, would trouble me. Look at them sitting here, they heard you were coming and going to pass — I have just come from buffalo; I heard you just come out on this prairie — then I think I will go and see you. I want to know what you think. I was talking to my children this past summer — when I found my children were going on war parties I would tell them to stop — be quiet — always tell my people I expect now we will see the chief — I talk to them that way. I expect he will talk to the Blackfeet again. I will stop very soon. I am telling you my mind — stop — wait — when the white man chief talks again you just listen. If the Blackfeet step over their words again we are not afraid of them my children — hold on to your minds my children, look out, danger might come my children — we will just be quiet, they have got arms those we are going to see. If we step over our word to the chief. It is two winters you passed here, every year since my horses have gone to the Blackfeet, last winter one, this spring two. I was going on a war party as your express passed along here. You say be quiet, I did not go, I will stop and wait — that is the reason I always stop my children — that is the way I spoke to my chiefs.

"Now when a chief will talk to the white chief don't be frightened — we are not going to fight each other, keep on that way; then I will let go my heart & speak to my children. I am not afraid of my enemies — you white man, you talk so smoothly, so well, therefore I tell you I am not ahead of you — I listen to you my father — we all like our children, take pity on them. Here this spring the Blackfeet put my daughter on foot — she packed the goods on her back — it made me feel bad; then I think of what I heard from you my father, and take my heart back and keep quiet. If I had not listened to your express I would have gone on war parties over yonder. I thought I would listen good — that is the reason I always checked those people — my heart said so — I don't want you to be put in trouble — I don't know your minds, you white men — I will stop talking. I am not thinking I am talking saucy. I have got a good deal more to say — I am tired now."

Governor Isaac Stevens
Photograph 76-1179, Toole Archives, Mansfield Library,
University of Montana, Missoula, Montana.

Document 19

Tempers at the 1855 Hellgate Treaty Negotiations
July 13, 1855

Source: Excerpt from "Official Proceedings at the Council Held by Governor Isaac I. Stevens, Supt. Indian Affairs, W. T., with the Flathead, Pend Oreilles and Kootenay Tribes of Indians at Hell Gate in the Bitter Root Valley, Washington Territory, Commencing on the Seventh Day of July, 1855," Robert Bigart and Clarence Woodock, eds., *In the Name of the Salish & Kootenai Nation: The 1855 Hell Gate Treaty and the Origin of the Flathead Indian Reservation* (Pablo, Mont.: Salish Kootenai College Press, 1996), pages 47-55.

Editors' note: The transcript of the July 13, 1855, negotiations for the Hellgate Treaty clearly showed Isaac Stevens' arrogance and impatience. Pend d'Oreille Chief Alexander accused Stevens of talking sharp: "you talk like a Blackfoot." Stevens insulted Salish Chief Victor, calling him an old woman and dumb as a dog. Somehow, Stevens seemed surprised when Victor walked out of the negotiations and did not return until three days later. After Stevens agreed to insert a compromise article dealing with the Bitterroot Valley into the document, all the chiefs signed the treaty on July 16, 1855.

Friday, June [i.e., July] 13th.

The Indians assembled at 12 p.m. and after the usual time spent in smoking, the council was opened.

Gov. Stevens said: "My children, you have had your feast; you have counciled together; you have, I am told, nearly agreed. I hope today you will all agree. You were told all go to the valley or all go to the mission. All wished to go to the mission at first except Victor; Victor does not like to leave his land; his children are buried there, but he has children living. His people have children and men will do for their children what they would not do for themselves.

"I ask now, are you ready to go to the mission, and sign the treaty? We must finish the council today; we have other work to do. I am ready now to explain the provisions of the treaty. My children, It is a treaty made between myself acting for the President, and the Flatheads, Kootenays, and Pend 'Oreilles. It provides for a reservation from the Jocko river to the Flathead Lake, and from the Flathead river to the mountains. You have the right however to pasture your animals at other places if those places are not occupied by the whites. You have in like manner the right to gather roots and berries, to take fish and kill game. You have also the right to go on the roads of the whites and take your produce to market. The Great Father has the right to make roads through your country if necessary. White people however cannot go there without your consent.

"The treaty provides you with a grist mill and a saw mill; it provides you with a blacksmith's shop, a carpenter's shop, and a wheelwright's and plow-maker's shop; you will have a school, you will have a physician, and especially an agent; and you will have all these things for twenty years. Besides this, we shall the first year expend in clothing, in tools, in building houses, in breaking up and fencing land, thirty six thousand dollars. The next four years we shall expend for the same objects six thousand dollars a year; for the next five years we shall expend for the same objects five thousand dollars; for the next five years four thousand dollars, and for the next five years three thousand dollars. For each head chief we will have a house; and they will be paid five hundred dollars each year for twenty years; The house will be furnished, and ten acres of land will be broken up and fenced for each of them. Those of the Indians who give up improvements outside of the reserve will be paid for their improvements.

"This treaty binds you to be friendly with other tribes, and with the whites. The whites and other tribes will be required to be at peace with you. If a white man takes your property, that property will be restored to you. If you take the property of a white person, that property you will restore to him. The treaty also requires you to refrain from drinking liquor. In making the payments provided for in the treaty, they will be made to each person of the tribe; he will receive his portion in his own hands. If any member of the tribe should be in debt, his indebtedness cannot be drawn by the trader from the several payments; that is a matter to be settled between the parties themselves. This treaty provides not only that no white man shall go on your land, but that no trader shall continue there without your consent. The whole of the land will be yours. (This refers to the paragraph concerning the Hudson Bay Company.) It finally provides that you accept the terms of this treaty as the children of the Great Father, acknowledging your dependence upon him.

"Are you ready to sign the treaty?"

Alexander said: "I am ignorant; I am an Indian; I am as it were in the dark. I see you here; it is good. I am glad that the Great Father talks about us. I am content with my people. Here you are — are you through with this treaty. Here are the Flatheads. I thought that the Flatheads were willing to go. You named a smaller place and they backed out. When you told us from [about?] the Jocko, they said it was too small. If you had said all on the other side of the mountains perhaps they would have taken it. We are four nations. When the stock increases where will they be? Suppose we put our farms here, where is the room for us."

Gov. Stevens: "You said the other day it was large enough."

Alexander: "I thought all the land on the other side was to be ours."

Gov. S.: "How far do you wish the land to extend? We told Alexander the place was not large enough; he said it was; Victor said it was; believing they could agree we have drawn it up. Do you bear in mind you can pasture your cattle at any place not occupied by whites?"

Alexander: "Sometimes there is a wide open place above filled with animals. I would rather accept the first proposition. When you first talked, you talked good; now you talk sharp; you talk like a Blackfoot."

Gov. Stevens: "I told Alexander I was afraid the place was too small. He said it was sufficiently large even with the Lower Pend 'Oreilles. I said there was a large place; I would rather you would go there. The white settler wants to go above; he does not want your place. You say the white man is smarter than you. I want to give you the place the white man would prefer. You have a feast, you talk with Victor. Victor says that is the best place. I agreed to give you that place; when you say I am sharp, I am like a Blackfoot, I am ashamed of you Alexander; you have changed your mind; you said one thing on yesterday, you say another today. Talk straight and then we will agree."

Alexander: "The Indians said your country is bad below; if one knows how to farm, it will do; if not, it will not do. They said there were few farming spots; they said that the horses would be mixed and lost. I said yes, that is very bad. You (the Gov.) knew it. You have it on paper, and I said it was good. I understand that nobody should put his foot on my ground, then I said I will stay, then nobody shall touch it, before that you never showed me the limits. It is true, it is quite large each side. I think both sides of the Flathead river will just be enough."

Gov. S.: "Are you through?"

Alexander: "I will take from course de femme [Evaro] on both sides of the river to the lake."

Gov. Stevens: "Do you understand that you have the privilege of pasturage for your animals on all lands not occupied by the whites?"

Alexander: "I do not understand perfectly."

Gov. S.: "Do you understand that the treaty secures to you all that land and the benefit?"

Alexander: "Yes."

Gov. S.: "The treaty gives you the right of pasturage and gathering roots and berries on all lands not occupied by whites."

Alexander: "Yes, I understand, I want the whole land marked out."

(Gov. Stevens again went over the treaty and explained it in all its details.)

Gov. S.: "Now we will sign the treaty."

Alexander: "They did not understand right the provisions — now we understand."

Victor said: "Where is my country: I want to speak."

Gov. S.: "When I call upon you to sign the treaty, you can make your objections."

Victor: "I have not agreed to accept this land (at the mission)."

Gov. S.: "Alexander has agreed and I call upon him."

Victor: "I was talking to you, and I told you no."

Gov. S.: "I now call upon Victor."

Ambrose (Flathead) said: "Yesterday Victor spoke to Alexander. He said, 'I am not headstrong. The whites picked out a place for us, the best place and that is the reason I do not want to go. Two years since they passed us — now the white man has his foot on our ground — the white man will stay with you — this is what I heard two years ago.' Yesterday when we had the feast then Alexander spoke; he said now I will go over to your side. I will let them take my place and come to your place. Then Victor did not speak and the council broke up."

Gov. S.: "Alexander, did you agree yesterday to give up your country and join Victor?"

Alexander: "Yes yesterday I did give up. I listened and he did not give me an answer; then I said I will not give up my land."

Gov. S.: "I speak now to the Pend 'Oreilles and the Kootenays. Do you agree to this treaty? The treaty placing the Kootenays and Pend 'Oreilles on this reservation? I ask Victor if he declines to treat."

Victor: "Talk, I have nothing to say now."

Gov. S.: "Does Victor want to treat? Why did he not say to Alexander yesterday, come to my place? or is not Victor a chief? Is he as one of his people has called him, an old woman? dumb as a dog? If Victor is a chief let him speak now."

Victor: "I thought my people perhaps you would listen — I said, I think this is my country and all over here is my country. Some of my people want to be above here. I sit quiet and before me you give my land away. If I thought so I would tell the whites to take the land there (the mission); it is my country. Long time ago you spoke to me here; then I thought I was very well pleased. I thought no one would touch it because you talked about it and I liked this place myself. I am listening and my people say take my country."

Gov. S.: "Alexander said yesterday that he would come up here. Why did you not answer and say come?"

1855 Hellgate Treaty Negotiations
Drawing by Gustavus Sohon, NAA INV 08603100, National
Anthropological Archives, Smithsonian Institution, Washington, D.C.

Victor: "Yesterday I did talk."

Gov. S.: "Alexander says yesterday he offered to give up his land and come to you — Alexander says you made no answer. Why did you not say, yes, come to my place."

Victor: "I did not understand it so."

Gov. S.: "Ambrose says he understood Alexander to say so. Alexander says he said so; you did not speak and say come to my place; but you were dumb — did not say a word."

Victor: "I do not insist upon staying here, but because you picked out my place [the Bitterroot Valley] I want to stay here."

Gov. S.: "Why did you not tell Alexander to come to my place; does Victor mean to say that he will neither let Alexander come to his place nor go to Alexander's?"

Ambrose: "The Great Father will know what we are talking about. We get a little stick and shove at it, perhaps we will hit it after a while. Here we are yet. If the paper is sent to the Great Father he will say here is a fool and here is a smart man; if the Great Father sees the fool's paper he will not be pleased (alluding to the notes taken). I say to the white chief, don't get angry, may be it will come all right. May be all the people have a great many minds, may be they will come all right. See my chiefs are now holding down their heads, thinking."

Tilcoostay (Flathead) said: "It is not our minds that we see each other here; your fore fathers did not expect to make a treaty; God is working it this way. His children are very poor; they are lost; only from their tongues, they work it different ways. We are all brothers, but we speak different tongues, that is all, and the color of our skins; we are all brothers, that is why you are travelling here. They are poor, these people; they don't know how to talk; a wolf can't talk; take pity on your children — I am done talking."

Red Wolf said: "I talked the other day and the Indians said I talked as though I was telling a story. I am proud, let them laugh at me, I am going to speak. Yesterday when we talked about this we studied all round — Victor is head chief and I am far below him. When we gathered up the first time I thought that he was making up his mind to stop at Flathead lake, but now he makes up his mind to stop here. Alexander spoke yesterday saying now I let it go — now I will come to the Bitter Root valley — I understood him so yesterday. I know Victor's heart, he does not speak quick — Alexander went off. I thought that Victor would agree and that we would all go there. I thought Victor would agree and would speak soon. Victor did not speak — I think this is the cause Victor did not talk, he was not ready to talk. Big Canoe talked then. He spoke as though a hand had been placed on Victor's mouth, that is the reason I think why Victor did not speak. I went home and told my lodge that

I thought our people would come together. Now when the people separated Alexander spoke. I know that if Alexander should come to the valley his people would not follow him. I think when Victor should talk if he did talk in favor of the other side all his children called Flatheads, it would all be right. I think if Victor goes there, though his people will not like to follow him, he cannot take it back and his people will have to go. I think that Victor is the head chief; we are in the same place that we were at first. I have no share in this country — my father's land is below — my mother's country is here. The Kootenays are my relations. This is my opinion — They dislike to leave their country."

Beartrack said: "We are trying to make a treaty. I will speak to you as though you were the Great Father. We met each other — you are my chief — we talked — when we talked we did not talk above or below, only one thing we talked about, we talked about what we wished to get. I want an agent — I want a doctor — I want a teacher — I want a farmer, a blacksmith, this is what we were talking about. Our chief (Lt. [John] Mullan) says look at this just as though it were before eyes. I looked at it and I was content and glad. He was on his horse, I told him to get down, I was glad, I wanted help, that is what I was talking about, then I spoke, 'I tell you my chief, you know me I am suffering, what for? My enemies.' He said, 'Ah, I will help you,' he said 'my people are coming, you will see them.' I said, I am glad, I will look for them. Now we see each other — you are my chief and father. You spoke; they have two minds, I am lost, I am very sorry. I might as well lie down, I am ashamed my father. I have considered, I am poor, I made up my mind, I will talk, I will show my mind. I speak as though to the Great Father, I will talk about the land. I think there is only one thing I am sorry for, I have a very poor country. I do not know what to do if my father tells me to go away. There are my old people I am sleeping with them; when they rise I rise. I think there is only one thing that we cover ourselves with. I studied. I am poor. I looked at my children. What will I do with my children? What will they be? It appears to me there is not room enough at the mission. You might as well tell me to go far to a big place. My country is about as large as my finger nail. I look at my nail; if I break it, it will not be good — something big it is good for me to break; this [is] my mind and the reason my heart is heavy. If you wish you are my father, tell me, break off your piece of land. I look over my country and study about it. May be I would break it off — I say yes, good. You my father, I think it is not bad making this treaty; it would [be] good to make this treaty; this is my mind; this is what I am telling you."

Gov. Stevens: "Ambrose, I am glad you think it is good to make a treaty; the treaty that we make will make you better off. The land reservation is much more than the same number of whites would want. We wish you to live together so that the agent can attend to you. When I met other tribes, many did not want to leave their lands, but they have made up their minds and all gone. I will tell you what a great chief said on the other side — he said, I do not want schools, farms, or mills, but my people want farms, schools, and mills and they want to make a treaty; I therefore will make a treaty and he did make a treaty, and his people approved and signed with him. He was a Yakima chief — Kameiakan. I hope Victor will do as Kameiakan did — I hope Victor's people will do as Kameiakan's people. Owhi signed the treaty also — you know him. Trust your father and trust your chiefs.

"My children, I find that things are nearer to an agreement than when we began talking this morning. Ambrose says the people are not quite prepared, they will be by and by; and Ambrose says be patient and listen. I am patient and have been patient and have listened to them. Others of you have said they were hiding their thoughts (minds) and did not speak; hence I reproved you and said speak out — let me have your hearts. It seems that many of the Flatheads are ready to go to the mission; if their chief says so, they will go. Victor says I am ready to go, but my people will not, but the people say they are ready to go. We want all parties to speak straight, to let us have their hearts, then we can agree. If Victor's people will go, we want Victor as chief to say I will go."

Victor here arose and left the council. After a pause of some minutes Gov. Stevens said: "I will ask Ambrose where is Victor?"

Ambrose: "He is gone home."

Gov. Stevens: "Ambrose speaking of Victor said he wanted time. Victor is now thinking and studying over this matter. We don't wish to hurry or drive you in this business. Think over this matter tonight and meet here tomorrow. I ask Ambrose to think over the matter; to speak to Victor and tell him what I say. Ambrose loves his chief — let him take my words to him."

The council is adjourned to meet tomorrow morning somewhat earlier than usual.

The council then adjourned at 5 p.m.

— — — — — — —

Saturday, June [i.e., July] 14th.

Word was sent by Victor about 3 o'clock p.m. to the Governor that he had not yet made up his mind; and that as it was too late to open the council, it was postponed till Monday morning.

Document 20

Treaty with the Flatheads, Etc.

July 16, 1855

Source: "Treaty with the Flatheads, etc., 1855," Robert Bigart and Clarence Woodock, eds., *In the Name of the Salish & Kootenai Nation: The 1855 Hell Gate Treaty and the Origin of the Flathead Indian Reservation* (Pablo, Mont.: Salish Kootenai College Press, 1996), pages 9-16.

Editors' note: The Bitterroot Salish, Upper Pend d'Oreille, and Kootenai chiefs signed the treaty on July 16, 1855. Article 11 had been added to the document to provide for a provisional reservation in the Bitterroot Valley for the Salish. This article was the source of friction between the Salish and the government for the next forty years. There were some problems with the boundaries of the Jocko Reservation laid out in Article 2; but the biggest threat for the tribes was Article 6, the sleeper clause which Senator Joseph Dixon exploited in 1903 and 1904 to get the allotment policy imposed on the Flathead Reservation tribes. The treaty was not faithfully implemented by the United States government, but it did provide the legal foundation for the Flathead Reservation into the twenty-first century.

Treaty with the Flatheads, etc., 1855

Articles of agreement and convention made and concluded at the treaty-ground at Hell Gate, in the Bitter Root Valley, this sixteenth day of July, in the year one thousand eight hundred and fifty-five, by and between Isaac I. Stevens, governor and superintendent of Indian Affairs for the Territory of Washington, on the part of the United States, and the undersigned chiefs, head-men, and delegates of the confederated tribes of the Flathead, Kootenay, and Upper Pend d'Oreilles Indians, on behalf of and acting for said confederated tribes, and being duly authorized thereto by them. It being understood and agreed that the said confederated tribes do hereby constitute a nation, under the name of the Flathead Nation, with Victor, the head chief of the Flathead tribe, as the head chief of the said nation, and that the several chiefs, head-men, and delegates, whose names are signed to this treaty, do hereby, in behalf of their respective tribes, recognize Victor as said head chief.

ARTICLE 1. The said confederated tribe of Indians hereby cede, relinquish, and convey to the United States all their right, title, and interest in and to the country occupied or claimed by them bounded and described as follows, to wit:

Commencing on the main ridge of the Rocky Mountains at the forty-ninth (49th) parallel of latitude, thence westwardly on that parallel to the divide between the Flat-bow or Kootenay River and Clarke's Fork, thence southerly and southeasterly along said divide to the one hundred and fifteenth degree of longitude, (115°) thence in a southwesterly direction to the divide between the sources of the St. Regis Borgia and the Coeur d'Alene Rivers, thence southeasterly and southerly along the main ridge of the Bitter Root Mountains to the divide between the head-waters of the Koos-koos-kee River and of the southwestern fork of the Bitter Root River, thence easterly along the divide separating the waters of the several tributaries of the Bitter Root River from the waters flowing into the Salmon and Snake Rivers to the main ridge of the Rocky Mountains, and thence northerly along said main ridge to the place of beginning.

ARTICLE 2. There is, however, reserved from the lands above ceded, for the use and occupation of the said confederated tribes, and as a general Indian reservation, upon which may be placed other friendly tribes and bands of Indians of the Territory of Washington who may agree to be consolidated with the tribes parties to this treaty, under the common designation of the Flathead Nation, with Victor, head chief of the Flathead tribe, as the head chief of the nation, the tract of land included within the following boundaries, to wit:

Commencing at the source of the main branch of the Jocko River; thence along the divide separating the waters flowing into the Bitter Root River from those flowing into the Jocko to a point on Clarke's Fork between the Camash and Horse Prairies; thence northerly to, and along the divide bounding on the west the Flathead River, to a point due west from the point half way in latitude between the northern and southern extremities of the Flathead Lake; thence on a due east course to the divide whence the Crow, the Prune, the So-ni-el-em and the Jocko Rivers take their rise and thence southerly along said divide to the place of beginning.

All which tract shall be set apart, and, so far as necessary, surveyed and marked out for the exclusive use and benefit of said confederated tribes as an Indian reservation. Nor shall any white man, excepting those in the employment of the Indian department, be permitted to reside upon the said reservation without permission of the confederated tribes, and the superintendent and agent. And the said confederated tribes agree to remove to and settle upon the same within one year after the ratification of this treaty. In the meantime it shall be lawful for them to reside upon any ground not in the actual claim and occupation of citizens of the United States, and upon any ground claimed or occupied, if with the permission of the owner or claimant.

Guaranteeing however the right to all citizens of the United States to enter upon and occupy as settlers any lands not actually occupied and cultivated by said Indians at this time, and not included in the reservation above named. *And provided,* That any substantial improvements heretofore made by any Indian, such as fields enclosed and cultivated and houses erected upon the lands hereby ceded, and which he may be compelled to abandon in consequence of this treaty, shall be valued under the direction of the President of the United States and payment made therefor in money or improvements of an equal value be made for said Indian upon the reservation; and no Indian will be required to abandon the improvements aforesaid, now occupied by him, until their value in money or improvements of an equal value shall be furnished him as aforesaid.

ARICLE 3. *And provided,* That if necessary for the public convenience roads may be run through the said reservation, and, on the other hand, the right of way with free access from the same to the nearest public highway is secured to them, as also the right in common with citizens of the United States to travel upon all public highways.

The exclusive right of taking fish in all the streams running through or bordering said reservation is further secured to said Indians; as also the right of taking fish at all usual and accustomed places, in common with citizens of the Territory, and of erecting temporary buildings for curing; together with the privilege of hunting, gathering roots and berries, and pasturing their horses and cattle upon open and unclaimed land.

ARTICLE 4. In consideration of the above cession, the United States agree to pay to the said confederated tribes of Indians, in addition to the goods and provisions distributed to them at the time of signing this treaty the sum of one hundred and twenty thousand dollars, in the following manner — that is to say: For the first year after the ratification hereof, thirty-six thousand dollars, to be expended under the direction of the President, in providing for their removal to the reservation, breaking up and fencing farms, building houses for them, and for such other objects as he may deem necessary. For the next four years, six thousand dollars each year; for the next five years, five thousand dollars each year; for the next five years, four thousand dollars each year; and for the next five years, three thousand dollars each year.

All which said sums of money shall be applied to the use and benefit of the said Indians, under the direction of the President of the United States, who may from time to time determine, at his discretion, upon what beneficial objects to expend the same for them, and the superintendent of Indian affairs, or other proper officer, shall each year inform the President of the wishes of the Indians in relation thereto.

ARTICLE 5. The United States further agree to establish at suitable points within said reservation, within one year after the ratification hereof, an agricultural and industrial school, erecting the necessary buildings, keeping the same in repair, and providing it with furniture, books, and stationery, to be located at the agency, and to be free to the children of the said tribes, and to employ a suitable instructor or instructors. To furnish one blacksmith shop, to which shall be attached a tin and gun shop; one carpenter's shop; one wagon and plough-maker's shop; and to keep the same in repair, and furnished with the necessary tools. To employ two farmers, one blacksmith, one tinner, one gunsmith, one carpenter, one wagon and plough maker, for the instruction of the Indians in trades, and to assist them in the same. To erect one saw-mill and one flouring-mill, keeping the same in repair and furnished with the necessary tools and fixtures, and to employ two millers. To erect a hospital, keeping the same in repair, and provided with the necessary medicines and furniture, and to employ a physician; and to erect, keep in repair, and provide the necessary furniture the buildings required for the accommodation of said employees. The said buildings and establishments to be maintained and kept in repair as aforesaid, and the employees to be kept in service for the period of twenty years.

And in view of the fact that the head chiefs of the said confederated tribes of Indians are expected and will be called upon to perform many services of a public character, occupying much of their time, the United States further agree to pay to each of the Flathead, Kootenay, and Upper Pend d'Oreilles tribes five hundred dollars per year, for the term of twenty years after the ratification hereof, as a salary for such persons as the said confederated tribes may select to be their head chiefs, and to build for them at suitable points on the reservation a comfortable house, and properly furnish the same, and to plough and fence for each of them ten acres of land. The salary to be paid to, and the said houses to be occupied by, such head chiefs so long as they may be elected to that position by their tribes, and no longer.

And all the expenditures and expenses contemplated in this article of this treaty shall be defrayed by the United States, and shall not be deducted from the annuities agreed to be paid to said tribes. Nor shall the cost of transporting the goods for the annuity payments be a charge upon the annuities, but shall be defrayed by the United States.

ARTICLE 6. The President may from time to time, at his discretion, cause the whole, or such portion of such reservation as he may think proper, to be surveyed into lots, and assign the same to such individuals or families of the said confederated tribes as are willing to avail themselves of the privilege, and will locate on the same as a permanent home, on the same terms and subject to the same regulations as are provided in the sixth article of the treaty with the Omahas, so far as the same may be applicable.

ARTICLE 7. The annuities of the aforesaid confederated tribes of Indians shall not be taken to pay the debts of individuals.

ARTICLE 8. The aforesaid confederated tribes of Indians acknowledge their dependence upon the Government of the United States, and promise to be friendly with all citizens thereof, and pledge themselves to commit no depredations upon the property of such citizens. And should any one or more of them violate this pledge, and the fact be satisfactorily proved before the agent, the property taken shall be returned, or, in default thereof, or if injured or destroyed, compensation may be made by the Government out of the annuities. Nor will they make war on any other tribe except in self-defence, but will submit all matters of difference between them and other Indians to the Government of the United States, or its agent, for decision, and abide thereby. And if any of said Indians commit any depredations on any other Indians within the jurisdiction of the United States, the same rule shall prevail as that prescribed in this article, in case of depredations against citizens. And the said tribes agree not to shelter or conceal offenders against the laws of the United States, but to deliver them up to the authorities for trial.

ARTICLE 9. The said confederated tribes desire to exclude from their reservation the use of ardent spirits, and to prevent their people from drinking the same; and therefore it is provided that any Indian belonging to said confederated tribes of Indians who is guilty of bringing liquor into said reservation, or who drinks liquor, may have his or her proportion of the annuities withheld from him or her for such time as the President may determine.

ARTICLE 10. The United States further agree to guaranty the exclusive use of the reservation provided for in this treaty, as against any claims which may be urged by the Hudson Bay Company under the provisions of the treaty between the United States and Great Britain of the fifteenth of June, eighteen hundred and forty-six, in consequence of the occupation of a trading-post on the Pru-in River by the servants of that company.

ARTICLE 11. It is, moreover, provided that the Bitter Root Valley, above the Loo-lo Fork, shall be carefully surveyed and examined, and if it shall prove, in the judgment of the President, to be better adapted to the wants of the Flathead tribe than the general reservation provided for in this treaty, then such portions of it as may be necessary shall be set apart as a separate reservation for the said tribe. No portion of the Bitter Root Valley, above the Loo-lo Fork, shall be opened to settlement until such examination is had and the decision of the President made known.

ARTICLE 12. This treaty shall be obligatory upon the contracting parties as soon as the same shall be ratified by the President and Senate of the United States.

In testimony whereof, the said Isaac I. Stevens, governor and superintendent for the Territory of Washington, and the undersigned head chiefs, chiefs, and principal men of the Flathead, Kootenay, and Upper Pend d'Oreilles tribes of Indians, have hereunto set their hands and seals, at the place and on the day and year herein-before written.

Isaac I. Stevens, [L. S.]
Governor and Superintendent Indian Affairs W. T.

Victor, head chief of the Flathead Nation, his x mark.	[L. S.]
Alexander, chief of the Upper Pend d'Oreilles, his x mark.	[L. S.]
Michelle, chief of the Kootenays, his x mark.	[L. S.]
Ambrose, his x mark.	[L. S.]
Pah-soh, his x mark.	[L. S.]
Bear Track, his x mark.	[L. S.]
Adolphe, his x mark.	[L. S.]
Thunder, his x mark.	[L. S.]
Big Canoe, his x mark.	[L. S.]
Kootel Chah, his x mark.	[L. S.]
Paul, his x mark.	[L. S.]
Andrew, his x mark.	[L. S.]
Michelle, his x mark.	[L. S.]
Battiste, his x mark.	[L. S.]

Kootenays.

Gun Flint, his x mark.	[L. S.]
Little Michelle, his x mark.	[L. S.]
Paul See, his x mark.	[L. S.]
Moses, his x mark.	[L. S.]

James Doty, secretary
R. H. Lansdale, Indian Agent
W. H. Tappan, sub Indian Agent
Henry R. Crosire [Crosby],
Gustavus Sohon, Flathead Interpreter.
A. J. Hoecken, sp. mis.
William Craig.

Document 21

Judith River Treaty Negotiations: Intertribal Peace and Common Hunting Ground October 16-17, 1855

Source: From "Official Proceedings of the Commission Appointed to Hold a Council with the Blackfeet, and Other Indian Tribes on the Head Waters of the Missouri River, in the Year 1855," U. S. Bureau of Indian Affairs, "Documents Relating to the Negotiation of Ratified and Unratified Treaties with Various Tribes of Indians, 1801-69," National Archives Microfilm Publication T-494, Reel 5, Ratified Treaties 1854-55, frames 965, 974, 1030-1039.

Editors' note: The October 1855 treaty negotiations between the United States government, the Rocky Mountain Indians, and the Plains Indians sought to establish peace between the various tribes. The agreement was to provide for a common hunting ground in the Musselshell Valley where the Rocky Mountain Indians could hunt buffalo in peace. Pend d'Oreille Chief Alexander played a prominent role in the negotiations. The punctuation and capitalization in the original text were hard to read, but it has been rendered as accurately as possible.

Official Proceedings
of the
Commission
appointed to hold a council with the Blackfeet, and other Indian Tribes
on the Head Waters of the Missouri River, in the year 1855
October 16th Tuesday.

The Commission met at 10 A.M., and the following papers were received, and after considering various points relating to the Council and Treaty the Commission adjourned to 12 M.

Commissioner Stevens recommends daily the following distribution of Provisions.

Bloods. 57 Lodges — 11 in a lodge — 627.

2 Boxes Hard Bread, 3 bags Flour, 2 Bags Sugar, 1 Bag Coffee.

Piegans. 78 Lodges — 858.

2 Boxes Hard Bread, 3 bags Flour, 2 Bags Sugar, 1 Bag Coffee.

Blackfeet. 5 Lodges — 55.
1 Box Hard Bread, 1 Bag Flour, 1 Bag Sugar, 1 Bag Coffee.
  Gros Ventres. 7 to 13 in a Lodge. 762
2 Boxes Hard Bread, 3 Bags of Flour, 2 Bags Sugar, 1 Bag Coffee.
  Flatheads. 101 Lodges — 7 in a Lodge — 707.
2 Boxes Hard Bread, 2 Bags Sugar, 3 Bags Flour, I bag Coffee.
  Nez Perces. 46.
1 Box Hard Bread, 1 Bag Flour, 1 bag Sugar, 1 bag Coffee.
  Indians about Camp 40 — in all 3295.

— — — — — —

Sir:

"Commissioner Cumming believes that it would be improvident to make any further partial distribution, as it necessarily tends to produce great inconvenience, in the final distributions. If however the Council be not concluded to day, he proposes that an issue be made to each band, and deducted from the Distribution Share in the general distribution."
Oct. 16th, 1855, Council Ground

James Doty Esq, Secretary.

— — — — — —

Council Ground.
Oct. 16, 1855.

Sir:

Commissioner Cumming considers it proper to state that he was under the impression that the Commission adjourned on the 6th inst. to meet at the Judith on the 13", that being the day fixed for the assembling of the Indians at that point, and that on examining the record he finds that Friday 12th and not Saturday 13th was the time to which the Commission adjourned. As his absence, at that time has been adverted to on the record, he will state for the information of the Commission that he was compelled to resort to a skiff as a means of going from Fort Benton to the Judith. the weather being boisterous on Wednesday evening his departure was deferred till Thursday Morning, and his voyage continued throughout every hour of daylight, till his arrival at this point on Saturday 13th (he believes) about noon."

James Doty, Esq.
Secretary

— — — — — —

The following Programme of Arrangements for the Council was adopted.
Arrangements for Council.
Commissioner and attendants in front of Office Tent.
Chiefs. In front Rank. 26 in number.

Braves. next behind.

Camp. In rear of braves.

Commissioners — Alfred Cumming, Isaac I. Stevens.

Secretary — James Doty.

Assistant — A. J. Vaughan.

Agents — Major Hatch, Blackfoot Agent. Dr. Lansdale, Flathead Agent. Thomas Adams, Special Flat Hd. Agent. W. H. Tappan, Nez Perce Agent.

Interpreters — Blackfeet, Mr. Bird, Mr. Culbertson, Mr. Roché; Flatheads, Ben. Kiser, G. Sohon; Nez Perces — Wm. Craig, Delaware Jim.

Reporters — Thomas Adams, A. J. Vaughan.

———————

October 16th Tuesday.

Pursuant to adjournment the Commission met at 12 M. At 1 P.M. the Indians had collected at the Council Ground, and the Council was opened.

Commissioner Stevens said: "The Council is now assembled and the first thing is to have faithful Interpreters. We have selected as Interpreters for the Blackfeet, Mr. Bird, Mr. Culbertson, and Mr. DeRoché.

"We have selected for the Nez Perces, Mr. Craig and Delaware Jim as Interpreters. Are you satisfied with these men?

"We have selected for the Flat Heads, Ben Kiser and Gustavus Sohon. Are you satisfied? No objection is heard. The Interpreters will now be sworn." And the following oath was administered to them by Commissioner Stevens.

"I solemnly swear that I will faithfully discharge my duties of Interpreter at this Council, and that I will truly and to the best of my ability interpret the speeches of the Commissioners on the one side, and of the Indians on the other. So help me God."

Commissioner Cumming said: "I wish my children to understand that I have been sent here with my friend on the left [Stevens], by my Great Father in the East.

"Your Great Father has been very much grieved to hear that you had difficulties among yourselves, and has sent us up now to arrange them. To-day we will open a paper in which we will all agree to live in peace and friendship, after which we will give you presents, which the Great Father has sent to show he is in earnest. By and bye, when you have signed this paper, the presents will be given.

"I am glad to see, and the other Commissioner is glad to see, that the hearts of the Indians are disposed for peace and to meet the wishes of their Great Father.

"When my Colleague has said a few words more to you, we will open the paper and the Interpreters will explain it to you, clearly, so that you can understand, and if you do not you must ask for explanations.

"The Great Father told me to tell you that if you kept your promises he would send goods to you every year, and people to show you how to farm, so that you can raise plenty to eat.

"I met the Assiniboines before coming here. They sent by me Tobacco, to be given you at this Council, saying that they wished to live in peace with you and all the Indians in this Country.

"I will quit by saying I hope the Great Spirit will put good sense in your heads about what you have to do at this Council."

Commissioner Stevens said:

"My children, My heart is glad to day — I see Indians, East of the Mountains and Indians West of the Mountains sitting here as friends. Bloods, Blackfeet, Piegans, Gros Ventres, and Nez Perces, Kootenays, Pend d'Oreilles, Flat Heads. And we have the Cree sitting down here from the North and East, and Snakes further from the West.

"There is Peace now between you all here present. We want Peace also with Absent Tribes. With the Crees and Assiniboines. With the Snakes, and yes, even with Crows. You have all sent your message to the Crows, telling them you would meet them in friendship here. The Crows were far and could not be found, but we expect you to promise to be friends with the Crows here.

"I might have some doubts did I not know from experience the hearts of these men. You have known me long. You have always found me your friend. You have trusted me once, I know you will trust me again. Peace, I say with the Crows!

"It was Low Horn, who, two years since, said to me, 'Peace with the Flat Heads and Nez Perces.' The Lame Bull said, 'Peace with the Flat Heads and Nez Perces.' The Little Dog, Little Gray Head, and all the Blackfoot Chiefs said, 'Peace with them, come and meet us in Council.' And here they are. Here you see them face to face. I met them the same year. I told them your words: they said, 'Peace also with the Blackfeet.'

"And both my Brother (Comm. C.) and myself have seen the Great Father, and he has sent us among you to be witnesses of this Peace and Friendship.

"And the Great Father has said, 'Peace with the Crees and Assiniboines, the Crows and all neighboring tribes.'

"I shall say nothing about Peace with the Whites. No White man enters a Blackfoot or a Western Indian's Lodge, without being treated to the very best. Peace already prevails. We trust such will continue to be the case forever.

"My heart must express its gratitude to you all for the kindness you have shown to me and those connected with me, for nearly three years.

"We have been travelling over your whole Country, both East and West of the Mountains: In small parties, ranging away north to Bow River, South to the Yellow Stone, and from Ocean to Ocean.

"We have kept no Guard. We have not tied up our horses, all has been safe. Therefore, I say Peace has been, is now, and will continue between these Indians and the White Man. There is no need of more words. It is a fixed fact.

"We will read the paper to you."

Commissioner Cumming said:

"I wish you to say to the Blackfeet and the other Indians, that the Cree here present, who came up with the 'Little Dog' is with him, a witness to the friendly spirit manifested by the Assiniboines and Crees, and their sending by me some Tobacco as a token of their friendship and desire for peace, and I will now distribute it."

(The Tobacco was given to the Cree, who accompanied by the Little Dog, gave it to the principal chiefs present.)

Commissioner Stevens then said:

"Thus you have the message from the Assiniboines. By and by you will have from my Brother here, a message of Peace from the Crows: but from this Ground send Tobacco to the Crows, through these men (pointing to the Nez Percés) who know the Crows."

The Commissioner then proceeded to explain the treaty. He said, "Here is the paper. But before I explain what is in it, I will state what is not in it.

"A story was told among you that your Country was to be taken from you and that you were to be driven North to the Saskatchewan, among the Crees and the Assiniboines.

"You see Mr. Doty writing at that Table. He told you it was a lie. You know Mr. Doty, and that he has never told you a lie.

"I tell you that story is a lie, and you have always had the truth from me.

"We want to establish you in your Country on farms. We want you to have cattle and raise Crops. We want your children to be taught, and we want you to send word to your Great Father, through us where you want your Farms to be, and what schools and mills, and shops you want.

"This Country is your home. It will remain your home. And as I told the Western Indians we hoped through the long winters, by and bye, the Blackfeet would not be obliged to live on poor Buffalo Meat but would have domestic Cattle for food. We want them to have Cattle.

"You know the Buffalo will not continue forever. Get farms and Cattle in time.

"I will now explain this paper to you."

The treaty was then read and explained — Article by article, and having reached the third — Commr. Stevens said:

"A few words before I explain the next point in the paper.

"The Blackfeet know that the Western Indians go to Buffalo on the other side of the Missouri. They use certain Passes. The Medicine Rock, the Big Hole, and others further South.

"They pass over through those Passes, go to the Muscle Shell, and the Yellow Stone and return home by them.

"There the Western Indians have hunted, and there the Blackfeet have hunted. We propose that all the Indians here shall continue to hunt on that Ground and that it shall be a Common Hunting Ground. I will explain that Ground more carefully in a moment.

"I have a word to say to the Western Indians: They have hunted at the Three Buttes. The Blackfeet complain of them. They say give up hunting here, and you may hunt on the Common Hunting Ground.

"We think that talk is good, and wish the Western Indians should not hunt there. I think, Alexander will think it good.

"I told you a few moments since that I should explain more fully the position of the Common Hunting Ground."

A map was then shown to the Chiefs, and the Boundaries of their Country and the Hunting Ground fully explained by Comr. Stevens, who then said:

"I have now explained to the Blackfoot and Flat Head Chiefs about this Common Hunting Ground, on the map — I will now explain it to the Nez Percés."

(After which he continued) — "We have now explained to all the Indians their Country and the Common Hunting Ground. Now Alexander the Pend d'Oreille Chief wishes to speak."

Alexander said:

"A long time ago our people, our ancestors belonged in this Country. The Country around the Three Buttes. We had many people on this side of the Mountains, and now you have shown us only a narrow ridge to hunt on.

"You do not see all of our people here. There are many beyond the Mountains. It is a very small place you give us for a hunting Ground.

"A long time ago our old people used to hunt about the Three Buttes and the Blackfeet lived far north. When my Father was living he told me that was an old road for our people.

"We Indians were all well pleased when we came together here in friendship. Now you point us out a little piece of land to hunt our game on. When we were enemies, I always crossed over there, and why should I not now, when we are friends? Now I have two hearts about it. Why cannot I go there? What is the reason? Why do you point us out a small place?

"Which of these Chiefs (pointing to the Blackfeet) says we are not to go there? Which is the one?"

The Little Dog, a Piegan answered — "It is I, and not because we have anything against you. We are friendly. But the North Blackfeet are bad, it might produce a quarrel if you hunted near them. Do not put yourselves in their way."

Alexander continued — "Here is this White Chief who has just been talking to us. He said all your nation was here to make peace. Why is it then that they do not?

"The Chief tells us that we are all, all us Indians, to eat out of the same plate, one plate. Now you tell me to quit crossing in the North. I wonder how this can be!"

The Little Dog said: "I went to the North with Mr. Doty. Those Indians would not come to the Treaty. I do not know what they intend to do."

Comr. Stevens said, "I will Explain to Alexander why the Commissioners think their plan about the Hunting just and good."

Alexander said, "All of these Blackfeet Chiefs spoke but one word. I was glad to have the Treaty. I was following only what they said. Now I do not know how it is. I thought they came here to make Peace. When Peace is made we should be mixed together freely. Here am I, and many of us. If they wish to come to our Country we will not tell them to go back. If in my Country, I saw you coming I would be very glad. Below here Gov tells us that we must all come together, all of us Everybody. If I see us all come together, then I shall be very glad. I like all of you. Now we are trying to learn Everything. We are only trying. Our Children will have better sense. I want you to speak. What are your minds?"

Little Dog said, "Since he speaks so much of it, we will give him liberty to come out in the North."

Commissioner Cumming said, "I wish Alexander to understand that all that Country North of these lines, (and here the Comr. pointed out on the map the boundaries of the Blackfoot Territory as laid down in the Treaty of Laramie) is recognized by the [1851] Laramie Treaty as belonging to the Blackfeet; and the Blackfeet in a desire for peace and friendship, give that to them for a Common Hunting Ground. It is not so large as some Countries, but it is pretty large, and appears to be sufficient for their use."

Comr. Stevens said: "In making this Division we looked to the Indians obtaining their living. The Blackfeet need all their Country here. The Western Indians have enough in the piece given them in proportion to their numbers.

Alexander does not want the Blackfeet to starve. The Blackfeet also want Alexander to have food. The Blackfeet agree as my Brother has said, that this shall be a Common Hunting Ground. We want Alexander to agree to it. The Western Indians are only one fourth as numerous as the Blackfeet. Let Alexander think of this. He does not get all his food from the Buffalo. He has farms and Cattle. The Blackfeet have none."

Alexander said, "I speak for this, because when I am hungry, I go in the North and hunt a few Buffalo and return home soon."

Commr. Stevens said, "Alexander has spoken of friendship and peace. It is right. We expect him to be good friends with the Blackfeet. Let him pause and not give a quick answer. But to listen to his Father."

The Big Canoe (Pend d'Oreille) said, "I am glad now we are together. I thought our roads would be over all this Country. Now you tell us different. Supposing that we *do* stick together, and *do* make a peace. That is the way we talk on the other side. Now you tell me not to step over that way. I had a mind to go there."

Comr. Cumming said, "The object is not to prevent social intercourse between the Tribes. It is only to preserve their Hunting Grounds distinctly apart. The Blackfeet will always be glad to see the Flat Heads. The Whites make these lines to show where each must hunt, so that there shall be no quarrels. The Blackfeet invite you to come and see them at all times."

The Lame Bull (principal Chief of the Piegans) said, "It is not our plan that these things are going on. I understood that what the White Chiefs told us to do, we were to do, both sides. It is not we that speak, it is the White Chiefs. Look at those tribes (pointing to the Western Indians) they are the first to speak, making objections this morning. We intend to do whatever the Government tells us: we shall take care to try and do it. We shall consider what the White Chiefs wish us to do, and I think we shall do it. They have done much, and intend much more for us. Let us listen. We shall abide by what the White Chiefs say. I hope these Indians will make friends with us and that it may be shown by a friendly exchange of property."

The Big Canoe said, "Dont let your war parties hide from me. Let them come to our Camp as friends."

Commissioner Cumming said, "I wish to say to the Western Indians that upon this Land no permanent settlement shall be made for ninety-nine years. Although it is recognized as Blackfoot Country by this Paper (pointing to the Treaty of Laramie). I wish Alexander to decide upon this proposition, that I may repeat it to the Blackfeet if he agrees to it."

Alexander declined replying —

Comr. Stevens then said, "I will say a few words to all the Indians present. We will try this Treaty again tomorrow. Think over the matter in your Lodges to night. I will say to the Western Indians that the proposition made to them I believe to be just and good. Let them council together and see tomorrow, if it will not suit their hearts. When you separate talk in friendship with the Blackfeet and see if your hearts cannot be one."

The Council then adjourned till to morrow at 10. A.M.

October 17th Wednesday.

The Indians assembled and Council was opened at 12. M.

Comr. Stevens said, "My Children you separated in friendship last night. You meet as friends now. The Blackfeet said last night, they say now, we will agree to what our Fathers recommended us to agree. We will give to the Western Indians the liberty to hunt on the Trail down the Muscle Shell to the Yellow Stone. Thus the Blackfeet give to you the right to hunt in their country down the Muscle Shell."

Comr. Cumming said, "Say to the Blackfeet that the Muscle Shell continues to be the boundary of their Country. Say to the Flat Heads and Nez Percés that the Muscle Shell continues to be the boundary of the Blackfoot Country; but the Blackfeet give them the right of hunting in their country along the trail passing down the Muscle Shell."

Comr. Stevens said, "Here is a map and I will now explain carefully the boundaries we have spoken of." And the Commissioner then proceeded to explain them in detail by means of a map, and a rough sketch of the Country drawn on a Buffalo Skin. Having thus fully explained Articles III, IV & V the Commissioner said, "If no objection is made to these Articles, my brother will explain to you the next articles."

The Indians appearing fully to comprehend and assent, no objections being made:

Comr. Cumming proceeded to say, "It is the wish of your Great Father that the Indians remain within their own Countries except when going to the Country of neighboring Tribes for the purpose of visiting or trading. The arrangements we have made, will not prevent you from visiting each other as friends. The Great Father wishes to encourage you in this."

The Comr. having taken up and carefully explained the VI, VII & VIII. Articles, continued as follows: "I hope this will be agreeable to my Red Children. It is what the Great Father says to them. Is there anything to which they object?"

The Indians expressed an entire comprehension and satisfaction with the agreements required of them, and the Comr. proceeded to take up Article IX relating to annuities and said:

"In consideration of the goodness of his children and the promises which they make, the Great Father has sent those goods to you," pointing to the goods which were piled up near the Council Ground.

"These goods he tells us to give to the four bands of the Blackfeet, and the Indians from the West, according to their numbers. There are some of the Four Tribes absent. The Great Father has sent an agent to live at the Forts above who will be your Father. When you have any trouble, go to him as you would to your Father. As soon as I can get the goods fixed I will divide them out among the Indians perhaps to morrow, it may be the next day, but I will do it as soon as I can. I know you are anxious to get away. Some of the Indians who live far off had no horses and could not come to the Council. We will give a plenty of goods to every body here. For those who are absent, my brother and myself have agreed to place them in the hands of the agent sent to them by the Great Father, till he can see them. When they come to the Forts they will find him there, and he will give them their Goods. I presume this arrangement is agreeable to the Blackfeet, let them say if it is not."

The Commissioner then explained in detail, the consideration to be paid, contained in Articles IX and X and,

Comr. Stevens in continuation of the subject said: "The Great Father thinks much of Farms, Schools, Mills, and Shops, and he wants you to consent, if he thinks best, that no goods shall be sent you, but all be given to Farms, &c. Your own wishes will be much consulted in this respect, but the Great Father does not want you to starve when the Buffalo passes away. Therefore he will do all he can to get for you farms, cattle, &c., and teach your children trades. We want, as we have said, the Indians to be friends of each other, to be the friends of the Whites. If the White man takes your property the Great Father will make it good to you. If any of you take the property of a White Man, you will make it good to him. If Indians steal from each other the same rule will apply as in case of Indians stealing from Whites."

Article XI in relation to their dependence upon the United States was minutely explained, as also were the remaining Articles of the Treaty.

The Commissioner continued, "Now, what we have said to you is written in this paper. If you like it, you will sign it, and from the time you sign it, you will agree to be friends with the Western Indians. This paper will be sent to your Great Father. If he thinks it good he will send it back. It is a long distance there and you cannot hear from it till next year. It is sometimes the case, the Great Father thinks it may be changed a little. He is very wise; wiser than my

Brother, and myself. But he will send back the alterations to see if you consent to them; if you do then it is a bargain. But I think and my Brother thinks that the Great Father will think the paper good and will approve it. You have heard the paper. Is it good? Do iyou like it? Speak out your hearts and let us know if you all like it. We are now ready to sign the paper. If any Indian wishes to speak, let him do so."

The Lame Bull wished to know what they should do in case their enemies the Assiniboines & Crees or Crows came to steal their horses.

The Commissioners advised that they should follow the thieves, retake their property, if possible, and on returning report the affair to their agent.

"Three Feathers" a Nez Percé Chief said, "I came here to hear what the Blackfeet would say concerning a Peace. We on the other side have already received the laws from the Whites. We came to see the Blackfeet receive Laws and make Peace with all their neighbors. We are friendly to them. Let the Blackfeet show their hearts."

The Blackfeet expressed a desire for Peace and Friendship with all the Tribes West of the mountains. They were determined to make a Peace now.

"Three Feathers" said, "It is good. The Blackfeet agree. *We* of course agree. We came here to make friends with these people and we are ready to sign the Treaty."

Onis-tay-say-nah-que-im, Head Chief of the Bloods, said, "I wish to say that as far as we old men are concerned we want peace and to cease going to war; but I am afraid that we cannot stop our young men. The Crows are not here to smoke the pipe with us and I am afraid our young men will not be persuaded that they ought not to war against the Crows. We, however, will try our best to keep our young men at home."

Comr. Stevens said, "Your Great Father wishes you to be on friendly terms with all the tribes, to keep peace with the Crows as well as with all others, but he does not wish you to lie down and be killed. You have a right to defend yourself, and if the Crows come into your country to make war and to steal your horses, drive them out and kill them, but do not go into their country to war. Your Father here (Col. C.) has an agent among the Crows. He will let the Crows know your wishes. That you want peace. Send messages to them and if they come to your Country as friends treat them friendly. I trust that they will not come as Enemies."

In reply to this remark of the Blood Chief, Comr. Cumming said, "I am alike the Father of the Crows and the Blackfeet, the words I have this day said to the Blackfeet I will also say to the Crows. I will tell them that the Blackfeet have made a Treaty of Peace, and that you will all consent to send out no more War Parties. Where a Young Man of the Blackfeet is lost in Battle, there is a great lamentation in your Lodges, and so when a young man of the Crows loses his life, he lays down in death upon the prairie, but in the Lodges of the Crows there is weeping and every night they cry for the dead. Tell your young men that your Great Father wishes all his Children to live in Peace; if you do not live in peace, and continue to go [to] war, he will be mad with his Children, he will be ashamed of his children, and will not send you Blankets and provisions, Coffee and Tobacco. Tell your young men to take wives and live happily in their own Lodges, then the old men will see their sons. Your sons will see their children, and you will all be happy. Remember my words. I will say the same words to the Crows."

The Commissioners then signed the Treaty, and were followed by the Chiefs, Headmen and Delegates of the various Tribes present. Great satisfaction prevailed, and every chief of any importance signed the treaty.

At 4 P.M. the Council was declared, concluded.

———————

October 18" 19" & 20" were occupied in distributing the goods, provisions &c to the Indians who were all assembled, each tribe being by itself.

On Saturday the 20th the Commissioners presented the Medals and coats to the principal Chiefs, and made to them suitable addresses admonishing them to faithfully keep the promises they had made to their Great Father.

The distribution of the Goods, provisions &c was made upon a basis determined upon by the Commission. The list of distribution was certified by the Commissioners and placed on file in the Office of the Commission, and will there be found. . . . .

Document 22

Peace Treaty with the Blackfeet

October 17, 1855

Source: "Treaty with the Blackfeet, 1855," Charles J. Kappler, ed., *Indian Affairs: Laws and Treaties: Vol. II (Treaties)* (Washington, D.C.: U.S. Government Printing Office, 1904), vol. 2, pages 736-740.

Editors' note: This treaty of peace between the Blackfeet and the Rocky Mountain Indians was the culmination of Gov. Isaac Stevens' efforts to end the intertribal wars on the Northern Plains in the 1850s. Article 3 of this treaty provides for a common hunting ground in the Musselshell Valley for the Rocky Mountain Indians to hunt buffalo. Articles 5 and 6 regulate the use and access to the common hunting ground. In addition to the Blackfeet tribes, the treaty was signed by chiefs of the confederated Flathead Nation and the Nez Perce tribe.

Treaty with the Blackfeet, 1855.

Articles of agreement and convention made and concluded at the council-ground on the Upper Missouri, near the mouth of the Judith River, in the Territory of Nebraska, this seventeenth day of October, in the year one thousand eight hundred and fifty-five, by and between A. Cumming and Isaac I. Stevens, commissioners duly appointed and authorized, on the part of the United States, and the undersigned chiefs, headmen, and delegates of the following nations and tribes of Indians, who occupy, for the purpose of hunting, the territory on the Upper Missouri and Yellowstone Rivers, and who have permanent homes as follows: East of the Rocky Mountains, the Blackfoot Nation, consisting of the Piegan, Blood, Blackfoot, and Gros Ventres tribes of Indians. West of the Rocky Mountains, the Flathead Nation, consisting of the Flathead, Upper Pend d'Oreille, and Kootenay tribes of Indians, and the Nez Percé tribe of Indians, the said chiefs, headmen and delegates, in behalf of and acting for said nations and tribes, and being duly authorized thereto by them.

Article 1. Peace, friendship and amity shall hereafter exist between the United States and the aforesaid nations and tribes of Indians, parties to this treaty, and the same shall be perpetual.

Article 2. The aforesaid nations and tribes of Indians, parties to this treaty, do hereby jointly and severally covenant that peaceful relations shall likewise be maintained among themselves in future; and that they will abstain from all hostilities whatsoever against each other, and cultivate mutual good-will and friendship. And the nations and tribes aforesaid do furthermore jointly and severally covenant, that peaceful relations shall be maintained with and that they will abstain from all hostilities whatsoever, excepting in self-defense, against the following-named nations and tribes of Indians, to wit: the Crows, Assineboins, Crees, Snakes, Blackfeet, Sans Arcs, and Aunce-pa-pas bands of Sioux, and all other neighboring nations and tribes of Indians.

Article 3. The Blackfoot Nation consent and agree that all that portion of the country recognized and defined by the treaty of Laramie as Blackfoot territory, lying within lines drawn from the Hell Gate or Medicine Rock Passes in the main range of the Rocky Mountains, in an easterly direction to the nearest source of the Muscle Shell River, thence to the mouth of Twenty-five Yard Creek, thence up the Yellowstone River to its northern source, and thence along the main range of the Rocky Mountains, in a northerly direction, to the point of beginning, shall be a common hunting-ground for ninety-nine years, where all the nations, tribes and bands of Indians, parties to this treaty, may enjoy equal and uninterupted privileges of hunting, fishing and gathering fruit, grazing animals, curing meat and dressing robes. They further agree that they will not establish villages, or in any other way exercise exclusive rights within ten miles of the northern line of the common hunting-ground, and that the parties to this treaty may hunt on said northern boundary line and within ten miles thereof.

Provided, That the western Indians, parties to this treaty, may hunt on the trail leading down the Muscle Shell to the Yellowstone; the Muscle Shell River being the boundary separating the Blackfoot from the Crow territory.

And provided, That no nation, band, or tribe of Indians, parties to this treaty, nor any other Indians, shall be permitted to establish permanent settlements, or in any other way exercise, during the period above mentioned, exclusive rights or privileges within the limits of the above-described hunting-ground.

And provided further, That the rights of the western Indians to a whole or a part of the common hunting-ground, derived from occupancy and possession, shall not be affected by this article, except so far as said rights may be determined by the treaty of Laramie.

Article 4. The parties to this treaty agree and consent, that the tract of country lying within lines drawn from the Hell Gate or Medicine Rock Passes, in an easterly direction, to the nearest source of the Muscle Shell River, thence down said river to its mouth, thence down the channel of the Missouri River to the mouth of the Milk River, thence due north to the forty-ninth parallel, thence due west on said parallel to the main range of the Rocky Mountains, and thence southerly along said range to the place of beginning, shall be the territory of the Blackfoot Nation, over which said nation shall exercise exclusive control, excepting as may be otherwise provided in this treaty. Subject, however, to the provisions of the third article of this treaty, giving the right to hunt, and prohibiting the establishment of permanent villages and the exercise of any exclusive rights within ten miles of the northern line of the common hunting-ground, drawn from the nearest source of the Muscle Shell River to the Medicine Rock Passes, for the period of ninety-nine years.

Provided also, That the Assiniboins shall have the right of hunting, in common with the Blackfeet, in the country lying between the aforesaid eastern boundary line, running from the mouth of the Milk River to the forty-ninth parallel, and a line drawn from the left bank of the Missouri River, opposite the Round Butte north, to the forty-ninth parallel.

Article 5. The parties to this treaty, residing west of the main range of the Rocky Mountains, agree and consent that they will not enter the common hunting ground, nor any part of the Blackfoot territory, or return home, by any pass in the main range of the Rocky Mountains to the north of the Hell Gate or Medicine Rocky Passes. And they further agree that they will not hunt or otherwise disturb the game, when visiting the Blackfoot territory for trade, or social intercourse.

Article 6. The aforesaid nations and tribes of Indians, parties to this treaty, agree and consent to remain within their own respective countries, except when going to or from, or whilst hunting upon, the "common hunting ground," or when visiting each other for the purpose of trade or social intercourse.

Article 7. The aforesaid nations and tribes of Indians agree that citizens of the United States may live in and pass unmolested through the countries respectively occupied and claimed by them. And the United States is hereby bound to protect said Indians against depredations and other unlawful acts which white men residing in or passing through their country may commit.

Article 8. For the purpose of establishing travelling thoroughfares through their country, and the better to enable the President to execute the provisions of this treaty, the aforesaid nations and tribes do hereby consent and agree, that the United States may, within the countries respectfully occupied and claimed by them, construct roads of every description; establish lines of telegraph and military posts; use materials of every description found in the Indian country; build houses for agencies, missions, schools, farms, shops, mills, stations, and for any other purpose for which they may be required, and permanently occupy as much land as may be necessary for the various purposes above enumerated, including the use of wood for fuel and land for grazing, and that the navigation of all lakes and streams shall be forever free to citizens of the United States.

Article 9. In consideration of the foregoing agreements, stipulations, and cessions, and on condition of their faithful observance, the United States agree to expend, annually, for the Piegan, Blood, Blackfoot, and Gros Ventres tribes of Indians, constituting the Blackfoot Nation, in addition to the goods and provisions distributed at the time of signing the treaty, twenty thousand dollars, annually, for ten years, to be expended in such useful goods and provisions, and other articles, as the President, at his discretion, may from time to time determine; and the superintendent, or other proper officer, shall each year inform the President of the wishes of the Indians in relation thereto: *Provided, however,* That if, in the judgment of the President and Senate, this amount be deemed insufficient, it may be increased not to exceed the sum of thirty-five thousand dollars per year.

Article 10. The United States further agree to expend annually, for the benefit of the aforesaid tribes of the Blackfoot Nation, a sum not exceeding fifteen thousand dollars annually, for ten years, in establishing and instructing them in agricultural and mechanical pursuits, and in educating their children, and in any other respect promoting their civilization and Christianization: *Provided, however,* That to accomplish the objects of this article, the President may, at his discretion, apply any or all the annuities provided for in this treaty: *And provided, also,* That the President may, at his discretion, determine in what proportions the said annuities shall be divided among the several tribes.

Article 11. The aforesaid tribes acknowledge their dependence on the Government of the United States, and promise to be friendly with all citizens thereof, and to commit no depredations or other violence upon such citizens. And should any one or more violate this pledge, and the fact be proved to the satisfaction of the President, the property taken shall be returned, or, in default thereof, or if injured or destroyed, compensation may be made by the Government out of the annuities. The aforesaid tribes are hereby bound to deliver such offenders to the proper authorities for trial and punishment, and are held responsible, in their tribal capacity, to make reparation for depredations so committed.

Nor will they make war upon other tribes, except in self-defense, but will submit all matter of difference, between themselves and other Indians, to the Government of the United States, through its agents, for adjustment, and will abide thereby. And if any of the said Indians, parties to this treaty, commit depredations on any other Indians within the jurisdiction of the United States, the same rule shall prevail as that prescribed in this article in case of depredations against citizens. And the said tribes agree not to shelter or conceal offenders against the laws of the United States, but to deliver them up to the authorities for trial.

Article 12. It is agreed and understood, by and between the parties to this treaty, that if any nation or tribe of Indians aforesaid, shall violate any of the agreements, obligations, or stipulations, herein contained, the United States may withhold, for such length of time as the President and Congress may determine, any portion or all of the annuities agreed to be paid to said nation or tribe under the ninth and tenth articles of this treaty.

Article 13. The nations and tribes of Indians, parties to this treaty, desire to exclude from their country the use of ardent spirits or other intoxicating liquor, and to prevent their people from drinking the same. Therefore it is provided, that any Indian belonging to said tribes who is guilty of bringing such liquor into the Indian country, or who drinks liquor, may have his or her proportion of the annuities withheld from him or her, for such time as the President may determine.

Article 14. The aforesaid nations and tribes of Indians, west of the Rocky Mountains, parties to this treaty, do agree, in consideration of the provisions already made for them in existing treaties, to accept the guarantees of the peaceful occupation of their hunting-grounds, east of the Rocky Mountains, and of remuneration for depredations made by the other tribes, pledged to be secured to them in this treaty out of the annuities of said tribes, in full compensation for the concessions which they, in common with the said tribes, have made in this treaty.

The Indians east of the mountains, parties to this treaty, likewise recognize and accept the guarantees of this treaty, in full compensation for the injuries or depredations which have been, or may be committed by the aforesaid tribes, west of the Rocky Mountains.

Article 15. The annuities of the aforesaid tribes shall not be taken to pay the debts of individuals.

Article 16. This treaty shall be obligatory upon the aforesaid nations and tribes of Indians, parties thereto, from the date hereof, and upon the United States as soon as the same shall be ratified by the President and Senate.

In testimony whereof the said A. Cumming and Isaac I. Stevens, commissioners on the part of the United States, and the undersigned chiefs, headmen, and delegates of the aforesaid nations and tribes of Indians, parties to this treaty, have hereunto set their hands and seals at the place and on the day and year hereinbefore written.

A. Cumming. [L. S.]
Issac I. Stevens. [L. S.]

Piegans:

Nee-ti-nee, or "the only chief," now called the Lame Bull, his x mark. [L. S.]

Mountain Chief, his x mark. [L. S.]

Low Horn, his x mark. [L. S.]

Little Gray Head, his x mark. [L. S.]

Little Dog, his x mark. [L. S.]

Big Snake, his x mark. [L. S.]

The Skunk, his x mark. [L. S.]

The Bad Head, his x mark. [L. S.]

Kitch-eepone-istah, his x mark. [L.S.]

Middle Sitter, his x mark. [L. S.]

    Bloods:

Onis-tay-say-nah-que-im, his x mark. [L. S.]

The Father of All Children, his x mark. [L. S.]

The Bull's Back Fat, his x mark. [L.S.]

Heavy Shield, his x mark. [L. S.]

Nah-tose-onistah, his x mark. [L. S.]

The Calf Shirt, his x mark. [L. S.]

    Gros Ventres:

Bear's Shirt, his x mark. [L. S.]

Little Soldier, his x mark. [L. S.]

Star Robe, his x mark. [L. S.]

Sitting Squaw, his x mark. [L. S.]

Weasel Horse, his x mark. [L. S.]

The Rider, his x mark. [L. S.]

Eagle Chief, his x mark. [L. S.]

Heap of Bears, his x mark. [L. S.]

    Blackfeet:

The Three Bulls, his x mark. [L. S.]

The Old Kootomais, his x mark. [L.S.]

Pow-ah-que, his x mark. [L. S.]

Chief Rabbit Runner, his x mark. [L.S.]

    Nez Percé:

Spotted Eagle, his x mark. [L. S.]

Looking Glass, his x mark. [L. S.]

The Three Feathers, his x mark. [L.S.]

Eagle from the Light, his x mark. [L.S.]

The Lone Bird, his x mark. [L. S.]

Ip-shun-nee-wus, his x mark. [L. S.]

Jason, his x mark. [L. S.]

Wat-ti-wat-ti-we-hinck, his x mark. [L. S.]

White Bird, his x mark. [L. S.]

Stabbing Man, his x mark. [L. S.]

Jesse, his x mark. [L. S.]

Plenty Bears, his x mark. [L. S.]

    Flathead Nation:

Victor, his x mark. [L. S.]

Alexander, his x mark. [L. S.]

Moses, his x mark. [L. S.]

Big Canoe, his x mark. [L. S.]

Ambrose, his x mark. [L. S.]

Kootle-cha, his x mark. [L. S.]

Michelle, his x mark. [L. S.]

Francis, his x mark. [L. S.]

Vincent, his x mark. [L. S.]

Andrew, his x mark. [L. S.]

Adolphe, his x mark. [L. S.]

Thunder, his x mark. [L. S.]

    Piegans:

Running Rabbit, his x mark. [L. S.]

Chief Bear, his x mark. [L. S.]

The Little White Buffalo, his x mark. [L. S.]

The Big Straw, his x mark. [L. S.]

    Flathead:

Bear Track, his x mark. [L. S.]

Little Michelle, his x mark. [L. S.]

Palchinah, his x mark. [L. S.]

    Bloods:

The Feather, his x mark. [L. S.]

The White Eagle, his x mark. [L. S.]

Executed in presence of —

James Doty, secretary.

Alfred J. Vaughan, jr.

E. Alw. Hatch, agent for Blackfeet.

Thomas Adams, special agent Flathead Nation.

R. H. Lansdale, Indian agent Flathead Nation.

W. H. Tappan, sub-agent for the Nez Percés.

James Bird, A. Culbertson, & Benj. Deroche, Blackfoot interpreters.

Benj. Kiser, his x mark (Witness, James Doty), and Gustavus Sohon, Flat
   Head interpreters.

W. Craig, and Delaware Jim, his x mark (Witness, James Doty), Nez Percé
   interpreters.

A Cree Chief (Broken Arm,) his mark (Witness, James Doty).

A. J. Hoeekeorsg,

James Croke,

E. S. Wilson,

A. C. Jackson,

Charles Shucette, his x mark.

Christ. P. Higgins,

A. H. Robie,

S. S. Ford, jr.

Document 23

News from St. Ignatius Mission

October 18, 1855

Source: Adrian Hoeken to Rev. and Dear Father, Oct. 18, 1855, P. J. DeSmet, *Western Missions and Missionaries: A Series of Letters* (New York: James B. Kirker, 1863), pages 296-303.

Editors' note: Hoeken tells of two Lower Kalispel chiefs, Loyola and Victor, the move of St. Ignatius Mission to the Mission Valley in what is now western Montana, and the two 1855 treaties with the United States government.

Flat-Head Camp, in the Black-Feet Country, Oct. 18, 1855.
Rev. and Dear Father:

You will thank God with me for the consoling increase he has given, through the intersession of Mary, to the missions which you began in those remote parts. During the many years that I have passed among the Kalispels, though my labors have not been light and my trials have been numerous enough, God has given me in abundance the consolations of the missionary, in the lively faith and sincere piety of our neophytes. We have found means to build a beautiful church, which has excited the admiration of even Lieutenant [John] Mullan, of the United States army. This church is sufficiently large to contain the whole tribe, and on Sundays and festival days, when our Indians have adorned it with what ornaments of green boughs and wild flowers the woods and prairies supply; when they sing in it their devout hymns with fervor during the Holy Sacrifice, it might serve as a subject of edification and an example to quicken the zeal of many an old Christian congregation. There is among our converts a universal and very tender devotion to the Blessed Virgin, a most evident mark that the Faith has taken deep root in their souls. Every day, morning and evening, the families assemble in their lodges to recite the rosary in common, and daily they beg of Mary to thank God for them for having called them from the wild life of the forest, spent as it is in ignorance, rapine, and bloodshed, to the blessings of the true religion and its immortal hopes.

The Kalispels have sustained a great loss in the death of their pious chief, Loyola, with whose euphonious Indian name, *Etsowish-simmegee-itshin*, "The Grizzly Bear Erect," you are familiar. Ever since you baptized this excellent

Indian chieftain, he was always steadfast in the faith. He daily made progress in virtue, and became more fervent in the practices of our holy religion. He was a father to his people, firm in repressing their disorders, and zealous in exhorting them to be faithful to the lessons of the missionaries. In the severe trials to which Divine Providence subjected his virtue in his latter years, when within a short space of time he lost his wife and three of his children, he bore the heavy stroke with the edifying resignation of a Christian. During his last illness, of several weeks' duration, he seemed more anxious to do something still for the promotion of piety among his people, than to have his own great sufferings alleviated. His death, which occurred on the 6th of April, 1854, was lamented by the Indians with such tokens of sincere grief, as I have never before witnessed. There was not that false wailing over his tomb which Indian usage is said to prescribe for a departed chieftain; they wept over him with heartfelt and heartrending grief, as if each one had lost the best of fathers, and their grief for the good Loyola has not died away even at this day. Never had I thought our Indians capable of so much affection.

As Loyola, contrary to Indian customs, had not designated his successor, a new chief was to be chosen after his death. The election, to which all had prepared themselves by prayer, to lead them to a proper choice, ended in an almost unanimous voice for Victor, a brave hunter, whom you as yet must remember as a man remarkable for the generosity of his disposition. His inauguration took place amid great rejoicing. All the warriors, in their great custume, marched to his wigwam, and ranging themselves around it, discharged their muskets, after which each one went up to him to pledge his allegiance, and testify his affection by a hearty shaking of hands. During the whole day, numerous parties came to the mission-house to tell the Fathers how much satisfaction they felt at having a chief whose goodness had long since won the hearts of all. Victor alone seemed sad. He dreaded the responsibility of the chieftainship, and thought he should be unable to maintain the good effected in the tribe by the excellent chief Loyola.

In the following winter, when there was a great scarcity, and almost a famine among the Kalispels, Victor gave an affecting proof of his generous self-denying charity. He distributed his own provisions through the camp, hardly reserving for himself enough to sustain life, so that on his return from the annual chase, when yet at a considerable distance from the village, he fell exhausted on the ground, and had to be carried by his companions, to whom on that very day he had given all the food that had been sent up to him for his own use.

The Indian is often described as being devoid of kind feelings, incapable of gratitude, and breathing only savage hatred and murderous revenge; but, in reality, he has, in his untamed, uncultured nature, as many generous impulses as the man of any other race, and he only needs the softening influence of our holy religion to bring it out in its most touching forms. We need no other proof of it than the grateful remembrance of all the Indians of their late chief Loyola, the generous character of Victor, and the affectionate feelings of all our converted tribes for their missionaries, and especially for you, to whom they look up as to their great benefactor, because you were the first to bring them the good tidings of salvation.

Among our dear Flat-Heads, Michael Insula, or Red Feather, or as he is commonly called on account of his small stature, "The Little Chief," is a remarkable instance of the power which the Church has of developing the most amiable virtues in the fierce Indian. He unites in his person the greatest bravery with the tenderest piety and the gentlest manners. Known amid his warriors by the red feather which he wears, his approach is enough to put to flight the prowling bands of Crows and Black-Feet, that have frequently infested the Flat-Head territory. He is well known and much beloved by the whites, who have had occasion to deal with him, as a man of sound judgment, strict integrity, and one on whose fidelity they can implicitly rely. A keen discerner of the characters of men, he loves to speak especially of those whites, distinguished for their fine qualities, that have visited him, and often mentions with pleasure the sojourn among them of Colonel Robert Campbell, of St. Louis, and of Major [Thomas] Fitzpatrick, whom he adopted, in accordance with Indian ideas of courtesy, as his brothers. He has preserved all his first fervor of devotion, and now, as when you knew him, one can hardly ever enter his wigwam in the morning or evening without finding him with his rosary in his hands, absorbed in prayer. He cherishes a most affectionate remembrance of you, and of the day he was baptized; he longs ardently to see you once more before his death, and but yesterday he asked me, when and by what road you would return. In speaking thus, he expressed the desire of all our Indians, who all equally regret your long absence.

It was proposed, during the summer of 1854, to begin a new mission about one hundred and ninety miles northeast of the Kalispels, not far from the Flat-Head Lake, about fifty miles from the old mission of St. Mary's, among the Flat-Heads, where a convenient site had been pointed out to us by the Kalispel chief, Alexander, your old friend, who often accompanied you in your travels in the Rocky Mountains. Having set out from the Kalispel mission on the 28th of August, 1854, I arrived at the place designated on the 24th of September, and found it such as it had been represented — a beautiful region, evidently fertile, uniting a useful as well as pleasing variety of woodland and prairie, lake and river — the whole crowned in the distance by the white summit of the mountains, and sufficiently rich withal in fish and game. I shall never forget the emotions of hope and fear that filled my heart, when for the first time I celebrated mass in this lonely spot, in the open air, in the presence of a numerous band of Kalispels, who looked up to me, under God, for their temporal and spiritual welfare in this new home. The place was utterly uninhabited, — several bands of Indians live within a few days' travel, whom you formerly visited, and where you baptized many, while others still remained pagan. I was in hope of gathering these around me, and God has been pleased to bless an undertaking begun for his glory, even beyond my expectation. In a few weeks we had erected several frame buildings, a chapel, two houses, carpenter's and blacksmith's shops; wigwams had sprung up at the same time all around in considerable numbers, and morning and evening you might still have heard the sound of the axe and the hammer, and have seen new-comers rudely putting together lodges. About Easter of this year, over one thousand Indians, of different tribes, from the Upper Koetenays and Flat-Bow Indians, Pends-d'Oreilles, Flat-Heads, and Mountain Kalispels, who had arrived in succession during the winter, when they heard of the arrival of the long-desired Black-gown, made this place their permanent residence. All these Indians have manifested the best dispositions. Besides a large number of children baptized in the course of the year, I have had the happiness to baptize, before Christmas and Easter, upwards of one hundred and fifty adults of the Koetenay tribe, men of great docility and artlessness of character, who told me that ever since you had been among them, some years ago, they had abandoned the practice of gambling and other vices, and cherished the hope of being instructed one day in the religion of the Great Spirit.

By the beginning of spring, our good Brother [Michael] McGean had cut some eighteen thousand rails; and placed under cultivation a large field, which promises to yield a very plentiful harvest. Lieutenant Mullan, who spent the winter among the Flat-Heads of St. Mary's, has procured me much valuable aid in founding this mission, and has all along taken a lively interest in its prosperity. I know not how to acquit the debt of gratitude I owe this most excellent officer, and I can only pray, poor missionary as I am, that the Lord may repay his generosity and kindness a hundredfold in blessings of time and eternity. We are still in want of a great many useful and important articles — indeed, of an absolute necessity in the establishing of this new mission. I am confident, many friends of the poor Indians may be found in the United States, who will most willingly contribute their mite in such a charitable undertaking — we will be most grateful to them, and our good neophytes, in whose behalf I make the appeal, will not cease to pray for their kind benefactors.

Please make arrangements with the American Fur Company to have goods brought up by the Missouri river to Fort Benton, whence I could get them conveyed in wagons across the mountains to the missionary station.

The Right Rev. Magloire Blanchet, bishop of Nesqualy, who in his first visit confirmed over six hundred Indians, although he arrived unexpectedly, when a great many families had gone to their hunting grounds, among the Kalispels and our neighboring missions, intended to give confirmation here this summer. I was very desirous of the arrival of this pious prelate, who has done so much good, by his fervent exhortations, to strengthen our neophytes in the faith. It had already been agreed upon that a party of Indians should go to meet him as far as the village of the Sacred Heart, among the Cœur-d'Alènes, about two hundred miles from St. Ignatius' mission, when our plans were broken up by a message from Governor [Isaac] Stevens, summoning all our Indians to a council, to be held some thirty miles off, in St. Mary's or Bitter Root valley, at a place called Hellgate, whence a number of chiefs and warriors were to accompany him to a Grand Council of Peace among the Black-Feet. I was absent on a visit to our brethren among the Cœur-d'Alènes, the Skoyelpies, and other tribes, when I received an invitation from the governor to be present at the councils. I had found, in my visit, all our missions rich in good works and conversions, though very poor in the goods of this world — all the Fathers and Brothers were in the enjoyment of excellent health. Father [Joseph] Joset, among the Skoyelpies, at the Kettle Falls of the Columbia, had baptized a large number of adults and children. During the late prevalence of the small-pox, there were hardly any deaths from it among the neophytes, as most of them had been previously vaccinated by us, while the Spokans and other unconverted Indians, who said the "Medicine (vaccine) of the Fathers, was a poison, used only to kill them," were swept away by hundreds. This contrast, of course, had the effect of increasing the influence of the missionaries.

While mingled feelings of joy at all the good effected, and of sorrow at the miserable death of so many of God's creatures — thankful to God for all his blessings, and submissive to the mysterious judgments of his Providence, I set out, accompanied by my neophytes, for the Black-Feet territory. The grand council took place in the vicinity of Fort Benton. Our Indians, who were in great expectation of seeing you with Majors [Alfred] Cummings and [Alexander] Culbertson, were indeed much disappointed at not finding you. The Black-Feet, although they are still much given to thieving, and have committed more depredations than ever, during the last spring, are very anxious to see you again, and to have missionaries among them. Governor Stevens, who has always shown himself a real father and well affected towards our Indians, has expressed a determination to do all in his power to forward the success of the missions. The establishment of a mission among the Black-Feet would be the best, and indeed the only means to make them observe the treaty of peace which has just been concluded. Until missionaries are sent, I intend, from time to time, to visit the Black-Feet, so as to do for them what good I may, and prepare the way for the conversion of the whole tribe. I hope a new mission may soon be realized, for it is absolutely necessary, both for their own sake and for the peace of our converted Indians on the western side of the Rocky Mountains.

From all I have seen, and from all I have learned during this last trip, I may say, that the Crows and all the tribes on the upper waters of the Missouri, as well as the various bands of Black-Feet, where so many children have already been regenerated in the holy waters of baptism, by you and by Father [Nicholas] Point, are anxious to have the Black-gowns permanently among them, and to learn "the prayer of the Great Spirit." The field seems ripe for the harvest. Let us pray that God may soon send zealous laborers to this far-distant and abandoned region.

The chief, Alexander, the Kalispel, Michael Insula, and the other Flat-Head chieftains, the leaders of the Koetenay and Flat-Bow bands, and all our neophytes, beg to be remembered in your good prayers — they, on their part, never forget to pray for you. Please remember me.

Your devoted brother in Christ,
Adrian Hoeken, S.J.

Document 24

A Blackfeet Winter Count of Fighting with and Against the Pend d'Oreille

1855-1870

Source: Extracted from James Willard Schultz, *Blackfeet and Buffalo: Memories of Life Among the Indians,* ed. by Keith C. Seele (Norman: University of Oklahoma Press, 1962), pages 264-266. Copyright © 1962 by the University of Oklahoma Press, Norman. Reprinted by permission of the publisher.

Editors' note: Three Suns' war record includes accounts of fighting in alliance with the Pend d'Oreille and against the Pend d'Oreille on the plains between 1855 and 1870. The war record lacks many details, but it does emphasize just how fluid tribal alliances and friendships were during the plains wars.

Three Suns' War Record
Told by Three Suns

Seele and Schultz note: Events in the life of *Ninókskatosi* — ("Three Suns," otherwise known as "Big Nose"), last war chief of the Pikuni Indians, were portrayed by him on an elk skin. This elk skin was given by Big Nose to Captain L. W. Cooke (later Brigadier General, U.S.A.), Third United States Infantry, while he was acting Indian agent for the Blackfoot, Blood, and Pikuni Indians in 1893-94. The following notes, interpretative of the various pictographs on the skin, were made by Captain Cooke from verbal descriptions given by Big Nose himself. At that time Big Nose was about seventy years old.

Scene 5 (1855):
Sweetgrass Hills, the east butte. At this time the Piegans and the Ponderas were at peace, and sixty lodges of the Piegans and ten lodges of the Ponderas were camped together. Late at night, when soundly sleeping, Big Nose heard a gun fired and then another. They all sprang to arms and when they emerged from their lodges, they discovered that they were surrounded by about four hundred Sioux. So close had been the fire that the Piegan horses corralled inside the circle of lodges were nearly all killed. Those not killed made their escape, except for the sorrel pinto horse ridden by Big Nose. The Sioux by this time had possession of half of the Piegan lodges. Big Nose on his pinto, which was wounded in the neck and then exchanged for the yellow horse, held

his people together in the other half of the village, fighting till morning. The yellow figure was a Sioux, wounded by a Pondera, and he ran off followed by Big Nose, who pursued and stabbed him to death. The Sioux then withdrew with a loss of sixteen killed; the Ponderas and Piegans lost eleven.

Scene 7 (1860):

In the Judith Basin in Montana. Big Nose crawled up on a Pondera lodge under cover of night, taking the horse shown picketed there. In the meantime the owner opened fire, shooting Big Nose through the coat. There were thirteen Piegans in the party and sixty lodges of Ponderas. The Piegans were a hundred miles from their own people. The horse shown was the only one taken, owing to the early discovery of the raiders by the Ponderas.

Scene 4 (1861):

Near White Sulphur Springs, Montana. A surprise by the Ponderas. The Indian shown falling was the brother of Big Nose. The Piegan party numbered eleven, and the Pondera, sixty. The former retreated to the brush. The brother recovered, and one Pondeara was killed.

Scene 1 (1870):

Represents the capture of eight Pondera (Pend d'Oreille) Indians by the South Piegans, with whom they were at war. A large village of the Piegans were in camp in the Cypress Hills near old Fort Walsh, Northwest Territory. The Piegans succeeded in surrounding their foes and were about to kill them when Big Nose interceded in their behalf, thus saving their lives and permitting them to return to the Flathead country from whence they came. It seems that at some previous time Big Nose had received a large silver medal from the United States government in Washington; he was told at the time that he must not kill or permit his people to kill anyone and that he and his people must make peace with all tribes as well as with the whites, hence his efforts to save the lives of this party.

Document 25

Lower Pend d'Oreille Treaty Council

March 24, 1856

Source: R. H. Lansdale, "Proceedings of Council held with Kalispel tribe of Indians upon treaty proposal, March 24, 1856," U.S. Bureau of Indian Affairs, "Records of the Washington Superintendency of Indian Affairs, 1853-1874," National Archives Microfilm Publications M5, reel 26, frames 53-57.

Editors' note: Flathead Indian Agent R. H. Lansdale presented the Lower Pend d'Oreille Indians with a draft treaty left by Gov. Isaac Stevens for them to sign. It provided for goods and services in exchange for relocating to the Flathead or Jocko Reservation with the Upper Pend d'Oreille and Kootenai Indians. Chief Victor of the Lower Pend d'Oreille would not agree to move to the new reservation and wanted a home in their traditional territory lower on the Pend d'Oreille River.

Proceedings of Council held with Kalispel tribe of Indians
upon treaty proposal, March 24, 1856.

At a council held at the mission St. Ignatius, on the Flathead Reservation, on Monday, March 24, 1856; present, R. H. Lansdale, Indian Agent for Flathead Nation, representing the president of the United States, and I. I. Stevens, gov. & sup. Ind. affrs and comr. for forming treaties for Washington Ter.; and Victor, head chief, and other headmen & delegates of the Lake or Lower Pend d'oreilles tribe of Indians, the following proceedings were had. Michael Rivet having been appointed and sworn as interpreter.

Agent Lansdale said: — My Red Brothers of the Kallispelm nation: The Great Spirit whose name is Jehovah, who made the heaven & the earth, and all things that are in them, has also made from blood all nations and peoples, to dwell together on the face of the earth in peace and friendship: — and all who hear his voice and all who receive his word, have received into their hearts a spirit of love and friendship for their fellow men, of all portions of the earth, whatever may be their color or condition. That is the reason why I, a white man, and these other white men, your fathers & friends are before you today: it is not because we have a spirit of ill will & enmity, but a spirit of good will, that we are here: — therefore what I say to you, but let it enter into your ears and sink deep into your hearts, for it is the truth.

Your great father, the president of the United States, and his children, the people of the United States, claim the domain of all these lands from the great sea in the east to the great sea in the west; he claims his red children to be his, as well as his white children to be his, and that he has a right to rule them all, and to extend his laws over them all; and amongst all the great & Christian nations of the world, it is agreed that he has the right to extend his laws over all these lands & peoples.

That they might get a more perfect knowledge of his laws; the president sent last year Gov. Stevens, as his commissioner, to talk and treat with all the people of this country, to make known to them the wishes of the president and his white people, to form treaties of perpetual peace and friendship between the president and all his red children, and to make arrangements with them about their lands, by which arrangements he would secure to them certain portions as permanent homes, and to confer other benefits and blessings upon them, by means of which they would be elevated and made to acquire additional knowledge of farms and trades, and the white man's way of living.

I shall now proceed to explain to you all the advantages that will accrue to you by reason of the treaty left for you to sign.

Whatever rights you have in lands below, the president through Gov. Stevens proposes to purchase from you, and Gov. Stevens left with me a paper for you to sign, and after you have signed it, it will be sent to the governor to sign, and after he has signed it, the treaty will be sent to the president and the great council, and if approved of, he will sign it, and then it will be a law never to be broken.

The paper provides as follows.

That you sell and convey to the president all your rights in lands below; and that you agree to be united and made one with the Flathead Nation, and that you be removed to and settle upon the Flathead reservation, which reservation is secured to the Flathead nation by the treaty made last summer by Gov. Stevens at the Bitter Root; and that you are to remove to the reservation within one year from the time the treaty is approved by the president. And, in order to enable you to remain and to open farms, build houses, &c, the president proposes to give you a large sum of money, to wit, ten thousand dollars, in one year after the approval of the treaty. In the mean time, until this money is paid and used for your good, it will be lawful for you to live upon & cultivate your lands below for one year; and after you leave your improvements, they will be valued, and the value paid to you in addition to the ten thousand dollars, and no one of you having houses & places there will be made to leave, till you are paid for them, or others are made for you here.

In consideration of your leaving your lands and coming to this reservation, the president proposes to give you forty thousand dollars, in all, as I have already stated, ten thousand the first year for removing, opening farms, building houses, &c. For the four years after the first year, twenty-five hundred dollars each year; for the next five years, eighteen hundred dollars each year; for the next five years, twelve hundred dollars each year; and for the next five years, one thousand dollars each year: — all which moneys are to be applied to the use and benefit of the Kallispelm or Lower Pend d'oreilles, under the direction of the president, as he may from time to time determine.

Besides these sums of money, other and great advantages will be enjoyed by you in Common with the other tribes of the Flathead Nation, and which are secured to the Flathead nation by the treaty in the Bitter Root last summer, and I will now state them. There will be built on this reservation, by the president & kept in operation for twenty years, one grist-mill, one saw-mill, one hospital & physician for the sick; an agricultural and industrial school with teachers; one Blacksmith shop, one Carpenter shop, and tin shop, one gun shop, one wagon maker and plow shop, with men to work in them for the Indians and to instruct them in these trades.

The remaining articles of the programme was then explained in order, item by item.

I have now explained the treaty, and the views of the governor; — I want to Know if you understand the treaty, and agree to it.

Victor, chief of the Lower Pend d'oreilles: We intend to give the half of the Kallispel lands. We want to give what land we have on the south side of Clarke's Fork, and keep the north side. I do not Know the Maps, but I take the River for my line. If you approve of this, it is well. As you speak about land, we spoke together about it, and we concluded to give what I said, that is the half, taking the river for the line. Are you satisfied with what I said?

Agent L. It is not for me to say. Gov. Stevens left with me a treaty which I was to explain to you, and see if you liked it. That paper I have just explained to you: — it provides, as I told you before, that you should give up all your lands below, and receive lands up here on this reservation, and certain other payments and advantages in lieu of your lands down there. I myself have not the power, or the will, to change this paper. The president authorized the governor to make a treaty with you; I am not authorized, but I will give you my mind on the subject.

Victor: It is not for my own part; I have no difficulty to agree: if they give for my people a piece of land that I can set my foot on. My people can't remain always in the same place. The big chief calls us his children; a father has care of his children and sees that they have what is good for them. Now the father is far away don't know what is for the good of his children. I would be glad if the g. father would give to his red children a small piece of land in their own country. I would be glad if it was agreed in this way.

Agent: I have explained the paper I believe, fully. I have not the power to change it. I have also tried to explain the good intentions of the president and the people of the United States. The desire of the president and people is not to get more land, for they have already more land than they need. The intention is not to take your lands, but to secure to you a permanent home. For, when you are dead, & your children come after you; when the white men come into the country and begin to settle — then your children will have no home. The object now is to give you a permanent home; to teach you to farm and to learn trades, and to become like your white bothers in other respects. For if you don't now commence to settle down, and to farm your lands, after a short time you will be swallowed up by the whites — you will have nothing, and you will melt away like snow before the summer sun. I who know the history of the red men in the east, know that all this will happen, unless you secure the friendship of the president of the United States, and throw yourselves under the protection of his wings; because if you do not, your lands will be taken, after a few years, forever without the permission and against the will of the president. The greedy white men will come & take your lands, and the president can't help, cannot prevent it. You cannot expect the president will pay you so great a price for your lands below, give you lands, mills, farms, schools, shops, &c. and give you a large part of the lands below back to you.

Victor: I want only a small spot; a big spot I give. The big chief calls us his children; he ought to have pity on his children. The big chief is mistaken; he ought to give us a small spot of our own native country. We want to be able to return. The price is good.

Simon; (brother to Victor): In all things we wish to do what the big father tells us: we don't want to go against his will. But we would wish if he had pity on us to give us a small spot where we might return in safety. We call our country a Safe country; — we have no enemy there. As they are now fighting below — the whites and Indians — if any of our nation would Kill a white man, we would Kill him.

Agent: there is no provisions in the treaty to prevent your going down the river to hunt fish, and travel and trade, dig camas, & graze your horses.

Simon: We understand that we might go to fish &c.; and though we understand the white people may come there — still we would wish the big chief to give us a small spot which we may call our own.

Victor: Has the chief said, that if we speak we should not be listened to? That he should pay no attention to what we say.

Agent: I have been directed to put down all you say, whether you agree to this treaty, or not.

Victor: We wish that the great father should be made acquainted with our wishes. If our chief sees what we have said, and if he could allow what we desire, it is well: — If he does not approve of it, then we will not be content.

Matthew: If the governor himself had been present, we could easily arrange by giving one half of our lands; but it does not do well to do it only by letter, for now our chief does not know what to decide. For one thing I suffer, and all the Kallispel suffer — for powder. Far off the people fight; we Kallispel are quiet; we have nothing to do with it. Now we heard that we are to suffer with the others, for they tell us that we will have no powder, — as if the Big Chief wanted to starve us to death by hunger. We have children — it is only with powder that we can get something for them to eat in order to live.

Never would we take our guns to kill a white man; we could not. I wished that the chief had pity on us, that in the fall he would give us powder to hunt in the winter. I don't want to talk too much. We don't like to see our children suffer. Hearing that powder is forbidden, we are anxious for our children. We have nothing; — we have no horses, no cattle, no pigs, no fields, nothing to live on but powder. If they refuse us powder, they might as well send us to die.

Agent: The object of the treaty is to do you good, not harm. The object of the great father is to give you homes, farms, every thing that will enable you to live. As to forbidding you powder, the president never forbids it to his friends: it is not yet forbidden — so that your fears are groundless. My opinion is that it is far better for you to make the treaty with the president, — to secure his protection. It is not because the president is afraid of you that he wants to make a treaty with you, it is for your good. Think over it tonight, and to morrow we will have another talk.

Upon a private consultation with Victor on the morning of the 25th, I found that his people had talked the treaty propositions over at night, and a majority still adhering to their first resolution not to sell without a reservation be allowed them upon their own lands, I concluded it was unnecessary to call the people together, but dismissed all hope of their agreeing to the treaty.
Flathead Agency
March 31, 1856.

R. H. Lansdale Ind Agt
Flathead Nation.

Document 26

More News from St. Ignatius Mission

April 15, 1857

Source: Adrian Hoeken, S.J., "Letter of Rev. Father Adrian Hoeken," Apr. 25, 1857, P. J. DeSmet, *Western Missions and Missionaries: A Series of Letters* (New York: James B. Kirker, 1863), pages 307-318.

Editors' note: Much of this letter concerns transport and supply for the St. Ignatius Mission, but Hoeken also mentions news about the tribes. He detailed the assistance the mission gave the Indians in agriculture, blacksmithing, and carpentry. Michael Insula got a gift from two fur traders he knew, and most of the Bitterroot Salish leaders came to St. Ignatius for their religious obligations despite the recent closing of St. Mary's Mission. Hoeken also noted a visit to St. Ignatius by the Blackfeet Chief Little Dog and the number of Indians of different tribes killed in recent intertribal warfare.

Letter of Rev. Father Adrian Hoeken.
Mission of the Flat-Heads, April 15, 1857.

Rev. and Beloved Father:

Before entering into a few details, I beg you to excuse the want of order in this letter. Much time has elapsed since I had the pleasure of receiving news from you, who have so many titles to my love and gratitude, and whose name is frequently on the lips, and always in the hearts, of each of the inhabitants of this remote region. Your letter of the 27th and 28th of March reached us towards the end of August, it was read, or rather devoured, with avidity, so dear was it to our hearts. It was remitted to us by our chief Alexander, who accompanied Mr. R. H. Lansdale to the Cœur-d'Alènes. Scarcely had we cast a glance at the address, and recognized your handwriting, than, not being able to contain our joy, all, with one consent, cried out, "Father de Smet! Father de Smet!" You cannot imagine the delight your letters afford us and our dear Indians. God be praised! Your name will be ever held in benediction among these poor children of the Rocky Mountains. Ah! how often they ask me these questions: "When, oh when! will Father de Smet come to us? Will he ever again ascend the Missouri? Is it true that he will not come to Fort Benton this fall?" These, and many other similar questions, show how dear to them is the remembrance of their father in Christ; of him who first broke to them the bread of eternal life, and showed them the true way to happiness on earth and bliss hereafter. It is not strange, then, that your letters should have been read several times, and that every time they gave us new pleasure and excited new interest.

I can never cease admiring Divine Providence, which presides over all, and which in particular takes care of our beloved missions. Among the unnumbered proofs of its continual protection, your assistance in our late distress, and the liberality of our benefactors, are not less remarkable, nor less worthy of gratitude. Our storehouses were empty, and the war between the Indians nearest the seaboard took away all hope of procuring other resources. Never, never was charity more appropriate, nor received with greater joy. May Heaven prolong your days and those of our benefactors! May you continue to foster the same interest towards us that, until the present moment, you have never ceased to testify! Yes, beloved father, let the recollection of our missions be ever equally dear to you. They are the fruit of your own heroic zeal, fatigues, and labors. Ah! never forget our dear Indians; they are *your* children in Christ, the offspring of *your* boundless charity and your unwearied zeal!

During the months of June, July, and August, disease raged cruelly in our camp, as well as in that of the Flat-Heads. However, there were few victims of its terrible attacks.

Father [Joseph] Ménétrey, my co-laborer, visited the Flat-Heads, where he had been asked for by the chief, Fidelis Teltella (*Thunder*), whose son was dangerous ill. Later, I visited them myself in their camash prairies. A second time, in the opening of the month of June, I remained some days with them, at Hellgate, and I distributed medicines to all those who had been seized with the epidemic, and a little wheat flour to each family. Victor, the great chief, Ambrose, Moses, Fidelis, Adolphus, and several others, came here of their own accord, to fulfil their religious duties. Since last spring there has been a notable amelioration in the whole nation. Ambrose has effected the most good. He had convened several assemblies, in order to arrange and pay off old debts, to repair wrongs, etc. The Indians appear, however, very reluctant to part with their lands; they will scarcely hear of the dispositions to be taken.

Father [Anthony] Ravalli labored as much as he could to pacify the tribes which reside towards the west, namely; the Cayuses, the Yakamans, the Opelouses, etc. As our neophytes hitherto have taken no part in the war, the country is as safe for us as ever. We can go freely wheresoever we desire. No one is ignorant that the Black-gowns are not enemies; those, at least, who are among the Indians. Almost all the Cœur-d'Alènes, in order to shield themselves from the hostilities of the Indians, and to avoid all relations with them, are

Father Adrian Hoecken, S.J.
Photograph 823.01, Jesuits West Archives at Gonzaga University,
Spokane, Washington.

gone bison-hunting. A few days since, Father [Joseph] Joset wrote me that Father Ravalli had already written to him several weeks before: "I fear a general uprising among the Indians, towards the commencement of spring. Let us pray, and let us engage others to pray with us, in order to avert this calamity. I think that it would be well to add to the ordinary prayers of the mass, the collect of peace."

If the less well-intentioned Indians from the lower lands would keep within their own territory, and if the whites, the number of whom is daily augmenting in St. Mary's valley, could act with moderation, and conduct themselves prudently, I am convinced that soon the whole country would be at peace, and that not a single Indian would henceforward imbrue his hands in the blood of a white stranger. Were I authorized to suggest a plan, I would propose to have all the upper lands evacuated by the whites, and form of it a territory exclusively of Indians; afterwards I would lead there all the Indians of the inferior portion, such as the Nez-Percés, the Cayuses, the Yakomas, the Cœur-d'Alènes, and the Spokans. Well-known facts lead me to believe that this plan, with such superior advantages, might be effected, by means of missions, in the space of two or three years.

Our Indians here are doing well. Last spring we sowed about fifty bushels of wheat, and planted a quantity of potatoes, cabbages, and turnips. God has graciously blessed our labors and our fields. Here all generally like agriculture. We give the seeds gratis to everybody. Our ploughs and our tools are also free to be used by them. We even lend our horses and oxen to the poorest among the Indians, and we grind all their grain gratuitously. But our mill, which goes by horse-power is very small, and we are not able to build another.

Mr. R. H. Lansdale, agent of the government, a very just and upright man, has assumed his functions at the Plum-trees, a place situated quite near the place where we cross the river, a few miles from this. We gave him all the assistance of which we were capable. I had indulged the hope that the government would come to our aid, at least for the building of a small church; but so far my expectations have been frustrated. Alas! are we never to cease deploring the loss of our little church among the Kalispels? Several of these latter-named, and among others, Victor, on seeing the chapel, formerly so dear to them, but now forsaken and neglected, shed tears of regret.

When, oh when! shall the oppressed Indian find a poor corner of the earth on which he may lead a peaceful life, serving and loving his God in tranquility, and preserving the ashes of his ancestors without fear of beholding them profaned and trampled beneath the feet of an unjust usurper?

Several among the Kalispels, Victor and others, already have possessions here. However, they have not yet renounced those which they own in the country lower down. Twelve very poor habitations are the beginning of our town called St. Ignatius. Our little abode, although very modest, is sufficiently comfortable. To any other than you, this word *comfortable* might sound singular; but you, Reverend Father, who understand perfectly what it means when applied to a poor missionary, will comprehend the relative application of the word. Our community numbers six members. Father Joseph Ménétrey, who is missionary, prefect of our chapel, and inspector in chief of our fields, etc.; Brother [Michael] McGean, farmer; Brother Vincent Magri, dispenser, carpenter, and miller; Brother Joseph Spegt, blacksmith, baker, and gardener; Brother Francis Huybrechts, carpenter and sacristan.

I intend going to Colville after the harvest and during the absence of the Indians.

Father Ménétrey, of his own free will, went to Fort Benton with a pair of horses. The distance by the great road is 294 miles. He took horses because we could with difficulty spare our oxen, and also because, according to information received from Mr. Lansdale, the road is impassable to oxen which have not, like horses, iron shoes. Father Ménétrey arrived at the fort on the 17th of September, and was very favorably received by the occupants; but he was obliged to wait some time for the boats. He speaks with high eulogiums of the Black-Feet, and regrets that he has not jurisdiction in that part of the mountains. He returned on the 12th of November.

How express to you, Rev. Father, the joy that filled our hearts, when we opened your letters and the different cases which you had the charity to send us? We each and all wept with grateful joy! In vain, the night following, I strove to calm the emotions that these missives, as well as the liberality of our benefactors, had produced in my heart; I could not close my eyes. All the community, yes, the whole camp, participated in my delight. In unison we rendered thanks to Divine Providence, and that day was a perfect holiday. The next day, having a little recovered from my excitement, I was ashamed of my weakness. You who know what it is to be a missionary; you who know so well his privations, his trials, his pangs, you will easily forgive my excessive sensibility.

I had agreed with Father [Nicholas] Congiato that he would send your Reverence my lists, as well as the money that he might allow me. I was bolder in soliciting your charity and your benevolence in our favor, because I knew the love and interest that you bear to our missions; and that, on the other hand, I only executed a plan that yourself had conceived and suggested, when, in consideration of the circumstances, it would have appeared to every one else illusory and incapable of execution.

Scarcely had Father Ménétrey gone than I received a letter from Father Congiato, in which he said to me: "If you think that your supplies can be furnished at a more reasonable price from Missouri, order them thence, I will pay the cost. Write on this subject to Rev. Father De Smet." Had I received this letter somewhat later, I scarcely know what would have been my decision; for it is very doubtful that we should have been able to find any one who would return to Fort Benton. I entreat you, be so good as to excuse the trouble that we give you; our extraordinary situation is the sole excuse that I can offer in favor of our importunity. A thousand thanks to you, and to all our benefactors who concurred so generously in the support of our missions. I also thank our kind brethren in St. Louis, for the very interesting letters that they had the kindness to write me. Receive too, our grateful sentiments. Rev. Father, for the catalogues of the different provinces, the classical books, Shea's Catholic Missions, the works of controversy, etc., etc. I should never conclude did I attempt to enumerate all your gifts, which we were so overjoyed to receive. Brother Joseph was beside himself with gladness when his eyes fell on the little packages of seeds, the files, scissors, and other similar objects. Accept, in fine, our thanks for the piece of broadcloth you sent us; by this favor we continue to be "*Black-gowns*." Ah! with my whole heart I wish that you could have seen us as we were opening the boxes. Each object excited new cries of joy, and augmented our grateful love for the donors. All arrived in good order. The snuff had got a little mixed with clover-seed, but no matter; my nose is not very delicate. It is the first donation sent into these mountains, at least since I have been here. We bless God, who watches over all of his children with so much care and liberality, even over those who appear to be the most forsaken.

On the following day I sent Father Joset his letters. I found an opportunity that very day.

It would have been very agreeable to me to receive a copy of all your letters published since 1836. The portraits were very dear to me. I could not recognize Father [John] Verdin's, but Brother Joseph knew it at the first glance. Yours was also recognized at once by a great number of the Indians, and on seeing it they shouted "Pikek an!" It made the tour of the village, and yesterday again, an inhabitant of Koetenay came to me with sole intention of "paying a visit to Father De Smet." This did them an immense good, only seeing the portrait of him who was the first to bear them the light of faith in these regions, still overshadowed with the darkness of moral death; and who first dissipated the mists in which they and their progenitors during untold ages had been enveloped. Believe me, reverend father, not a day passes, without their prayers ascending to heaven for you.

In what manner can we testify our gratitude in regard to the two benefactors who so generously charged themselves with the care of transporting and delivering to us our cases without consenting to accept the slightest recompense? Undoubtedly they will reap a large share in the sacrifices and prayers that daily rise to Heaven for all our benefactors, and which are with a grateful heart and the remembrance of the beneficence towards us, the only tokens of our thankfulness that we can offer them. How noble the sentiment which prompted them gratuitously to burden themselves and their boats, with the charitable gifts destined by the faithful, to the destitute missionaries of the Indians! Heaven, who knows our poverty, will reward them with better gifts than we could have imagined suitable to their liberality.

The package destined for Michael Insula, the *"Little Chief,"* lies here for the present. He has not yet opened it. The good man is abroad on a hunting excursion; but we expect him back in a few days. I doubt not that he will be very sensible to these marks of friendship, or, as he usually, expresses it, "these marks of fraternity." He set out from here, when he had harvested the grain he had sowed. Always equally good, equally happy, a fervent Christian, he is daily advancing in virtue and in perfection. He has a young son, Louis Michael, whom he teaches to call me *papa*. It is a real pleasure to him to able to speak of your reverence and of his two adopted brothers, Messrs. [Robert] Campbell and [Thomas] Fitzpatrick. I will give him the packet directly after his return, and will inform you of the sentiments with which he will have received it, as well as his reply.

Here in our mission, we already observe all the conditions stipulated in the treaty concluded last year by Gov. [Isaac] Stevens, at Hellgate. Our brothers assist the Indians, and teach them how to cultivate the ground. They distribute the fields and the seeds for sowing and planting, as well as the ploughs and other agricultural instruments. Our blacksmith works for them: he repairs their guns, their axes, their knives; the carpenter renders them great assistance in constructing their houses, by making the doors and windows; in fine, our little mill is daily in use for grinding their grain, *gratis*; we distribute some medicines to the sick; — in a word, all we have and all we are is sacrificed to the welfare of the Indian. The savings that our religious economy enables us to make, we retain solely to relieve their miseries. Whatever we gain by manual labor and by the sweat of the brow, is theirs! Through love of Jesus Christ, we are ready to sacrifice all, even life itself. Last year we opened our school; but circumstances forced us to close it. Next spring we shall have a brother capable of teaching, and we intend opening it a second time; but in the interval we shall not earn a cent. During last October, the snow forced Fathers Joset and Ravalli and Brother [Natalis] Saveo to return to the Cœur-d'Alènes.

We have done, and shall continue to do, all that lies in our power for the government officers. Still our poor mission has never received a farthing from the government. Do not think, reverend father, that I complain — oh no! you are too well assured no earthly good could ever induce us to work and suffer as we do here. As wealth itself could never recompense our toils, so privations are incapable of leading us to renounce our noble enterprise. Heaven, heaven alone is our aim; and that reward will far exceed our deserts. On the other hand, we are consoled by the reflection that He who provides for the birds of the air will never abandon his tenderly loved children. Yet it is not less true, that, if we had resources (humanly speaking), our mission would be more flourishing; and that many things that we now accomplish only with great patience and sore privations, and which again frequently depend upon contingencies, could be effected more rapidly and with less uncertainty of success.

In our mission, there are persons of such a variety of nations, that we form, so to speak, a heaven in miniature. First, our community is composed of six members, all of whom are natives of different lands. Then we have creoles: Genetzi, whose wife is Susanna, daughter of the old Ignatius Chaves; Abraham and Peter Tinsley, sons of old Jacques Boiteux; Alexander Thibault, a Canadian, and Derpens. There are some old Iroquois: old Ignatius is settled here, as well as the family of Iroquois Peter. The death of this venerable old man is a great loss to the mission. Then we have creoles from the Creek nation; Pierrish, and Anson, with his brothers; then some Flat-Heads; Kalispels; two camps of Pends-d'Oreilles; then several Spokans; some Nez-Percés, Koetenays, Cœur-d'Alènes, and Kettle-Falls Indians; a few Americans, settled a few miles from here; and some Black-Feet. All, though of different nations, live together like brethren and in perfect harmony. They have, like the primitive Christians, but one heart and one mind.

Last spring, and during the summer following, we had several Black-Feet here. They behaved extremely well. Among others, the Little Dog, chief of the Pégans, with some members of his family. They entered our camp with the American flag unfurled, and marching to the tones of martial music and an innumerable quantity of little bells. The very horses pranced in accordance with the measure, and assumed a stately deportment at the harmony of the national hymn.

We held several conferences with the chief concerning religion. He complained that the whites, who had been in communication with them, had never treated this so important affair. So far the best understanding reigns between us, and it would appear that all the old difficulties are forgotten. May Heaven keep them in these favorable dispositions. Last summer the Crows stole about twenty horses from our nation. A few days after, others visited our camp. The remembrance of this theft so excited the people that, forgetting the law of nations, which secures protection to even the greatest enemy as soon as he puts his foot within the camp, they fell upon the poor guests, and killed two of them ere they had time to escape.

May God bless the government for establishing peace among the Black-Feet! However, as hitherto the means have not proved very efficacious, I fear that the quiet will not be a very long duration. I trust that our society will one day effect a more enduring peace. A mission among them would, I am persuaded, produce this blessed result. And if to bedew this hitherto ungrateful soil requires the blood of some happy missionary, it would bring forth a hundredfold, and the Black-Feet would respect our holy religion.

I am much distressed at learning that an epidemic disease is making terrible ravages among the Black-Feet. According to the last news, about 150 Indians had perished in one camp alone, near Fort Benton. When the malady had ceased scourging men, it fell upon their horses. Many are dead already, and many are dying. We have lost five. Our hunters are forced to go to the chase on foot; for, according to their account, all the horses are sick. If the Nez-Percés lose their horses in the war with government, horses will be very dear here.

Michael, the Little Chief, has arrived. I presented him the gracious gift of Col. Campbell. He was astonished that the colonel should think of him, and was much moved at this mark of attachment. Then he cited a long list of kindred, dead since his last interview with Col. Campbell, and entertained me at length with the great number of Americans that he had seen annually passing Fort Hall. He told me with what solicitude and anxiety he sought his friend among those successive multitudes, and when at length he could not discover him, he believed that he was dead.

Our Indians are bison-hunting, and quite successful. Five Spokans have been killed by the Banacs, and six of these last killed by the Spokans and Cœur-d'Alènes. The Flat-Heads have had a man killed by the same Banacs. Louis, Ambrose's son, was killed last fall by the Gros-Ventres. All last winter a good understanding prevailed among the Black-Feet. Many of them will come, I think, and reside with us.

The Nez Percés and Spokans endeavor to spread a bad spirit among the Indians who reside in the country below. They endeavor to communicate their hatred of the Americans; but our chiefs are firm, and will in no wise acquiesce in the desire of their enemies. Victor, the great chief, and Ambrose, are here again, in order to accomplish their spiritual duties. Unfortunately a great antipathy prevails among these tribes.

Mr. [Neil] McArthur, formerly agent of the Hudson Bay Company, has now settled at Hellgate.

To conclude, Rev. Father, I entreat you to believe that, notwithstanding your reiterated exhortations to assure me, it is not without a feeling of restraint that I inclose you anew the list of things we need this year. I am aware that you are weighed down with business; but who, as well as yourself, can know and understand our position?

I entreat you to present my respects to all my kind friends who are at the university, at St. Charles, and elsewhere.

Your reverence's most respected servant,
A. Hoeken, S.J.

Document 27

Chief Victor Refuses to Leave Bitterroot Valley

April 25, 1857

Source: Jno. Owen to My Dear Doty, Apr. 25, 1857, U.S. Bureau of Indian Affairs, "Records of the Washington Superintendency of Indian Affairs, 1853-1874," National Archives Microfilm Publications M5, reel 22, frames 121-122.

Editors' note: The United States Senate ratified the October 1855 treaty with the Blackfeet soon after it was presented but did not ratify the Hellgate Treaty until 1859. That meant that the Blackfeet were getting annuities long before the Flathead Reservation tribes. According to this letter, Bitterroot Salish Chief Victor renounced any agreement that might result in the Salish leaving the Bitterroot Valley. The copy of Owen's letter that was preserved in the Washington Superintendency Records omitted the final part of the letter.

Fort Owen W.T. April 25th 1857.

My Dear Doty

Many thanks to you for your interesting and lengthy letter per Finley the Agency expressman, also the late file of papers by same conveyance. The news very satisfactory, [James] Buchanan is elected and Governor [Isaac] Stevens sustained by the administration and Ind. Dept. at home. May the snows of many winters rest lightly on his brow. When I wrote you from the Agency I expected ere this to have been on my way down the Mo. bound for the land of Oysters in the Shell. I did not deem it prudent to leave. My Brother has gone for me. Our camp has been in a state of excitement all winter. Some of the hostile and disaffected Indians from below have passed the winter in the jurisdiction of this agency; but what could be done with them. The Flathead Indians say that we are dogs — They say that two years ago they made a treaty with their great friend Gov. Stevens, and have never heard anything of it since. The Same year Some moons later a treaty was made with the Blackfeet which was responded to immediately by their great Father in the shape of Blankets, Guns, Groceries, &c! Why Should the Blackfeet stand so much better with the Great Father than we who have never shed the blood of a white man.

I was called up from the agency some three weeks since by Victor for the purpose of holding a council with the Flatheads. I was far from well but Still I came, and in my office at the fort Victor told me that he was sorry for one thing that they had promised the Governor, which was to vacate the Bitter Root valley if it was though[t] best for them, and have the reservation elsewhere. They now say they will never leave this valley. They say we have buried our fathers and Children here, which endears to us the soil. They went so far as to warn some white men here from fencing and farming telling them you are only tiring yourselves for nothing, you will sow the crops but we will reap them.

On Easter I killed two Beeves and gave them a feast here and made a short speech to them it was shortly after Finley returned and they were anxious to hear the news. I did it without authority but the good effects of the feast and the talk is plainly to be seen. I told them — you are not forgotten by your great Father for by his orders I give you this feast. They harped upon the treaty not being ratisfied. I told them to be patient and that all would turn out well yet. But they say our big friend Inta-ki a kin (Gov. Stevens) said we would hear our great Father speak long before this about our lands, the snows have now passed it is long, probably he has forgotten us. But we love to listen to what our big friend says, it may do us good.

It would have taken but but [sic] a very little to have Kindled the war flame in this camp last winter. The Ponderielles are not to be trusted too far as a body. There has been some unprincipled white men prowling through this section of country and by their talk and conduct are well calculated to poison the Indian mind. one Jonny Crapeau of Dalles notoriety and a most consummate scoundel [sic] was one. I ordered him out of the country still I believe he is prowling about the mission at this time, he belongs to the church, it is all well. But set this down in your book and that it came from me too. That is this, There will be the tallest Kind of Mess here when the reservation is settled, particularly if it is removed from the Vicinity of the Mission. There is an under current at work and the peacable [sic] foundations of this little community will be undermined and the fabric will fall with one stupenduous [sic] crash. New timbers should now replace old and doting ones before it is too late to save the Barque. An Agents duty is unpleasant as things are, law is impotent. You are not Sustained in things you may deem for the good of the Indians for want of troops to enforce the laws. In fact we talked seriously of organizing a vigilence [sic] club here this winter for the protection of the few law abiding people here.

At Beaver Head this winter, one Mr. Ponell the son of a gentleman of Va. I believe, brought about a difficulty between the Snakes, Bannacks and Nez Perces. He went in person with some three or four other men and drove off some 200 head of horses. Said he, had won them gambling and intended having them. The Spokans were also brought into the difficulty they were returning from the Buffaloe. Many horses were lost and some lives. When it will end remains yet to be seen.

I would like to see the Governor and yourself together and talk these things over. I am far from being an alarmist neither do I wish to be frightend [sic] by a Shadow. But I do assure you my own position may not be tenable long and that too among the friendly Flatheads. They are Indians and have their sympathies with other tribes that have never done them any harm. My own people have been cautioned this Spring about riding too far from the fort without cause. I hope that in seven years sojourn among these people I have been able to attach to my interest some few stern friends who would give me timely notice of approaching danger. I wish there was more of them. I shall leave for the agency this week although report reached me yesterday of a feast having been given in that vicinity by a Nez Perces & Cayuse Frank and a general invitation sent to the Spokans and Ponderills the object of which was to consult about the policy of their coming and Killing me at the agency Simply because I was the acting agent and was writing to the Governor about them. As for the truth of this report, I Know not, but I think the party at the agency far from being safe at this time. God send that the Doctor [Richard Lansdale] or some one else soon arrive to relieve me. I cant for my life see why the doctor selected such an out of the way place neither farming land nor grazing land and the Snow falls deeper and lays longer than in any other Section of the mountains. A much better location could be found on the Jocco further up, where he would have a plain some twelve miles in length by an average breadth of from five to Seven with favorable wintering ground. But rest assured that these Indians will never yeald [sic] cheerfully to being moved. They say this is all our country and the Ponderrills are merely here on sufferance. Their country is below the Lake and why should we be moved because they are living near the mission. It is due us as the Flathead Tribe to have more to Say about the reservation then they have. If things remain quiet this summer you may see me below.

* * * * * * * *

The remainder of Mr. Owens letter does not refer to the Indians.

(Signed) Jno Owen

To Mr. James Doty.

Document 28

Life of Baptiste Aeneas, Ferryman and Farmer

1857

Source: W. F. Wheeler, "Baptiste Aeneas — Biography," box 1, folder 13, William F. Wheeler Papers, MS 65, Montana Historical Society Archives, Helena.

Editors' note: Baptiste Aeneas was born in Tobacco Plains in 1817 to an Iroquois father and Kootenai mother. The family had various adventures and traveled across the Missouri River Valley. Part of the family was kidnaped by the Crow Indians. When Baptiste reached maturity, he had various jobs and adventures across the Missouri River Valley and Washington Territory until he finally took up a farm in the Jocko Valley in 1857. In 1846 he married a Kalispel Indian widow. After 1869 he operated a ferry across the river at the south end of Flathead Lake. This biographical sketch was compiled by Wheeler based on an interview with Baptiste in 1885. Typographical errors in the manuscript have been reproduced without using sic in order to make the manuscript easier to read.

Foot of Flat Head Lake
Baptiste Ferry,
May 21, 1885.

BAPTISTE AENEAS was owner of the ferry across the outlet of Flat Head Lake, and a resident there since 1869, was born in Missoula County, Montana. His father was an Iroquois indian, born near Montreal, Canada, and came to the Columbia river in company with some sixty other Iroquois, about the time of the war of 1812. They came on their own account to hunt and trap, having heard from returned voyageurs who had been in the employment of the Hudson Bay Company of the great abundance of beavers, mink and other fur bearing animals that were found in the country west of the Rocky Mountains. For permission to hunt and trap in this country, which was claimed by the Hudson Bay Company and its territory, they had to agree to sell all they procured to the H. B. Co. at a stipulated price.

Many of these Iriquois never returned to Canada, much preferring to live in this country on account of its better climate, and the ease which they could

[m]ake a living. They being Indians soon intermarried among the various tribes from the Rocky Mountains to the Pacific coast. Thus it was Mr. Aeneas' father married a Kootenais woman at Tobacco Plains Montana where he (Aeneas) was born in 1817.

About 1830, some half dozen or more families of the Flat Heads, the fathers of which were Iroquois, with quite a number who came out with the party of sixty started to go to St. Louis, with the intention of eventually visiting their old homes in Canada, and if not satisfied, to return here. On the Yellowstone they were joined by a number of trappers who were returning with the fruits of their labor and some furs purchased to St. Louis. Some traders of the American Fur Co. also joined them, so that the whole party amounted to over a hundred men, with the families referred to above. On the way down the Yellowstone, the father of Aeneas, stopped near the Powder river to trap up a small tributary, as signs of beaver were plentiful, while the main camp crossed that river and went on. During his absence, the family consisting of the mother, six children, and a young Snake indian, who had been captured by the Flat Heads, and held as a slave and a Flat Head woman and her child were surprised and captured by the Crows. The oldest boy was a son of the woman by a former husband, and had the misfortune of a short time before th break his leg while hunting Buffaloes, from his horse stumbling and falling on him.

The chiefs and head men, only participated in the capture. The women ans others were camped on a bluff in plain sight. Every thing was taken and carried off. The chiefs then had a consultation, and selected one of the Flat Head boys, Aeneas' brother boys and took him with them, and it is supposed they adopted him into their tribe for he has never been heard of since. They also took the Flat Head woman and child to their camp. The balance of the family they left, destitute of every thing. The Snake boy seeing some young indian on the top of the bluff, said he would go and se[e] them. The others tried to persuade him not to go, but he went and when near the top of the bluff was shot dead, and his body rolled down to the valley below.

When the Crows were first seen, the mother ordered all to run in to the brush and with her baby in her arms ans oldest child, a girl about 16, ran and hid. The lame boy and two smaller children, were captured but not harmed. After the chiefs had left with the boy they had selected to keep the mother & child left by them all hid in the brush.

The next day the father returned, but found his camp deserted and the dead body of his Snake slave. He then searched for his family, and happily found them, all except the one the indians had taken with them. He constructed a raft of drift timber and ferried his family over the Powder river in the night and about noon on that day overtook the main camp. A party was sent back to bring in the lame boy. They found him hid in the brush and brought him in. (Note. Overcome with the fatigues of the long journay across the plains and the suffering from his broken leg, on reaching Council Bluffs he died. W.F.W.)

The whole camp then moved on, and after many hardships arrived at the Platte river. Unknown to them, the Crows who had captured the family of Aeneas had followed them, and early one morning captured every horse belonging to the party. Thus they were left without any means of transportation. But many of the men of the party, being Iroquois from Canada, were familiar with the making of canoes, and for that purpose made frames of willows, and covered them with the hides of buffalo, which they had killed.

In these they descended the Platte river. When they reached the Pawnee Camp, they were kindly received, and cared for.

An express was sent to Council Bluffs for horses. In a few days they arrived. The whole party was then well mounted, and proceeded safely to Council Bluffs where was a U.S. Fort and an Indian Agency. Here Mr. Aeneas and his family remained for two years, while most of the party went on the St? Louis, and some of the Iroquois returned to Canada. White [Quite?] a few went to Santa Fe, N.M. Three of them subsequently returned to the Flat Head Country, and lived there until they died there a few years since.

Mr. Aeneas, at the end of two years hard effort or about 1832 or '33 succeeded in persuading the military to go up the Missouri and Yellowstone, to try to recover his son anf the Flat Head woman and her child, from the Crows who had captured them on their journay to Council Bluffs. Baptiste is not certain but thinks the name of the officer who commanded th[e] expedition was Col. Lewis. They filled seven boats which were propelled by side wheels, worked by the soldiers. The command was well armed and carried small howitzers. Mr. Aeneas accompanied the troops. His family went down the Missouri with a man who had been a beef contractor at Council Bluffs and for whom Mr. A. had worked while there. The family remained here a year, when the mother died.

The military expedition to the Yellowstone was partially successful. The Crow camp was found, and after a great deal of negotiation, and a threat to destroy the camp by the military, for they were so posted as to completely surround it, and could rake it with fire of the howitzers, the head chief, who had taken the Flat Head woman as one of his wives, most reluctantly gave her and her son up to the military force, and with them returned to Council Bluffs, the same season. The son of Mr. Aeneas could not be found and was probably concealed or sent to another camp by the Crows.

The next year Aeneas and his family returned to Council Bluffs, where the Flat Head woman and her child died. 1834, While here one day the surgeon with a friend started to go to visit Aeneas. His cook, a soldier, asked to go along. He was permitted and walked. John Aeneas, a few days before had killed a wild goose a[n]d made a head dress of the larger feathers which he wore. As Sylvester, the soldier, was passing along the road by a creek hw thought he saw a wild goose or swan in the weeds and fired and killed it. On going to get it, to his horror it was John, one of Aeneas' sons. The father was informed. The affair was investigated, the soldier acquitted of the intention to kill, an the boy was buried by his sorrowing family.

As Aeneas wife and son were now dead and another son a captive among the Crows, he took his daughter Mary and two remaining boys, Alexander and Baptiste, and proceeded to St. Louis. He left Baptiste in charge of the Governor (Wm. Clarke) to bt put to the Jesuit School, where he remained two years. The other brother and sister he took with him to Galena, Ill., where he went to work in the lead mines.

After leaving school, Baptiste worked with Micharl Crellee, a farmer, until 1839, until he was 22 years of age. He went up to Galena to visit his father and brother and sister. His sister had married a Canadian Frenchman named Pierre Ironchiel, and had several children. He, with Mr. Aeneas and son Alexander, were all working in the lead mines. The same year Baptiste returned to St. Louis and worked on the farm of Mr. Crelee until the sprinf of 1841, when he engaged in the service of the American Fur Co. and ascended the Missouri to Fort Pierre, where he worked for them for three years. In 1845 he worked for the company at Ft. Lorime [Laramie], and in the spring of 1846, crossed the plains, and went to the Willamet Valley in Oregon.

There he engaged in farming & stock raising until the spring of 1852, when he sold out and then settled in Walla Walla, and engaged in farming until 1856, when he moved up to Colville, W.T. to the new mines which had been discovered in 1855, and here went to mining. The gold mines were situated at the mouth of Clarke's Fork of the Columbia. Here he mined during 1856, but not meeting with success, he left in 1857, and came to St. Ignatius Mission, Montana. He here took up a farm in the Jocko Valley and engaged farming until 1869, when he left and removed to the foot of Flat Head Lake where he established the ferry at its outlet, which he still operates, to the great convenience of the traveling public, and to his own prifit.

In 1846 Baptiste, married a Callispel widow with one child in the Willamet Valley, and by her has had nine children only one of which survives. She has three children and lives near her father. Baptiste is a grey haired vigorous looking man. He has all except in color appearance of a white man. He has a heavy beard, a square, kindly and intelligent face and talks English like an

American, and is in every respect like one. He is well fixed and is glad to meet and talk with intelligent white man, and is well worth visiting.

By precept and example ha has done much in his life towards civilizing the Flat Heads, and he is as much respected by them as by the whites.

W. F. Wheeler.

Document 29

Starting Salish Farms in the Bitterroot Valley

September 20, 1858

Source: John Owen to Col. J. W. Nesmith, Sept. 20, 1858, in John Owen, *The Journals and Letters of Major John Owen, Pioneer of the Northwest, 1850-1871*, ed. Seymour Dunbar and Paul C. Phillips (New York: Edward Eberstadt, 1927), vol. 2, pp. 183-186.

Editors' note: Salish Chief Victor asked for half of their present from the U.S. government to be spent on plowing a field and planting wheat in the Bitterroot Valley so the tribe would have grain that could be ground into flour. Owen said that, "Some of these people are very anxious to farm." Victor was sick and could not accompany the tribe to the plains for the fall 1858 buffalo hunt. Some periods have been added to this transcription. The date was given as Sept. 18, 1858, in the published version but has been here corrected as per the microfilm edition to Sept. 20, 1858.

Owen to Nesmith Concerning His Work and Travel Among the Indians

Office Flat Head Agency
Fort Owen W. T., Sept. 20, 1858

Dear Sir

I wrote you last from Spokan river July 16 by George Monteur expressman. I am uneasy about him. he was to have returned here immediately but I have heard nothing of him. After starting the express I went to see Paul-Lot-E-Kon the only Spokan chief that had not met me in council at Schutes of Spokan river. I have Known him for eight years and always looked upon him as strong friend of the white man. I was astonished when I heard he had been in the attack against Col [E. J.] Steptoe. I had seen him but a short time before the fight took place, from what I could learn I believe he was lead into the fight by his son who is married to a daughter of Onahi the Yakima. He made no effort to excuse himself, said he would give me a safe conveyance through his country. Had no objection to me, but did not want to see any more soldiers in the country. I thanked him for the Kindness extended to me and endeavoured to show him the foolishness of of [sic] the undertaking they were about to embark in, the exterminating of the Soldiers. He however seemed very confident of success. After my visit to Paul Lot E Kon I rejoined my camp which I had left in charge of my Indian allies, my line of march was by Pen d'Oreille lake the Couer d'Alleine Indians having refused me a safe convoy through their country. The chiefs said they had no objection but was afraid the young men would molest me. In fact my Spokan friends advised me not to think of passing that way. The water was high and I was satisfied that the rout by the lake would be attended not only with difficulties but dangers. I reached Pen d'Oreille Bay safely, but my camp was entered during the night and seven horses that I had bought a few days before on a/c of the dept were Stolen. With all my vigilance up to the time of my late writing you I had lost twelve (12) head of animals including two mules. I was compelled to purchase animals to prosecute my journeys and still continue nightly watches in the camp. After reaching the Bay at which point I met a friendly band of lower Pen d'Oreills I relaxed my vigilance by allowing the guard to turn in after midnight, the result of which was the loss of the seven animals taken by a party of Colville Indians that had been on my track for some days which I only learned after they had secured the animals and rode them off. The Pen d'Oreille became alarmed as to our safety. said it was not safe for me to remain any longer in the neighborhood. They well knew I could not pass the lake yet with my packs. I might with difficulty pass the Animals around loose, They agreeing to furnish me with four bark Canoes with two men in each for five dollars per day each canoe — saying they would meet the party at the different arms and bays of the Lake and ferry them over. I had no alternative but to accept their offer. not that I considered the charge exorbitant — but that my remaining longer on the confines of the hostile Indians Country was unsafe for myself and party. From adverse winds on the Lake I was detained until the tenth day reaching its head. I paid the Indians the amount agreed upon with which they seemed satisfied. They had worked hard and justly earned the sum. After reaching the head of the Lake I felt myself pretty secure. Had the water been low my safety would not have been to certain. The rout was horrid. I came very near drowning two of my men but for the timely assistance of the Indians with the Canoes all would have been over with them. I had many talks with the Indians on the way and was astonished myself to find they had so light a conception of the strength of the white man. They think the whole white tribe has emigrated from the East to the West. I reached this point on the 6th ultimo without any further molestation from the Indians. I met the Flat Heads encamped at the Fort. they seemed delighted to see me rumors having reached them on my being rob'd and [the] party scalped. Victor the head chief I found sick confined to his bed and he still lingers in a very critical condition. I fear he will never recover. I delivered him your message. he was glad to hear from his Great Father. Tell my white father says he that he need never fear the firmness and friendly feeling of the Flat Head Nation. I told him you had authorized me to make them some presents not exceeding in amount one thousand dollars. The camp was destitute of many things to enable them to go on their Summer hunt. They said the amount would not go far in this country. I told them I would have brought the presents from the Dalles had the country been safe. That goods cost less there. But all the property I had started with had been expended on the way for conciliatory purposes and paying my expenses in reaching home. I asked them how they would like the amount laid out to receive the most benefit from it as a tribe. The answer was get us one half the amt in amunition and tobacco that we much need, the other half open us a field with and get us a plow. we will sow wheat and have flour to eat as Buffalo are growing scarce. We thank our great father for so Kindly thinking of us, he will probably do something for us yet for we are very poor. Our white father and friend Interkiacum (meaning Gov [Isaac] Stevens) whom we saw three snows ago said he would. His words begin to have some feeling in them now. I told them I would do as they wished which I thought would meet the approval of their father. I bought them Amunition, Tobacco, Knives, Pans a few Shirts and such things as they to my own Knowledge require. They also stood in need of a Blacksmith to mend their Traps, Guns Kettles, Axes &c. one was fortunately in the country out of work, he agreed to work for them Keep their Plow in order and do anything in his line for them for the rate per month of Five Hundred dollars year, which amounts to $41.^{66}/100 per month which I thought reasonable inasmuch as he was also willing to take his axe when there was no work in the Shop and make rails for their field, also assists them in plowing & attending the crop. Some of these people are anxious to farm & all they require is a little assistance and encouragement to put their wishes in force. The Camp is now off for Buffalo excepting the old chief Victor and three Lodges. the expenses of feeding the old chief will devolve on the agency. he justly merits it from the Government. Now in his destitute & helpless condition it is nothing more than humanity. After reaching the agency and taking a few days rest I left with a few of these Indians for Fort Benton to be present at the payment of the Blackfoot annuities. The Indians wished to see the payment & try and secure some lost horses. They were Kindly received by Agent [Alfred J.] Vaughan who made them some presents in the name of their Great Father. they returned well pleased. The Mormon settlement at Salmon river has been abandoned, report here is that one or two of them were Killed by the Bannac Indians and the rest ran off leaving everything they could not well carry away. Report reached us here a few days ago of a band of Coeur d'Aleine Indians having been seen in the vicinity of Hells Gate. It is my present intention to visit Salmon river and the Indians at Fort Hall. they are not all-together quiet, and while [I am] in the vicinity [I intend to] visit Salt Lake with a view of procuring a Couple of plows, and some Iron to work up for these Indians. It is necessary for the Dept to have some Animals here for the use of the Agency say three yoke of Work Cattle and a waggon and a few more pack and riding horses. I have three horses belonging to the Dept. of those I purchased in the Spokan Country. It is impossible for me to do anything satisfactorilly till I am put in funds. I have allready so far advanced my own means in defraying the Expenses of the agency. I have engaged Francis La Moosse as interpreter temporarily at the rate of five hundred dollars per anum. The expenses incurred in hiring animals for my different visits to the Indians will soon amount to what will pay for them. good horses can be bought for fifty dolls each. Work Cattle per yoke $125.00. I still continue the two men in the employ of the Dept as laborers that left the Dalls with me in June last. I am paying them $40.00 per month and finding [feeding?] them. Equipages such as Pack Saddles, Riding saddles, Pichamores, Parfeches, Cords. I have purchased on a/c of the Dept. inasmuch as there was nothing of the Kind belonging to this Agency. The property I expended on my way up for ferrages, p[r]esents to Indians for concilliating purposes. Pay to the Indians that escorted me to Pend' D' Orielle Bay and sundry other such expenditures all of which I deemed necessary for the good of the service. I could take no vouchers for you are well aware that [while] travelling through an Indian Country it is almost impossible to get vouchers for all expenditures made. I shall make out a fair statement of what [I] paid & on what a/c which I will have certified to by responsible persons that were present with me. I can do no more. I sincerely hope the Dept will take a liberal view of the matter and act upon the a/cs promptly —

Respectfully Your Obt Servt

John Owen Special Agent Flat Head Nation

To Col J. W. Nesmith Supt Ind Affs

O & W Terrs.

Document 30

From Clark's Fork to Sun River, with a Flathead Indian Camp October 12-19, 1858

Source: Excerpt from William T. Hamilton, "A Trading Expedition Among the Indians in 1858, from Fort Walla Walla to the Blackfoot Country and Return," *Contributions to the Historical Society of Montana* (1900), vol. 3, pp. 48-53.

Editors' note: Hamilton's traveling companion was Alex McKay who Hamilton described as "a one-eyed half breed" and "one of the bravest men I ever came across." Hamilton was employed as a scout by the U.S. Army and had been sent to learn the feelings of the Rocky Mountain Indians regarding the recent battles between the Lower Columbia River Indians and the U.S. Army. His manuscript was a remarkably detailed description of camp life among the Salish Indians while on their plains buffalo hunts. The Flathead or Salish Indians he traveled with between October 12 and 19, 1858, had been careful to stay out of the Indian-white wars on the Lower Columbia. Hamilton described the intense social life and singing and dancing in the camp. The buffalo hunts were basically military operations which had to keep constant watch for Blackfeet attacks and horse raiders. The manuscript uses an offensive term for Indian women.

[From Clark's Fork to Sun River, with a Flathead Indian Camp]
by William T. Hamilton

On the [October] 12th we camped at the post [Fort Owen]. On the 13th while packing up, two Flatheads rode up and asked us where we came from and where we were going. After we answered them they informed us they were going to the buffalo country and that their village was over the divide on Blackfoot River. This river also retains its Indian name. They informed us it was the shortest route to the Blackfoot country and that the Flatheads would be glad to see us in order to get the news from Walla Walla. We told the Indians to take the lead and we would follow and at sundown we came in sight of their village. The Flatheads had discovered us coming and about fifty young bucks came like a whirlwind to see who it could be with a mule outfit. As soon as they got to us some ten of the oldest of them looked closely at me. It had been some years since I had seen any Flatheads and I did not recognize any of them at first, but they evidently recognized me and gave a warwhoop, a signal of gladness. We soon arrived at their village. Nothing would satisfy their head chief, Victor, but our entire outfit must be put inside of his lodge, which was done by the s....s. They would not allow us to either cook, or open our packs. Victor's son took care of our packs. After supper we all took a smoke and all of the principal men of the village assembled in old Moese's lodge, which was a large one. Moese, as well as Victor, was an old acquaintance of mine and the second chief of the tribe. Their village was located in one of the most beautiful and romantic places to be found in the Rocky Mountains. They were anxious to hear all about the termination of the late war, known as the Spokane and Yakima war.

William Hamilton
Photograph 942-529, Photograph Archives, Montana Historical Society, Helena, Montana.

The tribes engaged in that war, had tried hard to involve the Flatheads in it, but failed in their object, the Flatheads remaining firm friends of the whites and also keeping the majority of the Pend d'Oreilles from joining the hostiles. For this conduct alone on their part, the government ought to respect and treat the Flatheads justly in all dealings with them.

We remained up most of the night conversing on all matters of interest to an Indian, they being highly elated in receiving direct news from the seat of the late Indian war. The "Haranguer," as they call him, had to harangue the camp in order to let all those who could not get inside of the lodge have a place adjacent, so that the information could be imparted to them. Indians are just as keen, as whites, to hear the news from a distance. I know that it will appear strange to very many that any person can hold counsel for hours with a tribe of Indians, who is not acquainted with a single word of their language. By the sign language thought can be communicated more rapidly, than by oral speech and with a certainty of being distinctly understood. A man who had a perfect knowledge of the sign language can converse readily with the Indians from Mexico to Alaska, and I never came across any Indians who did not prefer to hold conversation with a white man by signs, rather than in their own tongue. My knowledge of the sign language has assisted me many times in extricating myself and others from many tight places.

Just after sun-up Bear Track, another chief, called us to breakfast. After breakfast, another council was held, and we were requested to remain with them another day, and on the next day travel together as far as the buffalo country. We accordingly remained another day and spent the time in visiting the different lodges, making the chiefs daughters and wives presents of fancy calico and brass buttons, which at that time were held in high esteem, and with which we were well supplied. We compelled Victor to receive some flour, tea, coffee, sugar and tobacco, since we had to be his guests while we remained in camp and on the journey. I informed Victor of my intention of locating on Rattlesnake Creek in the near future and opening a trading post and asked his opinion with reference to the matter. He and the other chiefs were highly pleased and pressed me not to delay, but as soon as I returned to Walla Walla to come back, advising me to return through the Nez Perces country, as it would be the safest route.

On the 15th at daylight, the village was all astir, and breakfast soon over. Forty young bucks were ordered as advance scouts and were requested to secure plenty of fresh meat and informed that the village would camp at a designated place. It will here be remembered that the Blackfeet were their ancient enemies. Indians move camp with something of a military system. It is necessary for them to do so, for they are likely at any time to be attacked by their enemies,

if they are in their vicinity. In moving they not only have flankers but front
and rear guards. We had to go through about four miles of dense forest, a good
place for an enemy to attack a moving village with hundreds of horses and
trevois, with s....s and pappooses, strung out for about two miles. We kept our
outfit in the rear with a dozen picked warriors in company, stripped to their
breech clouts and armed at all points.

About 3 P.M. we arrived at the place selected for camping without being
annoyed by any enemies, though the scouts reported having seen Indian signs
upon the top of a bald butte about a mile distant. They thought the sign was
about two days old; at all events they kept guard out with their ponies. They
had an abundance of fresh meat, there being plenty of deer and antelope in this
section. At dark our stock was brought in and picketed. The young bucks and
s....s kept the village alive until a late hour with the Indian drum, dancing and
singing. Nothing occurred during the night except two false alarms.

On the 16th we were up early with scouts in advance moving across
an open country and crossed the main range at Cadotte's pass. Camped on
Dearborn River and saw plenty of hostile signs, but no hostile Indians. The
Flatheads scouted the surrounding country until sundown and reported that
Indians were around and gave instructions to look out close for stock. This
night another dance and song. The Indians stood guard all night.

On the 17th by 8 A.M. traveling north, keeping along the base of the
mountains. Camped on the South Fork of Sun River; that is the Indian name
for the stream. The Flatheads were friendly with the Piegans and Blood Indians
and expected to meet some of them at this place, and we also were greatly
desirous of interviewing them. We concluded to remain here today at least.
The Flatheads expected to remain here several days; their young men had seen
a few buffalo at a distance.

On the 18th Victor invited me to accompany him and some others to the
Piegan Agency, which was some twenty-five miles down the river. He requested
me to ride one of his horses. As I had a long distance to travel I accepted his
offer. Fifty of us mounted, each armed to the teeth and arrived at the Agency at
11 A.M. Some fifty Piegan and Blood Indian lodges were scattered around the
Agency. The agent came out when he heard that the Flatheads and one white
man were there. He was fine looking old man. It was Col. [Alfred J.] Vaughan
from the State of Mississippi. He invited us in and held a short council with
the Flatheads. After the council, he ordered the cook to prepare a feast for them
and invited me to his office. On this occasion I was first aware of the contents
of one of the papers which I had in the envelope. It was simply a request to
any Indian Agent, or any government officer to render any assistance which I
might need in executing my orders. Col. Vaughan asked me what he could do

for me. I asked him to give me a short statement, showing the condition of the Indians which he had in charge and their disposition towards the whites, and also what tribes were hostile, or were inclined to be hostile. He fully answered all my inquiries to my entire satisfaction and further informed me where Little Dog, the head chief of the Piegans was camped and advised me by all means to see him, as he might render great assistance, also informing me that the Piegans had very many fine robes.

After partaking of a lunch I informed the Colonel it was time to return to camp, as the Flathead chiefs had then assembled to bid the Agent goodby. The Colonel invited us to remain all night, but his generous offer was declined. The Agent and the Flatheads were old friends and he made them many presents. He made me promise if I ever passed through that section again not to fail to pay him a visit.

A few Piegans and Bloods returned with us to our camp, where we arrived at dusk. All the Flatheads were elated when shown the presents the Agent had made to their friends, and when they heard of the reception they had received. Dancing and singing as usual until a late hour and enjoying a great feast, as some of the young bucks had killed a few very fat buffalo, the tongues of which, with some of the choicest of the meat they presented to Victor. We had a supper fit for a prince.

On the 19th up early, and presented chiefs with some ammunition, which they were short of, and some presents for their s....s. The mules and horses were then brought in, and turning to our packs we found six of the finest robes I had ever seen, presents to us from the Indians. When we were finally packed up and ready for starting, the whole village surrounded us, each one wishing to shake hands and saying they were sorry at our leaving. I assured them they would see us again. They warned us, however, to be careful. The chiefs said they believed our medicine was stronger than any man's they had ever come across. I presume it seemed to them a great venture to go through the late hostile tribes with such a big and rich outfit. If they had been thoroughly posted they would not have thought it so difficult after all. The hostages held by the government and the magic envelope which they could not comprehend was the secret.

We bid them "How." . . . .

Document 31

Interior Salish Chiefs and the U.S. Army

May 25 and November 10, 1859

Source: P. J. DeSmet, S.J., to A. Pleasonton, Captain 2d dragoons, May
25, 1859, in *Affairs in Oregon*, House Ex. Doc. No. 65, 36th Cong., 1st Sess.
(1860), serial 1051, pages 141-143; [Pierre DeSmet, S.J.] to "Reverend and
Dear Father," Nov. 10, 1859, Hiram Chittenden and Alfred Richardson, eds.,
Life, Letters and Travels of Father Pierre-Jean De Smet, S.J., 1801-1873 (New
York, Francis P. Harper, 1904), vol. 2, pages 762-768.

Editors' note: Father Pierre DeSmet escorted a delegation of seven Interior
Salish chiefs to Fort Vancouver to meet with U.S. Army General W. S. Harney
and assure Harney of the desire of the Interior Salish to keep the peace with
the whites despite the Indian-white wars then raging lower on the Columbia
River. No transcript of their meeting with Harney has been found, but they
assured Harney that the Interior Salish tribes were not interested in joining
the hostilities. While the delegation was on the coast they had their picture
taken, which was one of the earliest photographs of Salish leaders. A copy of
the photograph is reproduced here from the Jesuits West Archives at Gonzaga
University, Spokane, Washington. The second letter is DeSmet's account of
the trip sent to a priest in the church hierarchy. Notice his testimony to the
honesty of the Kootenai Indians. This letter also has information about Pend
d'Oreille Chief Alexander's reaction to seeing the white man's prisons.

[Father Pierre DeSmet's Report Relative to Escorting a Delegation of Interior Salish Indian Chiefs to Visit Fort Vancouver, Washington Territory]

Fort Vancouver, *May* 25, 1859.

Dear Captain:

Towards the end of last March, owing to the deep snows and impractica-
bleness of the mountain passes, I received your kind favor of the 1st of January
of the present year. I am happy that my request to the general, concerning the
bringing down to Vancouver a deputation of the various chiefs of the upper
tribes, met with his approval. I have no doubt, from the happy dispositions
in which I left them at Walla-Walla, the general's advice and counsel will be

cherfully [sic] and punctually followed out by them, and will prove highly beneficial to their respective tribes, and consolidate the peace established last fall by Colonel [George] Wright.

During my stay among the Rocky mountain Indians, in the long and dreary winter, from the 21st of November last until the end of April, I have carried out, as far as lay in my power, the instructions of the general. I succeeded, I think, in removing many doubts and prejudices against the intentions of government, and against the whites generally, which were still lurking in the minds of a great number of the most influential Indians. I held frequent conversations with the chieftains of the Cœur d' Alénes, the Spokanes, several of the Shuyelpees or Kettlefalls, and lower Kalispels, who had chiefly aided, particularly the two first-mentioned tribes, in their lawless and savage attack on Colonel [Edward] Steptoe and in their war with Colonel Wright. These various tribes, with the exception perhaps of a small portion of lawless Kettlefalls Indians, are well disposed, and will faithfully adhere to the conditions prescribed by Colonel Wright, and to any future requests and proposals of treaties coming from government. The upper Pend d'Oreilles, the Koetinays and Flatheads, I found, as years ago, strong friends and adherents to the whites, and I have every reason to think that they will remain faithful; they ever glory, and truly, that not a drop of white man's blood has ever been spilled by any one of their respective tribes. When I proposed to them that from each tribe a chief should accompany me down to Fort Vancouver to pay their respects to the general and listen to his advice, all eagerly consented, and they kept in readiness for the long journey as soon as the snow would have sufficiently disappeared. Meanwhile Major [John] Owen, agent among the Flatheads, arrived at St. Ignatius' Mission, and made known to me that he had received orders from the superintendent of Indian affairs and from Commissioner Mot [Charles E. Mix] to bring down to Salem a chief of each tribe of the upper country. Upon this declaration I persuaded the Indians that as Major Owen had received orders from the highest authority he superseded me, and they should look upon him as their leader in this expedition, whilst I would follow on with them as far as practicable and I would be allowed. The major having brought no provisions for them, I lodged the chiefs in my own tent, and provided them with all the necessary supplies from the 16th of April until the 13th instant, the day on which we reached Walla-Walla, and where the chiefs were liberally provided for by Captain [Frederick] Dent, in command of the fort. The deputation of chiefs was stopped at Walla-Walla by Major Owen, to await an express he had sent on from the Spokane prairie, with instructions to the superintendent at Salem. My own instructions from the general, according to your letter of the 1st of January, "to return to Fort Vancouver as early in the spring as practicable,

Father Pierre DeSmet and the delegation of Interior Salish chiefs to
Fort Vancouver, 1859.
Seated are (left to right) Victor of the Lower Pend d'Oreille, Alexander of
the Upper Pend d'Oreille, Adolph or Red Feather of the Salish, and a Coeur
d'Alene chief; standing are Colville and Coeur d'Alene chiefs, Father Pierre
DeSmet, and Francis Xavier Saxa (Iroquois/Salish).
Photograph 802.21a, Jesuits West Archives at Gonzaga University,
Spokane, Washington.

for some contingency might arise requiring the general's presence elsewhere," hurried me down in compliance with said order. With regard to Kamiakin and his brother, Schloom, I held several talks with them in February, March, and April, and acquainted them with the general's order, wish, and desire, in their regard, videlicet, of following me, and of their surrendering into his hands, assuring them, in the general's own words, that "the government is always generous to a fallen foe, though it is at the same time determined to protect its citizens in every part of its territory," &c. They invariable listened with attention and respect. Kamiakin made an open avowal of all he had done in his wars against the government of the country, particularly in the attack on Colonel Steptoe, and in the war with Colonel Wright. Kamiakin stated that he strongly advised his people to the contrary, but was at last drawn into the contest by the most opprobrious language the deceitful Telgawax upbraided him with in full council, in presence of the various chiefs of the Cœur d' Alénes, Spokanes, and Pelouses. Kamiakin repeatedly declared to me, and with the greatest apparent earnestness, that he never was a murderer, and, whenever he could, he restrained his people against all violent attacks on whites passing through the country. On my way down to Vancouver, from St. Ignatius' Mission, I met him again, near Thompson's prairie, on Clark's-fork. Kamiakin declared he would go down and follow me if he had a horse to ride, his own not being in a condition to undertake a long journey. I had none to lend him at that moment. At my arrival in the Spokane prairie, meeting with Gerry, one of the Spokane chiefs, I acquainted him with the circumstance, and entreated him, for the sake of Kamiakin and his poor children, to send him a horse and an invitation to come on and to accompany the other chiefs to Walla-Walla, and hence to Vancouver; the best opportunity for him to present himself before the general and the superintendent, and to expose his case to them and obtain rest and peace. Gerry complied with my request and Kamiakin soon presented himself and joined the other chiefs. I had daily conversations with him until we reached Walla-Walla. He places implicit confidence in the generosity of the general. I believe him sincere in his repeated declarations that henceforth nothing shall ever be able to withdraw him again from the path of peace; or, in his own words, "to unbury and raise the tomahawk against the whites." My candid impression is, should Kamiakin be allowed to return soon, pardoned and free, to his country, it will have the happiest and most salutary effect among the upper Indian tribes, and facilitate greatly all future transactions and views of government in their regard. The Indians are anxiously awaiting the result; I pray that it may terminate favorably with Kamiakin. The sight of Kamiakin's children, the poverty and misery in which I found them plunged, drew abundant tears from my eyes. Kamiakin, the once powerful chieftain, who possessed thousands of horses and a large number of cattle — he has lost all, and is now reduced to the most abject poverty. His brother, Schloom, if he lives, will come in in the course of the summer. I left him on Clark's fork, sickly and almost blind; he could only travel by small journeys. Telgawax, a Pelouse, I think, is among the Buffalo Nez Percés; from all I can learn he has been the prime mover in all the late wars against Colonel Steptoe and Colonel Wright. His influence is not great, but he remains unceasing in his endeavors to create bitter feelings against the whites whenever he can meet with an opportunity.

With the highest consideration of respect and esteem for our worthy general and his assistant adjutant general, I remain, dear captain, your humble and obedient servant,

P. J. De Smet, S.J.,
Chaplain U.S.A.

A. Pleasonton,
Captain 2d dragoons, A. A. Adjutant General.

* * * * * * * *

[Another Report on DeSmet's 1859 Trip to Fort Vancouver with the Salish Chiefs]

St. Louis, Nov. 10, 1859

Reverend and Dear Father:

In accordance with my promise, I resume the little story of my long voyage. On my return to St. Louis, I tendered to the Minister of War my resignation of the post of chaplain. It was not accepted, because a new war had just broken out against the Government, among the tribes of the Rocky Mountains. I was notified by telegraph to proceed to New York, and to embark there with General [W. S.] Harney and his staff.

On the 20th of September, 1858, we left the port of New York for Aspinwall; it was the season of the equinox, so that we experienced some rough weather in the voyage, and a heavy wind among the Bahamas. We coasted for some time along the eastern shore of Cuba, in sight of the promontories of St. Domingo and Jamaica. On the 29th I crossed the Isthmus of Panama on a good railroad, forty-seven miles long. The next day I had the happiness to offer the holy sacrifice of the mass in the cathedral of Panama. The bishop very earnestly entreated me to use my influence with the Very Reverend Father General at Rome, to obtain for him a colony of Jesuits. His lordship especially expressed his earnest desire to intrust his ecclesiastical seminary to the care of the Society of Jesus. New Granada, as well as many other regions of Spanish South America, offers, doubtless, a vast field to the zeal of a large number of our Fathers.

The distance from Panama to San Francisco is more than 3,000 miles. The steamer brought to in the superb bay of Acapulco to receive the mails, and to coal and water: this is a little port of Mexico. On the evening of the 16th of October, I arrived at San Francisco, happy to find myself in a house of the Society, and in the company of many of my brethren in Jesus Christ, who loaded me with kindness, and all the attention of the most cordial charity. The *"quam bonum et jucundum habitare fratres in unum"* is especially appreciated when one leaves a California steamer in which one has been imprisoned, sometimes with fourteen or fifteen hundred individuals, all laboring under the gold fever, and who think and speak of nothing but mines of gold, and all the terrestrial delights which this gold is shortly to procure them. However, the "shortly" is long enough to allow of the destruction or disappearance of many an illusion. "All that glitters is not gold."

We left San Francisco on the 20th, and in four days made more than 1,000 miles to Fort Vancouver, on the Columbia river. The news of the cessation of hostilities and of the submission of the tribes had been received at Vancouver. The task remained of removing the Indian prejudices, soothing their inquietude and alarm, and correcting, or rather refuting, the false rumors which are generally spread after a war, and which otherwise might be the cause of its renewal.

Under the orders of the general commanding in chief, I left Fort Vancouver on the 29th of October to go among the tribes of the mountains, at a distance of about 800 miles. I visited the Catholic soldiers at Forts Dalle[s] City and Walla Walla on my way. At the last-named fort, I had the consolation of meeting Reverend Father [Nicholas] Congiato, on his return from his visit to the missions, and of receiving very cheering news from him as to the disposition of the Indians. At my request, the excellent commandant of the fort had the very great kindness to set at liberty all the prisoners and hostages, both Cœur d'Alènes and Spokans, and he intrusted to my charge to bring them on their way, and return them to their respective nations. These good Indians, particularly the Cœur d'Alenes, had given the greatest edification to the soldiers during their captivity: these men often surrounded them with admiration, to witness the performance of their pious exercises, morning and evening, and in listening to their prayers and hymns. During the whole journey, these good Indians testified the utmost gratitude to me, and their punctual performance of their religious duties was a source of great consolation and happiness to me.

On the 21st of November I arrived at the Mission of the Sacred Heart, among the Cœur d'Alènes. I was detained at the mission by snow until the 18th of February, 1859. During this interval snow fell with more or less abundance on forty-three days and nights, on seven days it rained, we had twenty-one cloudy days, and sixteen days of clear and cold weather. I left the mission on the 18th of February with the Reverend Father [Joseph] Joset, who accompanied me until we met Father [Adrian] Hoeken, who had promised to meet us on Clark's river. The ice, snow, rain and winds impeded very much our course, in our frail canoes of bark, on the rivers and great lakes: we often ran considerable risk in crossing rapids and falls, of which Clark's river is full. I counted thirty-four of these in seventy miles. We met with several camps of Indians in winter quarters on every side. On the approach of the winter season, they are obliged to scatter in the forests and along the lakes and rivers, where they live by the chase and fishing. They received us everywhere with the greatest kindness, and, notwithstanding their extreme poverty, willingly shared with us their small rations and meagre provisions. They eagerly embraced the occasion to attend to their religious duties and other exercises of piety: attending at the instructions with great attention, and with much zeal and fervor, at mass, and at morning and evening prayers. On the 11th of March we arrived at the Mission of St. Ignatius, among the Pend d'Oreilles of the mountains.

The Kootenais, a neighboring tribe to the Pend d'Oreilles, having heard of my arrival, had traveled many days' journey through the snow to shake hands with me, to bid me welcome, and manifest their filial affection. In 1845 I had made some stay with them. I was the first priest who had announced to them the glad tidings of salvation, and I had baptized all their little children and a large number of adults. They came on this occasion, with a primitive simplicity, to assure me that they had remained faithful to "the prayer," that is, to religion, and all the good advice that they had received. All the Fathers spoke to me of these good Kootenais in the highest terms. Fraternal union, evangelic simplicity, innocence and peace, still reign among them in full vigor. Their honesty is so great and so well known, that the trader leaves his storehouse entirely, the door remaining unlocked often during his absence for weeks. The Indians go in and out and help themselves to what they need, and settle with the trader on his return. He assured me himself that in doing business with them in this style he never lost the value of a pin.

On the 18th of March I crossed deep snow a distance of seventy miles, to St. Mary's of Bitter Root valley, to revisit my first and ancient spiritual children of the mountains, the poor and abandoned Flatheads. They were greatly consoled on learning that Very Reverend Father-General had the intention of causing the mission to be undertaken again. The principal chiefs assured me that since the departure of the Fathers, they had continued to assemble morning and evening for prayers, to ring the angelus at the accustomed hour, and to rest on Sunday, to glorify the holy day of our Lord. I will not enter into long details here, as to the present disposition of this little tribe, for fear of being too long. Doubtless, in the absence of the missionaries, the enemy of souls had committed some ravages among them, but by the grace of God the evil is not irreparable. Their daily practices of piety, and the conferences I held with them during several days, have given me the consoling conviction that the faith is still maintained among the Flatheads, and still brings forth fruits of salvation among them — their greatest chieftains, Michael, Adolphe, Ambrose, Moses, and others, are true and zealous Christians, and real piety in religion and true valor at war are united in them.

In my several visits to the stations in the Rocky Mountains, I was received by the Indians with every demonstration of sincere and filial joy. I think I may say that my presence among them has been of some advantage to them, both in a religious and secular point of view. I did my best to encourage them to persevere in piety, and to maintain the conditions of the treaty of peace with the Government. In these visits I had the happiness to baptize over 100 infants and a large number of adults.

On the 16th of April, in accordance with orders of the commander-in-chief of the army, I left the Mission of St. Ignatius for Fort Vancouver. At my request, all the chiefs of the different mountain tribes accompanied me, to renew the treaty of peace with the general and with the Superintendent of Indian Affairs; I give their names, and the nations to which they belonged. Alexander Temglagketzin, or Man-without-a-horse, great chief of the Pend d'Oreilles; Victor Alamiken, or Happy-man (he deserves his name, for he is a saintly man), great chief of the Kalispels; Adolphus Kwilkweschape, or Red-feather, chief of the Flatheads; Francis Saxa, or Iroquois, another Flathead chief; Dennis Zenemtietze, or Thunders-robe, chief of the Skoyelpi of Chaudières; Andrew and Bonaventure, chiefs and braves among the Cœur d'Alènes, or Skizoumish; Kamiakin, great chief of the Yakimas; and Gerry, great chief of the Spokans. The last two are still pagans, though their children have been baptized.

We suffered through much and ran many dangers on the route, on account of the high stage of the rivers and the heavy snow. For ten days we had to clear a way through thick forests, where thousands of trees, thrown down by storms, lay across one another, and were covered four, six and eight feet with snow; several horses perished in this dangerous passage. My horse stumbled many a time, and procured me many a fall; but aside from some serious bruises and scratches, a hat battered to pieces, a torn pair of trousers and a *soutane* or black-gown in rags, I came out of it [the "Bad Forest"] safe and sound. I measured white cedars in the wood, which were as much as six or seven persons could clasp at the base, and of proportionate height. After a month's journey we arrived at Fort Vancouver.

On the 18th of May the interview took place with the general, the superintendent and the Indian chiefs. It produced most happy results on both sides. About three weeks' time was accorded to the chiefs to visit, at the cost of the Government, the principal cities and towns of the State of Oregon and Washington Territory, with everything remarkable in the way of industrial establishments, steam engines, forges, manufactories and printing establishments — of all which the poor Indians can make nothing or very little. The visit which appeared the most to interest the chiefs, was that which they made to the prison at Portland and its wretched inmates, whom they found chained within its cells. They were particularly interested in the causes, motives, and duration of their imprisonment. Chief Alexander kept it in his mind. Immediately on his return to his camp at St. Ignatius Mission, he assembled his people, and related to them all the wonders of the whites, and especially the history of the prison. "We," said he, "have neither chains nor prisons; and for want of them, no doubt, a great number of us are wicked and have deaf ears. As chief, I am determined to do my duty; I shall take a whip to punish the wicked; let all those who have been guilty of any misdemeanor present themselves, I am ready." The known guilty parties were called upon by name, many presented themselves of their own accord, and all received a proportionate correction. The whole affair terminated in a general rejoicing and feast.

Before leaving the parts of civilization, all the chiefs received presents from the general and superintendent, and returned to their own country contented and happy and well determined to keep at peace with the whites.

Document 32

Crow Chief Plenty-Coups' Horse Stealing Raid Against the Salish in the Bitterroot Valley 1859

Source: Frank B. Linderman, *Plenty-Coups: Chief of the Crows* (Lincoln: University of Nebraska Press, 1962), pp. 85-96 and 98-105.

Editors' note: One of Plenty-Coups principal war exploits was an 1859 horse stealing raid on a Salish Indian camp west of the Continental Divide. Plenty-Coups was about eleven years old when he went on this raid. The Crows captured a number of Salish horses but also suffered the death of one of Plenty-Coups' closest friends. Later Plenty-Coups led a revenge raid across the mountains to retrieve his friend's body. On the second trip his party attacked a Salish man, but ended up entering the Salish camp in peace.

[Plenty-Coups' Account of a Horse Stealing Raid on the Flatheads]
by Plenty-Coups via Frank B. Linderman

One night in the early spring of that year [1859], when our village was near The-mountain-lion's-lodge [Pompey's Pillar], a young warrior named Bear-in-the-water had a dream. In it he saw a camp of Flatheads far to the westward. Many horses were tied near their lodges, some of them our own. One horse was chestnut with a light-colored belly. He looked very fast. Anyhow he was a handsome horse, and Bear-in-the-water wished to possess him. When he told his dream, thirty-five of us young men agreed to go with him to steal the chestnut horse and as many others as we could. We had a score to settle with the Flatheads anyway.

We elected Bear-in-the-water to carry the pipe [to be leader], and very early next morning we set out toward our leader's dream-camp, crossing Elk River and following it upstream. We came out of the high hills near the present site of the city of Bozeman, and later on reached the three forks of the Big River. Here our Wolves brought us news. They had seen elk moving as though disturbed and had heard a gun. While they were telling us this, two more Wolves came in and told us more. These two had been on a high hill and had seen Flathead hunters packing elk meat on horses. They said the valley ahead was very good to look at and that there were rivers everywhere.

Crow Chief Plenty-Coups
Image 3c09715u, Photograph Archives, Library of Congress,
Washington, D.C.

Of course we knew the camp of the Flatheads which Bear-in-the-water had
seen in his dream was not far away now, and at once got ready for action by
hiding everything we had with us, which was not much of a task. We left Bear-
in-the-water with our things, because he had brought his woman along with
us to do our cooking, and somebody must guard our horses and robes. But he
would not stay until we promised him the chestnut horse if we got him.

The sun was in the middle of the sky, and black clouds were gathering when
twenty-five of us started out to locate the Flathead camp, while nine men went
searching for the loose horses belonging to the enemy. But when we found it
we could not count the lodges because of the heavy rain that had begun to fall
almost as soon as we started. We were obliged to wait for night anyway, and
when it came it was unusually dark, with rain as cold as snow.

We scattered and began moving in, each man for himself. I kept looking at
the lodge-fires through the driving rain that pelted my naked back, trying to
count them as I crawled nearer and nearer.

Suddenly I heard laughing. It was loud and came from a dark lodge I could
almost touch. I was in the camp without knowing it, and stopped to look
around me. There were three dark objects not far behind, and I knew they
were Crows. Only four of us had come to the camp! The others must have gone
round it to try to stampede the loose horses, I knew. But would they wait long
enough for me to cut a horse?

The rain had grown a little finer now, and I could see between twenty and
thirty lodge-fires ahead. I crept on, and soon there were lodges all around me,
and I could smell fresh elk meat everywhere. The Flatheads were living high. I
wondered how many of their men were asleep.

At last I stood up and moved forward between two lodges, the rain coming
again in torrents, shutting out all but the blur of a few lodge-fires. I thought of
the men who had gone round the camp to stampede the loose horses. I must
hurry.

Something bumped against me! The thing struck my thigh and was hard
and cold. I put down my hand to feel it. A rope! My fingers closed around it,
and I got down on my hands and knees to follow it up, to learn where it led,
and what it was tied to. I crept along the rope till I came to a deep puddle
of water. When I stopped to find a way around it I saw something black just
behind me and it moved! I bent lower, my eyes straining to make out what the
black thing was, when a voice whispered, "I am with you."

I knew it was Big-horn who spoke. "Wait where you are," I whispered, and
began again to follow my rope till it led me to a horse. At last I had a chance,
but just as I rose up to cut his rope a man stepped out of a lodge right behind
me, almost on Big-horn.

I sank my body to the ground and waited, with my hand still on the rope. The man had left his lodge door open, and I could see into the lodge. A woman sat by the fire, but I saw no children near her. The lodge was neat. The man merely looked at the weather a little, and as soon as he had gone back into the lodge I cut the rope. There was little time to spare, I knew, and I got out of there as fast as I could lead my horse. Not even a dog spoke, and outside the camp I ran on to Big-horn and the two others I had seen when I was entering the Flathead camp. "This is foolish," I said. "We cannot see in this rain. Let us get away from here."

"Listen!" Big-horn whispered.

Horses were coming! We four hurried to our hiding place as fast as we could go, reaching it just as the others came in with a large band of loose horses. Not a shot had been fired, no Flathead dog had spoken, and we were merry over our good luck, though quiet about it. Whoever carried the pipe for that Flathead camp was a careless man.

At daybreak we looked at our stolen property, and there, sure enough, was the chestnut horse with the light-colored belly, the horse of Bear-in-the-water's dream. He took him, of course; but my horse, the one I had cut in the camp, was a mule! I had seen one or two mules before, but in the black darkness and rain I had not known what I was getting. There was blood on his back, and by this we knew how he came to be tied to a man's lodge like a war-horse. They had been using the mule to pack meat and would need him again in the morning. But he wouldn't be there!

Bear-in-the-water told us the Flatheads had many guns and plenty of powder and balls. We had but four guns and very little ammunition for them, so that we must get ready for trouble. Six of us were sent to a high hill to learn what the Flatheads were doing and to count their lodges. I was one of the six.

The rain had now ceased falling, but the clouds were yet heavy with it, and more might come down any time. We hurried, but before we were halfway up the hill a shot rang out below us. It sounded as though it had been fired near our hiding place. There was no good in going farther. Our party had been discovered, it was plain, and we raced down again with plenty of shots popping in the vicinity of our hiding place. And our party was retreating into the timber. We soon saw the Crows, driving the stolen horses ahead of them, disappear among the trees, and I was astonished at the number of the enemy. We learned afterwards that there were fifty lodges in their camp.

Many of their warriors were between us and the Crows, and we must ride for it, go through them, to reach our friends. Bending low over our horses' necks we dashed for the timber in a sudden downpour of heavy rain that hid us a little but made us blind. Two arrows whizzed near my ear, and a bullet that had struck something cried like a crippled rabbit over my head, but we reached the timber untouched.

Not a Crow was in sight there, nor a horse. Our friends had got away with the stolen band, but we six were in a bad situation. There were Flatheads all around us in the timber, and our horses would hamper our escape. We sprang from their backs and left them, scattering out, each for himself, dodging away among the trees, expecting to be stopped by an enemy.

Twice I saw the trail of the stolen horses, but both times there were Flatheads between them and me, and I dared not follow it. Running on, my eyes everywhere, I caught sight of Goes-against-the-enemy beckoning me from behind a tree, and went to him. He had found a white man's log cabin and led us all to it. White trappers had built it the year before, and it would keep us dry while we planned a way out of our difficulties. But no sooner had the door closed, shutting us in the dark, than I thought I saw a Flathead through a crack between the logs. My eyes had just caught him when he moved under a big tree back of the cabin, and I held up my hand for silence. The five stood still as stones while I put my eyes to that crack.

Yes, he was there, right enough, with his back against the tree — a big man with a gun, and very wet. He had on a white blanket capote from the Hudson's Bay people up north and, if the crack had been wide enough, was a fine mark. But it was not, and all I could do was look at him standing still as the big tree itself. When at last he turned his head I looked the way he did, and saw two more Flatheads slipping toward the cabin, one with a gun. Had they seen us enter? Were they closing in on us, I wondered.

I turned around to tell my companions, but used to the light outside, my eyes were blind and I did not know that Big-horn, who had our only gun, had been looking too, until he opened the door and stepped out.

Instantly, before he could even raise his gun, a Flathead bullet smashed his right arm from the wrist to the shoulder, burying itself deep in his armpit. I dragged him inside and shut the door. He was bleeding badly, and I saw that it would be difficult to stop the blood because of the wound under his arm. But we tried, while bullets smacked against the cabin logs, some of them coming through between the cracks so that we had to move Big-horn several times while we worked on him.

If we stayed in the cabin they could starve or burn us out, even if they did not take the place by fighting. We had but the one gun, and had come near losing that. Our bows could not be used unless we went outside to fight, and the Flatheads were too many for us. Big-horn, leaning against the logs, clearly understood our situation. "You had better get out of this place," he said. "I shall die anyway, and you cannot help me by dying yourselves. I am no good any more."

He was my friend. "No," I told him. "I will not leave you."

"Nor will I," said Goes-against-the-enemy. "But the rest had better go if they can. Three had better die than six."

"Yes, go," I begged them. And so they stepped out into the pouring rain in the face of the Flatheads.

We watched them through the cracks, even Big-horn, as long as we could see them, until the dripping bushes hid them. Then for a long time we scarcely breathed, listening for shots. But none reached our ears, and we three were in for a hard time, we well knew.

There was no longer any good in silence. The Flatheads knew we were in the cabin as well as we did, but they did not know that three of our party had got out of their trap. Wishing them to know we were ready to die, we defied them with the Crow war whoop. Then we sang our Death Song and waited.

It was now that we tried to stop Big-horn's blood, but in spite of all we could do he continued to bleed. Not so badly, but enough to warn us that he could not last long. He was aware of this and said, "I can travel. Let us get out of this place when night comes. It is not far off now, and perhaps we may find our friends." He even laughed a little at my serious look when I tried to twist the thongs tighter about his upper arm.

I expected the Flatheads would burn the cabin when night came. I knew the logs would burn in spite of all the rain. The flames might not reach us for a time, and we might get good shots at our enemy in their light, but the smoke would not let us live very long. I counted the bullets in Big-horn's pouch — eleven. Not many to make a fight with, but better than none if we could keep the door open. "Let us get out of this place," urged Big-horn, when I put the string of his bullet pouch over my own head and took his gun.

"If he thinks he can travel we had better try," said Goes-against-the-enemy. And I agreed.

Dark came early. The rain was still falling when we three crept out of the cabin. Goes-against-the-enemy was ahead, Big-horn and I behind with the gun. Not once did we stop to look or listen. There was nothing one could see, and the rain stopped every small sound from going very far. Our great danger was that we might creep right in among the Flatheads who were watching the cabin, but we went swiftly over fallen trees and among bushes that showered our backs with water held in their young leaves, till we reached a creek. Here Goes-against-the-enemy stood up to wade across, and I helped Big-horn to stand. His head struck a leaning alder tree, and he staggered into my arms just as a gun flashed in our faces. I saw Big-horn's eyes in its light. They were dead.

Holding him from falling I led him into the water, expecting to be killed. But we got across, and dropping back to our hands and knees followed Goes-against-the-enemy, who was just ahead, until we came to another creek. This time I lifted Big-horn to his feet and saw that he was bleeding worse than when we left the cabin. "Can you walk across?" I asked him.

"No," he said. "I can go no farther. I am finished. Leave me and run." He sank down at my feet, and Goes-against-the-enemy, who had already crossed the creek, came back. "Sit down beside me," whispered Big-horn, "and sing with me while I go to my Father."

We sat down and sang there in the rain. And he sang with us until his heart was still. Big-horn, my friend, was dead in the enemy's country. My heart was on the ground beside him.

We gave him the best things we had, my necklace of bear's teeth and Goes-against-the-enemy's belt of porcupine quills, that he might offer them to our Father, and we left him lying on a bed we made in the dark. But we carefully covered him with willows so that the Flatheads would not find him, nor the wolves disturb his body.

"When we come back to get him, if we live to come," I said to Goes-against-the-enemy, "we will sing of his deeds and ask his spirit to stay always with us, as we stayed with him when he was here."

"Yes," he answered, "we will do as you say, and now let us make our hearts sing because our friend died unafraid."

Though we could travel faster now, there were many grizzly bears to trouble us. We ran close to them often. I did not like to meet so many in the darkness, but we kept on until morning came. The sight of the trail of the stolen horses lightened our hearts a little, but we were tired and hungry, needing rest and food. We killed a deer and camped on a high hill where we could look east and west, slept like stones, by turns, and took up the trail of the horses at daybreak. I could run from sun to sun in those days, and we ran most of the time till we caught up with our friends.

I have forgotten to tell you that we lost the trail where two rivers join their waters and that a Crow waiting on the bluff told us with a buffalo robe to follow the right-hand stream. I was glad to see that man and just as glad to get back to our village, which was then on Arrow Creek. It was much larger than when we left it, near The-mountain-lion's-lodge, because the clans had gathered to plant the tobacco-seed. . . .

We entered the village quietly because of the loss of Big-horn. . . . I dreaded the mourning of his family more than I can make your believe. I had gone with the party to help even up some old scores, and now, although we had many of their horses, I had another and a stronger reason for going again against the Flatheads. They had killed my friend.

Before we could tell our story the people missed Big-horn. His father cut off a finger, and both he and his woman, the mother of Big-horn, slashed their bodies with knives and wailed pitifully. Of course none of his close relatives could now enter the ceremony of planting the tobacco-seed, and all those who continued the preparations for it felt sad.

Big-horn had four fine war-horses. Before telling the story of our raid against the Flatheads we cut their tails short and roached their manes. "I will go back and fetch the body of Big-horn to his people," I promised his father, and I knew I should not rest until this was accomplished.

No members of our war-party took part in the planting of the seed, each of us instead taking a sweat-bath and fasting through the day and night. When morning came and the rest were beginning the beautiful ceremony, we painted our faces black, mounted our best war-horses, and rode away upon the knolls.

Each man was by himself, with his horse. There were thirty-four of us on thirty-four high points that looked down into the village. We neither ate nor drank water, but gave our thoughts to Big-horn, our brother, who was gone. To be alone with our war-horses at such as time teaches them to understand us, and us to understand them. My horse fights with me and fasts with me, because if he is to carry me in battle he must know my heart and I must know his or we shall never become brothers. I have been told that the white man, who is almost a god, and yet a great fool, does not believe that the horse has a spirit [soul]. This cannot be true. I have many times seen my horse's soul in his eyes. And this day on that knoll I knew my horse understood. I saw his soul in his eyes.

Down in the village I saw the planters start for the planting place, saw the people crowd too close to him, watched, only half perceiving, the War-clubs push them back. One man picked up a snake to strike those who were too near the sacred line of planters. I heard the singing as these people started, saw them stop, then start again, singing toward the planting ground. I felt glad that the seed would be planted, but my heart was not with the planters. It was on the ground in the enemy's country with Big-horn.

The next morning the village moved to Yellow-willows [Sage Creek] but did not stop there long, because our Wolves signalled us from the high hills that there were many buffalo on the Stinking Water. The tribe moved there and began to hunt.

But I could not rest, and so when the village moved to the Rapids [Rock Creek] I gathered five of my best friends and told them I proposed going after the body of Big-horn. When they said they would go with me my heart felt like a breath-feather.

We made panniers of rawhide large enough to carry Big-horn, put them on the back of a strong horse, and started, traveling all that day and night. On the third day we reached a country where we must not be seen, and after this moved only at night. One morning, just as we were hiding for the day, we heard a shot and raced for a high hill to learn who fired it. Goes-against-the-enemy beat us all to the top. I was nearest when he sprang from his horse and looked over the hill. By the time I had reached him he was up again and had signalled "The enemy is here." Then he mounted and dashed down on the far side out of sight.

I got off my horse and looked over the hill. One mounted Flathead was in sight, a fine-looking man, too. He wore on his head a rawhide hat and carried a beautiful gun. I saw its brass patch-box flashing in the sunlight. But it was a very heavy weapon, so heavy the Flathead carried two rest-sticks for it. I held up my hand and stopped our party quite a way down the hill. The Flathead rightfully belonged to Goes-against-the-enemy, who had seen him first, and I wished him to have his chance.

When our party stopped I watched Goes-against-the-enemy. He was riding very near the Flathead before the fellow saw him at all. The Flathead raised his heavy gun, fitting his rest-sticks against his side, and fired just as Goes-against-the-enemy struck him in the face with his quirt. I heard the lash strike, a beautiful coup!

I waited no longer, but jumped upon my horse and raced down the hill to count coup myself. I would take the Flathead's gun. Watching Goes-against-the-enemy, who had turned his horse to come back, he was trying to reload it. He had not seen me. His horse was running at right angles to my course, and my horse ran into his so violently that both nearly fell. But on the instant of collision I grabbed the Flathead's gun and held on, trying desperately to pull him from his horse. We wrestled, riding across the level ground as fast as our unmanaged horses could run, both holding to the gun, each trying to pull the other from his horse, and thus holding the racing animals together as though tied. Though I soon began to tire, I dared not let go. Where was Goes-against-the-enemy, I wondered. My arms were aching as though they must have rest, or break. I must end things somehow.

So with a last desperate effort I pulled the Flathead nearly over. His head was against my breast, and I pressed down, down, my eyes looking for friends. They saw none, but they saw something else that made my heart sink — the Flathead camp! We were racing straight for it.

"Shoot! Shoot!" I cried out, not knowing if friend or foe could hear me.

"Lean far over, quick!" The voice was Big-shield's.

My heart sang again. But though I tried to lean over, the Flathead was a strong man and I could not hold myself away from him enough so that Big-shield's bullet would hit him and not me.

"Push him away from you! Push him away!" Big-shield yelled. "I'll kill him when you do."

But I could not push him away. The Flathead, who knew just what was going on, hugged me to himself as we flew toward the camp of his friends.

Another Crow now came with advice. Whipping his horse to reach us, he was just behind Big-shield when he shouted, "Do not shoot! Be wise, and hold your arrow!" It was Shot-in-the-hand. "We are discovered," he said. "We are in their village and must make peace if we can."

I believed his advice was good. The Flathead was more than I could handle, and I let go. So did he. I believe he was glad of the chance. I know I was. That Flathead was a good man, a good warrior, but a little careless.

Shot-in-the-hand spoke to the Flathead in the Nez Perce tongue, and he understood. He knew we could easily kill him now, and he expected us to do it, I think. I wished to, myself, but in a way we had made peace, and when Long-Shoshone, who carried our pipe, came up, we took the Flathead to his lodge.

We were well enough off, but had we known there were only four lodges in the camp we might easily have avenged Big-horn while I still had hold of the Flathead. As it was we ate the meat of his people, and all the time I was in their camp I was sorry I had tasted it. However, there would come another time, and then there would be no peace between them and me. Goes-against-the-enemy felt the same as I did.

After leaving their camp we did not trust the Flatheads, traveling at night and each day putting out Wolves to watch the elk and buffalo. These animals are always quick to tell a war-party if the enemy is near. But we saw nothing, not even the smoke of an enemy's fire, and at last came to Big-horn's body. It had not been disturbed, and we carried it back with us to the Crow country, finding our village on the spot where Park City now stands.

Chapter 4

Documents of
Salish and Pend d'Oreille History
Between 1860 and 1864

Document 33

Worthless and Spoiled Annuity Goods

May 25 and November 29, 1860

Source: Jno. Owen, Flathead Indian Subagent, to E. R. Geary, Oregon and Washington Superintendent of Indian Affairs, May 25, 1860, and Nov. 29, 1860, Robert Bigart and Clarence Woodock, eds., *In the Name of the Salish & Kootenai Nation: The 1855 Hell Gate Treaty and the Origin of the Flathead Indian Reservation* (Pablo, Mont.: Salish Kootenai College Press, 1996), pages 152-154, 158-159.

Editors' note: Flathead Indian Agent John Owen was distraught on learning that, after a bureaucratic delay of five years, the first treaty payment of $36,000 for the Flathead Nation land was spent largely on consumable goods that would be of little or no use to the Indians. Instead of plows and stock to expand their farms and herds in the Bitterroot and Mission Valleys, the government was providing hardbread, blankets, shawls, and flannel. Owen insisted the Indians "know very well that the lands they sold were not to be paid for in hardbread & the likes." In November 1860, when he finally was able to get the annuity goods to Fort Owen from Fort Benton, he was doubly upset because the goods shipped by the Indian Office were not only inappropriate, but low quality, overpriced, and suffered from water damage.

Office Supt. Indian Affairs
Portland Oregon May 25" 1860

Dear Sir

Your communication 23rd inst with invoices of purchases made by Ind Dept on the Eastern side of the Continent has been recd. I regret exceedingly that the purchases were made without a requisition being furnished from my agency setting forth the articles most desired for the Flathead Nation. I have examined the invoice with care & find it will amount to some twenty five thousand dollars ($25000.00). The purchase could have been cut down one half & that amt. invested in heifers would have gone much further toward toward [sic] benefitting the Indians than the tons of coffee, rice & hardbread that are now en route for my agency & shipt too at very heavy expense. Hardbread is the last thing my Indians require & it would have been much better if flour was necessary to have purchased the wheat in the Bitter Root valley & had it ground there. You will see by this purchase that the thirty six thousand dollars, the first installment due the Flathead Nation, is over two thirds gone. I fear the Indians will not be satisfied in having so large an amt. of property a great deal of which is perfectly useless forced upon them in payment for their lands without their consent ever being asked or obtained. There is no building material shipt. No irons for either mill & in fact many things absolutely necessary for the Indians have been omitted such as guns, ammunition, kettles, tin ware, &c &c which if purchased in this market & shipd to Flathead Agency at the present rate of transportation which is 40 cents per # will involve a very heavy expense. One item of the invoice 650 prs Blue Blkts are seriously objectionable, another 120 dzn shawls equally so, another 1166⅓ yrds. flannel equaly so, & many other items of minor importance go on to swell the invoice to $25000.00 & this amt to be furnished to the Flathead Nation in the name of their Great Father in compliance with promises made them some five years ago. And what makes it appear doubly strange to me that so foolish a purchase should have been made is that the Ind. Dept. was advised from your office on 22nd day last December by letter a paragraph of which I here quote in part, "where you refer to articles required for the Flathead Nation such as plows, wagons, & other farming utensils tools for the shops of the carpenter, blacksmith, tinner, wagon & plow maker & machinery for the saw & flouring Mills &c &c." None of which save a few *hand saws*, arguers, drawing knives, & *gimblets*, a sufficient quantity in themselves to stock a half dozen shops. Six plows & a few hoes & forks sickles & scythes constitute the farming utensils. Twenty five plows would not have been amiss. How far will six plows go toward furnishing several hundred Indians.

If the Dept will keep the *hardbread, rice,* and *coffee* at home & encourage the Indians in farming I will make my self responsible for the result. The Flatheads are not a barbarous people. They know very well that the lands they sold were not to be paid for in hardbread & the likes. Assist them in producing a change in their herd of horses by purchasing some American breed mares, & a few hundred heifers. The Indians will be better pleased & infinitely more benefitted. The anxiety of the dept. to ameliorate the condition of the Indian is thwarted. Their advancement in the scale of social life is not promoted by the shipment of trash. They may be pleased for the moment but no permanently [sic] good results from the adoption of such a course. The Dept may rest assured that I will use every honorable effort to quiet the Nation under my charge & promote the friendly feeling that exists between them & the white Man.

I have the honor to
Remain My Dear Sir
Your obt servant
Jno Owen
Ind Sub agt
Inc Charge Flathead
Nation W. T.

To
E. R. Geary Esq.
Supt Ind Affairs
O & W
Portland, Oregon

* * * * * *

Office Flathead Agency
Fort Owen W. T. Nov 29" 1860

Sir:

Herewith I have the honor to Enclose Mess P. Choteau Jr & Co's withdrawal of proposition made me in June/59 for transportation of Flathead annuities from Benton to this place @ 10 cents per #.

The agency pack train could have transported nearly all the property in ample time had the goods not been witheld by Agt. [Alfred J.] Vaughan and the expense I have been compelld to incur saved for the Dept. leaving the pack train a nett gain. I felt it absolutely necessary for the peace of the country that the property should be brought over. I had not funds to meet the expense of transportation with parties here not willing to contract for less than 15 cents per #. I have promised it conditionally subject to your approval. To meet a portion of the expense I was compelld to use money in my hands intended for other purposes.

My position has been rendered doubly more embarrassing than it otherwise would be from the fact of my being so far remote from your office.

The annuities are in my warehouse with the exception of six bales of blks & a few boxes of hard bread which I will not regain before spring. How am I to pay for transportation which will amt to some thirteen thousand dollars less what was performed by pack train amting to nearly three thousand dollars leaving me in arrears of some ten thousand dollars now due.

The blankets are inferior to the Salem Blkts. The shawls & flannels are miserable flimsey things no earthly use. The cott. hnkfs cost $1.50 per doz. better goods can be purchased in Portland for 50 pr ct less money. The coffee nearly all damaged. Report from Benton says it had been sunk on the Mo. River & brt up by a house in St. Joseph shipd back to St. Louis & then worked in for filling contracts let out in St. Louis for Central Superintendancy. The cloths fall short some 175 yds but quality is fair. The cottons generaly are heavy serviceable goods with the exception of the calicos which are in excess full $^2/_3$ rds. The linseys fair only. In fact since examining the goods with the invoice I have no hesitation in saying I could have purchased the same bill in Portland for one third less money. And when I say this I speak knowingly and will submit the invoice to any of four business houses.

I have not examined the coffee in detail but shall do so and I do seriously think it will be necessary to have a board called to pass upon it, what I have opened is mouldy & musty. The sacks from their appearance evidently having been under water.

Respt Your &c.
Jno Owen In Sub Agt
&c &c
W. T.

To
E. R. Geary Esq.
Supt Ind Affairs
Portland
Oregon.

Flathead Agent and Trader John Owen
Photograph 944-236, Photograph Archives, Montana Historical Society,
Helena, Montana.

Document 34

Salish and Pend d'Oreille Farms
and Annuity Goods
October 30, 1860

Source: "The Indians of the Rocky Mountains," *New York Freeman's Journal & Catholic Register* (New York), Mar 30, 1861, page 3, c. 1-2.

Editors' note: Congiato described the beginnings of farming among the Salish and Pend d'Oreille Indians in the Jocko Reservation and Bitterroot Valley. He also emphasized John Owen's criticism about the type of annuities sent to the tribes in payment for their lands.

The Indians of the Rocky Mountains.

[From the San Francisco Monitor.]

We give below a letter addressed some months since by Very Rev. N. Congiato, S.J., to the Superintendent of Indian Affairs, residing at Portland. It will be read with interest, and it is to be hoped that the suggestions contained in it will receive attention in the proper quarter. Father Congiato, in his capacity of Superior of Missions, visited all the tribes under the direction of the Jesuit Fathers, and is thoroughly conversant with the feelings and requirements of the Indians. The United States Government acts in the most generous manner towards the red men, but it too often happens that the supplies furnished are not those of which they stand in need. What they require most are farming implements. The provisions distributed are often thrown away — the Indians complaining at the same time that they are furnished with commodities that they do not desire. We hope that the officers who make purchases at St. Louis will pay some attention to the real wants of the Indians, which are stated in the appended letter of Father Congiato:

Portland, (Oregon,) *Oct.* 30, 1860.

E. S. Geary, Esq., Superintendent of the Indian Affairs for Oregon and U.T.:

Sir:

You have kindly requested me to give you such information as I possessed respecting the condition of the Northern Indians in U. T., whom I have just returned from visiting. Knowing the great interest you take in promoting the welfare of the different Indian tribes confided to your supervision, I feel great pleasure in complying with your request.

As you are already aware, the Indians to whose spiritual wants the Jesuit Fathers have been attending for the last twenty years in U. T., are the following: The Flat-heads, the Upper Pends d'oreilles, the Lower Pends d'oreilles, or Kalispelems, the Colville Indians the Cœur d'alenes, the Coutonais, and of late the Spokane Indians. I do not mention some other tribes in the British possessions, nor the different Black-foot bands in the Territory of Nebraska, as they do not come under your jurisdiction. We have succeeded, through the blessing of Divine Providence, in converting into Christianity all the above mentioned nations in U. T. Their Christianity has naturally brought with it their civilization, which if not complete, is certainly rapidly progressing. They have abandoned their old superstitions, done away with polygamy, idleness, and waging war with each other. They are now engaged in farming to a considerable extent, and their operations in this respect are conducted with an ability and success which are encouraging indeed. They also raise stock largely, build dwelling-houses, barns, etc., and raise vegetables in abundance. Unfortunately, their means have not been adequate to their wishes. There is no doubt that they would have accomplished ten times more in regard to farming and cultivating the soil had they been provided with the necessary implements, seed, etc. But until now, they had to depend solely and exclusively on the missionaries for teems [sic], plows, seeds and other necessaries both for sowing and harvesting. Only a small number of the richest have been able to procure plows, teams, wagons, etc. But the large majority are, as yet, in a great measure, dependent on the missionaries for these things.

The Upper and Lower Pends d'oreilles and the Cœur d'alenes are the three tribes that are most extensively engaged in agriculture; and the traveler who happens to pass through their countries is struck with the number and good order of their cultivated fields. The crops have been very abundant this year throughout the country. During the harvest time, I happened to be at the Pends d'oreilles mission, where I found that the Indians were greatly embarrassed on account of not having the necessary implements for harvesting. We distributed to them a great number of reaping-hooks, but they were far from being sufficient. The consequence was, that many were obliged to pull up the wheat by the roots, in order to save the grain.

I can state with certainty that all the Indians under our charge are industrious and laborious, and are very anxious to cultivate more extensively, and thus better their condition. As to their mental capacity, we find them more liberally endowed than is generally supposed. They easily learn how to read and write, evince considerable taste for vocal and instrumental music, and acquire different useful trades with great facility.

While at Fort Benton, I had an opportunity of seeing the annuity goods sent by the government for the Flat-heads, Pends d'oreilles and Coutonais. I frankly confess that I was considerably surprised to observe that very little of what the Indians stand most in need of was to be seen in the large amount of goods sent for them. From the knowledge I have of the condition of these Indians, I consider that such articles as bread, biscuit, sugar, coffee, rice and other eatables are of little or no advantage to them. They are all able to provide their own subsistence, provided they have the necessary means of so doing; and what they want is — plows, yokes, axes, sickles, light horse wagons, and other such things as farmers generally need. And here permit me to suggest the propriety of furnishing, besides scythes, cradles, etc., a good number of reaping-hooks. The reason of this is that a great deal of the harvesting is done by the women, who cannot as well handle the cradle as they do the sickle. As for threshing their grain, they suffer no inconvenience. They do it easily with the flail or with horses, and would, in all probability, be unable to manage a threshing machine.

I left the Pends d'oreilles Mission about the 28th of August. The Indians, both Pends d'oreilles and Flat-heads, were on the point of starting across the mountains for the buffalo hunt. When I left the Rocky Mountains, a perfect tranquility prevailed everywhere among the Indians. But on my way down, I learned that some signs of discontent were beginning to appear among the Flat-heads and Pends d'oreills. Both these tribes are unwilling that the farm intended for them should be located by government in the Yoko [Jocko] Valley — the former because it is altogether out of their country, and they would derive no advantage from it; the latter because that valley was the only place in which they could keep their animals during severe winters; and its occupation as a farm would cut off their last resource. I have been also told that the Pends d'oreilles were greatly displeased for the above reason, on account of the large band of cattle which was brought up lately from Walla Walla, and placed in the Yoko prairie.

In conclusion, I would state my full conviction that all these Indians are friendly and well disposed towards the whites, and will continue to be so, if the government strictly comply with the terms of the treaties alaeady [sic] made, and proper persons be employed to see them carried into execution.

I have the honor to be, with the highest consideration, your obedient servant,

N. Congiato, S.J.
Superior of the Jesuit Indian Missions, in the Rocky Mountains.

Document 35

Assiniboine and Cree Attack
Pend d'Oreille Buffalo Hunters
Autumn 1860

Source: John Owen to Col. J. W. Nesmith, Dec. 21, 1860, in John Owen, *The Journals and Letters of Major John Owen, Pioneer of the Northwest, 1850-1871*, ed. Seymour Dunbar and Paul C. Phillips (New York: Edward Eberstadt, 1927), vol. 2, pp. 238-239.

Editors' note: The autumn 1860 Assinniboine and Cree attack on a Pend d'Oreilles buffalo hunting party on the Milk River was a devastating defeat for the tribe. According to the first report written by Owen on December 3, 1860, a nearby camp of Piegan Indians came to the aid of the Pend d'Oreille and prevented even further loss of life. Some periods have been added to the transcription.

Owen to Geary in Description of the Defeat of Chief Alexander by the Assinniboines and His Aid to the Beaten Indians

Office Flathead Agency
Fort Owen Bitter Root Valley W. T. Decr 21" 1860

Sir

I retd last Evening after an absence of two Weeks to the Jocko reservation. While there I heard of Alexanders approach with his defeated & Scattered Camp. I Went to See him. My feelings were Shocked at the Scene his camp presented. Women with their children slung upon their backs had traversed the whole 400 Miles on foot from the point on Milk river where they had been defeated. They were literaly worn out & Exhausted. The loss of horses they Sustained by the attack of the Assinnaboines & Crees Was So great that Most of their Camp Equipage had to be abandoned on the battle field. They were destitute of provisions & clothing. I imediately ordered the Ind. Dept pack train from the Jocko to this place for Stores. I issued them four head of oxen. Alexander had lost a Son in the fight a young Man of Much promise Some 20 Years of age. He found his Sons body in a horribly Mutilated State. Scalped Stripd & heart Cut out. Some of the Wounded have since died. Dr [James A.] Mullan was prompt & Efficient in rendering assistance to the Wounded that Succeeded in reaching home. They Numbered [— — — — — ?] Some fifteen

Operations of a difficult Nature had to be performed Extracting Arrow points, Bullets, &c &c. The Pend's Oreilles had twenty Killed & twenty five Wounded (five of the latter Since dead) and lost 290 head of horses. Mr Ogden a ½ breed who was one of the party gave Me a thrilling & interesting account of the attack & the battle. He Say the Assinnaboins Numbered Some two hundred or there abouts. They were a War party all on foot & unincumbered With families, Lodges, horses, &c &c. Nothing in the World Saved the Complete & Entire Extermination of Alexanders Camp but the Amt. of plunder the attacking party had come in possession of. The 290 head of horses which they were Eager to Secure beyond a doubt. The Pends Oreilles Made Every effort that a brave & gallant band could do to recover Some of the Animals they had lost. But they were overcome by Numbers & had to quietly Submit to their fate & beat a retreat toward their far distance home. It was hard. They had just reached the Buffalo. They were in fine Spirits. On the Evening of the Night of the attack the tired Camp on bended Knees offered their thanks to almighty God for the prospect then before them. Alexander in a short harangue told his Camp that here we will Make our Winters Meat & return. Secure your fleet horses for to Morrows Chase &c &c. Little did the unsuspecting Camp know what awaited them. Before the dawn the Camp was Surrounded & between the report of the rifle, the Wailings of the Women, the Neighing of the horses at the picket & the Sheet of fire that Encircled the Camp from the rifles of the attacking party you can form but a slight Conception of What followed. Mr Ogden says it was about one hour before day when the attack was Made. Alexanders Camp was Still asleep. The attacking party approached the Lodges Cut an opening with the Knife Through Which they thrust their rifles & discharged their deadly Contents. The heart bleeds at the thrilling Story. Alexander thirsts for revenge. He talked to Me with Moistened Eyes. He Says he must visit the Sleeping place of his Son & people. I tell him I appreciate his feelings. I Sympathise deeply with him. I had a long talk with him. I have No doubt Myself but there will be a large War party in the field this Spring.

I have had to purchase Ammunition for the Camp None having been Sent up with the Annuity goods from the East

Respt &c

Jno Owen Ind Sub agt &c &c W. T.

E. R. Geary Eqr Supt Ind Affairs
Portland Oregon

Document 36

Annuity Goods Problems and Assiniboine–Cree Attack on Pend d'Oreille Buffalo Hunters September 12, 1861

Source: John Owen to B. F. Kendall, Sept. 12, 1861, in John Owen, *The Journals and Letters of Major John Owen, Pioneer of the Northwest, 1850-1871*, ed. Seymour Dunbar and Paul C. Phillips (New York: Edward Eberstadt, 1927), vol. 2, pp. 261-264.

Editors' note: Owen's 1860 report refers to the problems with the annuity goods sent in payment for the lands ceded in the 1855 Hellgate Treaty, Alexander's losses in an 1860 attack by the Assinniboines and Cree Indians on the plains, and the unwillingness of the Salish Indians to leave the Bitterroot Valley. Some periods have been added to the transcription.

Owen to Kendall Submitting His Report for 1860 and Summarizing the Indian Affairs of the Region Under His Jurisdiction

Portland Oregon
September 12" 1861

Sir

I have the honor to submit this My annual report for the Year 1860. I observe that My report for 1859 does Not for Some reason appear in the last annual report of the Hon. Com. of Ind affairs. Pursuant to the orders of Your predecessor Supt [E. R.] Geary of May 1860 I Started without delay for Fort Benton to Make provisions for the transportation of the annuity goods purchased East for the Flathead Nation by the Dept. at Washington City & shipd up the Mo river to that place. On reaching the Flathead agency I found Myself too unwell to proceed any further in person. I therefore dispatched Mr L. L. Blake & Mr. C. E. Irvine two of the Ind Dept Employees to Fort Benton with My order on agent Vaughn [Alfred J. Vaughan] for the annuity goods the former in charge of the agency Pack train & the latter to remain at Benton as shipping agent after having recd the goods from agent Vaughn.

In Supt. Geary's letter of instructions of May 1860 I was clearly designated by him as the person authorised to receive the annuity goods. My instructions were Exhibited to Agent Vaughn. He however contended that his instructions from Supt. Robinson who shipd the goods from St Louis Would Not warrant him in turning them over to Me unless upon Supt. Geary's direct order to him to that Effect.

The consequence was that the Pack train Numbering Some Eighty Animals returned without loading & that the Men were Kept under pay until I could Send an Express to the Supt. for further orders in the premises.

The Season was far advanced when the Express retd with the required order. Snow was already Making its appearance on the Mts. The train could Make but one More trip & that Not with Safety. I was therefore compelled to Employ such transportation as could be obtained in the Country for which you will see by refering to My account rendered to the 16" May last that I have incurred an outlay of $8229.80 all of which could have been Saved to the Dept had the goods been promptly turned over when the train first reached Fort Benton Early in August. The Withholding of the annuity goods also prevented My carrying out My instructions relative to Visiting the Snake & Bannac Indians camping on or near the great Emigrant trail passing Forts Hall & Boise.

The Flathead & Pend'Oreilles were also much disappointed in Not receiving a portion of their presents before going to buffaloe.

The Scarcity of buffalo compelled them to remain out all Winter. The Camps returned in March Excepting a portion of the Chiefs Alexander band which returned in December after their defeat on Milk river by the Crees & Assinaboines. Alexander lost in Killed 20 persons his own Son being among the Number & 290 head of horses. His camp returned in a Most destitute condition.

In March last I had the census of the Flathead & Upper Pen d'Oreille tribes taken. The former gives 90 families With a total of 548 Souls & the latter 184 families with an aggregate of 895 Souls. The Kootenays are believed to Number over 2000 Souls but I have as Yet had no opportunity to take their census. It will thus be Seen that the total Number of Indians parties to the Flathead treaty is over 3443. The Indians are Not pleased with their annuities. Many articles which they Much Need Not having been purchased & Many of the Articles purchased Not being adapted to their Wants.

I Certainly regard the purchase a very injudicious one. But I have referred to this Subject in My last annual report (not published) & also in a Special report upon that Subject dated Nov. 30" 1860 transmitted to Com of Ind affairs by Supt. Geary pr his letter of 26" Feby 1861.

I have Made considerable progress in farming considering it was so late when the Seed Wheat & plows arrived from Portland. I will have some 150 acres under fence plowed Sowed & planted. The Material for the Grist Mill has Not been recd. Had I the Burrs & irons I Might possibly get it up for this harvest.

The Expense of the Mill dam was much More than was anticipated. It required an Excavation of 210 feet in length by 60 in Width but I can safely say that it is a Substantial piece of Work.

I have been visited by two delegations of Snake & Bannac Indians. Their Camps during the Winter were in a Most destitute condition & I am pleased to Know that the course I pursed in issuing them rations of Beef & flour to prevent their trespassing on the Stock of the Settlers has Met the approval of your office.

I am also happy to learn that the Steps which I have taken towards recovering the four White Children taken from the Emigrants last September as the horrible Massacre at Boise had also the approval of your office. I will again call the attention of the Dept. to the Wandering bands of Snakes & Bannacks & to the propriety of Making treaties with them & making Some provisions for their Welfare. The increasing Scarcity of Game & the Constant Encroachments upon their lands by gold Miners would Seem to require some such Steps on the Score of humanity as well as of justice.

They Say they had No hand in the Boise Massacre. that the Indians who Make the forays upon the Emigrant road are from the Sink of Humbolt & are called Snakes because they talk the Snake language.

From all I could learn of the Snakes last Winter I believe they Number some 600 Lodges with an average of Six Souls to the Lodge will give an aggregate of 3600. The Bannacks & other Small tribes on Salmon, Snake & Green rivers May be Safely Set down at 5000. Thus it will be Seen that the total Number of Indians in My district is Not less than 12043 of which 8600 are Not parties to any treaty with the United States.

I will again call the attention of the Dept to the justice of confirming to the Flathead tribe their conditional reservation in the Bitter Root Valley for a time at least as I am Satisfied that the Flathead's will Never leave it to remove to the Jocko Reservation.

The annuity goods I divided into three Equal portions for the Flatheads Pend d'Oreilles & Kootenays & Explained to them My reason for So doing.

The Kootenays Seem Not to be disposed to avail themselves of the provisions of their treaty which will account for So large an amount of the annuity Goods being on hand.

The 300 head of heifers I purchased I have Not Yet issued but shall do so this fall. I intend 100 head for Each tribe.

Much good work would result from liberal appropriations for farms &c provided the funds are faithfully applied to the object intended.

But it is of little or No use to Make such appropriations if the funds are to be Expended by the Indian Bureau in the purchase of articles Not Calculated to promote the permanent Welfare of the Indians.

The following buildings have been Erected by Me during the past Year on the Jocko reservation viz one Store house, one double dwelling, for farmers & assistants, one Black Smith Shop one Mill Wright Shop, & one dwelling house for Mill Wright & party.

Very respectfully Your obt Servt
Jno Owen Ind agt Flathead Nation W. T.

To B. F. Kendall Esqr Supt Ind affairs W. T.

Olympia P. S.

"Note" For Some cause Not Known the foregoing report does Not appear in the Annual report of W. P. Dole Com Ind. affrs. The undersigned declines Making any report for 1861.

John Owen

Document 37

Pend d'Oreilles Start a Gros Ventres–Blackfeet War
Autumn 1861

Source: Lieut. James H. Bradley, "Gros Ventres," *Contributions to the Historical Society of Montana,* vol. 9 (1923), pp. 313-315.

Editors' note: A ruse perpetrated by a Pend d'Oreille horse stealing party on the Gros Ventres in the fall of 1861 led to a long running war between the Gros Ventres and their former allies, the Blackfeet Indians. Lt. Bradley joined the U.S. Army in 1861 and served in the Civil War and later spent many years in the American West. He died in 1877 at the Battle of the Little Big Hole during the Nez Perce War.

Gros Ventres

The Gros Ventres are an offshoot of the Arapahoes. The separation was the result of a dissention, and, the Gros Ventres, migrating north and being kindly received by the Blackfeet and invited to remain in their country, have since about the beginning of the present (nineteenth) century dwelt about the waters of the Missouri and until of late years been regarded popularly as a band of the Blackfoot nation. They, however, maintained friendly relations with the parent tribe and formerly made periodical visits to their former home. Renegade Arapahoes are frequently to be found among them, and the Arapahoes have never ceased to regard them as a part of their own people. As late as about ten years ago, when the Arapahoes were at war with the whites, they sent envoys to the Gros Ventres to entreat their co-operation, but the latter held fast to their old traditions of amity toward the whites and only a small number were found willing to listen to the entreaties of the Arapahoe plenipotentiaries. These few, after having removed for a day or two to a separate camp to await accessions of strength, were fain to drop the project and rejoin their people in the general village.

From the earliest times that the whites were familiar with Blackfoot affairs they found them and the Gros Ventres on the most friendly footing toward each other. The hunting and war parties pursued the chase and sought the enemy in common, they intermarried, and the Gros Ventres though perpetuating their mother tongue were in danger of ultimately losing it, so general began to be the use of the Blackfoot dialect among them. This friendly state of affairs continued until 1861, and the rupture that then ensued was the result of a misunderstanding that a few calm words would have readily explained and the subsequent ill feeling with its train of petty hostilities been averted.

In the fall of this year the Pend d'Oreilles in a raiding expedition stole some horses from the camp of the Gros Ventres, then located upon the Missouri some thirty-five or forty miles below Fort Benton. Retreating with their spoils, they, to throw pursuers off the track, resorted to the vicinity of the Piegan camp on the Marias river, some twelve miles below Fort Benton, and left a number of the horses, continuing their flight with the remainder. The Gros Ventres pursuing in hot haste found the abandoned horses as they supposed in the hands of the Piegans, and, boiling with indignation at such perfidious conduct on the part of professed friends, inconsiderately and without seeking an explanation, attacked the Piegan camp. In the conflict that ensued an old Piegan chief was slain, and the enraged Piegans had no thought but of vengeance. The news of the outrage was spread by runners throughout the entire Blackfoot domain and for a time the tumult of preparation, the gathering of parties of excited warriors in all the bands, the threats of dire retaliation seemed to threaten the entire annihilation of the presumptuous Gros Ventres. But fickleness and inability for continued operations of any magnitude innate in the Indian breast resulted in the collapse of the threatened war, and the relentless hatred that has since existed between the Gros Ventres and the Blackfeet bands has found expression only in the petty marauding expeditions, the stealing of horses, the destruction of stragglers which usually constitute the warfare of the Western Indians. This state of affairs continued without interruption until the spring of 1874, when under the auspices of the government a council was held at Fort Benton, in which Blackfeet bands, Gros Ventres and Assiniboines were represented, which resulted in mutual pledges to preserve the peace that were almost immediately violated. The bitterness engendered between the Gros Ventres and Blackfeet in 1861 has yet to be provided with a cure. As late as the beginning of December, 1874, a Gros Ventres was killed in sight of Fort Benton by a war party of Piegans in ambuscade at the upper end of the Coulee through which the Milk river road ascends from the Missouri valley.

[Bradley note: Information obtained from Father [Camillus] Imoda and other sources.]

Document 38

Traveling with Salish and Pend d'Oreille Buffalo Hunters 1862-1863

Source: Excerpt from "John D. Brown: A Narrative of His Early Experience in the West," in Robert Vaughn, *Then and Now; or, Thirty-six Years in the Rockies, 1864-1900* (Minneapolis, Minn.: Tribune Printing Company, 1900), pages 209-212.

Editors' note: John D. Brown was a prospector in the Northern Rocky Mountains in the 1860s. He later settled on a farm in the Sun River area. Brown's account is another example of the friendship, hospitality, and alliance between the Salish and Pend d'Oreille Indians and the white invaders on the northern Great Plains.

[Prospecting in the Musselshell Area, 1862-1863]
by John D. Brown, via Robert Vaughn

As I desired to go prospecting east of the Rocky mountain range, I left Bannock about the latter part of October, 1862, in company with John Peeterson and Thomas Thomas. On top of the main range, and where the Mullan road crosses, we met the old frontiersman, John Jacobs. He told us that Captain [James L.] Fisk, in company with a lot of immigrants from Minnesota, were in camp in the Prickly Pear valley. I went to their camp, which was near to what is now called Montana Bar. James King and W. C. Gillette were there with a lot of flour; from them I bought a sack to go prospecting. With the same outfit came Jesse Cox, Jim Wiley, Albert Agnel, Jim Norton, Charles Cary, Alvin H. Wilcox, A. McNeal, James Fergus, Bob Ells, old man Olan and old man Dalton. They and others were in camp and had not decided where to go next. John Peeterson, Thomas Thomas, Jim and Bill Buchanan, Dick Merrill and I did some prospecting there that fall and got considerable gold.

Late in the fall, myself, a man named Thebeau, Nickolos Bird, and a fellow by the name of Gervais, who could talk the Flathead language, went off with the Flatheads and Pend d'Oreilles Indians to prospect the country they were going to travel through that winter. The Indians were on the way to the Musselshell country to hunt buffaloes. At this time the Flatheads and Piegans were at war with each other.

All the old Indians, who numbered from eight to twelve hundred, went through what is now called Confederate gulch. We found good prospects there, but the Indians would not let us stay. It appeared that they had some kind of understanding with the Crow Indians to go and hunt in that part of the country, but not to encourage any whites to go there, consequently we had to move whenever the Indians would move, and, by this time, they would not let us go back. We camped for several days on the little prairie at the head of Smith river, near where White Sulphur Springs, the county seat of Meagher county, now is. There the Indians had a buffalo hunt and killed many. After that we went down Shields' river and made three camps there. During all this time the Indians were killing buffalo and drying the meat. At the mouth of Shields' river we saw a large war party of Crows trying to capture some of the Flatheads and Pend d'Oreilles who were out hunting, and who belonged to the Indians we were with. We camped near where there was a lot of willows. Moise, the head chief of the Flatheads, came and asked me if I would fight; I said yes, and he said, "That is good." I had a good rifle and two revolvers. Soon our Indians got together and prepared for a battle, but the Crows did not follow, and it was good for them, for the Flatheads and Pend d'Oreilles were well armed and mounted on good horses and were eager for a fight. That night they placed their horses inside the camp and put pickets out in as good way as I ever saw in my life, but the enemy did not make an attack. From there we went east of the Little Snowys. There we met a war party of Piegans coming around what is called Wolfe mountain; there were about thirty of them. They came to our camp to stop all night, and were received as friends, and they played games during the evening with the Pend d'Oreilles. About midnight the Piegans sneaked out and stampeded many of the best horses belonging to the Flatheads and Pend d'Oreilles and started away with them. Chief Moise at once blew a horn and his son beat a kind of drum; this aroused the whole camp. The Pend d'Oreilles and Flathead warriors were in an instant on their best horses and went after the Piegans and captured them all and recovered the stolen horses and brought them to camp. The Pend d'Oreilles wanted to kill the Piegan thieves, but Chief Moise said, "No, we will not kill them, though they are dogs. They came to our tepees as friends, but at the time they were deceiving us. They are dogs; they came to our camp and we treated them as friends, but they got up in the dark of the night and stole our horses. No, we will not kill them, but we will mark them." Then he ordered his warriors to bring the Piegans to the front of his tepee. After this was done, he ordered them to take the younger bucks and cut their hair short, and to cut a piece off each ear of all the others. During the time this was being done, the Flatheads and Pend d'Oreilles stood with their bows strung, and others with rifles in their hands, ready to shoot if anyone made a move to get away. After the marking was done, the Piegans were taken outside of the camp and were told to go home as dogs and never return or they would be killed as dogs. I witnessed all this.

On Christmas eve, 1862, we were in camp at Wolfe mountain. Chief Moise invited us to his tent to eat a Christmas dinner with him. He knew that it was Christmas day and respected it as such, for he had been taught what the meaning of it was by Father [Pierre] De Smet. His wife cooked dinner for us. She had fried doughnuts as good as any I ever ate, and excellent yeast powder bread; we had buffalo tongue and all kinds of meats. In all my life I never enjoyed a Christmas dinner better than I did that Christmas eve of 1862 in the tepee of the Flathead chief near Wolfe mountain.

Christmas morning I went on the top of what the Indians called Heart mountain. My object was to try and look in the direction of Fort Benton, for I knew we were not far from there, as I could see the Bear Paw mountains plainly. We decided to leave the Indians and go to Fort Benton. The Flathead chief sent six Indians to escort us through. It took us two days and part of a night. The second day out we traveled on a trail where the sage hens were as thick as I ever saw turkeys in a barnyard, but the Indians would not allow us to shoot, fearing that it might draw the attention of other Indians who were hostile to all of us.

Before the Indians started back we gave them tobacco and some matches, and a fancy pipe for them to take to the chief. It was the 18th of January, 1863, when we crossed the Missouri river at Fort Benton, and the river at that time perfectly free from ice. there were only a few days of cold weather and but little snow that winter.

Document 39

White Trader Accuses Bitterroot Salish of Theft

Spring 1863

Source: Aug. H. Chapman, U.S. Ind. Agt., Office Flathead Ind. Agency, M.T., to D. N. Cooley, Commissioner of Indian Affairs, Washington, D.C., Aug. 31, 1866, U.S. Office of Indian Affairs, "Letters Received by the Office of Indian Affairs, 1824-1880," National Archives Microfilm Publication M234, reel 488, fr. 282-284.

Editors' note: Figuring exactly what happened between Thibedeau and Chief Ambrose and the other Bitterroot Salish Indians in the spring of 1863 is hard, but incidents of friction between individuals or communities must have been frequent.

Office Flathead Ind. Agency, M.T.

Aug. 31st 1866

Sir:

I have the honor to transmit you herewith a claim presented by Zeb. B. Thibedeau against Flathead tribe of Indians, for the sum of Eight Thousand Dollars ($8000 x/x).

I have carefully investigated this claim and find the facts in regard to it to be about as follows:

During the spring of 1863 the claimant was passing through this country on his way from Lewiston in Idaho Territory to Bannack in Montana Territory. He had with him quite a number of pack animals, loaded with groceries and Whiskey (mostly the latter). Between Hell Gate and Gold Creek he met the Flathead Indians returning to their homes from the winter's Buffalo hunt; and sold to many of them Whiskey; when they of course became intoxicated and behaved very badly. Several white citizens advised Ambrose a Flathead chief to take a party of his people, follow Thibedeau and destroy his liquors; this he (Ambrose) done; and Thibedeau and the men who were with him, became alarmed and fled. Ambrose and his men after accomplishing their object, also left without disturbing any other property of the claimant. But a short time elapsed when another party of Flatheads came along, saw the deserted train, and helped themselves to what goods they wanted and the horses. Upon

Ambrose ascertaining this, he had the horses returned to Thibedeau, also what other property he could collect together; but much of the latter was never returned to the claimant.

A Mexican who was with the Flatheads got Thibedeau's canteenos, and if he had any money it must have been taken by this Mexican; but no one in this country believes he (T) had any more money than sufficient to pay his expenses.

After Thibedeau had collected his train, he proceeded to Deer Lodge Valley, to a place now called Cottonwood; where he and his party met a small party of Flathead Indians and forcibly took from them their horses as a recompense for the damage he (Thibedeau) had sustained at the hands of the Flatheads. This latter party of Flatheads collected together quite a number of their friends and took by force, again, these horses from Thibedeau: here the process ended.

No one in this country who was acquainted with Thibedeau, and Knew of his difficulty with the Flatheads, believes that he had the amount of goods which he claims to have lost on that occasion, or that he had the amount of money, which he claims was taken from him; it is certain the Flatheads did not get any money from him. The two men whose affidavits accompany his claim, were not with Thibedeau at the time of the difficulty.

Had Thibedeau not sold Whiskey to the Flatheads he would not have been disturbed by them. Now after a lapse of over three years, and after he, (Thibedeau) thinks that most of the facts in regard to this difficulty with these Indians has been forgotten, he presents his claim to me for damages. I respectfully recommend that the said claim be disallowed.

Respectfully
Your Obt Svt
Aug. H. Chapman
U.S. Ind. Agt.

Hon. D. N. Cooley
Commr. of Ind. Aff.
Washington
D.C.

Document 40

Salish Chief Victor Wins Foot Race

1863

Source: "Victor Won the Race," *The Anaconda Standard*, Sept. 13, 1898, page 10, c. 2.

Editors' note: If the race took place 35 years before 1898, it would have been about 1863. Fortunately, Duncan McDonald frequently told stories about the early lives of Salish and Pend d'Oreille chiefs, some of which were recorded in the local newspapers.

Victor Won the Race
Heap Swift Indian Runners 35 Years Ago or So.
Trailed a Long Time

Finally, Encouraged by the Whoops of His Entire Tribe, He Dashed to the Fore and Made a Garrison Finish — Mr. McDonald's Tale.

Missoula, Sept. 12. — Duncan McDonald is spending several days in town. This is the first long visit that Mr. McDonald has made to Missoula for some time and he has been improving the opportunity to drive around town and up the canyon, as he expresses it, "to look over the old stamping ground." In speaking of the matter last night, he said: "I have just been up the canyon a little way. I had not driven up that way for a long time and the country has changed greatly since I was last up over the Marshall grade. I was reminded by my visit to the Marshall grade of the famous foot race that was run from that as a starting point, some 35 years ago, by old Victor the father of Charlot, the present chief of the Bitter Root Flatheads. At that time Victor was in his prime. You may remember that he died at Stevensville in the early '80's [i.e., 1870]. Victor was a great foot-racer and he was challenged to a contest by one of the runners of his tribe. The event attracted considerable attention among the Indians and there was a great crowd on hand to witness the race. The start was from the foot of the grade, near where the fine orchard is now growing on the De Long ranch. The course was down, along the river bank, where the old trail used to run, as far as the Rattlesnake and then up the Rattlesnake to the north end of Mount Jumbo and from there over the hill to the starting place. It was a great race. The challenger — I have forgotten his name — led all the way down the trail and up the hill. When the river came in sight again at the summit of the hill that flanks Jumbo, Victor made a dash and passed his rival. From that time on he was never headed. There was a crowd of Indians at the top of the hill that had assembled to witness the last of the race and their cries added to the excitement of the race. At any rate, Victor took encouragement at something and his leaps down the hill and across the valley to the finish were wonderful. He won by a good margin and his superiority was no longer questioned. It was one of the greatest races ever run in this part of the country. Old Victor used to say that, when he heard the shouts of the people of his tribe at the top of the hill, he made a supreme effort to pass his rival and he remembered nothing else of the race. He had no recollection whatever of the last part of the race. But he won very handsomely.

"There are several incidents of interest connected with that little valley or basin east of Jumbo. Near the Marshall grade the Blackfeet, in one of their raids, killed a Flathead woman. There used to be a clump of pines near the river bank, this side of the grade, about where the railway runs at present, and in this grove a party of Blackfeet once waylaid a Flathead hunting party. All of the Blackfeet were killed. This was a great place for those battles and there are many stories told of occurrences there."

Duncan McDonald
Photograph 943-624, Photograph Archives, Montana Historical Society,
Helena, Montana.

Document 41

Pend d'Oreille Chief Michelle Asks His Son to Give Life for Good of Tribe 1863-1864

Source: Excerpt from W. P. Clark, *The Indian Sign Language* (Philadelphia: L. R. Hamersly, 1885), page 301.

Editors' note: Clark interviewed Pend d'Oreille Chief Michelle before Clark's book was published in 1885. The account of Michelle asking his son to submit to lynching despite being innocent, apparently came from Michelle.

Pend d'Oreille
by Chief Michelle via W. P. Clark

The head-chief Michelle, ... in speaking of their beliefs and customs said to me, "The old, old people, a long time ago, believed that a good man — a chief — was in the far East, and they said that as he was good he took pity on them when they prayed to him. There was another old man in the far West, and they prayed for him not to see them. When the priests first came they asked us if we prayed, and, if so, to whom; asked if we prayed to the sun, and we said, No; we pray to a good man, a great chief in the far East. They told us not to do this, and instructed us to pray to other Gods and saints. In olden times we thought that after death, if we had been good, we went to the East, and if wicked, to the bad man in the West. Some five hundred years ago there was a man named Weosel, and he climbed a tree, and as he climbed the tree grew, until finally he was raised into the far heavens, and saw the world and people there. He came back, told his story, and died here. The old people said the good man of the East made the world, and everything in it. When the whites came they called this man a God, and said he was above; but we knew all about this before they came."

At the time of the Nez Perce war, in 1877, there was great turmoil and intense excitement at this agency, and even the agent feared that his Indians might be persuaded to join their old friends, and so fearing was about to remove his wife and children from the danger, when Michelle went to him and said that he and his warriors would protect the agent's family from all harm, and if they left it would cast the shadow of an unjust suspicion on his friendship for the whites. The agent was so deeply impressed with the loyalty of the old chief that he concluded to trust the lives of his wife and little ones to the care of these Indians, and in telling me the story was visibly affected.

In this connection it seems proper to say that some fifteen years ago a white man, a miner, was killed some eight miles below Missoula, and the murder was attributed to the Indians. Michelle's son was found near the place the next day, arrested by the enraged whites and speedily hung. Before his death his father saw him, and the young man swore that he was innocent; but his father told him that he could only be saved, or his death avenged, by a disastrous war with the whites, and asked him to sacrifice his life for the good of his people; told him to go bravely to death. There was good evidence afterwards to show that the murder had been committed by members of another tribe, and that the boy was, as he claimed, innocent of the crime.

Document 42

The Remarkable Life of Pend d'Oreille Chief Big Canoe 1863-1876

Sources: Charley Shafft, "Big Canoe," *The Council Fire* (Washington, D.C.), vol. 3, no. 11 (Nov. 1880), pages 174-175; and Peter Ronan, *Historical Sketch of the Flathead Indian Nation from the year 1813 to 1890* (Helena, Mont.: Journal Publishing Co., 1890), pages 72-76.

Editors' note: Big Canoe was a prominent Pend d'Oreille chief in the nineteenth century. His long speech at the 1855 Hellgate Treaty council is reproduced above. These two contemporary biographical sketches of Big Canoe's life were written by Flathead Agency officials. Shafft was a longtime agency clerk in the 1870s, and Peter Ronan was Flathead Indian Agent between 1877 and 1893. The sketches are valuable, but only give us glimpses into Big Canoe's remarkable life.

Big Canoe.

Big Canoe, ("Francois,") the late war chief of the Pend d'Oreilles, in Montana, was, probably, just before he died, the oldest inhabitant on the continent. No one could tell his age. He himself did not know it, but he remembered that he was a big boy when Lewis and Clarke passed through his country. He was a self-made man, who rose to the chieftainship of a very turbulent band through individual daring and intrepidity, and retained his position on account of sagacious management.

Nearly every white man on the border knew the old man, and volunteered a piece of tobacco to the centenarian, who still would ride a horse, although his fingers and eyes could no longer act together. Age had dimmed one sense and paralysis the other; but his brain, which expired within the last year, was vigorous to the end, and the most violent Indian of his band would readily succumb upon an admonition of its leader.

Poor "Big Canoe," your bark was worn out by long usage, and you were finally wrecked upon the rocks of civilization. May you float easily upon the silvery lakes of the happy hunting grounds. Your speech to an old time Indian agent should be immortalized, and I will give it here as nearly as I can remember.

"The government bought our lands and made us big promises: they promised to send an agent to us who would protect us in our rights. The first one sent here by the Big Father was a thief. He stole our goods and sold them to us at Fort Owen. The next one was a thief also, but he stole our goods and sold them to us right here on the reservation, and (said the old chief, pointing his forefinger to the United States Indian agent present) I believe you are a bigger thief than the others." And the old chief was right.

Charley Shafft.

* * * * * *

[Sketch of Big Canoe, of Montana Indian Fame.]
by Peter Ronan

Big Canoe, who was war chief of the Pend d'Oreilles, died in 1882 [i.e., 1880], at the Flathead agency, and was buried in the Indian burying ground at Fort [St.] Ignatius Mission. He was 83 years of age at the time of his death, and was considered by the Indians to be one of the greatest war chiefs the tribe of the Pend d'Oreilles ever had. The stories of battles led by him against Indian foes would fill a volume. As this aged warrior was well known to the old settlers of Missoula county, I feel tempted to give one of his stories, which was related to the writer in front of a blazing camp fire some years before his death, and which was noted down almost word for word as repeated from his lips by the interpreter.

Story of Big Canoe.

Many snows ago, when I was a boy, and while Joseph or "Celp-Stop" (Crazy Country) was head chief of the Pend d'Oreilles, I was one of a large hunting and war party who left the place where the white men call Missoula, for the purpose of killing buffalo and stealing horses in our enemies' country. We (the Flathead and Pen d'Oreilles) were at war with the Blackfeet, the Crows the Sioux, the Snakes and the Gros Ventres. The Nez Percies were our allies and friends and assisted us to fight those tribes.

While encamped in the Crow country Big Smoke, one of the bravest war chiefs of the Pen d'Oreilles, discovered Crow signs, and taking a party of his braves with him, followed upon the trail. The Crow camp was soon discovered, and, as Big Smoke started out more to get horses than to secure scalps, informed his warriors that he did not intend to attack the small party of Crows, who were now at his mercy, as the Pen d'Oreilles and Flatheads had crept upon their camp undiscovered, and the Crows were resting in fancied security, their horses grazing upon the pleasant slopes unguarded, while the old

Salish Chief Big Canoe
Drawing by Gustavus Sohon, Photograph 1918.114.9.35,
Washington State Historical Society, Tacoma, Washington.

warriors lolled about the camp smoking their pipes, and the young men were engaged in the wild sports and rude game[s] practiced among the tribe.

The announcement that we were not to have a fight was received with great marks of disfavor by our braves, and, as I was a young man and had not as yet taken my first scalp, I could not restrain myself, but cried like a woman. Big Smoke was known to be the bravest man in the tribe and no one of us dared impute his action to cowardise, and we therefore acquiesced in his plans, and when night came silently and cautiously we ran off the whole band of Crow horses and left our enemies on foot. We soon found our main encampment and the horses were divided up. One particular fine black horse was given to our head chief. The day after our return the chief announced to us that our powder and lead was nearly exhausted, and as there was no way of procuring any without going to the Crow trading post, asked if there was any of his warriors brave enough to undertake the feat.

Alexander, or Tem-Keth-tasme, which means No Horse, who afterwards succeeded Joseph as chief, and who was then a young warrior and burning to distinguish himself, immediately volunteered, and disguising himself as a Crow, after darkness came on, set out on his perilous journey. Arriving at the Crow stockade, he was immediately admitted by the trader, and was at once discovered to be a Pend d'Oreille by a Crow who was lounging about the post. Word was sent to the Crow camp that an enemy was in the stockade, and soon a loud demand was heard at the gate for admittance. The gate was opened and a single Indian was admitted. He was a tall, noble-looking fellow, dressed in the full war costume of a Crow brave. Halting immediately in front of Alexander, he reached out his hand and cordially grasped the hand of the Pend d'Oreille. "Canoe man you are brave. You have come among your enemies to purchase powder and lead. You are dead but still you live. I am Red Owl. Your warriors stole into my camp; they took my horses; they were strong, but stole upon us while we were unaware and spared the lives of my band. Canoe-man on that night I lost my war horse — a black horse with two holes bored in his ears. He was my fathers gift to me. Is there such a horse in your camp?["] Alexander replied that such a horse was given to his chief by Big Smoke after the capture. "Red Owl will go back with you into his enemies camp," and striding out of the stockade he harangued, and then picking out twenty of his braves desired them to accompany him. Alexander was then allowed to make his purchases and on the next morning accompanied by Red Owl and twenty of his warriors set out for the Pend d'Oreille camp.

When arriving there the Indians were astonished to behold their trusted brave, Alexander, leading the Crow warriors armed to the teeth, up to the lodge of their chief, who was soon surrounded by his brave Pend d'Oreilles in such overwhelming numbers that there was no escape or even hope to escape for the Crows. Red Owl dismounted and asked Alexander which was his chief. The person being pointed out Red Owl addressed him: "Chief of the Canoe Indians, your braves captured a band of horses from my people. Among them was my war [horse], and I love him for he was the gift of my father. I desire the horse and have brought you as good to replace him." Our chief, who did not like to part with the horse, and who perfectly knew the advantage he possessed, bent his head in silence. Red Owl repeated his speech, but our chief gave no reply but stood in stolid silence. "Chief of the Pend d'Oreilles," exclaimed Red Owl, "twice have I spoken to you, and you gave me no answer. I repeat it again for the third time!" We were listesing [sic] to the conversation, continued Big Canoe, and as young as I was; I could not but admire the brave Crow; surrounded as he was with his followers by implacable enemies, only awaiting the signal to begin the slaughter. But the brave bearing of the Crow, and his indifferent manner won the respect of us all, and we could not help but admire him; and to such an extent did this feeling prevail that a murmur of applause went around when the Crow concluded his last sentence. Straightening himself up to his full height, the Crow continued turning to us: "Pen d'Oreilles, you have heard me address your chief; he gave me no answer; he buried his head low; he changed his color; this the subterfuge of a woman. Pend d'Oreilles, your chief is a woman; I give him my horse!" And mounting at the head of his band he rode from our camp and not one movement was made to stay his progress. So overwhelmed was our chief with confusion that he gave no orders, and Red Owl, with his followers, returned safe to his camp.

Document 43

Fight Between the Pend d'Oreille and Bannack Indians in the Bannack, Montana, Area October 29, 1864

Source: "Two Notches on a Pilgrim's Staff," *The Montana Post* (Virginia City, Mont.), Oct. 29, 1864, page 1, c. 4.

Editors' note: It is quite likely that the author of this article witnessed a fight between the Bannack and Pend d'Oreille in the Bannack, Montana, area in 1864, but it is hard to tell where the observations end and the color begins. The account needs to be used with care and caution.

Two Notches on a 'Pilgrim's Staff.'
Notch No. 2 — The Indian Fight.

After many minor incidents of travel had been observed and registered in the office of "the warder of the brain," I began to think that the last stage of the route would be almost eventless, but I was soon undeceived. Arrived at the Junction, where the road forks, one leading to Bannack, and one to Virginia, we camped at a small creek fringed with willows, from which it derives its name. Our fire was made, bread baking, and that ever delightful operation, dish-washing, fairly under way, when two men rode up to the camp, and asked if we had been to see the Indian fight. The question seemed so odd, that we naturally sought an explanation, and were told that portions of two tribes, the Bannacks and Pen d'Oreilles were actually engaged in hot (Indian thermometre) conflict, about a mile off. Out came rifles and pistols, and away went our folks to see the scrimmage. The sun was near the setting when we started, and we found that the distance was a prairie mile, but at last we reached the ground and looked round for the combatants. By the aid of an older settler, that is to say, a man who had been there a half an hour, we discovered the following hostile operations: Every now and then, a puff of white smoke would burst from a clump of willows at the foot of a hill, on which were lariated some Indian ponies. Around three sides of this clump, rode a band of Indians at full speed, without any regularity. As each came to a favorable spot, he let fly with his rifle among the willows and received a return without any harm being done. The horsemanship was splendid, the yelling terrific, but the fighting a burlesque.

Eight of the Pen d'Oreilles had made a raid into the Bannack territory, with a view of recuperating their stock of horses, and lifting a little hair of the

Bannacks, if possible. Happening to obviate one gentleman of the Bannack persuasion they shot and scalped him, taking his rifle and horse. This being found out, the Bannacks started in pursuit, and had corraled the enemy in the bushes aforesaid, yet though the Bannacks were fifty, and the Pen d'Oreilles eight, not once did they even think of a charge. The noble savage is a coward at heart. Like a cat, he will spring on his prey, but, unless the odds are on his side, no Indian ever thinks of attacking an enemy. The whites took the matter as good sport, walked about, criticising the shooting, mode of warfare, &c., without interfering. It was evident that the Bannacks were no match for their opponents, for though six to one in number, they continued their circuituous operations until dark, and then off went the Pen d'Oreilles. We have heard of Yankee bargains, and tough ones at that, but we saw an instance of the "dollar fever" here that completely put everything else in the shade.

The Pen d'Oreilles, having possession of a scalp, was all the trouble; otherwise they would not have been attacked by the Bannacks, who have a wholesome dread of their superior prowess. A Yankee on the ground [sic] hearing of the *casus belli,* was immediately struck with the idea that a trade might be made, and so off, he started for the Pen d'Oreille lodgment, and offered an ounce of gold for the scalp, but he failed to get it for that or any other price. On being asked what he wanted with so disgusting an object, he replied that he "cac'lated them Ingens would give a good many poneys for that bit of har,["] if he could only manage to buy it. During the fight, both sides appealed to the whites for aid, and deprecated the affording any assistance to their adversaries.

The party in charge of the wagon was wondering when we intended to go back, when a long train of red cavalry appeared, howling lamentably, precisely as the keeners at an Irish wake or funeral. Not being posted on the variation of yells, the gentlemen thought that his hair was about undergoing some surgical operation, and felt accordingly. The howling company passed on, and were followed by a band of warriors, who surrounded the wagon with exclamations of "tabbak," "hiskeet," &c., and being attended to, departed. Two or three Bannacks were wounded, and one, on the next day, showed us a ball which had entered the stock of his gun between the heal plate and the butt and remained imbedded in the wood. His gun was presented in the act of firing, so his escape was a pretty close one. The Pen d'Oreilles, had two wounded, but bore off the scalp in triumph. Ten horsemen could have swept the Pen d'Oreilles from the face of the earth in half as many minutes.

When our party awoke in the morning, we were surrounded by Bannacks — "Good Injins," "no steal hoss," &c., who fed with an appetite not affected by the loss of the scalp on the preceding day. Powder, ball, and caps were what they wanted, and having obtained a supply in exchange for mountain sheep meat and dressed deer skins, they retreated to their mountain fastness and we bowled along to Virginia.

Chapter 5

Documents of
Salish and Pend d'Oreille History
Between 1865 and 1869

Document 44

Bitterroot Salish Chiefs Petition
Montana Governor
April 25, 1865

Source: Victor, et. al., to Chief of the Whites, Virginia, M. T., Apr. 25, 1865, Sidney Edgerton Family Papers, MC 26, Montana Historical Society Archives, Helena, box 1, folder 8.

Editors' note: This letter from Victor and the other Bitterroot Salish chiefs to the Montana Governor stated their concerns about not wanting to move from the Bitterroot Valley despite the 1855 Hellgate Treaty. They also wrote of their efforts to keep the peace notwithstanding horse raiders stealing both Indian and white owned horses. Their final plea was for the white authorities to stop the sale of whiskey to young tribal members. It is not known who actually wrote the letter, but presumably the writer was expressing the concerns of the Salish chiefs who signed it.

The chief of the flatheads to the Chief of the whites, Virginia, Montana Ty.

Four horses have been Stolen by some of our young men, but I cannot find them in the camp. Therefore I, Victor the chief, Send you four horses of our own to pay for; and I the Chief Send to you the Chief of the whites a horse of mine, which I present you with for yourself.

I Send back also five oxen found, not stolen by our men, far below the Marias. You will see to whom do they belong.

Last Summer we had been requested of four horses stolen. I, Victor, found them out and delivered them to Mr Thomas Harris, a white Settler of this our valley, to be Kept for the right owner, who can recover them addressing themselves to him. One of the horses died.

Now I address myself to you the Great Chief of the whites of this country. Some of the big men among the white Settlers in this our land spoke to send us away from our country. This thing vexed a great deal me, and all the other Chiefs, and all my children. I, Victor, therefore do Send you the horse above mentioned to pray you to take pity on us, and to put an end to Such talkings, and to Stop the whites from building themselves houses in our own land guaranteed to us by treaty. We are almost given to despondency seeing every day new houses started up, and farms taken by whites in our land. We got this spring Some ploughs from Government, and we are all busy, and in great earnest to make ourselves fields; but after a little while there will be no more room for us in our own country, if you do not Stop the whites.

Tell the Snake indians to come no more to steal our horses. We have always been good friends to them, and we are glad that they come to see us, but not to steal horses.

I, Victor, Spoke already to my children not to go to war. But you must tell your white children to give nothing to eat to these warriors or horse stealers both Snakes, or Flatheads, but to let them Starve. Though our boys go not much to war, but other indians of other tribes go, and say to the whites that they are Flatheads, because we are good friends of the whites.

The last favor that I and all my fellow-Chiefs beg from you, is, that you would give order to the whites Settled in our valley to Sell no Wisky to our boys, who go to buy it against our will. I, Victor, an old man already, I could not Sleep all the winter, because the whites and indians, both drunk, were always fighting in the camp. My heart was broken Seeing the whites compelling by force our boys and girls, young men and women to drink, you Know for what purpose.

I. Victor, I think I fall not short of my duty towards the Whites; Therefore I hope you will take into consideration my words, I have done.

From the Flathead camp in Bitterroot Valley, Apr. the 25th 1865th

+Victor the Chief of the Flatheads.

+ Ambroise a chief

+ Moys a chief

+ Adolphe a chief

+ Fidel a chief

+ Harry a chief

Document 45

Salish Chief Victor Visits Helena

August 11, 1866

Source: "Victor," *The Rocky Mountain Gazette* (Helena, Mont.), Aug. 11, 1866, page 3, col. 1.

Editors' note: Salish chiefs were prominent figures in early Montana and were celebrated as allies of the white men against hostile tribes.

"Victor," the Head Chief of the Flat Head Nation, passed through Helena last Thursday. He was welcomed by many old residents, who have well and favorably known him for years. He is the bosom friend of the Pioneer Missionary, Rev. Father [Pierre] De Smet, who has honored the old and friendly Chief, by making his portrait a prominent feature in the frontispiece of his valuable work entitled "Oregon Missions," "Victor," with a large number of his tribe, was returning from the usual spring hunt in the buffalo country. Their animals were well loaded with meat and robes, and were in good condition, and the natives in fine spirits. They have large herds in the Bitter Root Valley, and flourishing farms. Chief "Victor" is worth his thousands, and receives a regular salary from the government of five hundred dollars per annum.

Document 46

Flathead Agent Accounts for Shortages in Annuity Goods
October 28, 1866

Source: Aug. H. Chapman, U.S. Ind. Agt., Office Flathead Ind. Agency, M.T., to D. N. Cooley, Commissioner of Indian Affairs, Washington, D.C., Oct. 28, 1866, U.S. Office of Indian Affairs, "Letters Received by the Office of Indian Affairs, 1824-1880," National Archives Microfilm Publication M234, reel 488, fr. 325-333.

Editors' note: Chapman may have magnified his role in the talks with Big Canoe and other tribal leaders, but his letter is interesting. Chapman made a detailed argument that the government seriously mismanaged and shorted the Salish and Kootenai Indians on the annuities promised in the 1855 Hellgate Treaty. The letter was marked "Finance??" and "File," so presumably Chapman never got a reply to the letter.

Flathead Indian Agency
Montana Territory
Oct. 28" 1866.

Sir,

Your favor of July 23d with Statement of account of Confederate Flathead Indians, for beneficial purposes came to hand in due season; for which please accept thanks.

When I assumed charge of these Indians, I found great dissatisfaction existing among them on account of their beneficial fund. They claimed that there was a large amount due them, and former Agents [John] Owen and [Charles W.] Hutchins both assured me that such was the case; but there was not a single book or paper left in this office, relating to the business of this Agency or the Indians under my charge; by either Agents, Owen or Hutchins. I found it a hard task to investigate this matter, and could not possibly have done so without the Statement you forwarded me, and the help of former Agent John Owen, who kindly rendered me every assistance in his power.

Your Statement forwarded me shows a balance due these Indians for beneficial purposes of $1,180^{99}/100 while the Statement which I enclose you, shows there is a balance due them up to this date of $30,793.50. This is a pretty large difference; yet I feel very confident that when the whole account is thoroughly investigated in your office, my statement will be found correct in every particular.

In your account of disbursements made for the benefit of Flathead Indians, you charge them with $5240²¹/₁₀₀ remitted to Agent Owen. While in Washington prior to my starting to this Agency, I was informed that this amount was allowed Maj. Owen in the settlement of his account for cattle, which he had purchased and issued to the Indians. This, Major Owen informs me is the case, but as the cattle were purchased with funds remitted to Supt. E. R. Geary July 18" 1860, and by Geary paid to Owens; it is wrong to charge them with that amount, as the money was charged to them, when remitted to Supt. Geary; and when expended for cattle was charged to them again — a moments reflection will show you that this is an error, and a way of keeping accounts that is not very advantageous to the Indians, and should be rectified. I have charged them in my Statement of disbursements with amount paid John Creighton, which was for two different lots of cattle bought by Maj Owen of Creighton for these Indians, and for which he (Owen) issued Creighton certified Vouchers, which were paid in Washington. These Vouchers amounted to $4,550 and of course should be charged to these Indians.

Again in your Statement of disbursements you charge them with paid Buckley, Sheldon & Co. April 23" 1866 $829⁶²/₁₀₀. now if any such bill was bought of this firm for these Indians, of that date, I never received the Invoice of the goods purchased or the goods; but I did receive a bill of goods bought of this firm for these Indians March 19" 1866 amounting to 3030⁰⁰/₁₀₀. I have accordingly omitted the first amount in my Statement of disbursements and charged the latter amount, making a difference in favor of the Government of $2200³⁸/₁₀₀. In all other items I believe your Statement of disbursements is correct in every particular.

In your Statement of appropriations you fail to credit these Indians with Annuity goods and Stock sold by Agent Owen, to pay charges for transportation. The 5th Article of the treaty with these Indians expressly stipulates, "that all the expenditures and expenses contemplated in this Article of this treaty, shall be defrayed by the United States, and shall not be deducted from the Annuities agreed to be paid to said tribes; nor shall the cost of transporting the goods for the Annuity payment be a charge upon the Annuities, but shall be defrayed by the United States," consequently, if Maj Owen sold Annuity goods and stock belonging to these Indians, to pay for transportation, the amount sold $15,359⁴⁸/₁₀₀ is due and should be refunded to them. I have accordingly credited them with that amount in my Statement, which I enclose you; and respectfully refer you to the enclosed Statement of former Agent Owen, and to his Abstract

"N" of sales, dated June 30" 1862 which is on file in your office. I think this whole matter is so plain, and the justness of refunding this amount to these Indians so apparent to any one, that there cannot be a moments hesitation in allowing this credit on your books.

There was remitted to Supt Geary $5981^{20}/100 for beneficial purposes for these Indians (July 18" 1860) and to Supt. [B. F.] Kendall Aug. 2nd 1861 $5000 for same purpose, making a total of $10981^{20}/100; both of these amounts were paid over to Maj. Owen and by him expended as follows: $5950 was expended for cattle, which were issued to these Indians, and the balance of $5031^{20}/xx was used by him for other purposes than that for which it was designed; I have accordingly credited these Indians with that amount in enclosed Statement. By referring to Maj. Owens Abstract "B" of Disbursements, dated June 30" 1862, and to enclosed Statement from him, I think this whole matter will be explained so satisfactorily, that there will not be a moments hesitation on your part, in regard to allowing the amount to be credited to these Indians on your books. Maj. Owen informed me that he used this money by order of Supt. Geary, with the understanding, that it should be refunded as soon as he (Geary) received funds for contingent expenses.

Maj. Owen also issued to the "Bannacks" & "Snakes" Indians, Annuity goods belonging to the Flatheads amounting to $2431^{76}/100, this he done on the order of Supt. Geary. (I have seen the order in Maj. Owen's Office, also a letter from Supt Geary, approving of the issue after it had been made). Of course there can be no difference of opinion in regard to this matter; every one is bound to admit, that if Maj. Owen issued to Bannack and Snake Indians by order of his Superintendent, Annuity goods belonging to Flatheads, amounting to the above named sum, that the Flatheads are entitled to a credit for the same. I have accordingly credited them with that amount in enclosed statement. I enclose copy of invoice of goods so issued, and would again refer you to enclosed Statement of Maj. Owen.

Agent Hutchins informed me that he sold eight Annuity plows belonging to these Indians for $30 each amounting to $240, this he done by order of Supt. [Sidney] Edgerton (I have seen the order). Of course this amount Should be credited to these Indians, and I have so credited it in enclosed statement.

These Indians should also be credited with the gold premium on all monies expended for them, since the passage of the law providing that their Annuity goods should be furnished them at gold premium prices.

At the time of making the treaty with these Indians Governor [Isaac] Stevens, made them the most extravagant promises in regard to what the Government would do for them and raised expectations in their mind that can never be realized. This of itself would create great dissatisfaction among them, and when the Government comes so far short in complying with the provisions of the treaty, it is no wonder that they feel to have been badly treated by the Government. Were they not the kindest disposed Indians belonging to the Indian Department, there would have been serious trouble with them long since.

The entire population of the three tribes were present at the Agency when I issued them their Annuity goods in September last. I had many long talks with the chiefs and head-men of the Nation in regard to the grievances which they complain of. They say the Govt and white traders have furnished their enemies the "Bloods" "Piegans" and "Blackfeet" arms and amunition in large quantities, and that it is very dangerous for them to go to the Buffalo grounds to hunt; that the above named tribes of Indians are their enemies, and always have been, and have killed about 50 warriors belonging to the Flathead Nation during the past 12 months (this is true) and that they will have to abandon the Buffalo grounds, and rely on tilling the soil for their future subsistence. They are poor, and need ox-teams to break their ground, haul their rails and lumber; they need stock-cattle; Agricultural and other tools and implements, and especially plows, harness, wagons, and seeds; and if these are not furnished them, they might as well give up. Unless the Government assists them, they will all, or nearly all starve. This is all true, you can form no idea of the poverty of a large portion of two of these tribes, and of their utter inability to get a proper start in the world, that is in agricultural pursuits. Something will have to be done for them and that at once; their necessities are such that delay is death to them. Could you have been present at their interviews with me, and heard them talk of their grievances and sufferings, you would have pitied them from the bottom of your heart, and blushed that the Govt had treated them in such bad faith — said "Big Canoe" (a Pend d'Oreille chief) to me, "Why is it that the Government arms our enemies the "Bloods," Piegans" and "Blackfeet"? They kill us, and the whites, with these same arms and amunition on all occasions. Why don't the Government furnish *us* arms and amunition? we are the friends of the white man. no white man's blood has ever been shed by any one belonging to either of our three tribes — we always fight for, and with the whites. the foes of the Government as [are] also our enemies. we have no arms or means of self-defence except bows and arrows (they have but few guns, and those of the poorest quality) we now have to go to the Buffalo grounds or starve, and are at the mercy of our enemies when we get there — this may be the last time you will ever see me, and I appeal to you as our chief, to ask our great father to help us. We are now willing to work; get us seed, stock, harness, Oxen, wagons, and farming and other tools, and see what we can do. pay our head chiefs what is due them, make them their homes as the treaty promises, start our agricultural and industrial school, give our youths opportunities to learn trades at your shops, have your men learn us how to build houses, fence and break ground and till our lands, pay us what is due us, regular and then if we don't prosper , we will not complain of anyone."

I promised them that their accounts should be investigated at once, that the Government would do them full justice in every thing, that my employees and myself would do all we could to assist them, but they say that they have had so many promises, that they have no longer any faith in them, but that they will trust me this time, for they believe me to be their friend, but if disappointed now, that they will never have any faith again in the promises of a white man. Now there is too much truth in what they say, and everything should be done for them, that can be at an early a day as possible.

If on investigation there is the amount due them that I claim, the amount will be amply sufficient to relieve all their necessities, and give them a fair start in the world. That is, if it is judiciously expended; and I appeal to you as the head of the Indian Department to have their acts investigated at once, and full justice done them in this matter. Will you please attend to this for them and when through write me the result and the exact amount due them, so that I may make my estimates in season, for the articles they need to be shipped me by the first boat that leaves St. Louis for Fort Benton next spring.

I have a large amount of seeds, raised on the Agency farm, to issue to them; and the beneficial fund I have in my hands will enable me to purchase more if needed, and other articles that they cannot wait for. A breaking team and plow should be purchased and put in operation for each of the three tribes at an early day. I can furnish wagons, such as they are, until others can be provided, and promise you, on my part, that if properly assisted, and that in time — that I will have all three of the tribes in a comfortable situation in twelve months, and in a position that they can live independent of the Buffalo, in two years. Please ship no Annuity goods to me for these Indians until my estimate approved by my Superintendent is forwarded you.

Respectfully
Your Obt Svt
Aug. H. Chapman
U.S. Ind. Agent

Hon. D. N. Cool[e]y
Commr of Ind Affs
Washington
D.C.

Document 47

Missoula Flour Mill Grinds Indian Wheat; Visit with Salish Chief Victor and Delaware Jim December 12, 1866

Source: Philip Ritz, "Journal of an Overland Trip to the Atlantic States," *Walla Walla Statesman* (Walla Walla, Wash.), Jan. 18, 1867, page 1, c. 3-4.

Editors' note: Ritz described a Missoula flour mill grinding Indian grown wheat into flour for Indian buffalo hunters. Ritz also included some useful personal information about Salish Chief Victor and Delaware Jim. Ritz was a promoter and entrepreneur for the Walla Walla settlement in Washington Territory.

Journal of an Overland Trip to the Atlantic States.

Hell Gate, M.T., Dec. 12, 1866.

Editor Statesman: — Having got through with business, I will start for Washington tomorrow via Virginia City. We have the new machinery mostly in the mill and will be ready to commence operating in a few days. We have about 12,000 bushels of wheat to grind this season yet.

It is rather a novel sight to see a flouring mill in operation in so wild a looking place as this, and surrounded by Indian wigwams. The Indian trade is no inconsiderable item here; the Indians in some instances, bring their wheat some 200 miles with their packs on their horses, when on their way to hunt buffalo, to get flour to take with them.

When in Bitter Root Valley, I had a talk with "Victor," the head chief of the Flat Head nation. He is some 68 or 69 years old and has lived on the same place most of his life. He was 6 or 7 year old when Lewis and Clark wintered on this very spot in 1804 — 62 years ago. He recollects distinctly all the particulars, and how the Indians were frightened, and how they came flocking in from all directions to see the strange men, they being the first white men these Indians had ever seen. There is another rather noted Indian here, "Delaware Jim." He is of the Delaware nation. His father is a noted chief of the Delawares, in Kansas, and has recently found out where Jim is and has written him to come back and see them. Jim told me he was going to the States next season to see his people. Jim is quite a farmer; some of his white neighbors have went as far as 35 miles to get wheat from him for seed, paying $4 per bushel, when they sold their own for $3. Jim's word is considered as good as any man's note. I sold him a bill of goods on short credit, and found him very prompt in making payment.

There are a great many Rocky Mountain sheep around this Valley. Their flesh is most delicious, resembling antelope. They are very readily tamed when taken young, and are the most affectionate and interesting animal that I ever saw. One that I saw in the upper part of this Valley, was constantly amusing itself by jumping on top of the house, walking on the very verge, or on top of the chimney or some other place where it seems almost impossible for an animal to balance itself. At night it would always select a small niche some 5 feet from the ground beside the chimney. It is a timid animal; when feeding from the house at a distance, if it would hear the howl of a wolf it would run to the house, and if the door was open rush in under the bed.

—— —— —— —— ——

Cottonwood, Deer Lodge Valley,
Dec. 16, 1866.

Arrived here to-day, horse back, and will take the stage in the morning for Virginia City, 120 miles. This little Valley is nestled down just along the West base of the Rocky Mountains.

The weather is delightful; no snow, the ground froze solid and the road dusty. This has been a noted wintering place for the buffalo from time immemorial till within two or three years. I never could understand before I came here, how the winters could be so mild away up in latitude 47, and within 4 miles of the summit of the Rocky Mountains. But as soon as I crossed the Hell Gate River and turned South up the Deer Lodge, and felt that warm familiar breeze that we call the "Chinook," at Walla Walla, I comprehended it all in a moment. It is the same and produced by the same natural laws that causes the trade winds on the Pacific, and that warms up the whole North Pacific coast. The earth in its rapid revolutions from West to East, causes a spiral current of air on the West side of each prominant ridge or chain. This current accumulating at the Equator, the highest point of the earth, flows rapidly down towards the North pole, as water would seek its level, carrying a current of heated air from the Gulf and the heated sands of Mexico, along the Western base of the Rocky and Blue Mountains, and the mountains that skirt the Pacific coast, warming up the atmosphere as far North as the 60th parallel of North latitude. Any one who will examine an isothermal chart of the American Continent, will observe that as soon as the lines cross a range of mountains Westward, they suddenly indicate a much warmer temperature.

—— —— —— —— ——

Virginia City, M.T., Dec. 18, 1866.

Arrived here this evening and start in the morning for Salt Lake. Crossed the summit last evening, the weather beautiful; not a particle of snow and road dusty all the way to Virginia. The summit at this place is a low pass, a valley 3 or 4 miles wide and covered with splendid grass. In fact, the whole mountain for a long distance is covered with good grass.

—— —— —— —— ——

Pleasant Valley, I. T.,
85 miles South of Virginia,
Dec. 21st, 1866.

Since leaving Virginia we have crossed the main range of the Rocky Mountains, and have been detained here 36 hours in a most terrific storm. We are now just starting out to shovel out the coach and try and make another start.

—— —— —— —— ——

Pleasant Valley, Dec. 23, 1866.

We are still lying by here waiting on this miserable Company to open the road, which there was no necessity at all in allowing to be closed. There was not even a sled nor a shovel on the mountain when we came here. It would not have required one-half the exertion to have kept it open that it took to keep the road open over the Blue Mountains last winter. Henry Meacham is worth more to keep a mountain road open in the winter, than any dozen men I have seen belonging to this Company.

Besides, after getting a lot of passengers together at their stand (they own all stations on the road) the landlord told us the custom of the Company was to charge $2 for the first meal (as that is the price charged for a single meal at all their stations) and then $1 for all subsequent meals, as long as the passengers were compelled to lay over; but when we came to settle our bills he said they had new instructions to charge $2 for all meals, and poor grub it was at that. I hope all Walla Wallaians and all others who can will avoid this miserable route. Nor have I seen the least disposition to treat passengers with proper courtesy and respect; on the contrary, I have seen some treated with meanness and insolence that was really shameful.

The more I see of Montana the more I like it. You may rest assured that it is one of the richest mining countries ever discovered. There are almost innumerable ledges here that are all the way from fair to immensely rich. Besides, it is such a magnificent grazing country, with timber, water and sufficient arable land to render the Territory self-sustaining within a very short time. The trade from Montana during the next five years will be immense, and you can depend positively on getting the greatest share for the Pacific side, if you will only make the proper exertion.

My theory is, merchandise to be bought to advantage must be bought in the eastern cities of the manufacturers. It will cost $23 per ton to Portland, or

$70 to the Mississippi; and it can certainly be taken from Portland into the mines as cheaply as from the Mississippi, with the advantage of replenishing three times from the Pacific in one season, which can be done only once from the other side.

— — — — —

Crossing of Bear River.
85 miles North of Salt Lake City,
Dec. 29, 1866.

We have finally succeeded in getting out of the snow; were 8 days in making 14 miles. Some days we would make but 1½ miles; once we left our baggage and treasure in the snow some 36 hours. The second night I hired a man to go back with me and sleep by it. It was Christmas night, one of the coldest nights I ever experienced. We dug a pit in the snow over three feet deep and spread down our blankets. After getting warm we slept quite comfortable till morning. Some of the passengers froze their feet considerably that night in walking back to Pleasant Valley; the distance is six miles but it took them from 11 o'clock at night till 7 the next morning. Yesterday noon we passed Port Neuf Canon. The spot was pointed out to me where those brave men were murdered so inhumanly for their money, by the road agents two years ago. Most of those wretches have already paid the penalty with their worthless lives. The driver, Frank Williams, who drove the unsuspecting men into the snare, is, it is thought, to be in Texas. I hope vengeance will never sleep until he is caught and shared the fate of his comrades.

Sunday, Dec. 29th. 1866

We had a beautiful drive down Salt Lake Valley along the shore of the lake to the city, passing a number of pleasant villages on the route.

— — — — —

Salt Lake City, Dec. 30th, 1866.

Spent the day in looking around the town and in taking some notes and dimensions of the Tabernacle and Temple, which, when completed, will not be excelled, in some respects, on the American continent. I have secured five pictures of the city, and of most of the public buildings, which I will take back to Walla Walla with me. Will send you a full description in my next. I take the stage in the morning again over the mountains for the Missouri River, 1500 miles; expect to be twelve days and nights in making the trip.

Yours,
Philip Ritz.

Document 48

Bitterroot Salish Chief Moese Dying on Return from Buffalo
May 9, 1867

Source: "A Native Patriarch Near the End of His Trail," *The Helena Weekly Herald*, May 9, 1867, page 3, c. 2.

Editors' note: Bitterroot Salish Chief Moese was a noted and important personage in early Montana. Newspaper articles such as this one give important clues to his life story.

A Native Patriarch Near the End of His Trail

Mo-ese, head war chief of the Flatheads, is now lying in his tent, in this city, in a helpless condition — the effect of old age and general decay. Over his head nearly a thousand moons have waned. It is his proudest boast — and although we can scarcely credit so much good of any Indian or tribe of them, old white settlers say it is well founded — that, as a leader on a hundred bloody fields, he never personally witnessed the shedding of a drop of the white man's blood, and that none of his people, in carrying out tribal measures, were ever known to lift the tomahawk against him. When Lewis and Clark arrived in these mountains, in the second year of Jefferson's Presidential life, Mo-ese was old enough to run buffalo. Prior to that time, he says, the reports the Blackfeet [i.e., Flatheads] had heard concerning the pale faces, were vague and bordering on the superstitious; but, as the "big canoe captains" camped with them many days, treating them kindly and giving them many presents, a familiarity sprang up which dispelled these vagaries, and resulted in a friendship which the vicissitudes of sixty summers have not shaken. Mo-ese led his party, old as he is, (the cause of his prostration,) in their late skirmish with the Blackfeet on the Muscleshell, when his ancient enemies, though in overwhelming numbers, were badly whipped. But the old warrior has fought his last battle, and is near the end of the trail that leads to "the happy hunting grounds;" with his family around him, and rich in flocks and herds, his way is cheered by the consoling faith of the Cross, the love and loyalty of all his own people, and the friendship and respect of many good white men. There are only three other Indians who remember the advent of Lewis and Clark.

Salish Chief Moiese
Drawing by Gustavus Sohon, NAA INV 08502400, National
Anthropological Archives, Smithsonian Institution, Washington, D.C.

Document 49

Flathead Agent John W. Wells Meets with Bitterroot Salish Chiefs
June 6-7, 1867

Source: John W. Wells, U.S. Indian Agent, Flathead Indian Agency, M.T., to A. G. Taylor, Commissioner of Indian Affairs, Washington, D.C., June 14, 1867, U.S. Office of Indian Affairs, "Letters Received by the Office of Indian Affairs, 1824-1880," National Archives Microfilm Publication M234, reel 488, fr. 561-564; "From Missoula," *The Tri-Weekly Post* (Virginia City and Helena, Mont.), July 2, 1867, p. 2, c. 3.

Editors' note: Well's letter does not say what was discussed in his council with the Bitterroot Salish Indians. It is interesting that in middle May he could not hold the meeting because the Salish were busy plowing and sowing their fields. The newspaper report on the council gives some detail about what the Salish wished to discuss and included a very negative evaluation of Wells as agent.

Flathead Indian Agency, M.T.
June 14th, 1867.

Sir,

I have the honor respectfully to inform you that I visited the Flathead tribe belonging to this Agency, on the 14th. Ulto. at their residence in the Bitter Root Valley near Fort Owen, about 54 miles from the Agency proper.

My object in making this visit to the Flatheads, was principally to make their acquaintance, and have them appoint a day when I should hold a business council with them; as, like myself, I told them, I found many ploughing and sowing and a future day for the council would suit us both, better than at the present time.

I remained there two days, and they, after a very agreeable interview we had together, appointed (that day 3 weeks), Thursday the 6th. of June ensuing, as the day upon which my first business council should be held with them, to which I readily assented.

Accordingly, on the 6th. instant, at 20 minutes past 2 P.M. we met at the same place, in a large tent, capable of holding 100 persons which the Flathead Chief, Victor, had caused to be erected, and prepared, for our accommodation:

the centre being surmounted with the Old Flag, which imparted to the rude scene, a cheery, and enlivening appearance.

There were present at the council, Victor the Chief; Ambrose; Isaac, Adolph, Henry, and Alexander, headmen; Stanislaus a young brave who spoke: the Hon. Angus McDonald Chief Factor Hudson Bay Company; Captain Fitz Stubbs, officer of the Hudson Bay Post near the Agency proper: Judges [Charles W.] Pomeroy, and Rand of the Missoula Courts: Majr. John Owens of Fort Owen: Majr. L. L. Blake, Superintendent of Farming on the Reserve; Father Joseph Giordi, Priest and Teacher of the Flatheads: Delaware Jim, (as he is called, James Sarcoxie a son of the present Chief of the Delawares of Kansas, being his name) and Francois, Interpreters; and myself: together with about 100 Flatheads, mostly adults.

In opening the Council, I told the Indians, it was a rule of the white legislators in Washington, to open their Council house when they met for business every day, with prayer; and that we would look to our Heavenly Father now, for a blessing upon our deliberations: at the same time, asking Father Giordi to invoke a Throne of Grace. The good Father assented.

The assembled crowd, rose orderly with the venerable Priest; and then knelt down reverently upon their knees; repeating after him in their native tongue, the Lords Prayer, and the solemn audible utterances of the customary responses of their Church.

In all the continuous and lengthened business of this Council for two days, there was no subject or remark introduced by them, or myself, before us, which marred the harmony of our deliberations. Every subject was discussed in an unimpassioned manner; there were no angry utterances, and no criminations; and when the Council broke up the second day, every body seemed pleased, and glad of the occasion which convened us together.

There were two subjects, which if introduced into the Council, I thought would arouse contention and ill-feeling; and, I concluded that if they were not introduced by the Indians themselves, they should not be (by my agency at this time) brought forward for discussion; believing it to be the very best mode by which they should be disposed of, to bring them to the notice of the Indian Department, in my Reports, at the end of this month; and await your instructions in reference to them.

They are

1st – The subject of removing the Flatheads from their present location to the Agency proper; throwing the Bitter Root portion of the Reserve open to settlement, now much demanded.

2d – The subject of damages claimed by White citizens from the Flatheads for cattle killed by them.

I have therefore thought it best that I should bring those subjects before you, (with the best information I may be able to obtain) in my Reports, separately, at the close of the month current; meanwhile, contenting myself with this breif [sic] allusion to my first business council with this interesting people; producing, as it did, in my mind the most unalloyed gratification.

I have the honor to be
Very Respectfully
Your Obdt Servt,
John W. Wells,
U.S. Indian Agent.

Hon. A. G. Taylor
Commissioner of Indian Affairs,
Washington, D.C.

* * * * * *

From Missoula.

Regular Correspondence.

Pow Wow at Fort Owen — "Union" Puts in an Opinion Thereafter — The Crops, Potatoes and Politics — Mining, Milling and Merchandizing.

Editor Post: —

On the 6th and 7th inst., J. W. Wells, Esq., U.S. Indian Agent Flat Head Agency, held at Fort Owen, what he was pleased to term, a business council. Outsiders could not see the point. The Flat Heads to the number of one hundred were assembled, headed by their great chief, Victor, supported by Ambrose, Isaac, Alexander and others of lesser note. The council was opened by prayer by Rev. Father Giorda, after which Mr. Wells informed the Indians that he was ready to hear what they had to say, what business they had to transact through their great chief, Victor; that he was glad to meet them, glad to see them all looking so well. Victor arose and said, "You see my people. We see our chief. Glad to see him." Ambrose followed. Desired to know what was to be done in regard to the Stevens treaty. He said they had received nothing for it; their annuities were behind; that their best lands were all being settled upon by whites; that the present Indians were poor, not as well off as their forefathers; their lands were barren; his heart was crying, for the Indians were afraid that the trail to their hunting grounds was in danger. He desired to know where the Agent was who was not a trader; where the articles were that were promised them when the treaty was signed — they had never received them. Isaac, Adolph, Alexander and others spoke, all desiring to know the object of the council; all expressed great regret at having made the treaty with Stevens, as the Government had not complied with the terms thereof; they complained that they had been unfairly dealt with, that their best lands were being settled upon by the whites; that the tribe was very poor, and wished their Great Father to help them.

Mr. Wells closed the council by saying that he was glad to see them all looking so well, strong and fat, not sick, for which he thanked the Great Spirit; that he was a stranger to them; that he hoped to know them all in time; that their Great Father told him to send them a medicine man to see that their children were educated; that he had talked with their good Priest about it; would talk again; that he wished to do what was right with them, old and young, that he wished them to judge him by his actions not by his words; that he would do the best he could for them; that their Great Father told him to do so; that he wished to do right, advising them to do right, be good and not to be unhappy; that his ears were always open to hear what they had to say; advised them to lay their troubles before Victor and their good Priest; that Indians should not quarrel, but love one another; all men should love each other; if we do not, God will not love us; white man is Indian's brother; Indian white man's brother; Indian and white man should love each other; that he loved them and would try and do what was right towards them; that he would talk with their good Priest about all things; that he hoped the Good Being would help them all; thanked them for the good order they had kept and the kindness in which they received him, and hoped they should become better acquainted.

Thus ended the farce — it can be called nothing else — no business of any kind transacted. I have no doubt this council will be the subject of a lengthy report to the Department. These gatherings are of no use except it be to breed discontent among the Indians, and are often productive of much harm.

All are of the opinion that Mr. Wells is totally unfit for the position he holds; he may do as a clerk in the Department at Washington, but he has no tact to manage Indians in the Rocky Mountains or get along with the employees on the Agency, and the sooner he is relieved of his present duties the better will it be for all concerned. Many think him to be insane at times. He certainly acts very strange occasionally, especially when under the influence of stimulants, which I am sorry to say, is often.

The weather is fine and warm; crops look remarkably well, and unless they are destroyed by the crickets and grasshoppers, we look for a large harvest. These pests have done considerable damage in some portions of Bitter Root valley — [i]n some instances destroyed entire fields of both grain and vegetables. So far, this valley has escaped.

Politics are looking up. The unterrified Democracy have called a County Convention to be held on the 6th of July, for the purpose of nominating a county ticket and electing delegates to a Territorial Convention at Helena, July 15th. Little interest is manifested here as to who is nominated for Congress. the fight will be on County officers. Most, if not all, of the old officers will have to take a back seat. The Republicans will nominate a full County ticket, and if they select good men, have a fine chance of carrying the county.

Thompson river mines are pronounced a bilk, yet most of the original prospectors have remained there and are sanguine of success.

Business dull; money scarce; no sale for produce, of which large quantities are on hand waiting a market. Most of our flouring mills have suspended work, or are grinding only occasionally for farmers.

Yours, truly,
Union.

Missoula, June 23, 1867.

Document 50

Salish Chiefs Ambrose and Adolph Complain About Hellgate Treaty Failures August 22, 1868

Source: W. J. Cullen, Special Indian Agent, Montana Territory, Helena, Mont., to Hon. N. G. Taylor, Commissioner of Indian Affairs, Washington, D.C., Aug. 22, 1868, *Annual Report of the Commissioner of Indian Affairs* (1868), pages 676-681; "Minutes of the remarks of 'Ambrose'. . .," U.S. Office of Indian Affairs, "Letters Received by the Office of Indian Affairs, 1824-1880," National Archives Microfilm Publication M234, reel 489, fr. 306-309.

Editors' note: Cullen's report included a transcript of the remarks of Salish Chiefs Ambrose and Adolph at an August 1868 council at Fort Owen. The chiefs' remarks capture their complaints about the failure of the government to carry out its obligations under the 1855 Hellgate Treaty. They especially note that many of the annuity goods were not received and those that were received were not the farming implements and tools that they needed to develop their farms.

Helena, Montana Territory,
August 22, 1868.

Sir:

I have the honor to report, that in pursuance of my instructions from the department of the 30th April, 1868, I have visited the Flatheads, Pend d'Oreilles, and Kootenays. On account of the many complaints which I have heard from this quarter, I induced the Hon. James Tufts, acting governor and *ex officio* superintendent of Indian affairs, to accompany me on a tour of observation.

We arrived at the Flathead agency on the 10th of the present month. We found the agency situated near the head of the Jocko valley, in a very beautiful and attractive spot. The valley is about ten miles long by five or six miles wide, and is surrounded by a chain of towering snowcapped mountains. It has a good soil, well adapted to the productions of all the cereals and vegetables which can be grown in this latitude. The valley is skirted by heavy bodies of timber, affording some of as fine lumber as I have ever seen. The Jocko, a beautiful, clear mountain stream, abounding in trout, and large enough to afford a good mill privilege at all seasons of the year, meanders through the valley, affording plenty of water for all purposes.

We found the Flathead agency in charge of Special Agent A. J. McCormick [i.e., W. J. McCormick], and, I regret to say, in very bad condition. Everything looks dilapidated and seems fast going to ruin. The agency building, now occupied by the farmer, is a small frame house with only two rooms, inconvenient in every particular, and very much dilapidated. The mess-house, or boarding-house for the men, is an old log building, which was erected several years ago by Major [John] Owen, and was never designed for anything more than a mere temporary concern. The roof of this building has fallen into such a state of decay as to afford but little shelter from either rain or snow. The barn, if the venerable pile of logs which compose it may be so termed, is without roof, save a few boards very badly warped up by the sun, laid at irregular intervals. The blacksmith and carpenter shops are pretty good buildings, but the former is entirely without iron, and the latter without nails. These indispensable articles were very scarce, there not being a pound of either to be found at the agency. The grist and saw mills are good buildings, and in very fair condition of repair, but both are lying idle on account of the mill-dam having been swept away. The dam was carried away some time last summer, and has not since been rebuilt. The farm cultivated for the employés, contains something over 100 acres. They are growing this year wheat, oats, and barley, besides a variety of vegetables. Everything looks very well, but how they have managed to grow such fine crops, with the stock and the farm implements at their command, is something of a mystery. Upon taking a careful inventory of farm property we found it to consist of two yokes of work-oxen, two old worn-out horses worth about $10 each, two milch cows borrowed from the mission of St. Ignatius, 45 head of hogs and pigs, three old wagons torn apart, four old broken ploughs, together with a few antiquated hoes, picks, shovels, &c.

The agency is very much in debt, and there are loud complaints among the employés on account of the non-payment of their wages. I could find no record, letter, report, or data of any kind at the agency, by which I could determine the amount in which it is involved, but as near as I could approximate to it I should judge the total indebtedness to be something over $30,000. Most of it is in the shape of vouchers issued by the agents. Over $25,000 of this sum has been issued by Agent McCormick, who claims that he has never received any money, and that it has cost him this sum to keep up the expenses of the agency.

On account of the very unsatisfactory condition of affairs at his agency Major McCormick asked to be relieved from duty at the Flathead agency, which was promptly done by Governor Tufts, and the property turned over to

Mr. L. L. Blake, the farmer, with instructions to save the harvest immediately and then employ his men in repairing the mill-dam.

While at the agency I had my attention called to the condition of the Flathead annuity goods for the present year. These goods, consisting of 15 bales of blankets, were shipped by Major George B. Wright, agent for the Blackfeet, from Fort Benton, Montana Territory, where they were received by him. The cost of transportation from Fort Benton to the Flathead agency should not be over eight or ten cents per pound, but Major Wright, in a spirit of extended liberality, contracted these at 20 cents per pound. These goods had but recently arrived, and a very casual observation convinced us that some of the bales had been opened, as they had been sewed up with a different kind of thread from that use in putting up the packages originally. Governor Tufts and myself, in the presence of Agent McCormick, Mr. L. L. Blake, and others, proceeded to open the bales which appeared to have been meddled with, five in number, and counted the blankets. We found that the inside wrappers of these bales were missing, and that the five bales were 113 pair of blankets short of the number they should have contained. Mr. Blake testified that the goods had not been opened or disturbed in any manner since they had been received, and from his and other affidavits which we took relative to the matter I am of opinion that the blankets must have been abstracted before they reached this agency. These peculations and frauds upon the Indians should be closely looked into, and the perpetrators of them dealt with summarily. They give rise to much dissatisfaction and complaint among the Indians, many of whom know very well what amount of annuities they should receive. Besides, rumor, with her thousand tongues, is sure to spread anything of this kind far and wide, and magnify it a thousand fold. There were a number of charges of fraud in the disposition of Indian goods, property, &c., which came to my ears during my stay at the agency, but the proof not being in my possession I shall refrain from mentioning them in detail at present.

With regard to this agency I may say further, before leaving this part of my report, that there never has been any hospital built or agricultural school established, as provided by the treaty. There is no physician residing at the agency, but there is one at Missoula Mills, 25 miles away, under pay as Indian physician.

Pend d'Oreilles and Kootenays.

On the 12th instant, in company with Rev. Fathers [Lawrence] Palladino and Van Zaio [James Vanzina?], of the St. Ignatius mission, who kindly came to accompany me, I started on a visit to their mission and to the Pend d'Oreilles and Kootenays, who are located there. The mission is situated in the St. Ignatius

Ambrose (in baptism)

Adolphe (in baptism)

Top: Salish Chief Ambrose
Bottom: Salish Chief Adolphe
Drawings by Gustavus Sohon, NAA INV 08502000 and 08502500.
National Anthropological Archives, Smithsonian Institution,
Washington, D.C.

valley, about 15 miles from the Flathead agency. It was founded in 1844 by Father P. J. DeSmet, the veteran missionary of the Rocky mountains, and has been instrumental in doing much good among the Indians. At present the mission is in charge of Fathers Palladino and Van Zaio, who are assisted in their labors by four sisters of charity and several lay brethren. The mission consists of a large fame church, a large log school-house, dwelling-houses for the clergy, a grist and saw mill, shops for the mechanics, &c., surrounded by a great number of Indian houses. These latter are built of logs, and seem to be well tenanted. The Pend d'Oreilles who reside here number 895 souls, and the Kootenays number 300 more. Some of these Indians are in destitute circumstances, but others are comparatively comfortable and well off. They have raised this year about 80 fields of wheat, besides other grains and vegetables, all of which are in splendid condition. Most of these Indians have embraced the Catholic religion, and are in some degree civilized. During my stay I attended church twice, once in the morning and once in the evening. There were present each time about 500 persons, men, women, and children, and seldom have I seen a more orderly or devout congregation. The Indians all joined in the services, which were held in their own tongue.

The Sisters have here an orphan school, and many of their pupils are full-blooded Indian girls. These little Indian girls showed great proficiency in the branches taught, particularly as all instruction is in the English language. The mission is very poor, and the school-room is in an unfinished condition. In view of this and of the great good they seem to be accomplishing among the Indians, I sent each of the little girls a new dress, and the Sisters five kegs of nails to complete their school-room, besides some other needful articles of smaller importance.

The lay brethren employed oversee, instruct, and assist the Indians in all their mechanical and agricultural pursuits, and under their instructions the Indians have made good progress in farming as well as the more necessary trades. The grist-mill and the saw-mill have been run entirely for the benefit of the Indian, and indeed everything that has been done here seems to have but that one common object. It would be hard to speak in terms of too high praise of the efforts for the civilization and improvement of the Indians which have been made by the devoted men having this mission in charge.

The Flatheads.

Upon the 14th instant I returned to the Flathead agency, where I rejoined Governor Tufts, who had busied himself in the mean time in taking an inventory of the farm property, and in preparing affidavits relative to the missing blankets. We then repaired to Fort Owen, in the Bitter Root valley, where the Flathead nation resides, and 53 miles from the Flathead agency. This tribe numbers about 550, and though in destitute circumstances, they are remarkably peaceable and well disposed. We made them a feast, and invited the chiefs and headmen of their tribe to a council inside the fort. The Indians complained, and we thought with good cause, that the provisions of the treaty made with them by Governor [Isaac] Stevens, July 16, 1855, had not been faithfully observed on the part of the United States; that they had received annuities but five years since the treaty, and then, they believed, in deficient quantities; that there had been no hospital or school-house built for them as provided for in the treaty; that the mills in the Jocko valley were inaccessible to them; that no houses had been built for their chiefs, land broken, &c. They also seemed very desirous of having a part of their annuities in farm implements, as they have scarcely anything to cultivate their farms with. One old man, showing his hands, said: "Look at these; they are my tools; I scratch the ground with my nails." Upon inquiry, we learned that the old man had planted a considerable crop this year, literally scratching it in with his nails. But I append to this minutes of the speeches of one or two of their principal men, taken at the time by Governor Tufts, which will serve to show the nature of their demands.

The removal of these Indians from the Bitter Root valley, where they have heretofore lived, to their reservation in the Jocko, is a question of deep interest to the Indians as well as to the white settlers of the valley, and is one by no means easy of solution. The Bitter Root valley is about 100 miles long by from 7 to 10 miles wide. It has a very fertile soil, a mild and genial climate, is well watered and timbered, and is one of the best, if not the very best, agricultural districts in Montana. In this inviting region have settled a large number of whites, many of whom have opened and cultivated large farms, and made valuable improvements thereon. These settlers, very naturally, are anxious that the Indians should be removed, so that they may retain their homesteads, and ultimately secure title from the government to the same. The Flatheads, too, who were the original owners of the soil, with all their strong Indian attachment for a locality which has long been their homes, and which contains the graves of their ancestors, are very desirous of being permitted to remain where they are. They would like to have a survey made, as contemplated by the 11th article of the treaty above referred to, and a reservation set off to them above the Loo-Loo-Fork. They say a reservation can be made there large enough to accommodate both themselves and the Pend d'Oreilles and Kootenays, and that they will then cede their interest in the Jocko, as well as all of the Bitter Root valley not embraced within their reservation. They think that a small deputation of their chiefs and headmen should be permitted to go to Washington, with a view of settling these difficulties. Unless it is settled soon, it will undoubtedly breed disturbances and cause bloodshed between the whites and Indians.

The matter may be settled satisfactorily to both the whites and Indians, I think, in either of two ways.

1st. If the provisions of the Stevens treaty were faithfully carried out, and particularly those contained in the 5th article, I have little doubt that the Indians could be induced to remove to their reservation in the Jocko valley. The improvements for their chiefs and headmen should be first made, land broken, houses built, &c. Then it would be well to make a treaty with them, by which they should receive a liberal compensation for the improvements made by them in the Bitter Root valley. Whatever may be given them on this account should be judiciously expended in the purchase of stock, farming tools, &c., to enable them to carry on farming upon a large scale on their reservation. The Flatheads have about 50 farms under cultivation where they are, and have made considerable progress in the art of farming. The miller at Fort Owen, where they have their flouring done, told me that the wheat raised by the Indians was of better quality and better cleaned than that grown by their white neighbors. Now, if these people could have $35,000 or $40,000 expended in the purchase of stock, farm implements, seeds, &c., with perhaps $5,000 or $10,000 per annum for ten years for incidentals, I think that they could be brought to see that they would be infinitely better off upon their reservation than where they are.

2d. If deemed most expedient, a suitable reservation for the accommodation of the three tribes might be made in the Bitter Root valley, as desired by the Flatheads. Four townships of six miles square each would probably be sufficient for all. This would necessitate the removal of a considerable number of white settlers, and in my opinion would not be so good for the Indians, as it would leave them on a main thoroughfare of travel, and liable to be outraged at all times by evil-disposed persons.

In conclusion, allow me most earnestly to recommend that something be done at once looking to the permanent settlement of these Indians upon a reservation. By reason of the encroachments of the white settlers upon them, these Indians are liable to cause serious trouble at any day. They are very peaceably and friendly disposed, and, as they claimed in council, have never killed but one white man; but they are nevertheless a very brave and warlike people, whose enmity is not to be scorned. Besides, until they are permanently settled no expenditure of money made by the government in their behalf can be of any appreciable benefit to them.

I would also recommend that the expenditures of money appropriated under the treaty here referred to be closely examined into, to the end that if any frauds have been committed the perpetrators of them may be brought to justice. The Flatheads have always conducted themselves with utmost good faith towards us. In all my experience with Indians I have never seen a nation whom I thought more deserving in every respect than the Flatheads, and I may add that I have never seen a tribe whom I thought had more just grounds of complaint.

With every consideration of respect, I have the honor to be your obedient servant,

W. J. Cullen,
Special Indian Agent, Montana Territory.

Hon. N. G. Taylor,
Commissioner of Indian Affairs, Washington, D.C.

* * * * * *

Minutes of the remarks of "Ambrose" one of the headmen of the Flatheads, at a Council held at Fort Owen M.T. Aug [blank space] 1868 —

"The provissions [sic] of the Treaty which we made with Govr Stevens long ago have never been complied with. Not one half of what was promised us has ever been received by us.

"We hear that a great road for the whites is to be built through the Jocko, if so it would be no place for us. The Bitter Root is our old home, here are the graves of our Fathers, our own and our childrens birth place and here we wish to die and be burried. We would be glad to have the Pen d Oreills and Kootenais come and live with us but we do not want to leave the Bitter Root.

"We wish our Great Father would send us a list of the goods which he gives us so that we may Know if it all comes. We are afraid that we do not get all the goods which are sent to us. We do not think that our Great Father will promise anything and not do it. He could not do wrong and will do justice.

"We want some farming tools, ploughs, axes, hoes &c. We hope our Great Father will send them."

"Adolphe["] another head man of the Flatheads spoke about as follows

"I am glad to welcome our friends here, who come with word from the Great Father. This fine day I call them our friends though I have never seen them before, because they talk and look like honest men. I know they are our friends and we can talk to them. The treaty which we made with Govr Stevens has not been Kept. We have received annuities only five years since our treaty. Gov Stevens promised us that we should live all alone and not be molested by the whites. He told us that our trail to our hunting grounds and camas roots should be Kept open. He promised us a hospital for our sick, a Doctor and a Blacksmith, and to build a school for our children. He also promised to build fences and houses for us all of which has never been done. The Grist mill and saw mill are far away we never see them. The young men are sometimes bad and we are afraid to live among the whites lest we have trouble with them. We want to Know if our Great Father allows the whites to settle upon our lands. Some of them threaten to shoot us. Old chief wants to stick to the word which he has promised the Great Father. The treaty promised us annuities twenty years, but the annuities do not come. We send for things which we want but do not get them. Our Great Father lives so far off we think he does not get our word. If we could go and see him we could tell him. The Agents have told us we could select such goods as we wanted. We want farming tools. My hands! Look at them!! They are my tools. I scratch the ground with my nails. The Great Father wants us to make farms. He ought to send us tools.

"Gov Stevens promised us a choice of of [sic] reservations. We want to stay in the Bitter Root Valley as long as we live.

"We are nearly naked. We want good clothes. This year again our Annuities have not all come. What is the reason? Our hands are not stained with white blood. We never Killed but one white man and he was a thief and a murderer. We had to Kill him or get Killed ourselves.

"Our Great Father I think at last takes pity on our old chief and on us, and that is the reason you have come to see us. You will tell him all that is wrong and he will make everything right."

Document 51

Angelique Eneas Tells of Life in Early Polson

1868

Source: Mrs. C. W. Buell, "Sixty-eight Years Ago Is Remembered by Local Character," *The Flathead Courier* (Polson, Mont.), July 1, 1937, page 1, c. 3; page 8, col. 4-6.

Editors' note: The daughter of Baptiste Eneas, who founded Polson, related some of the highlights about the early days in Polson and the changes that impacted the reservation during her long lifetime. As mentioned above in the Wheeler interview with Baptiste Eneas, the foot of Flathead Lake had always been a corridor for travelers heading west to the Lower Columbia Valley or east to the buffalo ranges.

Sixty-eight Years Ago Is Remembered by Local Character

———— ————

Angelique Tells of Polson in 1868

Imagine if you can the present site of Polson sixty-eight years ago. The grass was knee high and the flat was the favorite grazing ground of blacktail deer; they would jump up every where when a rider came along. There were no roads, only a trail over the hill. After July this trail was black all day long with moving pack trains of Indians on their way east to the buffalo range. They came from Spokane, Couer D'Alene, Bitter Root and farther to go with the Pend D'Oreille's to hunt; camped here to cross at the ferry and at night their cooking fires lit up the banks of the river. The ferry was kept constantly busy taking them across. In the fall they returned with pack horses loaded with meat and camped again as they returned to their homes.

Down along the lake shore, where there was cover the prairie chickens were so thick and so tame, that they would not bother to fly when a rider came along. In the spring their drumming could be heard all day long. The Indians copied many of their ceremonial dances from these feathered drummers.

At one side of the flat, where many years later was to be a town, was a cluster of log buildings built by Baptiste Eneas. Here he settled with his wife and little daughter Angelique. Baptiste was a Canadian of mixed French and Indian blood. He had a freight line from Hell Gate (later called Missoula) to the foot of the lake; from here the freight was taken to Demersville. Baptiste used a team of eight oxen and had Michel Pablo and his wife hired to drive the other freight wagons. Mrs. Pablo drove four horses.

Baptiste built and operated the first ferry across the Big River (as it was called then.) The ferry was built of huge cedar timbers large enough to hold a four horse team and wagon with room enough to spare on the side for riders. Before the coming of the ferry the Indians swam their horses across and towed their children behind in boats made of cow hide; high water or low made no difference, and according to Angelique they never lost a child.

Years after the coming of Baptist's family the Polson's moved out along the lake shore, and because their name was easily to pronounce Baptiste named the little settlement Polson. Occasional prospectors stopped for a day or two at the cabins, perhaps a lone rider or the mail carrier from Ravalli on his way to Ashley, the first town on the Flathead river. Father [Anthony] Ravalli, an old man even then, and according to Angelique a doctor as well as a priest, came at times to administer the last rites of the church or to help the sick.

Angelique's mother in company with other Indian women who came to fish would row out to the islands and camp for a couple of days and return with a boat laden with fish and wild goose eggs. The islands were swarming with ducks, geese, cranes, loons, and curlews, and other native game birds. Now the geese do not nest here; comparatively few even light on their way to the north, where they imagine they are safe from human vandals. The curlews are extint [sic] now. How many of you can recall their high clear call "curlew, curlew" and the fuss they made when you found their nest of brown speckled eggs?

The first trading post was built by Henry Lambert and the Indians used to come to trade and camp for weeks. Both sides of the river were dotted thick with tepees and every Sunday they would have horse races, wrestling and running. All the Indians had cattle and horses and always had plenty of money. The horse buyers were busy all summer. Cayuses sold for one dollar and fifty cents a head and there were thousands of them to sell. The Indians were glad to be rid of them as they wanted the grass for the cattle.

Angelique grew up to be an expert rider and could break a broncho as well as any boy. She says they called the lake Slick (giving the last letter the sound of a long a and pronouncing slick in a gutteral sound back in the throat — you try it). Somers was called Tsin Lop Ah. Pete Gingras says the lake used to get so high in the spring that they used a boat where the tourist park is now and he says there is still old drift wood on the top of the rocks that divide the falls.

Before coming to Polson, Baptiste lived at the Mission and with his ox team got out the logs for the first church built there. During the summer he accompanied the Sisters of Charity who were stationed there, to the more thickly populated section of the state to raise funds to keep their school going. The Sisters were very poor but strong and full of religious fervor. In recognition of the services he so faithfully rendered the Fathers and the good nuns named the Mission St. Ignatius. Eneas is the Indian pronunciation of Ignace or Ignatius [sic].

Angelique had ten children, all dead now. As she puts it, "The grass is gone, only weeds now; the deer and the geese are gone, the wild horses and most of the cattle; my children and most of my friends are dead." She has nothing but a host of memories where once was reality. Her much younger husband Pete Gingras, takes care of her but at seventy-nine she is near the end of the trail. Small wonder that she uses what diversions are at hand to help her forget for a time the days that are gone.

— Mrs. C. W. Buell.

Document 52

Early White Settlers Assisted by Bitterroot Salish Indians
ca. 1868

Source: Alex Matt, "Matt's Trip," *The Daily Missoulian*, Feb. 22, 1912, page 2, c. 5-6.

Editors' note: In the course of his report on his 1912 trip to Washington, D.C., Matt, talked about the relations between the Bitterroot Salish Indians and the white farmers in the 1860s and 1870s.

Matt's Trip

Editor, Missoulian: —

I left Arlee on the 10th day of January and arrived in Washington, D.C., on the 15th of January. Upon arrival there we went to the hotel and next day had a visit with the Indian office. In afternoon went in council with the Brotherhood of North American Indians, comprising over 60 different tribes. While in council all matters concerning the Indians were taken up. The following day I visited the Indian commissioners and had a very nice talk with Commissioner [Robert G.] Valentine. My treatment from this office was very encouraging. I explained to Mr. Valentine that the Indians were not properly treated; that they were in very poor condition. They all have 80 acres of land, which is naked; the majority of the Indians have nothing to work this land, and have no means of buying the necessary implements for working this land. In the early days it was not necessary; the Indians had considerable hunting ground and could make a living, but since these lands, monies and hunting ground have been taken away from them they are practically left on their own resources with practically nothing for their livelihood. They are now looking to no one but the government for protection. It is a fact also, that the Indian should have taken up their rights a long time ago. In making an address to congress I convinced them of the present conditions of the Indians. Congress was always aware that the Indians were in very good condition, but were very much surprised to hear of the present conditions. All the higher officials in Washington were in sympathy with the Indians, and their talk to me was very encouraging.

In the early days the Indians had a strip of ground which they called their own and was given to them by God. They had a large acreage of their own and lived very happy, but of later years most all this ground has been taken away from them.

The Indians would be very glad to have a little park of their own, where they could fish and hunt without the interference of the white man.

There are at the present time 93,000 Indian voters in the United States, and about 300,000 that are not yet citizens. It is not the policy of the Indians to favor any particular party in politics, but the man that is in sympathy with the just rights of the Indians, regardless of whether he is a democrat or republican, and if he will give some of his attentions to the Indians, then this man could have all the support of any and all Indians.

I can remember in the early days in the Bitter Root valley when the white people would come to the Indians and ask for land. I at that time was interpreter and know of many instances when old chief Victor would tell them to go and pick out land and use it; and all these white people had the protection of the Indians in the valley; and in later years all the thanks the Indians got was a petition for the removal of the Indians from the Bitter Root to the Flathead country. The Indians remembered these instances and it is one reason they feel downhearted.

When the Nez Perces came through the valley the Flathead Indians told them to go through, but to not harm even a chicken belonging to the white man.

The Indian made all efforts in the early days to help the whites, but since they have grown poor and become wards of the government they have no recognition from the white people. And they feel that the help they gave the whites in the early days should be returned to them by the whites in time of need, which is the present time.

Speaking of the conditions on the reservation now, there are several sections of land taken from the Indians and sold to the state. These lands are of the very best quality, but were sold to the state at the very lowest price possible. Such matters as these have been taken up through my efforts and I expect that a proper settlement will be made.

There are a great many appropriations being asked for (out of Indian monies) that do not entirely benefit the Indians.

The Indians feel that some of the appropriations asked for should be set aside, and if any is to made, then let an appropriation be made for the Indians, whereby they might buy farm implements, horses to work their land and lumber to build their homes. If the whites would look at it from the Indians' side of it and give him a little justice, he would not feel his hurts as he does now. Perfect harmony could exist between the Indians and the whites, if only the whites would jar loose and let the Indian have a few of the rights now held by all whites and some of which are not as entitled to them as lots of our good Indians.

Alex Matt.

Arlee, February 20.

Document 53

Salish Chief Victor Complains About Treatment by the Government May 3, 1869

Source: Victor, Hd Chief Flathead Nation, Fort Owen, M.T., to Our Great Am. Father, May 3, 1869, U.S. Office of Indian Affairs, "Letters Received by the Office of Indian Affairs, 1824-1880," National Archives Microfilm Publication M234, reel 489, fr. 454-456.

Editors' note: Victor outlined the history of Bitterroot Salish–white contact starting with the Lewis and Clark Expedition. The Salish were faithful in keeping the peace, but now needed government help to develop their farms to replace the buffalo hunt. Victor asked for the President to help the Salish. The letter is written in John Owen's handwriting, but presumably expresses Victor's ideas.

> Fort owen Bitter root valley
> Montana Territory
> May 3rd 1869

To our
Great Am. Father,

Victor Head Chief of the Flathead Nation wants to Speak his heart. Some 65 Snows ago My people saw the first Pale faced Men. I was then a boy. They gave My fathers people the first Tobacco & Blkts they Ever saw. Then we saw the first guns. & Many things the pale faced Men had were wonders to us. The pale faced Chiefs (Lewis & Clarke) told My father & his people that they were the Great Fathers Children & that he would be Kind to us if we would listen to what he told us. One of the "white" Chiefs (Capt Clarke [William Clark]) had an Indian wife. She had a son now among us. Who we call "Sintusensin" (Clarke) the son of the first pale faced chief we ever saw. He is a good Man. The pale faced Men looked Strange to us. They said they came from towards the rising Sun & were going to the great waters where the Sun set. Their horses were tired. We gave them fresh good horses in exchange. Which Made their hearts feel good. We have always loved the pale face Man. We have Never wet our hands with his blood. The Blkfeet our Enemies have Killed Many White

Men. Still our Great Father seems Kind to them. He gives them Guns, Powder & Ball, Blankets & provisions, &c. Why is this!

Our friend IntuKiaKin (Gov. [Isaac] Stevens) Made a treaty with us & our Enemies the Blkfeet some 14 Snows ago. We have Kept it. Our friend Simolsin (Mr [John] Owen) has lived With us some 20 Snows. He built a fort & Mill here. Was our trader. Married among us. He never had but one tongue. We love him for his Kindness. When our Meat is gone he gives us flour & Tobacco too. We are never hungry when he is with us. We shall Never forget him. My people love this valley. Their fathers & Children are buried here. & We hope you our Great Father won't drive us from here. Gov Stevens said he would speak a Kind word to our Great Father for us. But he is dead Now So who will be our friend but Mr. Owen. Last Summer two more White Chiefs Visited us (Gov [James] Tufts & Maj. [W. J.] Cullen). We had a long talk with them in Simolsin's house. We told them that we did not want to leave this valley. That we would give the Great Father the Jocko valley if he would give us this. The big road of the White Man runs through the Jocko valley. & the Whites are hauling thru all the Year round. Our Young Men get Whiskey from bad White Men & then they do Mischief, Abuse their Woman & Children. We Can't do any thing with our Young Men when their [hearts?] are on fire. I want this stopd. It will be better for us all. Then we can live on good terms with our White friends. My people are poor. We have No one to help us plow & farm as Gov Stevens promised us. Our white Chief (Ind Agt [Michael M.] McCaulay) lives Sixty Miles from here. It is a long way for us to go to get a plow, gun, or Kettle fixd. IntuKiaKins promises are fresh in my Mind. I dont forget what our White friends tell us. When the Indian, although friendly with us, have Strung their bows & filled their Quiver with arrows to Make War on the White Man We have Never joined them. Some Eleven (11) Snows ago when Kamiakin the great Chief, with the bands of our friends Made war upon the Whites in the Spokan Country we would not join him, although he offered My people Many horses if we would. But I said No. My word to Intukiakin & Simolsin was not a dry stick to be broken. Our word came from our hearts & We Must Keep it. And we have to this day & hope we always will. We Know the good Equilux (Revd Father [Pierre] De Smet) he is our friend & the friend of all good Indians. His heart is big & good. In council he talks Many good things to us. After all this talk we hope our Great Father Wont drive us from this Valley of our poor Fathers who sleep here. We have some fields & potatoes and if we had some one here to help we could raise all the wheat we would want. The country being filld up with White Men have driven the Buffalo off. They are not close & plenty as they were before the White Man Came among us to hunt for Gold, Which they seem to love so Much. We Must farm now or Starve.

May My words react from heart. Simolsin tells us You are a great Soldier. That Makes our hearts feel good. Please hear us & help us.

Victor Hd Chief
Flathead Nation
His Mark +
Witness
L. L. Blake

Document 54

Pend d'Oreille Warriors Attack Blood Indians at Sun River Trading Post 1869

Source: Edwin Tappen Adney, "Healy: Incidents of Indian-fighting and Fur Trader Days in Montana. . . .," Edwin T. Adney Papers, Stefanson Mss-1, Rauner Special Collections Library, Dartmouth College, Hanover, N.H., box 2, folder 10, pages 19-32.

Editors' note: Edwin Tappen Adney was an American-Canadian author, artist, and photographer. This manuscript is based on an interview with John J. Healy who operated a trading post on the Sun River in the 1860s and took part in the events described. Since Healy and the Flathead Agent went to Chief Big Canoe, it made it likely that the Indian raiders involved were Pend d'Oreille. This is one of several accounts Healy related over the years of the 1869 Pend d'Oreille raid on his Sun River trading post. The date came from Gordon E. Tolton, *Healy's West: The Life and Times of John J. Healy* (Missoula, Mont.: Mountain Press Publishing Company, 2014), pages 84-92. Some typographical errors have been corrected. Adney used an offensive term for Indian women.

The Battle of Sun River Crossing:
A Warrior's ruse that failed
by Edwin Tappen Adney

From the Astor Company's fort at head of steamboat navigation on the Missouri, Capt. [John} Mullan, of the United States army, had constructed a road west along the north bank of the river, and where this road crossed Sun River tributary (Captain [John J.] Healy built the bridge) was a government horse farm in charge of Healy. Note that Mr. Healy uses the good old Yankee word "farm." For this, you will understand, was *before* the cattle days and "cow boys" with their imported Spanish-Mexican things. The buffalo still covered the Plains, the Indians were everywhere at large, nor could be confined to reservations as long as there were buffalo. He could raid enemy tribes, get away with their horses, perhaps get a scalp by which he could prove his manhood. It was white men who exterminated the buffalo, and whatever we may think on that point, we must understand that the buffalo was the "commissariat" of every war party, and until they were gone the Indian was not really tamed.

The cattle and the cattlemen came only after the range had become entirely safe for white man — as far as the Indian was concerned, and that it was men of the stamp of Healy, who called themselves Prairie men, who made the Indian respect the white man by the only standard he accepted that of force and personal courage.

North of the Missouri in Montana was the great Blackfeet confederacy composed of the Blackfeet proper at the east, the Piegans at the west, and northward into Canada were the Kainas, or Bloods. They spoke a dialect of Algonquian. More to eastward was the great Siouan nations, speaking a different language, and of whom were the Absaroka, or Crows on the Yellowstone, great thieves, and like other Sioux mortal enemies of the Blackfeet. In the mountains about the heads of the Missouri was entirely different family of Indians, the Flatheads, regarded as "friendly" to the whites, from the beginning, but of course natural enemies of the Blackfeet, Sioux, all who spoke a different language. They raided each other, and when they met on the great buffalo plains, they fought.

Now we can return to Sun River, where both the Piegans and the Bloods from Canada were accustomed to come and set up their buffalo skin lodges during the summer buffalo hunting season, because besides the horse farm, Mr. Healy with his partner A. B. Hamilton, had a trading post. But it happened that this was not the usual strongly stockaded post. This "A. B." Hamilton must not be confused with "Wildcat Bill" Hamilton. Later it was A. B. who came into Canada with Healy. As the Indians nicknamed Bill "Wildcat" (read "My sixty years on the Plains," to understand why), and so Mr. Healy's partner was called "Long Hair," because he was one of the few left of the old long-hair race of frontiersmen.

Now this Sun River trading post and horse farm has been described for us by Mr. Healy. The trading post was a large low building built of cottonwood logs, the store in front with a stout door, kitchen and living quarters of the family and domestic servants at the rear. Besides Mr. Healy, there was the young wife he had brought out from the East (a Miss Wilson) and two little girls. Also a brother of Mr. Healy, a cook, and the half-breed interpreter Francois Vielle. Hamilton was not present, but there were stopping there that night two strangers passing by, who had been given blanket accommodation on the floor. Not far away was the corral for the horses. There were other usual buildings, but the one we have described was the "fortress." Not far away was a considerable village of friendly Bloods from Canada. Everyone was asleep, when Vielle came running into Mr. Healy's room, calling out, "Oh, Mr. Healy! Injun run off the horses!"

The rest is told in Mr. Healy's own words:

This night that I'm going to speak of there were also two men, strangers who were simply passing along; they were sleeping on the floor. In the night, Vielle's sharp ears heard something, and he came running in to me and called out, "Oh Mr. Healy! Injuns run off the horses!"

With that I jumped up and stepped outside the door and I could hear the horses jumping around and then a sound like someone trying to break down the gate. We all jumped up then and I got my buffalo gun, a Prussian needle-gun, and ran out in the direction of the corral. I had no sooner got there than down came the gate and out came the Injuns on horseback. It was dark but my eyes soon got so I could distinguish an Injun on horseback, and I let go and knocked one man off his horse. As I fired the others dropped behind their horses and they fired back toward the flash of my gun. But quick as I had fired I rolled behind a log that was there and the bullets rattled around me pretty close but never hit me. I took a look over the log and could see a man's legs behind a horse. I didn't want to shoot through the horse, so I took a line at the man's legs and let go. I hit him as I afterwards found out. With that they went off getting the horses off with them. In the distance I could hear more shooting, for at the first shot the friendly Injuns ran out and now were getting under fire. But there was nothing I could see. Just then I felt a heavy hand on my shoulder and a strange voice spoke, "For God's sake get back; they are surrounding us!"

It was one of the strangers, we ran back as fast as we could and just got the strong-door open and shut again when there came a rattle of bullets against the house. I made my wife and little girls lie close to the floor so the bullets wouldn't hit them. We could still hear the shooting. Just at that moment a man's head appeared outside at the window, and one of the strangers let go. "Did you get him?" I asked. "I hit him," he said. Afterwards we found him dead.

Just then I heard a voice outside in Blackfeet: "Kowpoke, nappt! Open, my friend!" Looking out I saw an object — I call it an object — coming straight towards the door. For an instant I didn't know what to do. But as he came he threw up his hands and gasped — Nesto smukaky-e. I'm shot! Let me in! Right behind me Vielle was standing, in his shirttail, scared to death. The Blackfoot fell so hard against the door as it opened to let him in that he fell right against Vielle. Vielle grappled with him and began to yell out, "He's murdering me!" I couldn't understand it. I gave them both a hard push and they went to the floor and as Vielle let go and jumped away, the Indian gave a gasp and Vielle with his Injun's quick ear recognized the voice. "It's Akyopaka!" Akyopaka, meaning "Many Braids" was a friendly Injun. Akyopaka lay on the floor, shot through the body. As Vielle called out his name, the cook came in with a candle and as he did so a shower of bullets came against the house. The cook snuffed the light out and all was dark again. The shooting kept up quite a while longer but after a while things simmered down and we could begin to count noses and take stock. It seems that at the first fire some of the friendly Injuns ran for the protection of the house, and as the back door into the kitchen opened to let them in there was a shower of bullets. One Injun woman was killed, shot through the heart. Another bullet struck over the bed where Vielle's s.... was lying and grazed her forehead. By and by we went out and as we went in the direction of the pig pen I heard a voice call out in Blackfeet — "Keep away! I'll shoot!" "We are friends," I called out. He was an old man and he had taken refuge in the pig pen, and he was sore wounded, and when we led him in, he kept saying "I'm very poor," in Blackfeet, and he pointed to a little blue dent in his side where he said a bullet had gone through him. His s.... came in to him, and she saw that he had probably only fallen against a sharp stick in the wood-pile. So she grabbed up some blue paint we had there, rubbed it onto the place, and made medicine, as the Injuns say, and in five minutes the old man was all right, laughing with the rest of us. There was a little Injun girl, shot badly with a bullet, and with an arrow. I said, "Bandage her up," but I didn't think she would live. But that s.... is alive now. There was another, a young Blackfoot, shot badly in the leg. He walked in, saying, "I'm very poor." He died in about an hour. He had lost his woman only a short while before, and he had a little boy. I knelt down beside him, and seeing he would die, I said to him, "Die easy, father! I will take care of your little boy." And I did, I kept him for many years.

I sent a runner immediately to Fort Shaw, and in the morning a lieutenant rode over. He said, "What can I do for you?"

I said to the lieutenant, "I want you to help me get my horses back."

"I couldn't do that," he said, "without authority from the captain."

"But you can see for yourself what has happened. Here are a lot of people shot up or killed. Why can't you simply detail some men, and make your report?"

"I didn't want to loose any time. I don't want to lose the time it will take to get to the fort and back. They've got six or seven hour's start, as it is.

"No," he said, "I can't positively take the responsibility."

I was angry then. I said, "Well then, I tell you what I am going to do. I am going after them myself!"

"You mean you are going alone?" he said.

"Yes, sir," I said, "and I won't have to go far from Sun River to get them." For the two strangers who had stayed in the post over night, had stepped up and quietly said they would follow me. I knew I could depend on these men. I was angry. For the Government had built a post at Fort Shaw and put soldiers into it to protect the citizens. But when had they done it? not until — I was going to say hundreds — but anyhow fifty white men had been shot down and murdered and the citizens had banded together and cleared the range themselves. Then they sent their soldiers, when we no longer needed them very much. And now when called upon, they wouldn't move a foot without "authority."

The lieutenant rode back to Fort Shaw. I had three good horses left, in the stable, that the Injuns hadn't got. We always kept some horses up, ready to be saddled and bridled, in case of an emergency just like this. I ordered them to be saddled.

But I must say I was puzzled. You see, when the firing began I didn't know what to make of it at all. At first it flashed through my mind that the friendly Bloods had gone on a tear. One could never tell what an Injun would do. He might by all appearances be very friendly. But he is superstitious. He is always looking for some "sign," to direct him what to do. The young brave is always looking for some message from the Unseen World telling him what to do in order that he may become a great warrior. That is his religion. It controls every action of his life. He may have a dream that he is to do such and such a thing, and he takes that as a message to himself, and if his "medicine" is "strong" he will persuade some other young men to go with him and the result is a war party. Every Injun carries his medicine with him. He consults it to know if everything is going right. It is his most valued possession.

But the Injun who had been shot dead just outside the window settled the question for the Bloods. I looked at him and saw that he was a Crow. I judged that he was a Crow from the Yellowstone by the cut of his hair. Injuns may look good deal alike but there is always some thing, some little thing, by which you can tell what tribe he belongs too. It is a knowledge of such things that would sometimes serve to save a man's life on the Plains. It might be a moccasin, or his medicine, or his hair, or some peculiar way of making camp. The Crows were a bad lot. They roamed a long way south toward the Yellowstone. They were supposed to be at peace with the white man but they scalped and stole whenever they saw opportunity to do so without detection. They were troublesome, and we had to admit they had done a pretty bold thing to come up here and steal our horses. So we were not surprised when we found the trail of the horses leading off to the south. The trail was troublesome to follow and there were a good many herds of buffalo roaming over the Prairie and we had to be very careful not to lose the tracks we were after. They had probably planned for this. We found where we had hit the fellow in the leg, by a little trail of blood. But we soon lost that. By and by we came to where they had stopped to let the horses graze and it was plain that they were now going more slowly. We knew what Indian custom was, to run the horses as fast as they could for the first day and the following night, and the next day, before they stopped to sleep. My plan then was to follow until they slowed down and then surprise them, cut the horses out and get them back. We might have to fight for it, but my intention was to let them think they were well out of danger and then surprise them.

But now a singular thing occurred. One of them had dropped his medicine-bag. I looked at and saw that it was not Crow medicine. A little further on, one of them had dropped an arrow. It was not a Crow arrow. Here we were, a hundred miles down in Crow territory, and it was not Crows we were following!

We studied pretty hard over this. If they were not Crows, who could they be?

Presently the trail began to swerve and turned — due west! We could think of no one but the Nez Perces and Flatheads off that way. They had always been friendly. They were Christian Injuns. The Jesuit fathers went among them in the early days and they practiced religion. It had been their boast that they had never made war upon the white man. No, it wouldn't be the Flatheads.

We kept on for thirteen days. On the fourteenth day we reached the Flathead reservation. The trail led there. I went right to the Indian agent. He was a well-meaning man. He refused to believe, at first, that the Flatheads had stolen my horses. But we had the proofs. We had followed the trail to their reservation. He thought there might be some mistake. But he would go with us and have a talk with Big Canoe. Big Canoe was chief of the Flatheads.

So we went down together to the lodge of Big Canoe. I could see a look of surprise in the Injuns when they saw us. As I stepped inside the lodge I took a quick glance around. I saw piled around one side a stack of dried fish. I went over and sat down with my back to this. If we were shot, we weren't going to be shot through the back, from behind, anyhow. I fully expected trouble so I prepared for it. By and by the warriors filed in until they filled the lodge. I could see that they were feeling pretty ugly. The agent began the talk.

He had not been speaking but a few words when I saw something was going wrong. For the s....s now began passing guns in to the men. I saw at once that something needed to be done. So I jumped up and I said to agent, "Stop! Let me talk!"

The Injuns were perfectly still. I started in. I talked to Big Canoe. I spoke the sign language. I said to him "You can kill us. We are only three white men against all of you. You can kill us, but we will die fighting as long as there is a breath left in our bodies. But I tell you this. If you as much as touch a hair of a white man's head, the Great Father will send his soldiers. There won't be left as much as a blade of grass to show that an Injun ever lived here. You will be wiped off the face of the earth! and I made the sign, one hand passed quickly over the palm of the other — You will be *wiped out, rubbed off the earth!*

I could see that they listened. It was having its effect. Went on the tell them, how I had trailed them. How they had disguised themselves to pass off for Crows and how they had traveled a hundred miles off their course so as to throw anyone off the scent. I showed them how the white man had discovered their ruse. I showed them the arrow. I showed them the medicine bag.

I talked for several minutes. I said: Your young men have gone on the war path. They have made war on the white man. They have attacked my house, they have run off my horses. They have killed friendly Injuns too, the Bloods, who were there under my protection. They had taken the Bloods' horses, too. You are at peace with the white man. You are at peace with the Bloods. It is a time of peace. It is wrong to steal horses in time of peace. Now we can't bring back the life of those people, but [you] can give me back the horses you stole. I want every one!

The young warriors I could see were feeling pretty ugly. But I could see my words were having their effect. For some moments not a word was spoken. Then the chief turned to the warriors and they talked together for a little while. Then he turned to the interpreter. He said through the interpreter that he was very sorry that it had all occurred. His young men had only supposed they were making war on the Bloods. They had no idea the white men would interfere. They didn't want to make war on the white man. He was very sorry. He would let me have my horses.

Now I had fully expected trouble and I had no idea that we would succeed as easily as we did. I was very glad at getting the horses back. So I turned to the old chief and said: Tell your young men, tell them this: I want every one who was in that party to keep a horse out for himself.

Well, you should have seen how that pleased them. They laughed and we all laughed. We all shook hands, the pipe was passed around and we were all good friends. But I have often thought the old chief, how mortified he was when he discovered how we had discovered his warriors' ruse.

"I might know," I said to Mr. Healy, "that Vielle did not go along with you."

"Vielle? Oh no!" he replied with a chuckly. "No Vielle! He had had enough of Injuns. The two men who went with me were Floyd Keating and John J. Kennedy. They were both good men. Kennedy was with us for many years and a braver and better man never sat in the saddle. Both are dead now."

Chapter 6

Documents of
Salish and Pend d'Oreille History
Between 1870 and 1874

Document 55

Death of Bitterroot Salish Chief Victor

July 1870

Source: "The Chief of the Flatheads Dead — A Feast Given in His Honor," *Rocky Mountain Weekly Gazette* (Helena, Mont.), Aug. 22, 1870, p. 3, c. 3-2; "Captain Mullan to the Flathead Indians — A Tribute to Victor," *The New North-West* (Deer Lodge, Mont.), Sept. 23, 1870, p. 2, c. 1; "The Dying Chief's Souvenir," *Missoula and Cedar Creek Pioneer*, Nov. 3, 1870, p. 3, c. 3.

Editors' note: These three newspaper articles indicate the importance of Salish Chief Victor in Montana life in 1870 and the significance of his passing.

The Chief of the Flatheads Dead —
A Feast Given in His Honor.

"Oh, how have the mighty fallen." Victor, chief of the confederate tribes, composed of the Flatheads, Pen d'Oreilles, and the Kootenais, which form the Flathead nation, died about a month ago, while returning from a buffalo hunt on the Yellowstone. He was the last of his tribe who remembers having seen Lewis and Clarke when they passed through the Bitter Root valley in 1803. He He [sic] traveled with them from Rosses Hole, on the Columbia, to and through the Bitter Root valley, when he was thirteen years of age. At this time these tribes received their first tobacco. On the 7th of the month a place was selected on the banks of the Bitter Root by Victor's wife, for the purpose of giving a feast to the Flathead nation in honor of their lamented chief. The location selected was one-half mile from Fort Owen. Four or five hundred were present. For the occasion they had evergreens so arranged as to form a shed, and had their lodges thrown over the evergreens so as to form a large hall. At the end of this hall sat the wife of Victor in a mourning position, and ten feet from her was piled the chief's wardrobe and all his toys which had accumulated from his boyhood. Around Victor's wife and apparel sat all the head men of the nation, and the remainder of the tribe were ranged in a circle round the hall of evergreens. The feast, which consisted of dried buffalo meat, dried salmon, berries of almost every description, four beeves, killed for the occasion, bitter root and Kamas root, was then handed round to each and every person by members appointed for that purpose. After the passing around of the viands all knelt in prayer in behalf of the departed chief. Then they arose and sang a hymn. When this was concluded the head men of the nation, one after another, arose and spoke of the merits of the deceased Victor. The last one that spoke was the head chief of the Pen d'Oreilles. He began by exhibiting Victor's wardrobe. At this juncture the whole tribe commenced wailing and lamenting, in a most pitiable manner, their departed chief, which they continued for half an hour, when quiet was again restored. They then proceeded to general business, and the principle men of the tribe held a caucus in regard to appointing a new chief. They all favored the appointment of Victor's son. They postponed further business till a future day when a new feast will be given and a chief appointed.

Victor, the chief of the Flatheads, was not only a great favorite of his tribe, bur was venerated by the whites for his kindness of heart. The question of appointing another chief is not only an important one to the tribe, but also to the whites, as a great deal depends on the temper of a chief in order to maintain a peaceful existence, where both are so closely allied, if not in relation, in close proximity to each other.

With the Nez Perces is a son of Clarke, who passed through Montana in 1803. He is sixty-six years old and has red hair.

* * * * * *

Captain [John] Mullan to the Flathead Indians — A Tribute to Victor.

San Francisco, California,
August 26th, 1870.

To the Indians of the Flathead Nation, Montana Territory:

Your friend, Captain Mullan, has learned with great sadness and regret the loss you have sustained in the death of your great and good Chief Victor.

As the long and oft-tried friend of the white man, Victor had no superior among the red men of America. Mild and gentle as a woman, and innocent of wrong as a child, he commanded his people for near a half century.

Your friend, while residing among your people, knew Victor well. He has eat and slept and smoked at his camp fires, traveled with him to the hunt, has seen him help the widow and orphan of his tribe, and to go in person on missions of peace to the Blackfeet, to the Crows, to the Sioux and to the Bannacks, endeavoring to maintain with them friendly relations. Brave in battle and generous in peace, he has set an example worthy of imitation, to all Indian tribes. To his many and constant acts of kindness do I chiefly attribute the fact that while I resided in your mountains I never had one of my men injured or one of my horses stolen.

Salish Chief Victor
Drawing by Gustavus Sohon, NAA INV 08502300, National
Anthropological Archives, Smithsonian Institution, Washington, D.C.

Victor's record as your Chief is on file in the archives of the government at Washington, and I shall use my best endeavors to have the Indian Department erect a monument to his memory to commemorate his worth and his acts, and at the same time to teach all Indians that their good deeds shall never die.

In reading the death of Victor I feel that the white man has lost a friend and I could not do less than say as much to your people.

In the selection of Victor's successor may you choose a Chief that possesses, if possible, all his virtues, and may the mantle of his wide-spread greatness fall on his shoulders.

Victor, to-day, is resting from his labors in the home which the Great Spirit has prepared in eternity for all his children who do right. May it be our good fortune to meet him again in the far off hunting grounds of the Spirit Land.

Father [Pierre] De Smet, Sahon [Gustavus Sohon], and all your friends among the whites, have many reasons for feeling exceedingly sad to hear of the death of the great and good Victor.

* * * * * * * *

The Dying Chief's Souvenir.

Our correspondent, "Don Felix," writing from Stevensville, sends us the following reminiscence of the late Flathead Chief Victor: "Our old and honored friend, Mr. [Angus] McDonald, of Colville, was the recipient of a present recently which was made under peculiar circumstances. It is, perhaps, well known to most of your readers that this gentleman has had charge of the Hudson Bay Company's interests in the Columbia District for about twelve years, but has been a resident of this part of the Northwest, in the employ of the Company, for the last twenty-five or thirty years. By his noble manliness and gentlemanly qualities, he has made himself the friend, not only of all the white settlers, but also among the Indians far and wide he has none but devoted admirers. This was especially shown a short time since, when Victor, the able and honorable Chief of the Flatheads, while on his annual buffalo hunt in the enemy's country, finding himself to be near the end of life, requested those who surrounded his deathbed to give his old war-horse to Mr. McDonald, as a present from a dying friend. A few weeks ago, when on a visit to Fort-Owen, Victor's widow, leading his old gray horse by the head, presented it to Mr. McDonald, with a last 'good-medicine' message from the old warrior, ere his spirit departed for the 'Happy Hunting Grounds.'"

Document 56

A Visit to Father Jerome D'Aste and Agnes, Widow of Victor in 1870 September 23, 1870

Source: [W. F. Wheeler,] "A Trip to the West Side," *The Helena Daily Herald*, Sept. 23, 1870, p. 1, c. 1-2.

Editors' note: Wheeler interviewed Father Jerome D'Aste, described the extent of Indian farming in the Bitterroot Valley, and wrote about his meeting with Victor's widow who owned 200 head of horses.

A Trip to the Westside.

To the Editor of the Herald:

Having within the year past had frequent occasion to visit every settled valley on the East side of the Rocky Mountains, I never have tired of admiring their beauty and productiveness. Business having required me to cross the range lately, I availed myself of an invitation to go down to Missoula in one of the magnificent new coaches of Huntley's line, in company with Governor [Benjamin] Potts, Secretary [Addison] Sanders, Colonel W. F. Sanders, of Helena, and full load of other passengers. We dined at Deer Lodge, the prettiest village in Montana, after a drive of six or seven hours from Helena, and then started down the beautiful Deer Lodge Valley, which has often been described. At six o'clock the next morning we drove into Missoula, in company with a fine coach of Gilmer & Salisbury's line, well filled with passengers, traveling on business or pleasure. Competition and low fares have caused great numbers to visit this part of Montana this Summer. We passed Hellgate Canyon in the night and could only see the dark sky above us between the high walls of mountains, which rise on either side, and hear the rush of the swift water of Hell Gate river as we drove along the narrow road, cut into the mountain sides, where they jut into the river. In places, the valley widens out, and we drove through several groves of pine, which thinly cover it.

To one who has never seen it, the view of the valley at Missoula as we first enter it, after a drive of forty miles through the narrow canyon of Hell Gate river, is one of infinite beauty and grandeur. The village is small, neatly built, and charmingly located. On the left, close by, rise in towering heights, the Bitter Root mountains; on the South, behind us, where we emerged into the valley, as if through a door in a wall, and to the east and north, the Rocky Mountains rise one above another, until they seem to unite with the Bitter Root range far to the North of us. Through the centre of the valley, and from the Southwest, can be seen the long line of trees which mark the meanderings of the Hell Gate and Bitter Root rivers, until they unite in one stream some miles to the North, and form the Missoula. Here is beauty all around.

On Tuesday it rained all day, but the hospitality of the citizens of Missoula made indoors pleasant for all.

On Wednesday, Captain Huntly, Dr. [John] Buker, Colonel Sanders and myself started with good teams up the Bitter Root valley and drove about thirty miles to Fort Owen. With not more detention than a half hour on the road, we shot snipe, wild ducks and prairie chickens, to the number of a dozen or so, and they made a dinner as fine as any sportsman could desire. We found Major [John] Owen at home. His castle gates were thrown wide open to us, and we were made to feel most welcome. Major O. has lived here twenty-two years, and loves his beautiful valley now, as well as on the day he first saw it. He was for many years Indian Agent here, and often entertained such men as Governor [Isaac] Stevens, General McLellan [George McClellan], Captain [John] Mullan and other officers of the Government, who were sent here to survey roads, make explorations, treat with Indians, etc. He told us of many visits he had had from Captain U. S. Grant, Lieutenant Phil Sheridan, and other officers who had been stationed on this coast, and have since risen to distinction. What a mine of valuable information his recollections and experiences written out, would be to the future historian of Montana. We sat up late listening to the interesting conversation of our host, but awoke early next morning, in order to get time to make further observations.

We called on Father Dasta [Jerome D'Aste], in charge of St. Mary's Mission, originally founded by Father [Pierre] De Smet. From this and other missions founded by this pious and benevolent man, have issued the influences which have made many Christians of the Flatheads, Pen d'Oreille, Nez Perces, and Kootenaie Indians, and also made them peaceable toward the whites. Some three hundred and fifty of these Indians make the Bitter Root Valley their home, and some twenty or more families live in log houses, cultivate from an acre to twenty acres of land with success, and raise large numbers of horses. The majority of the young men live by hunting and fishing, and upon the food raised by the industry of their relatives. Yet, all respect the influence of their church, and are restrained from making war on the whites, who are rapidly settling in this fertile valley, and are nearly, or quite equal in number to the Indians. This joint occupancy is becoming a very serious question, and the settlers and the Indians are alike anxious that the Government should decide who shall occupy the valley. If not satisfactorily settled it will lead to serious, and perhaps, deadly strife.

Father Dasta went with us to call upon the widow of Victor, the head Chief of the confederated tribes of the Mountains; the life long friend of the whites, and a thoroughly good man. She lives in a comfortable cabin, and is the owner of 200 head of horses. The Father acted as interpreter, and said we had called upon her out of respect to the memory of her good husband, who was highly respected by all the white people of Montana for his faithfulness and friendship. She seemed quite moved by these words, and said that her husband loved the white people because they had shown him how to live a good life here and to hope for a better one in the spirit land. She said she was very lonely now, but it would not be very long before she would go to her husband and be happy with him always, and she bent her grey head in thoughtful silence.

Our next visit was to Hon. W. E. Bass, member of the Legislature elect, who owns a farm that would do credit to Ohio or Illinois. We drove over early in the morning to the west side of the Bitter Root with Maj. Owen and Capt. Huntley and took breakfast. The hearty welcome we received precluded the idea that we were intruders. People living comparatively isolated, as do Mr. Bass and his excellent wife, are glad to see even strangers from the busy world as their cordial manner showed. The large fields of wheat, corn and potatoes, the vegetable garden, and especially the flower garden, excited our admiration. We saw 50 acres of wheat, averaging 40 bushels, 20 acres of corn, averaging 50 bushels to the acre, ripe and sound. Everything else was in the same ratio. I brought away specimens of corn, onions, melons, tobacco, broom corn, and even peanuts, which, for quality and size, cannot be surpassed anywhere. The flower garden was a gem of its kind, covered half an acre, and contained over one hundred varieties, with perfect form, and more varied hues than a thousand, sun-beams. It was a surprise itself, considering the location.

The barn is 165 feet long and 60 wide. The loft will hold 150 tons of hay, and the stalls below will accommodate his herd of dairy cows, fifty of which are milked, and the butter churned by water power, obtained from a small stream which irrigates the garden. The house is prettily located among shady pine trees, a forest of which extends back to the mountains. A saw mill furnishes the lumber used on the place. Industry and thrift are seen all around.

On the opposite side of the valley, ten miles away, is the farm of Thos. Harris, Esq. He has 70 acres of wheat, 50 acres of which were raised without irrigation, and the whole will average 40 bushels to the acre. Twenty acres were a volunteer crop, and is the best field. Mr. H. has an orchard of apple and plumb trees of four years growth, and they look very thrifty, varying from six to nine feet in height. Frost has never injured a twig. He has a field of

Timothy grass from which he cut twenty tons of excellent hay, or, two tons to the acre. Here were vegetables of the best quality in the greatest profusion, water melons, musk melons, squashes, tomatoes, beets, carrots and onions, of enormous growth.

The two farms above described were the only ones we had time to visit, but they fully sustain the reputation of the Bitter Root Valley as one of the best, if not *the* best valley in Montana for farming purposes. For twenty years, Maj. Owen says, stock have required no other food in winter than the bunch grass they pick themselves on the foot-hills. After a hearty dinner we returned to Missoula.

In my next I will describe our visit to the Jocko and Flat Head valleys.

W. F. W.

Document 57

Salish Farming Efforts

ca. 1870 to early twentieth century

Source: J. Verne Dusenberry, "Samples of Pend d'Oreille Oral Literature and Salish Narratives," in Leslie B. Davis, ed., *Lifeways of Intermontane and Plains Montana Indians* (Bozeman, Mont.: Museum of the Rockies, Montana State University, 1979), pages 118-120.

Editors' note: Martin Charlot's narrative of the efforts of the Bitterroot Salish to establish farms in the Bitterroot Valley, and later in the Jocko Valley, emphasized the willingness of the Salish to farm to replace the buffalo and other hunting resources and the obstacles they faced from changing government policies. Note the cooperative approach the tribal members used in their farm work.

Flathead-Salish Farming Experiences
by Martin Charlot

In the Bitterroot when my grandfather, Victor, was chief, we Salish started farming. The government told us to do it and we did. We had no equipment except the few things the agent gave us, such as harness and plows. We made fenceposts in the mountains and hauled them home by packing them on our horses. Each of the Indian families fenced small acreages and protected their grain. Then time went on and my grandfather died. My father, Charlot, became chief.

We continued farming. The agent told my father to tell the people they would receive wheat and oat seed. My father told the tribesmen to do more farming and get the seed. They did. We got more plows and harness. We helped each other with the farm work. One Indian farmer had two or three plows going at the same time. Everyone helped everyone else in the harvest. We didn't have any threshing machines. We put the grain on buffalo hides that the women had sewed together. They we led horses over the grain to separate it. Several of the men would lift the robes and shake them to let the wind blow the chaff out. We also had two mills going and we used to fetch the grain to the mill on pack horses. The mill was about 12 miles from where we lived.

Everything was going along fine. We were making a good living and learning the White man's way. Then [James] Garfield came to see us. He came to visit my father, for Charlot was the head man among the Salish. Garfield told my father that we would have to move out of the Bitterroot and go to the Jocko.

"I am doing some farming," my father said. "I am getting good crops and my people and I are living here as the agents and the priests have taught us to do. I am not going to move."

"If you don't move you will be treated like a fish in dirty water," Garfield said.

"This is my home," my father answered. "By the 1855 treaty, we don't have to move. We will stay in the Bitterroot."

A general who was with Garfield spoke up and told my father that he would send an army in there and kill us if we didn't move. Still my father would not agree to go. Some of the other tribesmen pulled out and went to Jocko. Arlee led them.

About a year later, the general came back and told my father that we had to move. He said that my father was no longer the head man of the tribe now that Washington considered Arlee the head man. That made my father mad because Arlee was not a full-blooded Salish. He was mostly Nez Perce. So every year for about three years this same general came back and asked us to go, and every time my father said he wouldn't do it. Finally, my father said that he would move to the Bannock tribe or the Shoshoni tribe and live with them on their reservation, but that he would not go to the Jocko to live. The government men would not agree to that so we stayed in the Bitterroot.

We tried to keep on farming, but Whites came in and homesteaded our land. We could not keep the little patches where we had fenced and had raised our crops. The wild game kept getting scarcer and scarcer. Nearly 20 years went by. We had no money or supplies from the government. Our young men were getting lazy, my father said. Also, many of them wanted to move to the Jocko. One of the leaders of the Salish, Vanderberg, asked my father to take us over. He said that the time had come for us to go. My father sent word that we would move.

A man from the government came to see us. He promised that we could have some livestock. Every family would get one cow and one calf of their own. Besides that, the government would have a herd of steers for us so that every Saturday seven head of steers would be butchered and distributed to us. My father knew some White men in the Bitterroot who had good cows, so he asked if the government would buy the cows and calves from him. The agent said "no," because the cattle would drift away and we would lose them coming over.

Salish Chief Martin Charlo
Photograph 954-501, Photograph Archives, Montana Historical Society,
Helena, Montana.

We were told also that we should leave behind our belongings such as furniture and equipment, for we would get new things once we got to the Jocko. Some of the people really owned some good machinery and some pretty good household equipment, and they hated to leave it but thought they would get new things, so they just left it. The government man also told my father that the government would buy him a new team and buggy to make the trip over in.

"When you go through Missoula," the government man said, "you look at the residences and see the best-made house that you like. Our carpenters will make one for you just like it."

But when we got to the Jocko, things were not the way we were promised. Whatever we got, we had to work for. There was no new machinery nor household stuff for those people who had left theirs behind. We never saw or heard of the seven head of steers that were to be butchered every Saturday. We never got the cow and the calf apiece like we were promised. My father did not get his new house. Instead, we cut logs and had to haul them to the mill to make lumber for our houses. Then we built our cabins, some near the Agency and more of them along Jocko Creek in the timber. Then, we were told to fence off the land we wanted. Only a few people did that. The next instruction we got was to start farming. Again, only a few people did that. My father refused to do it, although he had put in an irrigation system.

The men in the tribe did all that work digging ditches without getting much pay for it. After the irrigation system was in, many more people started farming. They were successful in farming on both sides of the Jocko River. In time, we even had a threshing machine. Just as we had done in the Bitterroot before the trouble began, we started helping each other out and got quite a bit of farming done. After the harvest, we took the grain to the flour mill and had it made up into flour for our winter provisions. The surplus grain we sold. All in all, we made a good living.

But those days didn't last either. Pretty soon, maybe in 15 years, engineers surveyed the reservation. When my father asked why they were doing it, they told him the government was just making a survey to determine the acreage. But it wasn't long before we were allotted and the Whites moved in. Then, the government took hold of the irrigation system. They made it bigger, all right, but the Indians didn't get the water when they wanted it and needed it. Their crops burned up. Some of them went in debt. Pretty soon, most of them quit farming. The White man took over everything.

Document 58

Piety and Penance at St. Ignatius Mission

ca. 1870

Source: L. B. Palladino, S.J., *Indian and White in the Northwest: A History of Catholicity in Montana, 1831-1891,* second edition (Lancaster, Penna.: Wickersham Publishing Company, 1922), pages 99-102.

Editors' note: Father Palladino's memories of life at St. Ignatius, probably about 1870, gave some of the details and texture of life at the mission and the importance of religion in the lives of tribal members at the time.

[Piety and Penance at St. Ignatius Mission]
by Lawrence Palladino, S.J.

Among them there are not a few daily communicants; a great many receive the sacraments weekly, others, every month; while those who receive them less frequently are the exception. On the principal feasts of the year, Christmas and Easter, and also on the feast of St. Ignatius, the Patron Saint, all the Indians gather at the Mission, some traveling as many as two or three hundred miles to be present on these occasions. The number of communions on such festivals varies from 800 to more than 1,000.

We cannot omit mentioning here a very peculiar feature, which, by the way of preparation, used to precede in our days and in fact up to a short time ago, these great solemnities. Some two or three days before the feast, a kind of general assizes or open court would be held by the chiefs and head men in the presence of the whole tribe, and be conducted in a most solemn manner. Offenders against the law of the land and good morals were brought before the whole assembly. But frequently the culprits came forward of their own free will, even before any accusation had been lodged against them, and would confess their wrongdoing and ask their due punishment.

At a signal given by the great chief, the whole crowd fell on their knees, all praying together aloud for a space. After this, the culprits were examined, and if found guilty, they were sentenced and punished on the spot. A blanket or buffalo robe having been spread on the ground, the culprit came forward and stretched himself flat upon it. At another signal given by the chief, all again fell upon their knees, praying aloud for the reformation of the offender, while those appointed carried out the sentence on the bare back of the victim. The whipping was done with a horse-whip or a raw hide, and the number of stripes was proportioned to the nature of the offence and the back of the offender, women and young people being, usually, let off with a short and light discipline.

One day two Indians, one of the them a Blackfoot adopted into the Pend d'Oreilles tribe, and the other a Kalispel, held a discussion among themselves, each claiming to be a better Indian than the other. The Blackfoot had been left by his wife and had taken unto himself another; while the Kalispel had left his first wife to go with another woman. The point of issue between them was, which deserved less blame. Unable to decide the question of themselves, they brought the case before the writer. The controversy, so far as stated, was easy enough the settle, and even in the mind of the Kalispel himself, the point would have been in favor of his opponent, but for the following circumstances which he now proceeded to relate.

"Black Robe," said he, "listen and then decide." He went on to say that he had been married by Father [Joseph] Menetrey to such a one of the tribe, and at such a time, and that the Father had given him a big head of cabbage, twice as large as their two heads put together, to feast upon at their wedding dinner, and then he himself had cooked the cabbage and set it before the bride. "She scowled, Black Robe," continued he. "She took a mouthful, one, two, three times, and each time spit it out, grimacing. I looked her in the eyes, and asked her why she acted so; and she made faces at me, Black Robe, saying: 'You shut up; had I not married you, no woman in the camp would have taken you for a husband!" I got angry, Black Robe, very angry; I rose without saying a word, and left her and the big cabbage and mounting my horse, went down to my people to get me another wife, to prove to my first wife that she had lied to me."

Some three years after, when he thought his first wife fully convinced that some other woman would have married him, he returned to St. Ignatius, and presented himself to the chiefs to be chastised for what he had done. He was told to go and live with his first wife, his offence being condoned. "No," said he "unless you give me my whipping, I go back to the other woman"; and off he started. Some of the men were sent after him, and upon his return he was given the coveted castigation. He then return[ed] to his first wife, and a happier couple could hardly be found thereafter.

The poor fellow did not know as yet that a good end does not make a bad means lawful, as evil may never be done that good may come of it; and with this ignorance in his favor, there is no doubt that the peculiar circumstances lessened considerably his guilt.

The custom of whipping did not originate with the missionaries, as some have wrongly stated. It existed among the natives before the coming of the Fathers. While still pagans, they believed that the chastisement wiped out the guilt of the action for which it was inflicted, and made full satisfaction for it. Hence the Fathers found it at times no easy task to convince them, even after their conversion, that they were obliged to confess the sins for which they had been whipped. Adultery, abandonment of one's wife, lying, stealing, slander, drunkenness and violent anger were the offences which the Indians, when still in the darkness of heathenism, punished by flogging. After becoming Christians, another offence was added to their penal code of their own accord, namely disorderly conduct at church or during prayer.

Document 59

Negotiations about Moving to the Jocko Valley

January 23, 1871

Source: C. S. Jones, Flathead Agency, to E. S. Parker, Commissioner of Indian Affairs, Jan. 23, 1871, U.S. Office of Indian Affairs, "Letters Received by the Office of Indian Affairs, 1824-1880," National Archives Microfilm Publication M234, reel 339, fr. 717-724.

Editors' note: Jones describes his negotiations with Arlee and Nine Pipes about removal from the Bitterroot Valley to Jocko.

Missoula, Montana
January 23d 1871.

Hon. E. S. Parker
Commissioner of Indian Affairs
Sir:

In the communication which I had the honor to address you on the 8th December last, I detailed the points of a conversation held with the chiefs of the Flathead Nation on the occasion of my first official visit to them during the month preceeding in reference to their continued residence in the Bitter Root Valley.

The developments on that occasion were anything but favorable to a proposition for their removal then or at any future period. Time, however, shows that the seed then sown is about bringing forth good fruit, for although I have not broached the subject to the chiefs or others of the Tribe since the date of the interview referred to in my communication of the 8th December last, yet on Tuesday last, January 17th, Arleck, or Henry, and Nine Pipes, or Joseph, two of the principal chiefs and speaking men of the Tribe, the same who participated so actively on the first occasion, came to the agency from their home, sixty miles distant, and spent three days with me, during which time I treated them with particular attention.

In the course of a long conversation during the afternoon of the second day, they gave me a detailed account of the harassments to which they were subjected in their present homes, and the demoralization which has ensued consequent upon the incoming of so many whites among them, concluding by asking me what I would advise them to do.

I gave them to understand that it was difficult, if not impossible to apply a remedy because of the temperament of our people, and the nature of our laws, which rather encouraged than prevented the settlement and cultivation of public lands everywhere, except upon the regular Reservations set apart for the Indians, like the one on the Jocko, repeating substantially the arguments which I had used at our first interview, together with such additional ones as subsequent reflection had inspired me with.

I then said to them, in view of all these facts, and of the bitter complaints which you have this day made to me, would it not be better for you to reconsider your determination not to remove from the Bitter Root Valley, and to make up your minds to come here. I advise you to do so as your friend and counsellor, having warm sympathies with you, and not capable of advising you to a course which I did not in my heart think would bring to you many blessings and benefits.

They said then do you think it will be a benefit to our people? In the first place, said I, by taking them from contact and association with the whites, and the attendant evils as you have to-day described them to me, and bringing them to this ground which the government regards as sacred forever to your occupancy, and which will be kept from the invasion and intrusion of the whites by all the armies at the command of our great Chief at Washington, if necessary. In the second place according to the stipulations contained in the Second article of the treaty made with you in 1855, the property you now have in the Bitter Root Valley, will be valued by the direction of the President, and the full value given you either in money or in other improvements here. And in the third place that I had no doubt they would be allowed to select any portion of this Reservation which they might prefer for their future homes, describing to them the beauty, fertility and advantages as best I could.

They asked me how their properties in the Bitter Root would be valued. I told them I had no authority to say, but supposed it might be done in this way: They to select one person and the government another, who would make a valuation, which would be adopted by the President as provided in the Treaty. After a pause Arleck the elder said: "We see as you do, and we would like to see the head Chief at Washington (meaning the Commissioner) in order to talk over all the matters connected with our removal and to make arrangements for it."

They evidently desire to come to Washington, and so intimated in my first interview with them; but I did not encourage the idea at that time, for the reason that I thought it better policy to bring them to the point of agreeing to remove before gratifying them in this respect. Now that They have indicated such a disposition I think it would be wise and politic to allow five or six of the principal men to visit you. Their business is really important; and they think you will deal more liberally with them than any delegated person. None of the Tribe have ever been to the seat of government, tho' sometimes promised that privilege by over anxious agents. They are worthy of it, having been the uniform friends of the Whites since the days of Lewis & Clark, and it is the boast of the Tribe that the blood of but one white man is on their hands.

Their trip hence will be worth more to the government than the cost of it, in view of the large area of valuable domain to which they quietly yield possession, but from which they could not be forcibly ejected upon any principle of law or justice. If, however, their application to visit you does not impress you favorably, then pardon me for saying, and I trust without egotism, that if delegated with proper authority, and suitable means I can bring this long contested question to a successful consummation; better perhaps than almost any other person, because of the confidence, indeed I may say affection, with which these people regard me.

The expense of their removal will be considerable, particularly because of the value of their improvements in Bitter Root Valley. Of the ninety heads of families composing the Tribe, forty four are well to do farmers, some of them making five or six hundred bushels of wheat annually. The expenses incident to payment for property and the removal of so many families a distance of sixty miles; as well as the preparation of their new homes, and subsistence for awhile after they reach there will probably not be less than $40,000, for which amount it will be necessary to make an appropriation. But the amount is inconsiderable compared with the incalculable advantages to result from it, not only to the Indians immediately interested, but to the hundreds of white settlers now in the Bitter Root Valley, to whom security and undisputed possession will be given, as well as to thousands more who are anxious to locate there, and only awaiting the period when Indian occupancy should cease.

I have the honor to be,
With sentiments of
Great respect,
Your Obdt. Servt,,
C. S. Jones
U.S. Indian Agent.

Document 60

Petition for the President to Honor the Hellgate Treaty
May 7, 1871

Source: Charlos, et. al., to Ulysses S. Grant, President, May 7, 1871, U.S. Office of Indian Affairs, "Letters Received by the Office of Indian Affairs, 1824-1880," National Archives Microfilm Publication M234, reel 491, fr. 351-353.

Editors' note: The Bitterroot Salish were anxious about the status of their claim to the Bitterroot Valley in 1871. Father Jerome D'Aste of St. Mary's Mission witnessed the marks, but the letter was not in his handwriting.

Flathead Nation,
Bitter Root Valley,
Stevensville P. O.
Montana Terry.
May 7th 1871.

To His Excellency,
Ulysses S. Grant,
President of the United States.

The undersigned, Chiefs and Headmen of the Flathead Nation of Indians, beg leave respectfully to represent to you the importance and necessity of some final and definite action in regard to our future continuance and residence in the Bitter Root Valley.

By the 11th article of the Treaty made by us with the United States at Hell Gate, in this Territory, during the year 1855, our right here was guaranteed until His Excellency the President should have ordered a survey of this Valley with a view to determine whether we should always remain here, or else remove to the regular Reservation set apart for this and other Confederated tribes on the Jocko River. Connected with this was an express provision that no part of this valley above the Loo Loo Fork should be open to settlement or occupancy by the Whites, until the survey and decision by the President under the Treaty as before stated.

Notwithstanding these solemn guarantees, no survey of the valley has as yet been made, although eleven years have elapsed since the U.S. Government ratified the Treaty; and still worse and what we most complain of is that almost

Salish Chief Charlo
Detail from photograph 954-526, Photograph Archives,
Montana Historical Society, Helena, Montana.

our entire valley is occupied and overrun by white settlers, who impose on us in many ways, subjecting us to annoyance, inconvenience and injustice, which seem to call aloud for redress at your hands, and to you, therefore, we respectfully appeal.

We are, in violation of Treaty obligations, as we conceive, encompassed on all sides by white settlers, even to the extent of villages in the midst of our settlement, and the results of the contact and association are, the drunkenness of our young men, to whom the whites will sell whiskey, as well as the demoralization of our women, which it seems impossible, with the greatest watchfulness on our part, to prevent.

In view of these and other details of trouble with which we will not burden you, we ask and urge that a delegation of our tribe be allowed to visit you at Washington for the purpose of arranging and finally settling the difficulties under which we suffer, superinduced mainly as we humbly suggest, by the failure of the United States to perform its duties under the Treaty made with us. We prefer to settle these difficulties at Washington, because we believe justice will best be secured to us there; or at any rate, it will be far more satisfactory to use [us?], as we have many grievances which we want the great Father to hear. None of our tribe, living or dead, have ever been to see you, although we hear of Chiefs of other tribes, who are always making war on you, being allowed that privilege, while we have always been the friends of the whites.

We do not desire to come for amusement, but for really pressing, important, and, to us, vital business, affecting the present happiness and continued existence of our people.

We ask this our Great Father, and will be thankful for such a favor.

    Witness Rev. J. D'Aste SJ Missionary Priest — Charlos his + mark.
    Witness Rev. J. D'Aste SJ Miss. Priest — Henry his + mark.
    Witness Rev. J. D'Aste SJ Miss. Priest — Adolph his + mark.
    Witness Rev. J. D'Aste SJ Miss. Priest — Francis, his + mark.
    Witness Rev. J. D'Aste SJ Miss. Priest — Laurence, his + mark.
    Witness Rev. J. D'Aste SJ Miss. Priest — Henry, his + mark.
    Witness Rev. J. D'Aste SJ Miss. Priest — Joseph Ngantà, his + mark.

Document 61

Sitting Bull Leads Salish Warriors into
an Ambush
July 11, 1871

Source: Stanley Vestal, "The Fight with the Flatheads," Material originally published in *Sitting Bull: Champion of the Sioux*. New edition copyright © 1957 by the University of Oklahoma Press, Norman, pages 118-124. Reprinted by permission of the publisher.

Editors' note: The eighteen Salish warriors killed in the ambush set up on July 11, 1871, in the Musselshell by Sitting Bull were listed in the St. Mary's Mission, "The Book of Deaths." (Robert Bigart, ed., *Life and Death at St. Mary's Mission, Montana: Births, Marriages, Deaths, and Survival among the Bitterroot Salish Indians, 1866-1891* [Pablo, Mont.: Salish Kootenai College Press, 2005], pages 128-130.) Vestal compiled his biography of Sitting Bull from Sioux oral sources. Unfortunately, no detailed account of the battle from the Salish perspective has been found.

The Fight with the Flatheads

The hunting Sioux were in camp on the Yellowstone at Big Bottom, below the mouth of the Rosebud. Hunkpapa, Oglala, Minniconjou, and Sans Arcs were there — a big camp, almost a thousand lodges. The summer hunt was over, the drying racks and parfleches were thick with meat. Young men began to say it was time to go on the warpath.

Beyond the mountains to the northwest, in Montana and Idaho, were the Flatheads, Pend d'Oreille, and Nez Percé. Ever since the white men had settled in their country looking for gold, these nations had been coming into Sioux country for buffalo, because their own game was killed off. Sitting Bull organized a war party to rub out these trespassers. It was a big war party — more than four hundred men. Sitting Bull and Flying-By were the principal chiefs. They set out in high spirits, horseback, leading their war horses, full of fight. They headed northwest toward the Musselshell.

There were many young men in this party, and they were a jolly cheeky bunch. One of the ringleaders was Sitting Bull's nephew, Big-in-the-Center, then just twenty-one, and now known as White Bull. When the party camped, they made shelters or war lodges in a circle: the seasoned warriors slept together and the younger men by themselves, every tribe separately. One day White Bull thought he would have some fun at the expense of these older honor men; they had been on the warpath for several days and had done nothing. So White Bull got on his horse and rode around the little camp circle, stopping before the shelters of famous warriors to sing a song he had composed:

My friends, when we go home to report,
What have I to report to my father and mother?

He would end the song with a sharp yell, then ride on to another group and sing again. It made the young men laugh: they praised White Bull for his song at the older men's expense. For as yet there was nothing to report.

When they had been out for some days, the chiefs sent scouts out to look for enemy camps. While they waited for the return of these scouts, some of the warriors became impatient, and went to Sitting Bull. They asked him to divine what was going to happen, to make a prophecy. He had often done this, and nearly always his prophecies came true.

Sitting Bull said, "I will try to find out something."

He walked away from the crowd some distance, and walked up and down, singing. They could hear him singing, but he was too far away for his words to be understood. After a while he came back. They had a pipe ready to light waiting for him.

Sitting Bull lighted the pipe and smoked. When he had finished, he said, "In the smoke I see a battle within two days. Many enemies and several Sioux will be killed." After a few moments, he added: "When I was out there singing, I saw a little ball of fire — a spark — coming toward me. But it disappeared when it reached me." The warriors all knew what that spark meant: it was a sign that Sitting Bull was going to be wounded.

Soon after, the scouts got back, and the war party struck out for the Flathead camp, reported to be on the Musselshell. They left their saddle horses hidden, and rode their war horses. All night they rode, and about dawn were close to the camp of their enemy. There they halted and Sitting Bull announced his plan for the attack. Said he: "Let's all act together; that's the best way. Let's pick a small party of young men with fast horses and send them against the enemy. The rest of us will stay behind, out of sight. When the Flatheads see how few they are, they will chase them. Then our young men can lead them straight into the trap we have prepared."

The arrangement was satisfactory to everyone. It allowed the young men to make the first attack — which they would probably do anyhow. And it gave the old men a chance to take part in the fight and distinguish themselves, since the young men would bring the enemy back to them. Old men and young men were jealous of each other. It is probable that strategy originated in a desire on the part of the old men to turn the young men's headlong courage to their own advantage.

The whole party was filled with martial ardor that morning. One of them, Badger, stood up, and, jerking off his breech-cloth, displayed the tokens of his virility, saying, "Look at me. I am brave. I want to distinguish myself. I can do anything. Go to war, kill the enemy. I am a *man*!"

Mole and Herald were chosen to lead the advance party. Other young men chosen to act as decoys were Bull Eagle, Hump, Owns-the-Warrior, Red Gun, Drops-Two, Red Circle, Looks-for-Enemies, Bear-Shoot-Him-as-He-Runs, Eagle Thunder, Red Thunder, Use-Him-as-Charger, Red Thunder (No. 2), Crane, Two Eagle, Red Tomahawk, White Shield, Turning Bear, Charging Bear, Long Ghost, and Running-Wild. Long Ghost was Sitting Bull's relative. White Bull, his nephew, went with this bunch on his own hook. Day was breaking as they started for the Flathead camp.

The reserves, under Sitting Bull and Flying-By, remained about two miles behind — to the west of the camp.

As the young men advanced, they could see the Flathead tipis, about one hundred of them, sharply outlined against the brightening east. They kept a sharp lookout, not making much noise. One of the Flatheads was driving his ponies out onto the prairie; he was heading south from the camp. As soon as the Sioux saw him, they rushed him. He was half a mile from his camp before he saw them coming. At once, he let his horses go and raced for his life, back to his friends among the tipis. The Sioux were after him yelling and lashing their horses, but he had a start, he rode hard, and got back to the camp. The Flatheads swarmed out of the tents like hornets. The Sioux rounded up the lone Flathead's seven ponies, and started back, as if they had got what they wanted. Sitting Bull's plan worked perfectly.

Away went the young Sioux, running off with their capture, back toward the four hundred warriors in the ambush. And after them, pell-mell, came a hundred mounted enemies, riding like mad. The Flatheads were well armed with guns and pistols, and were shooting all the time.

It was two miles back to the ambush. The young Sioux raced for that place. But White Bull wished to distinguish himself and keep the enemy coming. He kept charging back at them, as if trying to hold them so that he comrades could get away. He rode last of all the Sioux young men. All at once he gave two yelps and turned his horse back, charging his enemies. All alone he charged them, chased them back alone. One of the Flatheads was in the rear, waiting for White Bull. White Bull struck at the Flathead with his spear three times. The Flathead fired his revolver at White Bull, but missed. White Bull then drew his own revolver, pumped three bullets into his enemy's horse. The man's horse dropped, and White Bull thought he had him. But the man afoot ran in among the tents, and White Bull couldn't touch him.

White Bull then turned to follow his comrades, and once more the Flatheads pursued. Again White Bull chased them back a way, but was unable to strike anyone. And as he fell back, the Flatheads came after him. It was back and forth that day.

The third time he chased them, they nearly caught him. But the other Sioux stopped and waited for him, and he reached them safely. The Flatheads dismounted, and they all had a good fight.

One of the Flatheads came right after White Bull, and jumped off his horse to shoot. White Bull turned and charged him, with lowered lance. The Flathead did not run as White Bull expected, but stood his ground, with gun up, ready to shoot. White Bull, however, though all alone, wished to do as chiefs and chiefs' sons do; he was Sitting Bull's nephew. He had started after this Flathead,

Sioux Chief Sitting Bull
Image 39879u, Photograph Archives, Library of Congress, Washington, D.C.

and, if he did not strike him, people would say he was a coward. So he went right ahead, lance against rifle. The Flathead shot at him, and the ball broke his lance-shaft. White Bull struck the Flathead. This deed is reckoned the bravest of all White Bull's thirty *coups*.

By this time the Sioux reserves had come piling out of their ambush, the fight became general, and a hot fight it was. The Flatheads were well armed, fought on foot, and hit a number of Sioux, killing Standing Bull and Hunts-the-Enemy, and wounding Crow-Going-up-in-the-Air.

One of the Flatheads was very brave. The Sioux were all around him, and he had wounded three of them. White Bull saw his wounded comrades, and he got mad. He jumped off his horse and rushed this enemy. The Flathead had a bow, and just as White Bull came up, he loosed an arrow. *Tchk!* It went by — a miss. White Bull had thrown away his broken lance. He knocked the Flathead over with his pistol butt, jumped on him, and cut him about the face and throat. The Flathead was apparently dead. White Bull scalped him. While he was ripping off his hair, the man grunted, came to. He jumped up and ran around dizzily a few yards before he fell dead.

Seeing how many the Sioux were and how many of their comrades were killed, the Flatheads ran back to their camp. It was a regular stampede. The Sioux were eager to follow. White Bull and another young man raced to strike one of these men, who was afoot, with a revolver. But before they reached the Flathead, one of the Sioux behind them shot and killed him. They struck his dead body: White Bull counted the second *coup*.

Just then they could hear Chief-Flying-By shouting to the Sioux: "Stop! That will be all for this time! Some good men have been wounded already."

So they turned back, and let the Flatheads go. If Flying-By had not given that order, all the Flatheads would have been wiped out that day.

But Sitting Bull did not want to stop. He had not yet begun to fight. He paid no attention to the advice of Flying-By. Six young men felt just as he did. These were his "brother" Jumping Bull, His Cup, Bad Horse, Dresser, Top-of-Lodge, and one Crazy Horse (not the famous war chief). They all remained on the field. Pretty soon some of the Flatheads came back to see their dead, and these seven Sioux began to shoot at them. They chased these men back toward the Flathead camp.

Just before reaching the camp, the last Flathead got off his horse to fight. One of the Sioux captured his horse and ran it off. Sitting Bull, on horseback, charged the Flathead. He had no shield, only a gun, held in his right hand. The Flathead had a bow and arrows, and when he saw Sitting Bull coming, he jerked an arrow from his quiver, snapped it on the string, drew it back to the point, and waited. An instant later, Sitting Bull was right on top of him.

The Flathead let fly. Sitting Bull tried to avoid that deadly shaft. He threw up his left arm to shield his face, and dodged to one side. But the Flathead did not miss, the arrow found its mark. It hit Sitting Bull, passed clear through, between the bones of his forearm.

Instantly, Sitting Bull flung himself to one side of his racing horse and sheered off before another arrow could reach him. He rode back to his friends, carrying the bloody shaft through his arm. When he was out of range, they cut off the head of the arrow, and drew out the shaft. The wound was painful, dangerous, they thought. He "died" for a while; that is, he fainted. Back at the camp of the reserves, Sitting Bull found a number of wounded. The two dead men were laid out in state, and their horses shot alongside. They carried their wounded and the horses they had taken back toward home. On the way home three wounded men died: Crow-Going-up-in-the-Air, Dog Eagle, and Bull Eagle.

They found the camp of their people on the Yellowstone below the mouth of the Rosebud. Before they reached the camp, the war party sent in a messenger to break the news of the casualties. Because they had lost some comrades, they felt bad, and they wished to make the people feel better, and cheer them up. Therefore the messenger was ordered to say that Sitting Bull had died also.

When the news arrived, the family began to cry and rend their garments. And then, just when everybody was feeling so bad, here came Sitting Bull riding his own horse, still alive. Then the people laughed and almost forgot the losses they had suffered. Once more Sitting Bull had shown his courage and his strategy, and had survived a bad wound. Nearly everybody in camp came running out to embrace him and stroke him all over, they were so glad to see him again.

After they had mourned four days, a big victory dance was held, and the people danced over the scalps the men had taken. White Bull had a Flathead scalp with hair as long as his arm. He also brought home an enemy quiver and belt. These he gave away, according to custom. Sitting Bull was unable to dance at this celebration, because of his wound. But before long it had healed nicely, and he was all right again.

For all that, his mother shook her head. It looked as if that son of hers would never learn to stop playing with fire!

Sitting Bull, however, was content. The Flatheads never troubled the Sioux buffalo herds again.

Document 62

Return from the Buffalo Hunt, 1871

July and August 1871

Source: "From the Buffalo Hunt," *The Missoula Pioneer*, July 27, 1871, page 3, col. 1; and "The Indian Feast of Mourning," *The Missoula Pioneer*, Aug. 10, 1871, page 3, c. 2.

Editors' note: These two newspaper articles present an outsiders view of the grief of the Bitterroot Salish community over the loss of 18 warriors to a Sioux ambush on the plains.

From the Buffalo Hunt.

The Flatheads, Kootenais and Pen d'Oreilles are just returning from their spring and summer buffalo hunt. We have not as yet interviewed them, and cannot report their success. The Flatheads had the serenity of their excursion somewhat disturbed in the little massacre of eighteen of their number by a large band of Sioux. The latter, concealing themselves in ambush, sent out a number of their braves (?) to surround and capture a large number of Flatheads' horses. This freedom of appropriation the latter florid gentlemen proposed to contest, and eighteen of them at once boldly gave chase. The Sioux clung to the horses and drew their pursuers into the ambuscade, when the entire number were murdered outright. The Flatheads then pursued the Sioux in force, recaptured nearly all their animals and killed some three of the enemy.

Judging by intimations from official quarters, we hope soon to chronicle the removal of the Flatheads to their reservation on the Jocko. This effected, the Bitter Root Valley is at once subject to settlement in every part.

* * * * * * * *

The Indian Feast of Mourning.

On the return of the Flatheads from their recent buffalo hunt, the friends of the murdered Indians, as is their time-honored custom, made great feasts of mourning, to which the whole tribe was invited. Their first was held near St. Mary's Mission on the 31st ult., and was a grand affair. Two fine buffalo cows and two buffalo calves, besides some cattle were killed for the occasion. Flour, sugar, coffee, etc., were also furnished in great abundance for the feast, and several hundred of the mourners and friends ate till even buffalo meat ceased to excite their *gusto*. Their second feast — and perhaps, a larger one than the first — was held on Burnt Fork, some two miles above Stevensville. To this, we believe, the entire tribe and many distinguished members of the neighboring tribes were invited. The viands were furnished as before, but no buffalo, we understand, graced their table.

These mourning feasts are peculiarly *aboriginal* in their character. A share of the property of the deceased furnishes the feast, and this is general in the tribe according to the wealth of the estate. In the case of the above-mentioned feasts, the families of the murdered braves united, and, having considerable property, their entertainments were conducted on the grandest scale. Their meats are barbecued, and refreshments generally are dealt out somewhat after our picnic style. In the midst of their repast general speech making takes place, in which condolence and the sad feelings of the friends are expressed. At this juncture, also, the Chief, or some head man, having collected together all the remaining effects of the deceased, publicly invites all creditors to present their claims against the estate, and pays up till the effects are exhausted. This done, the feast proceeds, at the close of which the bitter wailings of the multitude for the dead are indulged in for about half an hour, then prayer, the interchange of social feelings, etc., and the final dismissal. Their crying is in many respects very impressive, they entering into it with apparently much more feeling than the ancient hired mourners who went about the streets begging bread.

The camp of the Flatheads has been almost a continual wail ever since their return some two weeks ago. This massacre has been to them a terrible calamity, especially when it is considered how it was brought about. Many years will have passed before it is forgotten.

Document 63

An 1871 Peace Treaty Between the Pend d'Oreille and Blackfeet Indians August 1871

Source: Frank Wilkeson, "The Last of the Indian Treaties," *The New-York Times*, Apr. 17, 1887, p. 11, c. 5-7; and excerpt from Frank Wilkeson, "Indian Trails," *The New-York Times,* Feb. 27, 1887, p. 6, c. 3-4.

Editors' note: The date Wilkeson gives in the article is 1870, but the events he described were likely in 1871. In 1870 John J. Healy moved to a trading post north of the border in southern Alberta. Wilkeson worked as a civil engineer for the Northern Pacific Railroad in 1871 and 1872, so he was probably in the area in 1871. An article in the Missoula newspaper ("Peace with the Blackfeet Indians," *The Missoula Pioneer,* Aug. 10, 1871, page 3, col. 3) noted that peace had been arranged between the Pend d'Oreille and Kootenai and the Blackfeet during the summer of 1871. One might be tempted to believe that Wilkeson added some color and drama to the story he told in *The New-York Times* newspaper. The last part of this document is Wilkeson's description of a buffalo hunting party of the Salish, Pend d'Oreille, and their allies crossing the Cadotte Pass, probably also in 1871.

The Last of the Indian Treaties.

In August, 1870 [1871?], I was in the land of the Blackfeet on British territory. The northern plains which stretch from the Hole in the Breast Divide to the thick woods lying beyond the North Saskatchewan River lay broiling in the sun. The air rose from the hot ground and rolled in heated waves across the sea of arid land, breaking into shimmering foam against the buttes and divides, and raging in angry tumult in the low-lying land. Every depression was a boiling sea of heat. Every hill was a sea-girt island, against which impalpable waves foamed, and long, silver tongues of heat swished far up their flanks. The wind, doubly heated sirocco, blew in puffs, and the scant, buffalo-trampled herbage was whipped into ribbons and ground into brown powder and flung into vast caldrons of boiling air. Between the puffs of hot, withering Mexican breath tiny whirlwinds rose from the caldrons to be blown into brown haze by the succeeding puff. Birds, with parted bills and drooping wings and heaving breasts, stood in the shade cast by low-growing cactus, and closely hugged the spiny plants. Spectre prairie fires chased one another across the arid, gravelly plains, and great tongues of seeming flames were thrust far in advance of the billows of heat. Seen through the heated air, rocks, antelope, buffalo, were transformed into awe-inspiring or fantastic objects. Nature was conjuring in the land of the Blackfeet. Groups of mounted and blanketed Indians dashed from behind hills and descended into valleys, to emerge as antelope or buffalo. Mirages sprang into life. Here was a mountain scene. There, on a tree-encircled lake, white-breasted swans and geese sported. Yonder the glories of the Cypress Hills were revealed, and there the cañons, snow-packed and pine-clad, of St. Mary's Lake rose out of the ground. The pictures changed continually. One instinctively listened to hear the sound produced by the shifting of the scenes. The low depressions, which had been filled with alkaline water in the Spring, were dry and paved with ill-fitting, loose-jointed tiles of sun-baked, white mud. The profound silence was broken only by the sad, mournful cry of a hawk, which circled high above the hot, parched earth.

In a deep valley, gouged in the plains by the cold water of the Belly River, at the point where the St. Mary's River joins the former stream, the Haley Brothers' trading post stood, apparently in a sea of flame. It was hot on the plains. It was hotter in this narrow valley. Men lay on the ground in the shade cast by the walls of the log fort and panted. Hatless, shoeless, with open shirts, they lay and suffered. At intervals Indians girls in bright-colored, flowing gowns walked slowly out of the dark recesses of the fort and stood in the blazing sun for an instant as they gazed at the quivering crest of the cañon-like walls of the valley. Then turned and, after speaking lowly to their white lovers, slowly re-entered the fort. The sullen, fierce-visaged men paid no attention to the girls, but lay silently suffering. Occasionally one of them would unbuckle his revolver belt and irritably casting it on the ground would pull off his flannel shirt and plunge into the river. The valley was absolutely silent, except for the murmuring of the rapidly flowing water.

Suddenly an old man, whose life had been spent in the service of the Hudson's Bay and Northwestern Fur Companies, and who had been lying on his back close to the wall of the fort, apparently in profound sleep, sprang to his feet, alert, active. He leaned forward, gazed up the valley, listened attentively for an instant, then called aloud to his comrades: "There is fighting going on up the St. Mary's Valley." Instantly all the men were on their feet and listening. Then they dashed into the fort. The doors were shut. Rifles were grasped, and the employes silently took their respective stations: Up the valley, far beyond the point which juts into the river, faint rifle shots could be heard, mingled with yells and Indian battle cries. Presently the battle sounds grew clearer and the firing increased in volume and the shouting was incessant. In a few minutes the contestants swarmed around the point in a seemingly confused mass, and it was seen that the Blackfeet were being whipped and in full retreat. Braves threw up their arms, wavered in their saddles for an instant, and then fell headlong from their horses. Others fell to rise again and to continue their flight. The band attempted to stand, then, panic stricken, wheeled their horses and galloped down the valley abandoning their dead and wounded. Behind them, naked, mounted on bareback horses, and causing the heated air to quiver again with their cries, came the Pend Oreilles and Flatheads, the bravest Indians on the continent. Their bowstrings twanged, and a cloud of arrows preceded their line, and tongues of smoke shot out of the few rifles their braves carried. As they galloped in pursuit, active men leaped from their horses and scalping knives flashed around the heads of their dead enemies, and scalps bloody and warm were twirled on high with exultant shouts.

The Blackfeet, flying before the Pend Oreilles, crowded into the stockaded corral of the trading post and dropped the heavy gate into place. The so-called scourges of the Northern Plains were corraled to the number of 250. They were frantic from fear. Outside, the valley was apparently abandoned by animal life, excepting a bunch of horses slowly disappearing up the valley. The victorious Pend Oreilles had comprehended the situation at a glance. They had dismounted and sank out of sight in the grass, behind trees, under the bank at the river. Wherever there was cover there lurked a Pend Oreille or a Flathead brave. At last, after two generations of robbery, and murder, and savage foray on the part of the Blackfeet, the Pend Oreilles had got the upper hand in a fight and they meant to exterminate that war party. They had driven them to cover; driven them to the protection afforded by white men and a fort.

The Blackfeet warriors belonged to the celebrated Piegan clan, famous for desperate valor and fearlessness. They were mighty men, few of them were less that 6 feet in height. They were broad-shouldered and lean flanked. Each brave carried a breech-loading rifle, two heavy Colt's revolvers, and short, powerful bow and a quiver stuffed with long, iron-tipped, grooved and feathered war arrows. Many of them were wounded. The feathered butt of an arrow stuck out of the abdomen of one of the Piegans, and its iron head was thrust six inches out of his back. The arms and legs of other Indians were skewered with arrows that they had not had time to extract during their disorderly retreat. Quickly the arrows were broken and pulled out and the wounds bound up. These wounded Indians were gray from fear and pain. All of them were greatly excited. They clamored for admittance to the heavy fort. They stood singly or in groups, chanting their sad death song. They made no organized effort to man the stockade and beat off their enemies. They were the most thoroughly demoralized troops I have ever seen. Haley, the trader, did not dare to admit them within the protective walls of the fort. Notoriously treacherous, the Blackfeet would have been unsafe allies. They might have murdered every white man in the fort if they were admitted. Outside the stockade the Pend Oreilles, slim, active men, bareheaded and almost naked, armed with bows and arrows and a few muzzle-loading rifles, flitted as spectres among the trees, their bowstrings twanging, and their long war arrows whizzing in swarms through the air. They gradually approached the stockade. It was evident that they meant to storm the fort. High above the din of battle sounded the directing voices of their chiefs. If anything was to be done to avert the final fight, which promised to be a slaughter, it had of necessity to be done quickly. Haley was torn by conflicting emotions. The Blackfeet had killed many of his friends and he hated them. But he depended on their trade for the support of his trading post. He was tired of hearing them boast, weary of seeing them swagger around his fort. He wanted them to be killed. But every Blackfoot represented a certain number of buffalo robes annually. He could not afford to have them killed. His commercial instincts triumphed. He entered one of the bastions which towered above the main fort, clambered to it summit, and there crouched. Then, after waving a white cloth for an instant, he stood erect and began to talk to the Pend Oreilles. Haley, slouch-hatted, flannel-shirted, rifle in hand, on a bastion addressing a war party of victorious Indians who were preparing to assault his fort, was an impressive spectacle. He was greeted with derisive yells. He stood calmly and waited until the woods became silent. Then he talked to the Pend Oreilles of the beauties of peace, of the benefits the Indians derived from commerce. He dwelt briefly on the causes of the hereditary war that raged between the Blackfeet and Pend Oreilles, and graphically set forth the advantages the latter would reap if they abandoned the warpath. He said that he was the friend of all Indians, and that it made him sad to see them kill one another. Finally, and by this time the Pend Oreilles were listening attentively to him, he said: "These Blackfeet braves whom you have driven into my corral are my friends. I have 15 white men in this fort. They have strong hearts. They shoot straight. I will not permit you to kill my friends. If you attempt to assault the corral my white men will kill you. You had better stop fighting and send your chief men into the fort to talk to the Blackfeet chiefs and make peace." Then he spoke briefly to the corraled Blackfeet, and they eagerly promised not to fire on the Pend Oreilles envoys.

Presently three young Indians, clad in breech-clouts, with their bows in their hands, came out from behind widely separated trees and walked on converging trails to the door of the fort. They were admitted and stood side by side, with their bows and fitted arrows in their hands, and gazed into the darkness through blazing eyes. Another door which opened into the corral was cautiously opened and five Blackfeet chiefs entered. They were wrapped in blankets, and carried their rifles openly in their hands. They were gigantic men and handsome. They looked curiously at the slight, alert Pend Oreilles, and the latter faced them in the gloom as though about to spring on them. I expected to see blood flow every instant. Silently the hostile envoys faced one another. Presently the eyes of the Blackfeet wavered, trembled, and sought to rest on the more friendly eyes of the whites. Haley interpreted for the Pend Oreilles, who voiced their determination through a young chief. He recounted the grievances of his people. He reproached, he invoked, he denounced, and his eyes ever blazed and his fingers toyed with his bowstring. His speech was listened to attentively by the Blackfeet. When he had finished talking he drew himself up proudly and gazed fearlessly and fiercely at his enemies. Haley turned to me and said: "He has been laying down the law to these thieves and cowards. He has been abusing their tribe, and he has consented to make peace and to let them out of the hole he has them in on his own terms, which are hard and degrading."

A Blackfoot chief dropped his blanket from his shoulders. In the dim light he looked like a bronze statue. He stepped forward a yard and began to talk slowly and with many gestures. Again Haley interpreted. Attentively the Pend Oreilles listened. Now their mobile faces lighted with amusement, then darkened with scorn and contempt. The Blackfoot's speech finished, it was scoffingly waved into a dark corner by the graceful hands of the Pend Oreilles. Then the leader turned to Haley, and in a few words dispensed with his services as interpreter. He strode close to the Blackfeet chiefs, who fairly cowered before him. He cast his bow and arrow on the ground, and began to talk in the sign language. His arms and hands moved incessantly. He rode horseback, he killed buffalo, he fished, he slept, he fought and scalped his foes, he cut lodge poles and pitched his lodge, and whatever he did did gracefully and well. While he was talking in signs the eyes of both whites and Indians were set on him. I heard murmurs of approval from the rough, half civilized traders, such as "Give it to the beggars," "Clean them out," "That is just," "That is true." To me the conversation was somewhat incomprehensible, but I gathered from the remarks of the white men and such of the signs as I understood that he was savagely scathing the Blackfeet and arrogantly dictating his terms of peace. Through with talking, he picked up his bow and arrow, shook hands with several of the white men, and walked out of the fort followed by his comrades. They separated and disappeared into the woods where their soldiers lurked.

He left the Blackfoot amazed at the audacity of his demands. He claimed every horse they had in the corral as prizes of war. He insisted that in the future the Columbia River Indians should be free to hunt and fish and camp in the land of the Blackfeet without molestation. All disputes about stolen horses were to be settled once for all by letting bygones be bygones, whoever then held the horses should keep them; but that no more horses should be stolen. In addition, and to hasten the making of the treaty, he said that he had sent runners to the main Pend Oreille tribe, in camp on the Milk River, to tell the warriors to hurry to the battlefield, and that he intended to have the horses that were in the corral and to scalp every Blackfoot in the party if his terms were not agreed to. And, he added, that he and his people had crossed the mountains expressly to fight the Blackfeet, and they intended to exterminate them, man, woman, and child, and use their country for a game preserve.

The Blackfeet chiefs were turned into the corral, first having been strongly advised by Haley to accept the terms offered. They talked for a few minutes with their men, and the terms were accepted. The horses were delivered. The Pend Oreilles withdrew from the river banks and adjacent woods. The cowed Blackfeet filed out of the stockade and disappeared down the valley, first having made arrangements to have their people come to the fort to solemnly ratify the treaty. The Pend Oreilles agreed to meet them at the expiration of two days on the tongue of land lying between the Belly and St. Mary's Rivers.

I was homeward-bound, but Haley told me that the ceremonies connected with the ratification of this treaty would probably be the last great Indian pageant to be witnessed on the continent, and that it would be well worth seeing. He urged me to remain to see the treaty made and to see the Summer trade he would afterward make with the Blackfeet.

On the afternoon of the second day about 150 Pend Oreille braves, well mounted and armed with rifles and bows and arrows, dashed into the valley at a gallop. They entered the river, and shouting and laughing, forded it and camped on the tongue of land. Quickly they posted sentinels on the summit of the bluff to watch for the approach of the Blackfeet. Presently some of the Pend Oreille braves forded the river and came to the fort. They were admitted. They were intelligent men, full of courage, and gay-spirited. They said that they desired to be at peace with the Blackfeet, whom they denounced as utterly villainous and treacherous. They said that they were going to have the privilege of hunting buffalo on the Saskatchewan plains or they were going to kill every Blackfoot they met. They held the courage and warlike skill of the Blackfeet in the utmost contempt.

That night the Pend Oreille camp resounded with merriment. Early the next morning, which fortunately was cool and pleasant, they put on gay-colored calico shirts and gaudy leggins made of blankets and painted their faces with vermillion. They gathered on the point and waited, their sentinels still posted on the bluffs. Down the river the faint barbaric music made by beating Indian drums arose. Presently the head of a column of mounted troops came into sight on the crest of the northern bluff of the river. Banners were flying, drums were sounding, and the Blackfoot warriors were chanting their marching song as they slowly advanced. They came to the Belly River, forded it, and marched past the fort to a level meadow, and there the head of the column halted. Long before the tail of the column had crossed the river their camp had been pitched. Conical lodges stood in regular rows, with wide streets between them. The s....s worked with ardor. Sentinels were posted on hills, from which they could overlook the plains which stretched toward the Sweet Grass Hills. The camp pitched, the Blackfeet braves gathered at the river bank. They were a magnificent body of warriors. They were perfectly armed with breech-loading rifles and Colt's revolvers. They were splendidly mounted on war horses. Their buckskin shirts were ornamented with many-colored quills of porcupines. Red and blue blankets, procured at the Hudson's Bay Company's trading posts, were wrapped carelessly around them. On their broad breasts hung ornaments and around their necks were necklaces of beads and of bear claws. Eagle feathers streamed fluttering from their coup sticks. Their faces were painted hideously.

A Pend Oreille chief advanced to the river bank, and using the sign language, told how many Blackfeet would be allowed to cross. About 200 warriors rode into the stream, forded it, dismounted on the other side, and strode in imposing array to where the council was to be held. There they sat on the ground. The Indian camp was silent. The children and s....s lined the river bank. Eight hundred warriors sat motionless on their horses. All looked at and strove to hear the words of the gesticulating figures standing on the council or treaty ground. For an hour the talk continued. A great pipe was brought to the treating braves. It was filled with tobacco, lighted, and passed from hand to hand, each warrior smoking it for an instant. A shout arose on the council ground. Quickly it was answered. Women and children began to talk and laugh. The treating Blackfeet sprang into their saddles, re-forded the river, and rode with joyful shouts into the ranks of their comrades. A war that had lasted for 60 years was ended. Presently the Pend Oreille braves mounted. Their sentinels left their posts. They formed into line. Then, singing their marching song, they rode into the river and crossed it. The ranks of the Blackfeet opened, and the two tribes assimilated. Together they rode into the Blackfoot camp. There the juicy humps of buffalo roasted before fires. Dogs were killed, cut up, and put into pots to boil. The Indian art of cookery was exhausted to do honor to the Pend Oreilles. That night the camp was a blaze of light, and a carnival of song and laughter and merry with feasting.

Early the next morning Haley sent one of his men into the camp with a message to the Pend Oreille chief, asking him to call at the fort. Soon the chief appeared. Haley explained to him that the Summer trade with the Piegan clan of the Blackfeet would begin the next day, that all the Indians would get drunk, that they would surely attack the Pend Oreilles if they were near by when they were drunk, and he urged the Pend Oreille chief to gather his men and return to his main camp and keep away from the trading post until after the Summer trade was over. The advice was good and the Indian accepted. He rode his horse through the streets of the village, calling to his warriors. He thanked the Blackfeet for their hospitality. His braves appeared. Indian maidens led their saddle horses to them and bade them farewell as they mounted. Lines of Blackfeet warriors stood by the lodges and shook hands with the departing Pend Oreilles, and exclaimed: "How! how! how!" as they rode off, laden down with gifts of blankets, painted buffalo robes, rifles, and presents of food. A group of Blackfeet warriors accompanied them, riding around and around them to display their admirable horsemanship. In a couple of hours the Pend Oreilles had disappeared beneath the gray horizon, the escort had returned, and the Summer trade and semi-annual "drunk" had begun.

That treaty made on the Belly River stood as long as buffalo grazed on the northern plains.

Frank Wilkeson.

* * * * * * * *

Some years ago, in late August, I was traveling from the land of the Blackfeet to Walla Walla, in Washington Territory. I had followed an Indian trail from the Saskatchewan Plains to the Cadotte Pass. In the pass I unsaddled my horse for his noon feed, and sat down to smoke. I had just left a noisy, buffalo-hunting Indian camp, and I presently conjured an Indian scene. Columns of Indians, painted and stripped to their breech clouts, filed past me and disappeared in the haze which hung over the eastern plains. Great herds of buffalo sprang into life in my brain, and bands of Cheyennes, Sioux, and Blackfeet pursued them. When the buffalo were falling, and the plains below me were a map of ever-shifting light and color and active life, the Utes, mounted and with bent bows and long, grooved war arrows drawn to their heads, dashed past me, and battle savage and bloody, raged below. I sat smoking and wondering why men ever became lonesome when they could repeople the remote solitude of highland and plain and enjoy scenes of human interest, when my horse threw up his head and sniffed inquiringly of the air and then trotted to me, and stood by my side looking at the summit of the pass, which was a few yards above us. Presently an Indian's head appeared above the crest of the range. I sat and looked at him and he looked at me. Soon another and another and another dark and savage visaged head rose above the crest, and then the head of a column of mounted Indians rode into sight. They were singing their marching song — much as the Indians in the Wild West Show do. Every trail was occupied. The Indians looked neither to the right nor to the left, but marched slowly past me. There were old men, and warriors, and young men, all with their rifles across their knees, and hundreds of women, some of who were handsome, and many children, and an army of dogs brought up the rear. I thought I had conjured to very good effect. For an hour this column swept past me, and I sat on a rock and smoked and looked at them. Not a word was spoken to me. Hardly a glance was cast at me. The migrating people talked to one another, and laughed, and had a good time generally. Three thousand Indians defiled in front of me. They were gay with bright-colored shirts, and gaudy blankets, and many-colored painted faces. I knew that these Indians were portions of the Nez Percé, Flathead, Spokane, Okinagan, Wenatchee, and Pend Oreille tribes, and that they were going to hunt buffalo on the Saskatechwan Plains and to fight the Blackfeet. These Indians riding past me in the Cadotte Pass made one of the most impressive spectacles I ever saw in the heart of the Republic.

That evening about dark, while I was riding westward on the Blackfoot River trail, I met a belated Indian who was hurrying after the main body. He made signs of inquiry to me, and I answered with signs. I did not fully understand the sign language, and the anxious Indian failed to interpret my meaning. Evidently I conveyed information of direful import. The dusky warrior started in his saddle. He slapped his mouth with open palm to express his great surprise, then wheeled his horse and galloped off before I had finished telling my story. I have often wondered what I really told that savage and to what I impelled him.

Document 64

Reservation Farming, Battle Losses, and the Whiskey Trade September 1, 1871

Source: C. S. Jones, United States Indian Agent, to Jasper A. Viall, Superintendent of Indian Affairs, Sept. 1, 1871, U.S. Commissioner of Indian Affairs, *Annual Report of the Commissioner of Indian Affairs* (Washington, D.C.: U.S. Government Printing Office, 1871), pages 840-842.

Editors' note: This annual report by Flathead Agent C. S. Jones was included because it contained considerable information about the farming on the reservation and a battle between the Salish Flathead and Sioux on the buffalo plains. A cricket infestation destroyed the 1871 crops on the Flathead Reservation. Jones' comments on the Kootenay reflect his bigotry and prejudice.

Flathead Indian Agency,
Jocko Reservation, Montana Territory, September 1, 1871.

Sir:

I have the honor to present herewith my first annual report of the condition of Indian affairs within the limits of this agency, of which I assumed control on the 17th of October last, having on that day relieved Lieutenant George E. Ford, United States Army, acting agent in charge.

The official receipts then passed, and now on file at Washington, together with the quarterly property returns subsequently rendered by me in accordance with regulations, will show the quantity, quality, and condition of the public property here at that time, since, and now.

Immediately upon assuming charge I caused the fences, which were in a very dilapidated condition, to be thoroughly repaired, and then completed the erection of a new log-building for kitchen and mess-room, the foundations of which had been commenced by my predecessor. During the present season about 40 acres of tolerable farming land have been under successful cultivation, planted as follows: 26 acres in oats, 8 in corn, 4 in potatoes, and 2 in garden vegetables. The product cannot now be estimated with accuracy, but that it will be sufficient for the subsistence, in part, of the employés connected with the agency, and for the animals belonging to it, as well as some to spare for destitute Indians, there can be no doubt. About 18 tons of hay have also been cut, and hauled from a distance of two miles to the agency, for the use of the animals during the coming winter. Wheat has not been sown this season, because past experience here proves it to be unprofitable, partially on account of the nature of the soil, but particularly at this time for the want of a good grist-mill, rendering necessary the transportation of wheat in bulk a distance of twenty-five miles to be ground into flour, and returned, the effect of which is so to enhance the cost as to render it more economical to purchase from time to time such supplies of ready-made flour as the necessities of the place may require.

The report made to the President by the Indian peace commission, January 7, 1868, and published in the reports of the Commissioner of Indian Affairs for that year, states the numbers of the tribes under the control of this agency, as follows: Flatheads, 558; Pend d'Oreilles, 918; Kootenais, 287; making a total of 1,763. An actual count of the Kootenais, made under my own observation shortly after arriving here, shows 318 members of that tribe, and excess of 31 over the estimate of the commissioners as above stated. Although I have had no opportunity to test the matter practically, as in the case of the Kootenais, yet I am satisfied from general inquiry, as well as from close observation, that the excess of numbers is quite as great *pro rata* among the Flatheads and Pend d'Oreilles as among the Kootenais, making the aggregate of the three tribes not less, probably, than 1,900. Their material condition will be seen from the following data, relating to the Pend d'Oreilles:

Number of farms cultivated, 70, varying in size from 5 to 60 acres, and averaging 15 acres.

Crop of 1870: Wheat, over 3,000 bushels; oats, about 900 bushels; potatoes, about 1,000 bushels; corn, about 100 bushels.

Amount of live stock: Horned cattle, about 800 head; hogs, about 100 head; horses, over 2,000 head.

Flatheads proper. — Number of farms cultivated, 35 averaging 12 acres each.

Crop of 1870: Wheat 2,000 bushels; oats, about 5,000 bushels; potatoes, about 650 bushels; corn, about 60 bushels.

Amount of live stock: Horned cattle, about 600 head; hogs, about 100 head; horses, about 1,100.

The Kootenais have nothing. They are idle, thriftless, improvident, and dishonest. They must not be confounded with the Upper Kootenais, living outside the jurisdiction of this agency, a very different class of people, moral, high-toned, and christianized, and from whom the branch here were driven many years ago on account of their vices and dishonesty. The sanitary condition of these tribes continues to be good, comparing favorably with that of other neighboring ones, as reported to me from time to time by Dr. [J. H.] McKee, the agency physician.

Spiritually, the Flatheads and Pend d'Oreilles are under the direction and teachings of the Roman Catholic church. Nearly forty years since some Iroquois from Canada, trading with the Flatheads, told them of the teachings of the Jesuit fathers, who for many previous years had been laboring among them, both for their spiritual and temporal good. The Flatheads, listening to these narratives of wonder and love, and as if directed by inspiration from above, selected some of their best men, rude and savage warriors, to proceed to St. Louis and ask a mission to teach them "the ways of the cross." Wending their way through the then almost trackless wilds between here and St. Louis, the delegation found itself among a hostile band of Sioux, on the western borders of Missouri, only to be murdered, but one escaping to tell the fate of the rest. In the following year, another and larger delegation was dispatched on this heaven-inspired duty, which succeeded in reaching the object of their destination, and prevailing of Father [Pierre] De Smet to accompany them to their wild mountain homes — the Flatheads thus becoming the first spiritual children among the red men of that venerated and distinguished Catholic missionary. Located among them, the Pend d'Oreilles soon sought his teachings, and bending their necks to the Christian yoke, both tribes in aggregate were duly received into the church, and, to this day, although subject to failings and short-comings, like the rest of humanity, they (particularly the Flatheads) will compare favorably, at least in morality, with a like number of people anywhere.

The earnest and energetic measures adopted by you in order to secure the entire suppression of the whisky traffic among the Indians have met with my zealous co-operation, and it is a subject of sincere congratulation that at the last term of the United States district court, held at Deer Lodge City, two white men, convicted of selling whisky to the Indians under my charge, were sentenced to the penitentiary, one for eighteen months, and the other, who plead guilty and asked for the mercy of the court, for a period of six months. The moral effect of these convictions, the first of the kind in the history of Montana, cannot be overestimated, and indeed it has ever since been sensibly felt in general quietude and exemption from violence prevailing at all points within the limits of this reservation to a degree not before known.

The supply of flour, which you so humanely authorized to be purchased during the past winter for the use of the necessitous among these tribes, was equitably distributed among them, and was productive of incalculable good by prevented a great amount of suffering, which I am confident would otherwise have occurred. Quite an equal amount will again be necessary for the coming season, for, in addition to the causes ordinarily operating to produce want among them, I have to report the entire failure of the crops belonging to the Pend d'Oreilles, caused by the depredations of immense swarms of crickets, which, during the absence of this tribe on the summer hunt, have devastated the little fields belonging to them, leaving nothing but a barren waste in their tracks. The Flatheads, though not so unfortunate in this respect, have more than an offset in the loss of eighteen of their best men, heads of families, killed in a fight with the Sioux about the 1st of July last, a terrible loss compared with the whole number of fighting men (about one hundred) belonging to the tribe prior to that time. The Sioux, who ambuscaded and attacked the party, afterward stated that it was done through mistake, under the impression that they were Crow Indians.

Subjects of great and paramount importance connected with the interests of this agency have from time to time been brought to the consideration of the Department at Washington through you, in communications from me, dated as follows: November 17 and December 8, 1870; January 23, January 19, and May 25, 1871. The first had reference to the removal of this agency to a central and more desirable point on the reservation. The second and third, and by far the most important, both related to the removal of the Flatheads proper from the Bitter Root Valley, where they now are, to this reservation. I say most important, because, considered in any and every point of view, whether in regard to the best interests of whites or Indians in that valley, there is no measure so indispensably necessary to the future well-being of both races as the one in question. Justice and good policy, as well as every consideration of common humanity united in demanding that this long-agitated subject should be definitely and promptly settled. The fourth of my communications, to which reference is herein made, was in response to the department school circular; and the fifth was in the form of a requisition for farming implements to supply the pressing wants of the tribes in that particular.

I cannot conclude without calling the special attention of the Department to the one relating to schools, dated January 19, 1871, accompanied as it is by a most interesting and valuable letter from the Rev. F. L. Palladino, S.J., in charge of the mission school on this reservation, in which the details connected with that subject are so fully given that I do not deem it necessary to duplicate the information in this report.

I am, sir, with great respect, your obedient servant,

C. S. Jones,
United States Indian Agent.

Hon. Jasper A. Viall,
Superintendent of Indian Affairs, Helena, Montana.

Document 65

Adventure on a Plains Buffalo Hunt

1871

Source: C. M. Russell, *More Rawhides* (Great Falls, Mont.: Montana Newspaper Assoc., 1925), pages 29-31.

Editors' note: McDonald referred to this buffalo adventure at various times over the years. Most of his accounts indicate the trip to the plains with the Pend d'Oreille occurred in 1871, but a few of the sources give the date as 1873. This adventure relates a valuable human-interest facet of the plains buffalo hunts in the 1870s. Russell probably added some color to the story. A Russell pen and ink drawing illustrated the story.

Dunc McDonald

"Dunc McDonald tells about a buffalo hunt he has when he's a kid," says Rawhide. "Like all things that happen that's worth while, it's long time ago. He's traveling with his people — they're making for the buffalo country. They're across the range — they ain't seen much — an old bull once in a while that ain't worth shootin' at, so they don't disturb nothin'. They're lookin' for cow meat and lots of it.

"Dunc's traveling ahead of the women with the men. As I said, it's a long time ago when Injuns ain't got many guns — they're mostly armed with bows and arrows. There's one old man packing a rifle. It's a Hudson Bay flint-lock but a good gun, them days. Duncan is young and has good eyes that go with youth. He sees a few buffalo in some broken hills, and tells this old man if he'll lend him his gun, he'll get meat. The old man don't say nothin', but taking the gun from the skin cover, hands it to Dunc. Dunc wants bullets and the powder horn but the old man signs that the gun is loaded and one ball is enough for any good hunter. The wolf hunts with what teeth he's got.

"Dunc knows he won't get no more so he rides off. There ain't much wind, but Dunc's gettin' what there is, and keepin' behind some rock croppin's he gets pretty close. There are five cows, all laying down. Pretty soon he quits his pony and crawls to within twenty-five yard and pulls down a fat cow. When his gun roars, they all jump and run but the cow he shoots don't make three jumps till she's down.

"There's only one hold," says Dunc, "shorter than a tail hold on a buffalo —
that of a bear."
Drawing by Charles Russell, C. M. Russell, *More Rawhides* (Great Falls,
Montana: Montana Newspaper Association, 1925), pages 29-31.

"When Dunc walks up she's laying on her belly with her feet under her. She's small but fat. When Dunc puts his foot again her to push her over, she gets up and is red-eyed. She sure shows war. The only hold Dunc can see is her tail and he ain't slow takin' it. The tail hold on a buffalo is mighty short, but he's clamped on. She's trying to turn but he's keepin' her steered right — and he's doing fine till she starts kickin'. The first one don't miss his ear the width of a hair. If you never saw a buffalo kick it's hard to tell you what they can do, but Dunc ain't slow slippin' his hold.

"There's nothin' left but to run for it. This rock croppin's ain't over two feet high, but it's all there is. These rocks are covered with ground cedar and Dunc dives into this. He gophers down in this cedar till a hawk couldn't find him. He lays there a long time, his heart poundin' his ribs like it will break through. When the scare works out of him he raises and there agin the rock rim lays the cow — it's a long shot and she's bled to death.

"'There's only one hold,' says Dunc, 'shorter than a tail hold on a buffalo — that of a bear.'"

Document 66

1872 Contract for Tribal Attorney

July 1, 1872

Source: Charlos, et. al., [Attorney contract with James Fullerton], July 1, 1872, "Treaty with United States" file, MONAC Papers, MS 184, box 124, Eastern Washington State Historical Society, Spokane, Wash.

Editors' note: A copy of this contract was found in a collection at the Eastern Washington State Historical Society which originally came from the Oregon Province Archives of the Society of Jesus in Spokane, Washington. No reference to the contract has been found in the Commissioner of Indian Affairs Papers at the National Archives or any other source. James Fullerton was a Washington, D.C., attorney in the late nineteenth century, but no record has been found of any suits or actions coming out of this contract. Presumably this was the first tribal attorney contract for the Flathead Reservation tribes.

Copy of the official copy.

Flathead Indian Agency
near Missoula, Montana Territory
July 1st 1872.

Know all men by these presents that we the chiefs and headmen of the Confederate Flathead Nation of Indians, have constituted, made and appointed, and by these presents do constitute, make and appoint James Fullerton Esqr. of Washington City, District of Columbia to be our true and lawful attorney for us, and in our name and stead, and to our use to ask, demand and recover from the United States of America, all such sum and sums of money, debts, dues, accounts and other demands whatsoever, growing out of or in reference to annuities from or treaties with the United States; or relating to lands as connected with or growing out of such treaties, which are or shall become due, owing, payable or belonging to us, or detained from us in any manner of ways or means whatsoever by the United States giving and granting unto our said attorney by these presents our full and whole power, strength and authority in and about the premises, to have use and take all lawful ways and means, in our name for the recovery thereof; and generally all and every other act and acts, thing and things, device and devices in the law whatsoever needful and necessary to be done in and about the premises for us and in our name to do, execute and perform as largely and amply to all intents and purposes as we might or would do if personally present or the matter required more special authority than is herein given: And attorneys, one or more under him for the purpose aforesaid to make and constitute and again at pleasure to revoke, satisfying, demand and recover from the United States of America, all such sum and sums of money, debts, dues, accounts and other demands whatsoever, growing out of or in reference to annuities from or treaties with the United States; or relating to lands as connected with or growing out of such treaties, which are or shall become due, owing, payable or belonging to us, or detained from us in any manner of ways or means whatsoever by the United States giving and granting unto our said attorney by these presents our full and whole power, strength and authority in and about the premises, to have use and take all lawful ways and means, in our name for the recovery thereof; and generally all and every other act and acts, thing and things, device and devices in the law whatsoever needful and necessary to be done in and about premises for us and in our name to do, execute and perform as largely and amply to all intents and purposes as we might or would do if personally present or the matter required more special authority than is herein given: And attorneys, one or more under him for the purpose aforesaid to make and constitute and again at pleasure to revoke, satisfying, allowing and holding for firm and effectual all and whatever our said Attorney shall lawfully do in and about the premises by virtue hereof.

In testimony whereof we have hereunto affixed our signatures and seals, on this First day of July A.D. One Thousand Eight Hundred and Seventy Two.

S. (L.S.) Charlos His x mark, Head Chief of Flatheads
S. (L.S.) Michelle His x mark, Head Chief of Pend d'Oreilles
S. (L.S.) Eneas His x mark, Head Chief of Kootenays
S. (L.S.) Arlee His x mark, Flathead Chief
S. (L.S.) Adolfe His x mark, Flathead Chief
S. (L.S.) Big Canoe His x mark, Pend d'Oreilles Chief
S. (L.S.) Andrè His x mark, Pend d'Oreilles Chief
S. (L.S.) Paul His x mark, Cootenay Chief
S. (L.S.) Kinlacko His x mark, Cootenay Chief
S. (L.S.) Lickoss His x mark, Cootenay Chief

S. Baptiste His x mark Marengo, Interpreter
S. Lorette Hix x mark Pablo, Interpreter.

Signed, sealed and delivered in presence of Chas Schafft (S) John W. Ragan (S) James House (S) Wm. W. Jones.

Certified to be a true copy from the Original. C. S. Jones U.S. Indian Agent.

I certify, on honor, that the above recited power of Attorney, was duly acknowledged and signed by the subscribers in my presence on this the first day of July A. D. One Thousand Eight Hundred and Seventy Two, and that before taking such acknowledgment I satisfied myself by personal investigation that is [sic] was fairly and duly obtained, and that I fully explained the contents and purports thereof to the parties acknowledging the execution of the same; and in accordance with letter of instruction from the department of the interior dated January 21st 1871.

(S) C. S. Jones
U.S. Ind. Agent.

Document 67

Gossip and News from Flathead Agency

August 6, 1872

Source: *The Pioneer* (Missoula, Mont.), Aug. 10, 1872, page 2, col. 4.

Editors' note: Kalispelm who signed this letter was Charles Shafft, long-time Flathead Agency clerk. Actual events were behind most of the incidents described in this letter, but it is very hard to determine where the facts ended and Shafft's creative writing began.

[Communicated]

Jocko, F. R.,
August 6, 1872.

Major W. J. McCormick:

Dear Sir,

The great Jubilee and peace festival which Uncle Sam semi-occasionally gives to his red children of the confederate Flathead Nation came off last week. Knowing that no representatives of the press would be present, on account of the intercourse law, which prohibits whiskey being brought on the Reservation, your humble servant mounted his wooden legged nag and started for the Flathead Agency in order to take notes.

I arrived at the ancient ruins just in time to be invited to dinner, and of course I accepted the invitation with the expectation of being regaled with camas, berries, buffalo meat, having understood that no other subsistence had been provided for the Indian Department here by the authorities that be; however Major C. S. Jones agreeably disappointed by leading me to a table, which his energy and private credit had supplied with civilized and substantial items of diet.

Being refreshed I was introduced to the chiefs of the Flathead tribe, who seeing me with note book in hand, supposed I was a medium of the great father and told me to make notes that they would take the blankets which they had just received to the Bitter Root valley and hoist them onto the backs of their s....s and papooses as emblimatical of the Stevens Treaty. I kindly tried to persuade them to spread their blankets in the valley of the Jocko, but they were unanimous in the sentiment that where their fathers died they would sustain themselves to the last bitter end — to the last Bitter Root. I left them to their fate.

Next morning the Pen d'Oreilles were to receive their cover of the red, white and blue — minus the star, blankets which Stevens had secured for them, and I retired early in order to spend a sleepless night and quietly to listen to the harmonious sounds emitted by the canine creation.

At about 9 o'clock, the flour of chivalry of the Pen d'O'reilles, consisting of about 15 men and an amazon, raised the war whoop at the S. E. corner of the Agency fence, and violently rushed around the encampments of about 100 lodges several times.

Having exhausted their steam they pulled up and said that Major Jones was their father, that he had done more for them than any other itlemakum had. They said that the Crows was bad people and had killed four of the Pen d'Oreilles, and regretted that the gunsmith shop of the Agency had been stolen years ago by the Kooteniais.

Then they wanted a smoke but the Indian Department at Helena, had not raised any tobacco for the confederate Flathead nation, and the pipe of peace could not be lighted.

The Pen d'Oreilles were hungry, and nothing had been provided but a vial of wrath by the Superintendent; but the Major had foreseen this and set the vial of wrath aside by laying some £2000 of beef, which with all spareable vegetables was freely given and cheerfully accepted.

The blankets were distributed agreeably, under the direction of the chiefs and the Major. There were enough to cover four fifths of the tribe, the other one-fifth, (principally females) has departed for Missoula to get covered with something else. All the Indians was well satisfied that Gov. [Isaac] Stevens was a big liar.

A horse race came off between a Prince and a subject, the head chief of the Pen d'Oreille and the cook of the Agency. The distance run was 1/2 mile, which the cook gained by several feet and the chief lost with $50, a $40 horse and pair of blankets. 40 blankets 6 pistols and 4 horses changed hands on the outside.

An eight mile race was made between Roman Nose and Aleck Bonaparte. 5 horses were gained by the latter on account of the former's horse bolting at the 4 mile turn. 45 blankets bet on the outside. A club race of 7 was won by Louison, together with 2 horses and 30 blankets.

The sports finished with a foot race between Stephen, an athlete and Pierre a stripling; distance 200 yards, the betting was heavy on Stephen, but Pierre got away with 20 blankets.

Most of the Indians are now departing to the fishing grounds (except the Kootenais who are waiting for the coming of the chief.)

The Agency employees are hard at work, getting in the crops. They are a very moral set of men and expect to get a holiday to pay their bills whenever their money is withdrawn from market and delivered to them. Some of them who have not received a cent for the last six months, are rather hostile, because they have neither credit nor money. Major Jones is sticking to his ship nobly and will no doubt bring it through the breakers. The painful accident which befell him last night has undoubtedly been reported to you. He is doing well.

Kalispelm.

Document 68

Letters from Indian Students at St. Ignatius Mission August 18, 1872

Source: "Letter of Rev. F. L. Palladin, in Charge of Saint Ignatius Mission," U.S. Board of Indian Commissioners, *Annual Report of the Board of Indian Commissioners* (Washington, D.C.: U.S. Government Printing Office, 1872), pages 186-187.

Editors' note: Father Lawrence Palladino's views on Flathead Reservation affairs were interesting, but the appended letters from two female Indian students at St. Ignatius Mission were even more valuable.

Letter of Rev. F. L. Palladin, in Charge of Saint Ignatius Mission.

Helena, Montana, *August 18, 1872.*

Honored Sir:

In compliance with your wish, expressed in the very kind conversation with which you were pleased to favor me, I beg to submit to your kind consideration the following statements, containing the substance of what I made known to you by word of mouth a few days ago in that conversation in regard to our Flathead, Pend d'Oreilles, or Kootenay Indians:

1. The Government has not kept some of the solemn treaty-stipulations entered upon with these Indians in 1855. One of the stipulations was that they would have houses built for them in the Jocko reservation, but not a single house, to my knowledge, has ever been built for any of our Indians at the Government's expense. If a good many of our Indians do live in houses they owe it principally to the missionaries. Many, however, are still houseless, and the missionaries have no means to furnish them with one.

2. One hospital, instituted and provide for them in the treaty, has not been established as yet. I feel confident in stating that nothing would prove a greater blessing to the sick and destitute Indians than such an institution. To make it really a blessing to the Indians, and beneficial to them in all its bearings, I should suggest that it be intrusted to the Sisters of Charity, who have devoted themselves for several years to the Christianization and civilization of these Indians, and this, under whatever point of view their assistance may be claimed, whether industrial, mental or moral, or economical.

3. That the Indians are capable of Christianization and civilization is beyond question, though it is necessarily a slow and tedious task. I here inclose some letters, intended for your honor, from some of the pupils who are being educated by the Sisters of Charity of our mission of Saint Ignatius. The letters will speak for themselves. Your little Indian correspondents are all pure Indian blood, and their letters are their own thinking, speaking, and spelling. I must here observe that the benefit for education of Indian children must necessarily be very limited where subsistence is not provided for them, Indian children being obliged to hunt and fish for a living. I do think, if there be any means of civilizing the Indians with success, and permanently, it is in industrial boarding-schools for children. But unless the Government affords some means to board and clothe the children it would be impracticable.

* * * * * * * *

I beg also to call your attention to some serious points connected with the Jocko reservation, and deeply affecting the future well-being of the Indians. White people are crowding around the reservation, and some of them of late are actually trespassing on the reservation, in open violation of the treaty and against the remonstrances of the local authorities. This also affects the Flatheads unfavorably to their removal from the Bitter Root Valley to the Jocko, since they judge from this that they shall be as little protected there on the Jocko against the rapacity of the whites as they have been in the Bitter Root Valley. I finally suggest the consideration that our Indians stand in need of some agricultural implements, such as plows, &c.

They have been asking for them for five or six years, but to no avail. If, also, the Indian women were furnished with some clothes it would prove a good means to preserve their morals.

Hon. Felix R. Brunot.

————————

Letters of Indian children.

Dear Sir:

I take the liberty to write you these few lines, to tell you that we are glad that you are charged of the Indians, since we are told that you take interest in what concerns them.

We are sixteen little Indian girls here, under the care of the Sisters, but we hope that many more will enjoy the same blessing one day.

Oh, how much we would like to see all the Indian children live as happy as we do. I know the Sisters would be glad to receive more children, but they have not the means to maintain them.

I know they would not refuse any that they could take, for they take as much care of little Indians as they would of their own friends. We did not even know how to serve God well until we were put under the charge of the good Sisters. If you can do some good for the Indian children, I hope you will give us many more companions, by helping the Sisters to keep them here. If you do you will have the prayers of all these children, for we pray every day for our benefactors here.

Yours, respectfully,
Mary, (aged fourteen years.)

Dear Sir:

As I am yet a very little girl I will only repeat what my companions told you on their letters. I will be very glad if you are good to the Indians, and will pray for you.

Therese Sophie, (aged ten years.)

Document 69

First Negotiations with General James Garfield in the Bitterroot Valley August 22 and 23, 1872

Source: "Indian Council," *The Pioneer* (Missoula, Mont.), Aug. 31, 1872, page 2, col. 2-4.

Editors' note: These negotiations brought together the desire of the Salish to have a reservation in the Bitterroot Valley and the intention of the white government negotiators to pressure them to remove to the Jocko Valley. Confusion over the final agreement reached with Garfield was to lead to years of hard feelings on the part of the Salish. Note Chief Adolph's complaints about his problems planting crops without proper farm equipment.

Indian Council.

Gen'l James A. Garfield, Commissioner on the part of the United States for the removal of the Flathead Indians from the Bitter Root valley to the Jocko reservation accompanied by Major Swaim, of the U.S. Army, Gov. B. F. Potts, Hon. W. H. Clagget, Col. J. A. Viall, superintendent of Indians affairs, and Col. W. F. Sanders, of Helena, met the Chiefs and head men of the Flathead tribe, in council about 1 o'clock on Thursday the 22d near the St. Mary's mission in the Bitter Root valley. Baptiste Maringo and Francois, two half-breeds were selected as Interpreters. As the day was intensely hot, three of the largest Indian tents made of dressed Buffalo and Elk sins had been constructed into one large tent or pavilion in which the council was held. The Chiefs, Victor [i.e., Charlo], Adolph and Arley came forward and took seats immediately in front of Gen'l Garfield and through the interpreters signified their readiness to hear what the General had to say to them. Addressing the Chiefs, the General said: I have been sent by the President from Washington to see the Flatheads in regard to their affairs in the Bitter Root valley. The President thinks very highly of the Flatheads. Since the time of Lewis and Clark, they have been friendly to the whites. He told me that the Flatheads were learning and doing well. Before we talk about the matter of business, I want to inquire whether the Chiefs understand the Stevens treaty in reference to the Bitter Root valley made 17 years ago with Victor. Do you understand under that treaty the Flatheads were to go to the Jocko, if the President should think best?

Chiefs. We understand the treaty.

Gen'l G. Do you know that the President last fall decided not to set the Bitter Root valley apart as a reservation for the Flathead tribe.

Chiefs. We understand that he did.

Gen'l G. Now the President has sent me here to find out what would be the most agreeable way for you to go to the Jocko. The President has heard that some of the Flatheads want to stay here on their farms, and leave the tribe, and that any such may remain, Congress has made a law allowiing [sic] such to remain and leave the tribe. Congress will give those who are farming and desire to remain from 40 to 160 acres of land. Congress thought that some bad white men might get these farms from you, so they provided that the Indians should not sell them.

The other Indians that have not been farming, the President and Congress will provide farming tools to help them start farms on the Jocko. They will have their annuities until the Stevens treaty runs out but the President knows for several years that some of the agents have cheated the Flatheads and he want[s] to make up for it. So the money for which there [sic] lands are sold shall be given to the Flatheads. The law which Congress made, provides that $5,000 shall be given each year for ten years to the Indians that go to the Jocko. Now the President will pay that $5,000 in any kind of goods, farming tools, or cattle that he thinks is best for them. He wants me to ask the Chiefs what they want this money in. Besides the $50,000 the President has given me $5,000 to be used in moving the Indians to the Jocko. I want you to tell me how you want that money expended. Those Indians that stay here and take farms will become citizens, and will not have any of the annuities, or any part of the $50,000. The Pen d Oreilles and Kootenais will get no part of the $50,000, it belongs to the Flatheads. The President thinks it will be better for the Flatheads to go to the Jocko where white men can't settle, and where they can have cattle then to remain here where white men and the railroad will come. The President and Congress are keeping all the treaties and paying all the money, that belong to them, and they know there are rascals that cheat them, but that is no fault of theirs. I am now ready to hear what you have to say to me, and will answer as best I can.

Charlois, the Chief rose, shook hands with the Gen'l and then spoke as follows: When the Flatheads made the treaty with [Isaac] Stevens it was understood they were to stay here. The great Father does not come here and see the Bitter Root valley, nor the land on the Jocko, where he wants us to go. Gov. Stevens gave us blankets and told us we could stay here. I have no more to say. Charlois presents to Gen'l G. copy of the Stevens treaty, and commission from Gov Stevens to Victor the old chief of the Flatheads, and invited Major [John]

Owen to a seat in the council as their friend. Arley, a sub-chief was the next speaker he said. Here is Major Owen, he has been here 22 years with us, he is our friend, he knows our wants, he can tell you all about us. We keep the treaty in our hands we know what it is. You may think that Steven and Victor are dead, but we don't take it so. We hold the treaty all the time. The President sent Gov. Stevens to make a treaty with us, we listened to him and heard his words. There are four things we have not got that was promised us, a Schoolmaster, a Blacksmith, a Carpenter and a Doctor.

They promised that the Flatheads should be taught for twenty years, how to read and write, and then they would be like white men, know how to do everything, but nothing has been done.

Gen'l G. Did you understand that you were to have these things here.

Arley. We understood that we were to have these things when our lands were given us. There is a man (pointing to Col. Viall) about my shape, with a big belly on, who told the Flatheads to put their names down. We don't understand anything, we are like the brutes of the valley. I felt very sorry when I put my name down. I think I have more right on this land than anybody. You white men belong to another tribe. I can't do things as you do. I have another way. You whites have different laws from the Flatheads. The whites have strong laws so have the Indians. The Indians are following their own laws, we don't want to be white men and live under their laws.

Now if I was to ask you to be an Indian and do like Indians would you do it?

If I was to find your people in another country as the white men found us here, and tell them to go away, that I wanted to put my people there would you like it? That is the reason I want to stay here, because we were here first. The Flatheads have always been here, they have lived and died here, the bones of our fathers and mothers are mixed with the dirt of this valley. There is not one of my people that thinks of going to the Jocko.

Gen'l G. The great father did not understand that he was to go and hunt other lands for the Flatheads, he understood that he was to have this valley and Jocko examined by his officers. He thinks that if there should be a railroad through this valley then it would not be a good place for the Flatheads. The Stevens treaty allows railroads to be built through the Indians land, and when we build railroads, the whites will come and settle for forty miles on each side of the road. By the order of the President which he made last fall this valley has been given to the whites, and he thinks it will not be good for the Flatheads to stay here. He has seen white men from this country and has received a great many letters and in that way he thinks it would not be good for the Indians to stay here.

Arlee. If this land is no account we don't see what the whites want to come here so thick for.

Gen'l G. We have to build railroads through low passes in the mountains.

Arlee. We dont get our money, we don't know what to think about what you say.

Gen'l G. If the President can get men honest enough to give you this money you shall have it. We dont want you to become white men. We want you to be by yourselves.

Arlee. God has given you a manner and he has given us a manner, and when we are dead we will know who was right and who was wrong.

Gen'l. I wan't [sic] you Chiefs to go with me to the Jocko, and show me where you want to settle and what kind of houses you want so I can tell the President.

Arlee. White men came among the Indians poor, the Indians took their part and took care of them. Now the white men are rich and the Indians are poor, why does the great father take the part of the white men now? We used to take pity on the whites when they were poor. Our chiefs told us to take care of the white men, our people obeyed their chiefs. We did not think that the white people would disobey their chiefs and steal our property. The Flatheads never drew the white man's blood.

Adolph. When Gov. Stevens made the treaty he told Victor that the Flatheads should never leave this land. Gov. Stevens put flour on his head, said he was a white man. I don't understand the line across the Lo Lo Fork. When Gov. Stevens held up his hands after making the treaty what did he mean? My hands are dry. I don't tell lies. I think you are a friend.

When the Flatheads made the treaty with Gov. Stevens, we took our bows and arrows and threw them away, made peace with everybody. Did God tell you to come and drive the poor Indians away from this land? You see morning and night they don't move, they are the same so are the Flatheads. God put the Flatheads here and when they are moved he will move them, in no other way will they be moved. I have showed you my hands my head and my heart, they are good.

Gov. Stevens promised us two horses and two cows each where are they, he promised us plows, where are they? I have ploughed with my hands, they are worn out.

Gov. Stevens asked us to do right and said the great father would do right, we have done right. The Sioux are whipping you. You ought to put them in the timber in bad places, and not the Flatheads. I don't want to spill my blood.

Gen'l. The Flatheads were in the Crow country when their 17 young men were killed and not on their reservation.

Adoph. We feel good when you are here. When you are gone white men will ask us to do wrong. We ought to be good and laugh all the time.

Gen'l. Do I understand the Chiefs to say, that their people will not leave the Bitter Root valley.

Charlois. We will not go, we will not accept the terms. I speak for my tribe.

General Garfield here explained to the chiefs at length the advantages to the Indians in removing to the Jocko. The order of the President directing their removal, the trouble that would come upon them eventually from contact with the whites, the building of the R. R. followed by the Bitter Root valley settling up with whites, that in seven years more their annuities would run out, that if they would go to the Jocko, they should have $5,000 each year for ten years, besides their annuities closing with the question, "are the chiefs willing to go with me to the Jocko and select their farms."

Charlois. We know the Jocko, we have been there many times, only wheat and potatoes can be raised there.

Gen'l. The $50,000 given under the law of Congress goes to the Flatheads alone. The Pen d O'reilles and Kootenais will get none of it. But you cannot have this $50,000 unless you go to the Jocko. I want you to tell me before I go if you want me to say to the great father when I go back that his children the Flatheads will not leave the Bitter Root valley, and will not obey his order. You can give me your answer in the morning.

Council adjournment until 9 o'clock in the morning.

Friday morning, Aug. 23. — On the reassembling of the council Charlois said I don't want you to go back and tell the great father that his children the Flatheads will not obey his order. The Chiefs will go with you to the Jocko as you desire, and will then tell you what you may say to the great father for his children.

Document 70

Partial Agreement on the Bitterroot and
Tragic Consequences
August 25, 1872

Source: "Conference of Hon. James A. Garfield, Special Commissioner, with the Indians of the Bitter Root Valley, Montana," U.S. Board of Indian Commissioners, *Annual Report of the Board of Indian Commissioners* (Washington, D.C.: U.S. Government Printing Office, 1872), pages 171-174.

Editors' note: These negotiations had some strange and tragic consequences. Despite recording and publishing the clear statement by Charlo that "I won't sign it," when Garfield's final report was published an x was entered next to Charlo's name suggesting that he had signed. Many Montana whites seized on this to say Charlo had broken his word and had promised Garfield he would move to Jocko. Charlo was always bitter about this charge and many historians have criticized this "forgery." The editors have never found a place where Garfield claimed that Charlo had signed the agreement, and there is no x on the original copy of the 1872 agreement in the Office of Indian Affairs file. General Garfield swore that the government would never take the Jocko Reservation away from the Indians or allow the land to be sold without their consent. This promise was violated by Congressman Joseph Dixon in 1904.

Conference of Hon. James A. Garfield, Special Commissioner,
with the Indians of the Bitter Root Valley, Montana.

General Garfield met the chiefs at the Flathead agency pursuant to the appointments. We report the following as having occurred at the interview:

General Garfield. The Great Father understands that the three tribes own this reservation and that the Flathead is the leading tribe, and he thinks it would be better for them to be here, near the agency farm and mill, where their goods are distributed, so that they can see to their own interests; and he made this order for their removal on their account and for their good. Would you like to know what this Great Father will do for you if you come over here?

Charlois. Will what I say be taken in good part?

General Garfield. Yes.

Charlois. We will not talk mean against the Great Chief. We do not like to come here, nor do we like to become citizens and remain on the Bitter Root.

How could I be a white man? My skin is red. This is my land as well as the Bitter Root. I do not see why he wants to put me here borrowing this land. I want you to tell me how it is going to be about this land.

General Garfield. This land belongs to the three tribes, and the Great Father will never take it away nor allow any one else to take it away, unless they want to part with it. In the Stevens treat[y] you agreed to let a railroad be built through it; but the Great Father will not allow the land to be sold without your consent. He does not know that he will want to build a railroad through here; but you gave the right to do so and no more. The Great Father has built a mill here to saw lumber and grind grain for Indians without expense to them, and here they have a farmer, blacksmith, and carpenter to teach them. Here you can learn to farm. The Great Father will have men here. He wants you to have horses and land and learn to work. Then you can go and hunt, but have homes to come to. The Great Father does not expect Charlois to be a white man, but wants him to learn some of their ways and have a home here. The Great Father is glad to know Charlois does not allow the Flatheads to drink, but punishes them for so doing; but he fears, if the Flatheads remain in the Bitter Root among the whites, that he cannot keep them from becoming drunkards. I want to know how many families you have among the Flatheads, and the Great Father will build them houses. We know you have been badly treated; your money and goods have not come as they should; but the Great Father does not intend this shall happen any more. He does not want you to come over here without homes, and has given me money to build houses, so that you can have places to live in when you come. He wants you to select the places where you want these houses built, and he will have them placed there.

Adoph. Only one thing, Charlois and I do not believe all we hear. Since I got sense enough to know I fear the Great Chief. You are a great chief. I am afraid of you. You are like Charlois; when we want a talk nobody comes to talk with us. I told you once before I do not mean any harm.

General Garfield. The Great Father told me to tell you just how he feels and what I promise you will be done. I want to know how many houses you want and I want you to see the crops, mill, and shops, and know what he has done to help the Indians. Lumber, shingles, flour, carpenter and blacksmith work will call you here. There are ten or twelve acres of wheat up here, and if you come over I shall give that to you. I shall plow you some ground and you shall have plows, harrows, hoes, shovels, and tools you need. I shall have the agent and superintendent go to work now and fix up places. If you do as he desires, the Great Father will take care of you.

Charlois's brother. Charlois says he will not come over here and live. Victor liked the Bitter Root, and took the land there, and as long as he lived he liked it, and when he died he dropped it to Charlois, who is in his place and feels just so and won't let it go. I want to know if the Great Father sent you to remove us over here?

Arley. Have what I say well written down. I shall talk to you and Charlois, both chiefs. I studied what I say; if you think it is so, it will be so. I have a place in the Bitter Root, — three houses, and fields, and good crops, like white man. I get money for it. Now over here when we get to talking about it, I have two hearts, one to come and one to stay. I have been there nine years; I go nowhere. Now you know what I think. You were to give us money for ten years; why is this? This land will only last ten years; it will wear out. The money does not go far enough. There is no end to the Bitter Root; there is to your money. My land is worth considerable; if I live long enough, I shall have considerable property. The man who is fat like me told us the Great Father would give us money as long as we lived about the houses. Perhaps your $5,000 would only last to build ten houses. I do not think $5,000 enough to start on. Some are afraid this land will go as the Bitter Root has. They told us we should always have that, but in a few years they take it away. I wish it could be always for Indians. This is the way my heart is for this place. The Flatheads feel as if they were getting lost for white men. I wish this place was always for the Flatheads; Victor would come again and should be a great chief once more over all our people. If the Flatheads should come here and be white men, then the Flatheads would be chief of all. If white men come we want troops to drive them out. I do not know how you feel, or how Charlois feels, but if you will give more money we will go with you; if not, we will go to the Bitter Root.

General Garfield. I see you occupy middle ground; you stand between us. I hope we shall all meet on Arley's own ground. If the superintendent said you were always to have $5,000 he was mistaken; it is for ten years — no longer. After that I can not promise, for I do not know as I could perform it. Colonel [Jasper] Viall does not mean that, I guess. I will build fifty or sixty houses if you need so many. I know $5,000 will not do it, but the Great Father has men, and all will be put in, so it will be as good as ten thousand. I know Arley loves the Bitter Root and has a nice farm, but fear his children will not love it. You must think of your children, and not yourselves. If you come here the Great Father will not let whites in here. Victor consented to whites going into Bitter Root at first. That was because they were not crowded by whites. Here it must be different. In this treaty I see Victor was chief of Flatheads, Pend d'Oreilles, and Kootenais. When Lewis and Clarke stopped at Lo-lo Fork, Victor was a little boy, but his tribe was a great nation. But now they have dwindled down. If they come up here I trust their tribes will increase and Charlois, Arley, and Adolph will be chiefs of the whole Flathead nation, because *they* do not drink nor fight.

Arley. Will you give more?

General Garfield. I cannot promise more; it is all I have. I will say to the Great Father he ought to give more to the Flatheads. The annuities are divided among the three tribes, but the $5,000 I have, and the $5,000 for ten years is for the Flatheads alone. Besides this, I am authorized to bring some presents for the chiefs and Victor's wife. You who have improvements in the Bitter Root can sell them to the whites. The fathers sold their houses twenty years ago for $250 to John Owen. So Indians can sell out. Do you think I am telling you the truth? If not you need not listen longer. I want to put it in writing, that the Great Father will build houses and fences, and pay this money, and that you will come here. (Here the chiefs requested that the agent, Mr. [C. S.] Jones, to examine General Garfield's credentials, and they were subject to a searching scrutiny and explained as being formal and genuine.)

General Garfield. I am in favor of whites being wholly excluded from this place.

Charlois. Is the land in the Bitter Root the Great Father's or ours? We want money one year, wagons next, teams next, tools next, not blankets all the time. (To Agent Jones.) Are you going to the Great Father?

Jones. I hope to.

Charlois. I want you to set us right before the Great Father, and tell him what I say and what white men are doing against us. I won't go to the Jocko. The young men of the Kootenais or Pend d'Oreilles will do something foolish, and then there may be a fight right there. When Stevens made the treaty, Lo-Lo Fork was made the line, and I never forget it and I stay there. If I go I shall go another way, but not to Jocko. Here they will steal. If Major Jones says the Great Father wants me to go, I will go the other way. If only my people where here, I would come, but there are bad people here. If you want me to starve, I tell you I am a chief too; I will go toward the buffalo country. Major Jones, you tell the Great Father what I say. The Flatheads about all feel as I feel.

A Young Brave. I feel as Charlois; where he goes I will go.

(General Garfield here resolved to reduce his proposition to writing, and a recess of an hour was taken, at the close of which there was a farther conference, in which the paper was interpreted to them and duplicates prepared.)

General Garfield, (to Charlois.) Have you a paper making Victor chief of three tribes?

Charlois. Yes.

General Garfield. I think you should be chief of all three tribes. Have you received a paper?

Charlois. No.

General Garfield. I am willing to ask the Great Father to give you such a paper. Do you want it?

Charlois. No.

Generl Garfield. We have had a long talk, and now I must go back to the Great Father. You have been very kind to me, and I must tell him all about our talk. I will carry this paper to the Great Father, and if you sign it, it is a contract between us. If you do not sign it, it will show the Great Father what I propose and what you are not willing to do. You have heard it read and know what it is. I want you each to answer, so that I can tell the Great Father whether the Flatheads will obey his order or no.

Charlois. I won't sign it.

Arley. I will sign it. When shall I come over? I do not want to leave until spring, until my cattle are wintered in the Bitter Root.

General Garfield. That will do; but you want to be here, so that you and your people can put in crops. How many will you bring; all your family?

Adolph. I know what you want, but I am not talking. I think may be it is so, may be not so. I have two hearts. Is it true that Charlois is to be head of three tribes?

General Garfield. It can be so I think, and I will ask the Great Father to make Charlois chief of three tribes.

Adolph. Will you move us from here if we come?

General Garfield. We should be everlastingly cursed if we do without your consent.

Adolph. Will the Great Father keep whites away?

General Garfield. Yes, I will ask him to take means to do so.

Adolph. (Showing hands blistered by hard work.) Will my hands get well if I come? The whites up in Bitter Root say you will drive us off in three days if we come.

General Garfield. There are some bad men who tell you these things. They told me you had got the Nez Percés there to fight the whites and pretended you were going to be bad Indians; but before I saw you I wrote back to the Great Father that it was not true, and now I want you here away from those bad whites, and I want Charlois to come and be chief of the three tribes and maintain the glory of Victor. He is young and we want him to live as chief of these tribes many years. Now I shall order the men to go to work and build houses for the Indians, and three houses for the chiefs, and Charlois's house will be very lonesome until he comes over to the Jocko. I will take this paper to the Great Father and tell him Charlois will not sign it; that Arley will; that Adolph won't say whether he will or no.

Charlois. Young men like this (selecting one) will go with me.

Adolph. I don't know what to say. If my chief was alive, I would answer. I don't know what the Great Father will say.

General Garfield. The Bitter Root will soon be settled up; the Great Father has so ordered, and he will not take that order back.

Charlois. I have told you once what I am going to do. When Major Jones goes east I will go the other way. My father felt so, and so do I. I would not like to be head chief over the three tribes.

General Garfield. I must say another word. The promises here are for those who come over. They will do all promised in this paper.

(Here Arley and Adolph signed the paper.)

(Charlois, to General Garfield.) I am not mad, but I must see what is done here and see my people.

Colonel Viall. When you (chiefs) come to Helena, call and see me at the Indian office.

Charlois. (laughing.) Do you want to whip me?

Colonel Viall. No, I want to give you some tobacco.

Charlois. You ought to whip me, I think.

This closed the negotiation. The three chiefs went out in the afternoon, and Arley and Adolph selected their farms and places of residence, and houses will be constructed at once.

Accompanying the chiefs to Missoula, General Garfield made them each some valuable presents and departed to go east, while they went to the Bitter Root.

Document 71

Indian Farmers and Fishing in the Bitterroot

November 23, 1872

Source: Calcium, "Up the Bitter Root: With Notes on the Side," *The New North-West* (Deer Lodge, Mont.), Nov. 23, 1872, p. 3, c. 4.

Editors' note: This travelogue includes some very useful information about Indian farming and fishing practices in the Bitterroot in the 1870s.

Up the Bitter Root.
With Notes on the Side.

Editor New North-West:

But of the Lo-Lo, or Travelers' Rest Creek, as Lewis and Clarke called it, I may have occasion to say more again, and will proceed on my journey. The first night I stopped at Mr. McWhirk's, 16 miles from Missoula, who came to this country last spring from Ohio, to try his hand at farming in the valley of the Bitter Root. A portion of his ranche is under a good state of cultivation. From sixteen acres sown in grain, he had some four ricks of wheat and one of oats — a crop any farmer in the East would be proud to take from four times that amount of ground.

Keeping on the right hand side of the river in the morning, I passed many
Fine Farms,
Whose crowded stockyards gave proof that a most bountiful harvest had been gathered, while the owners patiently awaited the arrival of the threshers.

The lands nearest the river are covered with a splendid growth of pine, which, with no underbrush, renders it easy of access. Some day this will all be valuable for lumber, most of the trees being clear of limbs for a distance of forty or sixty feet and from eighteen inches to three feet in diameter.
Prairie Chickens
Are seemingly as numerous in the valley as in Illinois or Iowa. They sat in the trees and on the fences by hundreds, enjoying the warm morning sun. They are not quite as large as the same specie of birds in the Western States, but they more than make up in sweetness of meat. Pheasants of the old fashioned kind are also found in great numbers near the river and in the brush along the creeks. This a fine

Field for Hunters and Sportsmen,

Deer, bear and elk abounding in the low hills and adjacent mountains; while trout of wonderful size are plentiful in the river and brooks. Ducks and geese, also, congregate on the little lakes and bayous by thousands; so that, take it altogether, the palate of the most fastidious can be fully gratified in the Bitter Root country.

Stopping a short time at the house of the Hon. W. E. Bass, I took a glance at his farm. It is one among the best in the Territory. His extensive fields had yielded enormous crops, and his system of farming gives his place the appearance of a well-regulated homestead in much older communities. The location is excellent, with all the conveniences one could wish for in any country. From there I turned in the direction of the river, over a mile away. On the road down, I saw, for the first time in my life,

Indian Women Threshing.

They lay their sheaves on a large cloth, and then with a pole a dozen feet in length, pelt out the grain. Each one of these noble women, of whom there were a number in the field, had taken a shock apiece and were laying on with a vim that was a caution to Woman's Rights. (Their "old men" and boys were at the same time engaged in the laborious task of inveigling fish from the river near by.) This style of threshing is but little below that of the old flatl, the thump, thump of which from morning till night, many of us can remember hearing in our childhood days. The operation appeared more striking, perhaps, to me, for the reason that I had seen the steam thresher at the lower end of the valley, which devours whole stacks without stopping to breathe. Nearer the river I saw the thing

As It Should Be.

An Indian splitting a big stump into slivers and extracting from thence grubs for fish bait. He had secured a handful of these and laid them on a piece of bark, while his wife, quite a pretty woman, with a bright eyed little girl at her side, sat by and watched the bait that it might not crawl away. They seemed very much interested in the operation, and no doubt were thinking what a nice string of trout those worms would bring home. The lesson taught is, that it is the man's duty to gather together the goods of this world, and the woman's to watch over them and see that by mismanagement or oversight they do not get away. This Indian, I might add, raised good crops and had his threshing done by the machine.

The Bitter Root this time of the year can be forded almost anywhere, the water being so clear there is no danger of getting into bad places, as in the Hell Gate. On the bank of the river, near the Stevensville crossing, in a quiet little home, lives

Æneas, the Iroquois,

Of whom I may have something to say in another letter, for I look upon him as one of the greatest men in humble life the West has ever seen, and his history is full of interest; yet

> "The world o'erlooks him in her busy search
> Of objects, more illustrious in her view
> And, occupied as earnestly as she.
> Though more sublimely, he o'erlooks the world."

A mile from the river brought me to

Fort Owen,

The quaint old walls and battlements of which, even now in a good state of preservation, contrast strangely with the style of architecture adopted by the settlers of these latter days. There is scarcely a spot or place in the whole Northwest so historically interesting as this, and which, when we come to consider the associations that surround it, might well be called

Sacred Ground.

Its loop-holes ranging in every direction, its massive gates and bullet-proof turrets, tell plainly it was not built for shelter from the rude elements alone, but to shield the occupants, and furnish a safe retreat for the few settlers, against the fierce attacks of the wily Blackfoot as well. These Indians, so far back as any knowledge of them is had, have made the Ritter [sic] Root Valley their particular foraging grounds, driving off stock and murdering residents when the least opportunity afforded. Maj. John Owen, under whose supervision the Fort was erected, and who has made there his home for more than 20 years, has, on different occasions, been a great sufferer by these treacherous Blackfeet. At one time they ran off 100 head of horses and mules he had imported at great expense, and killed a very worthy young man in his employ, named Dobson [John F. Dodson]. These savages were so bent on stealing horses they would crawl to the corral at night and attempt to undermine the walls to get at the stock.

Fort Owen is thoroughly identified with the settlement of the Northwest; it has been owned each by Oregon, Washington, Idaho and Montana; within its walls the lamented Gov. Issac I. Stevens issued his first proclamation as Governor of Oregon; it is hallowed by the blood of martyrs to savage ferocity, and made sacred by its many associations; its history connects the dark and bloody past with the bright future, and when truthfully written will furnish a most interesting and instructive leaf in the records of the great Northwest.

                                                                            Calcium.

Document 72

Stealing Crow Horses

ca. 1872

Source: Excerpt from "Kutenai Notes," Claude Schaeffer Papers, Glenbow Archives, Calgary, Alberta, folder 161.

Editors' note: This war story was related to anthropologist Claude Schaeffer in 1934 by Felix Barnaby. Some periods have been added to the text.

A party of three raiders. — Charlot was chief of the Salish, who were returning from the Spring hunt. They were Peter Sinátsi, Peter łcikákiepi and Isaac. Peter S was the leader. This occurred before 1875.

They were headed for the Crow Indians along the Big-Horn river. They were mounted and traveled three ~~or four~~ days. In the evening they looked around from the top of a hill and saw a small creek. There was a lone tipi there; There were some horses around it. They rode towards it and thought they would be near it by nightfall. When they came up they saw it was a large tipi, with about 30 horses grazing around it. They were glad to see this, as they thought they would get away with all the horses.

Before dark the horses were gathered up and picketed close to the tipi. The party remained close for awhile and then advanced to drive off the herd. Peter S went ahead and his companions remained near. Those horses picketed were tied by the ankle and he cut the ropes with his knife and drove all the horses off. Peter S moccasins were badly ripped and he returned to the tipi to get a pair for himself. (It was the custom in sleeping to throw the moccasins towards the entrance.) He found a pair that fit inside the tipi and he then left. As he went outside, he struck the tipi with his whip, to count coup, and yelled "Wake up, wake up. You have no more horses." He returned to his pardners [sic]. (He thought the Crow had no more horses and that they would never be overtaken.) They rode off with the horses, taking their time and not hurrying. Daylight soon came and they travelled on. Later in the morning, one of them looked back and saw that a party of about 30 Crows were pursuing them. They jumped off their horses and let them go and by that time they were surrounded by the Crow. Both started shooting at each other. Peter S charged at them and they retreated a ways. Isaac ran off Some distance and waited there. The two then killed one of the Crows, one of the best warriors. The Salish couldn't count coup as there were too many Crows. The latter picked up their dead and carried it away and left about 10 Crow left. Isaac kept running away from them, waiting for a chance to escape. Peter S was a fast runner but his companion wasn't and he didn't want to leave him, as the latter had fought well. They kept up a running fair and Peter S would occasionly [sic] charge the Crow. They finally came to a cut in the ground and his companion was ~~shot dead~~ here wounded here.

Peter S first thought that his partner was killed and he ran off for a long ways but then he thought that he should be able to tell the tribe where his companion was wounded, so he ran back. The Crows were beginning to come up to the body but retreated as he came up. Peter S chased off the Crows and then hollered at his partner "Where is your wound?" His partner replied "I'm not wounded at all but only had cramps in my leg." Peter S helped him to his feet and they ran off together. The Crows chased them for some distance and then rode off.

Isaac waited for them and they looked back to see the Crows weeping over their dead comrade and the Salish began their song of victory. The next year after this the Salish and the Crow made peace with each other. The Crows then inquired the names of the three raiders and were told that Peter S was there and they gave him the name of Crazy-Bear, because he fought so recklessly. They told the Salish that one in the tipi was sick at the time but that the main camp was only (4 miles) a short distance off. After Peter S struck the tipi one of them ran off to the main camp with the news.

The person who was cowardly, as Isaac was, was taunted and laughed at, to his face, thereafter.

Document 73

Two Leggings, Crow Warrior, Battles the Flatheads
ca. 1872

Source: Two Leggings, *Two Leggings: The Making of a Crow Warrior*, ed. Peter Nabokov (Lincoln: University of Nebraska Press, 1967, 1982), pages 89-93.

Editors' note: There is no dating in the manuscript, but Two Leggings was born about 1847 and he would have been about 25 in 1872. The account reinforces the conclusion that intertribal warfare in the nineteenth century involved continuous vigilance and significant injury and death.

[A Battle with the Flatheads near the Little Rockies]
by Two Leggings, Crow Warrior

I planned to stay in camp for the rest of that summer and not take any more chances. Our village moved from place to place until it was decided to visit the Black Lodges at the foot of Three Mountain in the Little Rockies along Big River.

We had a happy time there. Game was plentiful and enemies seemed to be staying away. War parties would occasionally return and this gave us more reason for dancing and feasting. Our two camps together held several hundred tipis and we had to hunt continually for food. We were here for nearly a moon when scouts reported a large herd nearby to the north. I needed fresh meat and the following afternoon rode my buffalo horse slowly out of camp, leading a pack horse. Usually I rode the pack horse to rest my buffalo runner, but I did not think I would be going far.

No enemies had recently been sighted, but I was accustomed to being careful. Before each ridge I dismounted and crawled to the edge to cover the country with my telescope.

Riding into the valley where the herd had been reported, I found nothing. I decided that if I did not see any game from a high hill a little to the north I would return to camp. It was hot and all the dancing and eating of the last days had made me sleepy. Tying my horse to a tree, I lay in the shade and watched the sun set. For a time I forgot what I was doing.

Before me the country was very broken; beyond lay a large meadow and then came more broken country. As I looked over those ridges and coulees I saw something which made my laziness go away. A buffalo herd was running out of the broadest coulee. Looking through my telescope, I knew no wolf pack could chase that many. Soon about six men appeared behind, and from their riding style and headgear I could tell they were Flatheads who had crossed the mountains.

I rode into camp as night fell. I should have informed the chief right away, but we had nothing to fear from a few Flatheads who would have left immediately if they discovered our tipis. I wanted to be the first to surprise them, and told only Young Mountain.

When we set out at sunrise I was on a roan, a good long-distance runner, and Young Mountain was riding a buckskin, also long-winded and fast. Young Beaver stopped us at the edge of camp, calling me brother and saying that I had a better horse. He asked me to kill him a nice cow and promised me the fat.

Young Beaver tried hard to provide for his father and mother but his buffalo horse had just been stolen by enemies. I liked him and his people, and they were my relatives. I told Young Mountain we would hunt before looking for the Flatheads.

We three started north, where Young Beaver had been told to find buffalo. I was sure these were the animals the Flatheads had been chasing. On the way we passed a few Crow hunters already butchering their kills. When we reached a ridge I dismounted to look over the edge. Two Flatheads were chasing buffalo. I ran back to the horses and told Young Beaver to warn our hunters and also to alert the camp. I said I was going to try and kill one and might be out all night.

Young Mountain and I tied our horses and hid behind sage and rocks along the ridge. While I looked through my telescope he watched the two men below. I could not find the other Flatheads but was sure their camp was nearby. Young Mountain pulled my arm, the two Flatheads were chasing a few stray buffalo in our direction.

I looked back but Young Beaver with help was not to be seen. Then I noticed someone skinning buffalo south of us. We galloped over, recognizing Hunts The Enemy and his long-legged sorrel horse stolen from Flatheads. I said that if we killed those two the women could dance the scalp dance for us and we could tell our children about this coup. But I said that if we were killed it would be a good death, for the Great Above Person was looking down to watch our bravery.

Meanwhile Medicine Bear had ridden up on a pinto mare and told me that two more men were just over the ridge. When we called to them Small Heart appeared on a buckskin and White From the Waist Up on a big bay.

Returning to the hill we now saw four Flatheads on the other side. I was glad to have collected more men. Then several more Flatheads appeared around a pine grove on a faraway hilltop. We also noticed that the four below were not the men Young Mountain and I had first seen. Those two had wounded a bull, now charging them as they rode in circles. They could have easily seen us but were too busy. We drew back and Hunts The Enemy and I dismounted, handing our horses to our friends. Crawling to the edge again, we saw the two hunters about a rifle-shot away. Hunts The Enemy said that everything dies sometime and that we should think about what we could tell our children and grandchildren if we scalped these men.

We all rode around the hill and into a deep ravine between the hunters and their pack horses. As Hunts The Enemy and I watched from the rim the others waited below. Finally killing the bull, the Flatheads came for their pack horses, one on a white horse and the other on a bay, both men about my age but larger than most Flatheads. They wore breechcloths and held guns. Bows and arrows hung on their backs, but they carried no medicines.

As soon as we crawled back all of us galloped out of the ravine. The Flatheads reined in so hard one horse almost fell backward. Its rider slid off and called for the other man, who was racing down the meadow to his friends.

When the man on the ground fired I tried to pull up, but my horse kept running. I felt a pain in my left shoulder and thought I was dying. As soon as possible I dismounted and he ran up, in signs calling us women.

He was brave but I did not notice that. Blood soaked through the light-colored shirt I had bought from the trader at the mouth of Plum Creek. At first I thought it came from my mouth. When I moved, my left arm hurt badly. I made signs to the Flathead that he was a woman and that I would kill him before I died.

When he saw me back on my horse he caught his again and I grew afraid. I do not know why I felt that way, but I rode back to the ravine. Just as I discovered my friends were gone after the other Flathead, a bullet missed my head. I turned and we began riding around in circles, hanging to the outside and shooting over or just below our horses' necks. Then I heard yelling and was glad to see Bear Looks and Hunts The Enemy. But it also made me want to earn this coup alone. I reined in and shot from behind my horse. The Flathead also dismounted, keeping up his fire as he walked with his horse in front of him. When I killed it he laid down, shooting from behind the carcass. As I started to ride around him I did not notice that Bear Looks was beside me until he fell from his horse, shot through the spine. Then I raced straight at the Flathead, but I was out of breath and my horse threw its head into my gun as I fired. Before the animal dropped I jumped off. The Flathead tried to grab my gun but I shot his left hand. He tried again and I shot him in the right side. Dropping his gun he rushed at me with a knife. I jumped away and he fell on the ground.

I shot my last bullet, but was so excited I hit his left hand again. I picked up his knife and gun, grabbed his long hair, and was about the scalp him when Hunts The Enemy asked me to help lift Bear Looks onto his horse. Then he stopped wailing over the body and pointed north. More Flatheads were heading toward us. I let the head fall back but told myself I would return. By the time we had Bear Looks' body tied to the horse we had to leave.

My horse was dead and Hunts The Enemy's had run to camp. As we reached a rise we saw Flatheads grouped around the man on the ground. I felt faint from loss of blood, but would kill some of them before I died. I told Hunts The Enemy to give me his gun and cartridges and go on with the body.

The Flatheads were pointing at me and I could find no hiding place so I tried to walk up the hill. Before reaching the top I saw someone on a horse. I held my gun but it was White From The Waist Up. As we rode double over the top I turned to see the Flatheads catching up.

I told White From The Waist Up that if they got too close we should dismount and fight. Then he pointed out Young Beaver riding with men from camp. We all started shooting as the Flatheads rode over the hill. When they spun around to escape, our men raced close behind and White From The Waist Up left me. Feeling weak and in pain, I started walking back to camp.

Men riding home stopped to tell me that the news had passed I was dead. They were glad to see me alive and wanted to see my wound. I rode double into camp. As I passed Bear Looks' tipi I heard his relatives crying. They buried his body in the brakes [sic] along Big River.

The chiefs decided to move camp early the next morning. All night we heard men riding in and singing victory songs. I felt glad because it meant they had been successful without losing any more men. Hunts The Enemy visited me and said they had revenged Bear Looks, returning with three scalps. When I fell asleep I dreamt of a scalp dance in which I was the chief.

(Many years later when we were friends I visited the Flatheads. That man told me that when he was on the ground he felt me lift his head by the hair, unable to move. He had waited for my knife and could not understand what had happened. But he was never able to use his left hand.)

Document 74

Negotiations with the Bitterroot Salish

April 24, 1873

Source: D. Shanahan, U.S. Ind. Agent, to Commissioner of Indian Affairs, Apr. 24, 1873, U.S. Office of Indian Affairs, Records of the Montana Superintendency of Indian Affairs, 1867-1873, National Archives Microfilm M833, reel 2, fr. 305-310.

Editors' note: Shanahan describes his interactions with Charlo and the Bitter Root Salish in some detail, but, of course, his account represents his viewpoint of what happened.

Flathead Indian Agency M.T.
April 24th 1873

Hon. Commiss'r of Indian Affairs
Washington DC
Sir

I have the honor to report that on the 16th inst I left this Agency for the Bitter Root Valley agreeable to instructions from Supt [James] Wright. I arrived at Stevensville on the 10th [19th?] and soon after visited Charlos Head Cheif [sic] of the Flathead tribe accompanied by Rev Father [Jerome] D'Aste and my Interpreter. Charlos received us very Kindly and after exchanging compliments I read and had interpreted to him your telegram sent to supt Wright also a letter from the Supt which I enclose herewith. But Charlos was unmoved and said he only could reafirm what he had already said to all the Agents and commissioners who had spoken to him about the matter. I then asked him if he would call his people together and I would have a talk with all, he said he could not call his people from their work, but said I had better wait until sunday when they would all be at church and he would then call them together and have a council. When leaving Charlos house on this occasion he rose and gave me his hand, and said he would be my friend, and he would leave the other members of the tribe to decide for themselves and he would not interfere with me in any effort that I might make toward the removal of the tribe. Here he again gave me his hand and said in a dignified manner if you use force to remove me you will not make me afraid, for I know no fear, but use what force you may I will suffer, I wont move, but no matter what you may do, I will never raise my hand against a white man. After my interview with Charlos I returned to the residence of the missionaries and in a short time there were three Indians called on me to settle cases of long standing between themselves and whites, two cases I settled without much trouble, but the third case being one of five years standing, I was unable to settle it. In this case I travelled about sixty miles of the valley and found so many conflicting statements that I concluded to abandon it, the Indian being satisfied that it would be impossible to bring it to a successful settlement. During my time in the valley I visited most of their lodges and houses and talked as much as possible with the white men of the valley, and notwithstanding the desire of the white settlers to have troops brought into the country they don't seem to be over anxious for those Indians to leave the valley, nor were they able to state more than one case in which an Indian had committed any offense against a white man, and this case is the shooting of a cow by an Indian who received One hundred and fifty lashes for the Offence by order of the cheif [sic]. On sunday the 20th gave them a feast of which over four hundred of all ages partook, about this time they all felt in good humour. I then had a council in which all the men took part. They made many complaints such as not getting what was promised them in the Stevens treaty, and said they have been promised much but got little. They dwelt much on the eleventh article of the treaty which they seemed to think guaranteed them a right to the Bitter Root Valley. This I fully explained to them and besides explaining it through my own interpreter Rev Father D'Aste did so in such an effectual manner that they were all convinced of the true meaning. They then dwelt on the promises made by Gen'l [James] Garfield and said that the houses promised to be built were not built, and they asked if they would get what Garfield promised. I told them that everything promised by Gen. Garfield they would be sure to get and as an evidence of the good faith of the Government they could see that in a very short time the seven who had selected their locations would have their houses finished, and as they have not been finished as soon as expected I would give to each family that would remove immediately five acres of land already under crop, and in addition to those seven, I could give the same to twenty more families and build their houses whenever they select their locations in the Jocko. They object to the limited amount of agricultural land in the Jocko and said they have now fifty two farms in the Bitter Root all under seed, mostly wheat, and they asked if they would be compelled to abandon their Crops and houses without any compensation. I then said that the Great Father did not wish to compel them to move, but he asked them to move in order that he may better protect them from the intrusions of the whites. I showed them in the plainest and most forcible manner I could, the good intentions of the President and the injury it would be to them to longer remain in the Bitter Root Valley. They having advanced sufficient reasons why they could not remove immediately, such as the impracticability of crossing the Bitter Root and Missoula rivers as well as abandoning their crop I deemed it advisable to tell them that in consideration of those facts such as wanted to remove had better visit the Jocko and select their locations and at the time they would have their crops in, the waters in the rivers and streams would be low and most of their houses would be ready for occupancy, and after some consideration fourteen families expressed a desire to come and three of them requested me to select locations for them and said they would be satisfied with such locations as I may select, two others desired the Interpreter to select for them and on monday morning Arley "and Adolf" 2d & 3rd Cheifs [sic] told me that they had other names and in a few days they would give the names of fourteen or fifteen other families that would come to the Jocko, and these Cheifs [sic] say that as soon as the tribe is thus divided the balance will remove before winter without any trouble, and such is the opinion of the catholic Priests to whom I am indebted for so much success for it was through them I have succeeded in gaining the confidence of the Indians and with their co-operation I have no doubt the removal of most if not all the Indians of this tribe before the next winter without any trouble, provided they get what has been promised them, and there being no cause for their immediate removal and in view of the circumstances I think it would be impracticable and impolitic to force them to remove immediately. I have asked if there were any who wished to become citizens, but there was not one who expressed any such desire or intention. They all want to live as Indians. They also spoke much about their religion and said they wanted a catholic church and school and black gowns (meaning Priests) to instruct them. I told them the great Father would give them those things as it is his desire to see them have all the advantages of their religion and always remain under the good influences of their spiritual Fathers the black gowns. I would therefore ask that means be provided for the erection of such buildings immediately as there is nothing could be more conducive to the good of these people.

Very respectfully
Your obt servt
D. Shanahan
U.S. Ind. Agent.

Document 75

A Battle with the Crows on the Dearborn

July 16, 1873

Source: "Dog Eat Dog!" *The Helena Daily Herald*, July 16, 1873, page 3, col. 1.

Editors' note: *The Helena Weekly Herald* on July 24, 1873, page 8, col. 1, corrected the number of dead Pend d'Oreilles in the battle to six. The buffalo hunt was wonderfully productive for the Pend d'Oreilles, but it was also very dangerous. The author's bigotry shows in the writing, but a bloody battle probably did occur.

Dog Eat Dog!
Fight Between the Mountain Crows and Pen d'Oreilles.
Numerous Dead Savages the Result.

A deadly hostility has existed between the Mountain Crow Indians and the Pen d'Oreilles, from the West Side, dating back into the generations gone by; and it is said that neither tribe ever lets and opportunity go by for a fight, skirmish, or horse-steal when they come within reach of each other.

A few weeks ago a party of the Pen d'Oreilles passed through Helena on their way out for a summer's hunt. They were bound for their usual hunting ground, the Judith Basin. Last week another, and quite a large party came up from below by way of the Big Blackfoot and started out on the prairie between the Dearborn and Sun rivers. In some mysterious manner they had come into possession of a supply of whiskey, and many of them were intoxicated, and consequently happy and brave. This was about the 10 inst., the date of their going out of the mountains. On the 13th they returned, in rather a sorry plight, indeed. On one of the intervening days (which one we are unable to learn) they had had a severe fight with a band of warriors from the Mountain Crows, and had come out second best. It appears that the Pen d'Oreilles were in camp on the Dearborn, with their tepees in a circle. Just after daylight in the morning they were attacked by the Crows, who were evidently bent on a grand horse-steal. At first the fighting was hand to hand, and, making due allowance for exageration [sic], for a time it must have been a desperate affair. Frontiersmen, who have witnessed and participated in Indian warfare and battles, can draw a vivid picture to their mind of the exciting scene — bucks fiercely whooping, s....s and children yelling, (and *such* yelling!) the rapid firing of the carbine and pistol, the barking of a multitude of dogs, and the running hither and thither of the Indian ponies — all conspire to make an unutterable chaos of sounds and figures that once seen can never be forgotten. The fighting after a time was reduced to skirmishing, which was kept up until noon. At this time, thinking discretion the better part of valor, the Pen d'Oreilles, putting their wounded bucks and s....s upon ponies, retreated to the mountains. The ride of the Pen d'Oreilles down the Blackfoot was quite in contrast with the happy hunting band that came up only a few days before, and it could hardly be recognized as the same party. The loss of the Pen d'Oreilles foots up as follows: Sixty [i.e., Six] killed, a number wounded, and one hundred horses killed and stolen. The Crows lost four killed.

We are indebted to Wm. Dilts, a resident of the Big Blackfoot, for the above facts.

Document 76

Cultural Friction Over "Stolen" Clothing

October 22, 1873

Source: "Search Among the Indians for Stolen Clothing," *Weekly Rocky Mountain Gazette* (Helena, Mont.) Oct. 22, 1873, page 3, col. 2-3.

Editors' note: The encounter described in this article emphasized the potential for misunderstanding and friction between white men who threw away valuable clothing and other items and Indians who rummaged through the trash cans for useful items. The Pend d'Oreille women showed the sheriff the rags and other items they had gathered while in Helena, but none of the valuable "stolen" items were found.

Search Among the Indians for Stolen Clothing.

Last week a large hunting party of Pen d'Oreilles encamped a few miles outside of town, being on their way to the Marias on their annual buffalo hunt. The hunters were accompanied by their old chief "Canoe," now in his ninetieth year, and still a hale and hearty old man, but no longer, the robust and athletic chief, as described in the reports of Governor Stephens [Isaac Stevens] as he appeared twenty years ago, when he saved that officer and his command from destruction by hostile Indians while making surveys through our country, long before a white man was known upon the spot where now stands the metropolis of our Territory. It appears that several robberies of clothing were made from premises during the encampment of "Canoe" and his band, and on Sunday Deputy Sheriff English and others armed with a search warrant, went to the Indian encampment to make a search, and through an interpreter announced their business. Old Canoe seemed much grieved to think that his hunters and their s....s should be guilty of trespassing upon the whites in any way, and announced his intention of finding the property if in camp. The old chief then stepped to the door of his wigwam and commenced calling aloud, something in the style of Travis when he wishes to draw a crowd to auction off a horse, and the Indians, s....s and pappooses gathered around him. After speaking to the crowd of Indians for a few minutes they all repaired to their tents and the s....s rolled out all the old rags and stuff gathered around the town since their encampment, but the officers failed to find the stolen articles for which they were in search.

Document 77

Arlee Asks for More Money from the Government
October 18, 1873

Source: "From Jocko Agency," *The New North-West* (Deer Lodge, Mont.), Nov. 1, 1873, page 3, col. 6.

Editors' note: This letter was written by Charles Schafft, the longtime Flathead Agency clerk in the 1870s. Arlee asked for an extension of the support payments under the 1872 agreement with Congressman James Garfield.

From Jocko Agency.
"Arley Makes a Speech."

Editor New North-West. —

The following address was made by Arley, second chief of the Flatheads, to Agent [Daniel] Shanahan, Oct. 18, 1873, and is placed on the official records. Arley and sixteen families of the Flatheads have elected to reside on the reservation, and the address will show Arley's feelings on the removal question.

Arley's Address:

"I left my place (in the Bitter Root valley) to come here, and stop here. I shook hands with you, and think you are glad to see me here. I do not know if the President likes it that [I] came here to stop on the Reservation. All the white people have a chief, and when he talks to them they are glad. I listened to the President, and came here to stop. It is for that I ask if he is glad. I am going to talk to the President. Last year I came here to have a talk with General [James] Garfield. He told me, 'You will get pay for your land ten years, then it will stop.' I said it was too short a time, and he told me, 'I can't tell you now, but when I go to Washington I will tell the President what you said, and I think he will give you more, perhaps for twenty years.' Since that I have not heard news.

"I am here to stop and now I speak. I ask to have five more years in addition to the ten promised: you all know what I said last year; it is on paper. I did not want the railroad to pass here. In the spring you will commence to give me my money promised last year. As the Flatheads come here I want the President to help me for three years — because the people are poor and have nothing to eat. I want him to listen to me, and what I say, and I will be glad. If this letter goes to the President he will be glad that I have come to stop here. I want you to tell the President to write a letter to my people, and I will give it to the Priest and he will tell them to come here, because many white men are in the Bitter Root Valley who told my people not to go to the Reservation, that we would be poor there and starve. I think they will believe the Priest, and he will tell the truth. If the letter comes to this office, I will take it to the Priest in the Bitter Root valley."

Yours truly,
K.

Flathead Agency, Oct. 28, '73.

Salish Chief Arlee
Peter Ronan, *Historical Sketch of the Flathead-Indians from the Year 1813 to 1890* (Helena, Montana: Journal Publishing Co., 1890), page 78.

Document 78

Theft and Murder by the Crow Indians

December 29, 1873

Source: Charles Schafft to Daniel Shanahan, Dec. 29, 1873, U.S. Office of Indian Affairs, "Letters Received by the Office of Indian Affairs, 1824-1880," National Archives Microfilm Publication M234, reel 500, fr. 268-272.

Editors' note: In December 1873 Flathead Agent Shanahan was in Washington, D.C. and Dr. Wright was the Montana Superintendent of Indian Affairs in Helena. The statements from Chiefs Michelle and Arlee illustrate just how complicated and dangerous intertribal war was on the plains in the early 1870s. Schafft was the Flathead Agency clerk. The punctuation in the original letter was hard to read, but is rendered here as accurately as possible.

Flathead Indian Agency
December 29, 1873

Major Daniel Shanahan
Dear Sir:

The enclosed letter from the Commissioner was received here on the 27th minus the enclosure from James Wright Esqr mentioned therein. I immediately mentioned the subject to the Chiefs and gave till to-day for an answer. Accordingly Arlee and Michelle came here at the appointed time and also were present Baptiste Robwain, Frank Robwain and Dandy Jim Louis as Interpreters. Having again read the Commissioner's letter to them, Michelle expressed himself as follows:

"We will not give up any horses to the Crows — the Crows are sorry because we steal their horses and we are sorry that they kill our people — they killed four of our people last summer — among them a chief named Cow-ackan my father-in-law — Last Spring they killed two of my people and wounded three women and a boy — one of the women is now lying before your door and will die" (Penama the woman who was shot through the hip) "Last fall a year ago the Crows stole 31 horses and a Jack-ass from my people while hunting on the little Blackfoot. We made peace with the Snakes once and the Crows came and stole 80 horses from us, that was 10 years ago — the Crows told us it was the Snakes and we made war on them but we found that the Crows were the thieves and they have been our enemies since that time and we made peace again with the Snakes and are at peace with them now. What our people have stolen from the Crows since last winter we will Keep — but after to-day when my people steal horses from the Crows or other I will have them returned and I want the Crows to do the same. When we go to the Crow country we always go in peace but the Crows always attack us first. I don't Know of any white man's horses but if you will get a description I will look around and see if they are here. That is all I have to say."

Arlee then said: (after having read enclosed description sent here by Dr Wright last fall and the only description of stolen stock from the Crow Country on file here) (as far as Dr Wright is concerned):

"I know about those white men's horses you have described they are with my people of the Bitter Root Valley.

"Kul-Kul-tui has the stallion.

"Charl Quall-che-nee has the brown mare and colt.

"Francois has the blue horse and the other brown mare was left behind on the way given out — the blue horse is now in the Bitter Root Valley and I will go and get it when the weather is more warm." (He is suffering with a bad cold just now) "The other two are with the people on the buffalo hunt but when they return with them I will get them also and deliver them to you — there is not a horse belonging to the Crows in the Flathead village — If my people stole any horses from them we have them no longer and cannot return them but if my people steal from them after to-day I will have them returned. I mean what I say. We have tried to be friendly with the Crows for a long time but whenever we make peace they are the first to break it.

"The first Flathead they Killed was an old man named 'One Night' while peaceably trapping near Heart mountain.

"Then they killed 2 of our people last spring — they went to the Crow village to eat and smoke. the Crows shook hands with them and then they killed them. one of them was the brother of 'Nine Pipes' and the other was Pascal the son of a chief. After these two were Killed we still were friendly to the Crows and we hunted together. When we were together we missed some of our horses and thought the Crows had stolen them but we found them in the Pend d'Oreille camp. Then we all camped at the Crow Agency and were happy. Then we moved camp and stopped about 8 miles from the Crow Agency. Here we saw some Blackfoot tracks in the snow and we sent a messenger to the Agency to warn the Crows to tie up their horses. The messenger went to the chiefs lodge but was told the Chief was with the Agent and he went to the house of the Interpreter and there they Killed him and threw his body into a well right at the Agency — that was last Spring and the messenger's name was

Chawl-paw-paw-tcheel. A young man who had accompanied the messenger"
(Baptiste Marengo's Cousin) "saved his life by the fastness of his horse but he
was shot in many places. The Crows said that the Flatheads had stolen their
horses the night previous, which we denied but the Crows said they had found
a hat belonging to a Flathead — but those horses were stolen by the Blackfeet
and they Killed this man for nothing. One of the white men working at the
Agency pulled his body out of the well.

"When I was over here my people stole those white men's horses while I
was gone. When I returned they were going to war and said they would Kill the
Crows wherever they would meet them. I said of course your hearts are sorry
because they killed our people.

"Now I will say something to the great chief:

"The Crows and Blackfeet have the best of us because the government gives
them good guns and plenty ammunition. I don't know what to make of it. Is
it because we have never spilled the blood of a white man that we do not get
guns from the great father also. The other Indians kill our people and they Kill
the whites and they get guns and ammunition and plenty of everything. I can't
understand it."

I asked him if he would consent to meet the Crow chiefs and try to make
some peaceable arrangements but he said, "No we have tried that too often.
The Crows will always break the peace."

I send you the remarks of the chiefs in full. what they said is true as you
know well yourself — and you have already done all you could do while
you were here and for reference I enclose you also copy of a letter you wrote
Dr Wright on the subject in October. I am satisfied that I can get back any
white man's horses now among them if I had a description of them but the
Commissioner did not enclose Dr Wright's letter referred to and I will have to
write the latter for information. When Arlee gets ready to go to Bitter Root I
will send an employ with him for that Blue horse according to his request. And
when here will notify Dr Wright of the fact. Whatever other horses there may
be I think are in the buffalo country.

Very Respectfully
Chas Schafft

Please call the Hon Commissioner's special attention to the matter and
have justice done to *our* Indians. it seems to be altogether a one sided question
with Dr. Wright.

The Flatheads who have located here will not go to the buffalo country
anymore — if promises made them are kept and if the government would
furnish them with a few good arms they would be to the Agency the same as
soldiers — these are certainly under the control of their chief Arlee — who

is worth half a dozen Charlots, and his salary as Head chief will be earned. Michelle should also have a few good carbines for his local police.

Document 79

A Novice Missionary Priest Among the Bitterroot Salish
April 11 and May 5, 1874

Source: Father Philip Rappagliosi, *Letters from the Rocky Mountain Indian Missions*, ed. Robert Bigart by permission of the University of Nebraska Press, Lincoln, copyright 2003 by the Board of Regents of the University of Nebraska, pages 31-40.

Editors' note: Father Rappagliosi described his dealings with the Salish soon after he arrived at St. Mary's Mission in the Bitterroot Valley. The Salish welcomed him as a teacher and a friend and included him in their memorial feasts and as a guest in their homes. These letters to his parents and neighbors in Italy were gathered into a book published in Rappagliosi's memory after he died on the Great Plains in 1878. Some footnotes have been omitted.

Piousness of the Catholic Indians at Easter
Stevensville, April 11, 1874

P. C.

Dearest Parents and relatives,

Almost all the Indians have come back from the buffalo hunt. Only ten lodges or families did not arrive in time for Easter, because with so much snow covering the country, their horses had suffered from hunger. But yesterday I heard that these families are closer and will soon arrive, and will go to confession like all the others. Oh, how nice the Easter holiday is among our Natives. When I say nice holiday, you shouldn't think a nice setup, many lights and what have you. In this regard we are very poor, but our poor wooden Church is adorned by the pious congregation of the Indians, by their faith and prayers. On Maundy Thursday family by family came to visit the pitiable Sepulcher and they prayed and sang. Of course their songs are the songs of Indians: it's not strictly speaking music: nevertheless, since the Fathers worked hard to teach them even singing, one can recognize amidst great shrieking this or that tune, this or that aria, but altered and counterfeited as they please. Nevertheless God is certainly fully satisfied with that. Then on Good Friday they came to the adoration of the Cross: one after the other approached the Cross laid out on a blanket on the floor to kiss it. In the evening they came to

Philip Rappagliosi, S.J.
P. Filippo Rappagliosi, *Memorie del P. Filippo Rappagliosi, D.C.D.G., Missionario Apostolico: Nelle Montagne Rocciose* (Rome: Bernardo Morini, 1879), frontpiece.

the sermon about the passion of Our Lord and they listened with feelings of faith and piety. The Indian who weeps so rarely is nevertheless moved to tears when he hears about the suffering of Our Lord. That very Good Friday I saw one leave the Church red-eyed and teary. At first I thought he was not well because, as I said, it's extremely rare to see a Native cry, and without thought I asked him, what happened to your eyes? Are you not well? And he answered: "Oh, blackrobe, I am not sick, but I cried in Church today because Our Lord died." On Easter Sunday a great number came to receive communion. I don't think there is one Indian who refuses to come to these highest sacraments especially during these more important feasts. The Church was full and some stood outside the door. While the Father was dressing for the Mass, one of the chiefs stood up and addressed the others in the following way: (I give you here his whole little speech in its entirety, and it's just as he said it, because I called him to my room, made him repeat it, and I wrote it down, and now I translate it verbatim into Italian for you.) "Men and women, you all went to confession and you all want to go to communion now. Will you perhaps again take up sins afterward? If you go to communion when you intend to sin again, that is a great sin, if you confessed when you intend to sin again, that's a great sin. I am finished." Then High Mass began. The Indians have learned (who would have believed it?) to sing the *Gloria*, the *Credo*, and all the rest and they sing it firmly: at least that was the intent of the Father who first taught them. The same with the *Regina coeli* during Easter time. In sum, much simplification, but much faith and piety. Of course that day they were all dressed up, that is those who had one had wrapped themselves in a new wool blanket, or else in the hide of a buffalo killed in the last hunt. Then red paint on their faces, only on the forehead, or only on the cheeks, or only on the chins, or all over the face, ears, and neck according to one's taste; and seashells, glass beads, shards, and brass or iron wire twisted around their braids, and necklaces of all colors and mirrors and Crucifixes and medals dangling on their chests, and all the rest which I will describe at greater leisure some other-time. In other words carnival wear for us, but for them the latest fashion.

This week I went to visit a few Indian huts either along the river or at the foot of the mountain, scattered at a distance of two or three miles from each other. Note, that there are only a few among the Natives who have frame houses, because they live wherever there is room to set up a few poles in a circle, tie them together at the top, and cover them with buffalo skins. This is their movable home. Nevertheless there are a few who have started to farm the land, and these have a fixed house, that is to say, a fixed one-room log structure. So I went to see them and to hang up in their houses a few nice icons of the Heart of Jesus and of Mary. I assure you that I returned home very happy that evening. They had received me with as much welcome as Indians can give. The little Indians were the first ones to see the Blackrobe approaching, and I saw them leave their games and go inside to tell the family, "Pilip, good day, Pilip." While I was inside someone would hold my horse or tie it to a tree, and not let me do it myself. Right away we talked, I asked if they had gone to confession, if they love Jesus and Mary, and if they shun sin; there is no need to wait for the right opportunity to talk about these things. The opportunity is always there, and you just have to talk to be understood.

Pilip (one said to me), a mile from here there is a girl who is not well and couldn't go to Church; go take her confession. In fact I found that poor girl and she did her confession. There I also found a blind old woman who had wanted to confess because she couldn't come to Church, not only because it's far away, but also because those houses are across the river which one has to cross on horseback. I led her to a tree, because the sick girl couldn't leave the one-room dwelling, and there I confessed the blind woman who stood up and thanked me profusely, shaking my hand as if I had given her back her eyesight. That's the faith of the Indians. In another house I said to a cripple, "How unfortunate you are, poor Michael," and he said, "Yes, indeed, but I shall not be unfortunate in Heaven." — Good lesson by a Catholic Indian.

I don't have to tell you how glad they were to receive those pictures. In general the Indians appreciate and love medals, Crucifixes, and rosaries because they are easier to keep, but those who have houses love the icons because they can hang them. They keep all these things like treasures. While I was in one house hanging those pictures an old woman took out a package and started to unwrap it: out came some rolled papers. What was it? A very old picture in pieces, as yellow as the wax of the Holy Week. These fragments of picture were wrapped around a stick of wood and the old woman said: "See, thirty snows ago (that is to say thirty winters, or thirty years ago) Father [Pierre] DeSmet gave this to me! and then she rolled everything up again and wrapped it like a treasure. . . .

I embrace you with all my heart.
All yours
Philip S.J., Apostolic Missionary.

＊ ＊ ＊ ＊ ＊ ＊ ＊

Way of Life Among the Indians and Good Deeds

Stevensville, May 5, 1874

P. C.

Dearest Parents and all relatives,

The thirtieth of April I received you dear letter of March 23. . . .

Dad asked me about the Baby Jesus. From my other letters you probably already know that it arrived in pieces. Now it's in the care of the Nuns of Missoula and we will see what becomes of it.

Now let's turn to our beverages. Our beverage is very simple, excellent, and it's always available. You already understand that I am speaking of fresh water which is really good in this region, and the trevi's water is no match. [The Trevi is a famous fountain in Rome.] For the Mass we get a little bit of wine from California; and since the purchase and shipping are so terribly expensive, we order only what we need, we use it only for the consecration during the Mass; for the two ablutions that follow, we have the permission to use just water; so the wine for the Mass lasts much longer. At meals one can have *Coffee* or *tea* if one wants to — We can get these two beverages more easily from the Whites who live nearby, they cost less and the Indians, too, often go sell deer and buffalo skins in order to get coffee, tea, and sugar from the whites. In almost the whole of North American this is the usual beverage for lunch and dinner: but many don't like hot drinks with their meals and therefore we turn to fresh and limpid water, which is a pleasure. As for food, we are much better off than I thought we would be; we have different kinds of meats, but mostly pork and beef. We have cows which give us good milk and hens which give us eggs when they are young, and broth when they are old. Then potatoes and carrots, much better than those from Belgium which are already big and good. We have good wheat, good flour, and good bread, made by a brother. In short, I came here prepared for the worst, and so this now seems a delight. And in fact I am in very good health and feel very strong. If God helps me I want to do some good to this good tribe, as well as to the other one, which is not yet good because not converted: I am talking about other tribes nearby. I forgot to tell you that when it comes to fish we are really the first lords of the world here. I have not seen such good and tasty fish anywhere else. The Indians often bring us some: if you saw how beautiful! You will never find the like in the fish-market. When you cross the river on horseback you can see them jump, as if to say: take me, take me. — The boys stand there with a hook and they eat them for lunch and for dinner. They come and ask us for fishhooks: we have obtained a good supply, a fishhook is a big present for the Indians.

The other day a boy said to me: "Give me a fishhook, blackrobe:" then in the evening he came back with a magnificent fish which we weighed, just out of curiosity. It was over seven pounds. And how did you manage to catch it with a hook, I asked him? He answered with a laugh that meant: The way we and others like us do it. . . .

Dad would like a new photo of me. But it's too soon, and you have one taken a few months ago: how different do you think I would be? And there is another reason why I won't send you one, there are no photographers around here. That's a good reason, I think. Maybe later we'll see if I can't let you have at least a drawing of my beloved Indians, or their true friend *Pilip*, and of our little wooden Church, etc. etc.

That's all as an answer to the letter of March 23. Now the news from here, but first the one who will read this letter to the others should take a break and have a drink to our health. For today, I'll rest my pen too. Until tomorrow.

May 6, 1874

P. C.

I continue my letter of yesterday, and first let me tell you that I am really happy because I am starting to speak the language of the Flatheads a little. Several times a week I go on my rounds on horseback to see them. I teach the Catechism with the youngsters who all know me and congregate by me. In Church, too, I do Catechism every day, morning and evening. With the Indians you can't get tired of repeating the same thing a thousand times. The Father Superior has already written to me that by July I should be ready to accompany him to the tribe of the Kalispels who also speak the same language. They are already baptized, but we go to give them a little mission, as we have done before with other tribes. Then if the Lord helps me I want to learn some other language.

There are many Native tribes and their languages are quite different. One is not related to the other. See, for example, how the Flathead say "Jesus, Joseph, and Mary, may my soul expire in peace with you [may I die in peace]":

They say:

Jesus Mary Joseph die with you in peace

Jesu, Mali, Zose, ilkamkemt, lanui ikaespopeulsem

my soul.

isingapeus.

The Kootenais instead say:

Jesus Mary Joseph die with you

Jesu Mali, Zosep machutsuan gamni ninkonissemil

in peace   my soul

kakannuckuaskommik kutuklululak.

The latter have some very long words. They call the *priesthood Jakaokualetiamkikam kokokolkatuumlat.*

Of course these are compound words and the one just cited, literally translated, doesn't mean Priesthood, but the *office of one who wears the black robe.*

The other day four Indians from the Nez Perce tribe came here, and they speak a third language which is as related to the others as Turkish is to Italian. They had come to be baptized. They were accompanied by another Nez Perce who is already baptized, knows the Catechism well, and also speaks the language of the Flatheads. With his help I now try to instruct the others. They'll come back tonight. In the meantime two Nez Perce women, Catholics, came running here. Oh, if you had seen their fervor: how they were trying to teach the others themselves! My room was full of Indians kneeling in front of an icon of Jesus on the cross and Holy Mary. Even those not baptized knelt down. I was moved to tears. I hope in two or three weeks they will be well instructed, and on their way to eternal salvation. In sum, we should learn at least six or seven Indian languages if we want to help everybody. With the help of God we will do as much as we can. Of course the good disposition of those Indians is of great encouragement to the Missionary, and you mustn't stop praying for me.

Last Saturday I was called to assist a dying woman; she was on the floor lying on a buffalo skin. The place was full of Indians who had come to pray. I felt real consolation seeing how the sick woman, until her last, gathering whatever strength she still had, lifted her arm and her hand touched her forehead, her chest, and her shoulders. [She crossed herself.] She was not able to speak anymore, but she did what she could, and with such faith that I stayed there watching her with admiration. Would you believe it? She died making the Christians' sign: her hand fell on her chest, and she was with our Lord just as I was giving her the last absolution. What do you think about that? Don't you bless our Lord? Aren't you happy about what you have done? For my part, I think that just one such single act is a great reward, and I'm sure you feel the same.

You should have heard the prayers the Indians were saying. One of the women said: "God, my Lord, have mercy on this dying woman. She is suffering now but soon she will be rejoicing with you, because she has confessed her sins. God, my Lord, have mercy on her; Mary, Mother of God, have mercy on her." She was silent for a moment, then she added: "Soon we might be lying like this, too, called by God. Lord, have mercy on us." — Then she received the act of contrition, and the others joined in, word after word. What a beautiful scene!

I thought that the Fathers had taught them these prayers, to be recited in such circumstances, and that was the custom. Then I learned, however, that it wasn't so, and that this Indian woman was just following her heart. One should know what these Indians were like forty years earlier to understand the sublimity of that prayer, and all the beauty of their faith.

I've done quite a few baptisms. May 1, the day of Saint Philip and Saint James, I gave one the name of Philip (Pilip). Usually they themselves propose names and it's better to give them the choice. Among these good Indians, I have found almost all the names you have.

(I interrupt again because the Nez Perces have come back to be instructed. We will continue later.)

Here I am again for you. I don't want to miss telling you about a custom that prevails among the Natives here, that is to give a feast for the whole tribe two or three days after one of their relatives has died. Two or three oxen are killed according to one's means, and on that day everybody is invited. I don't know where this custom comes from but I think that, while it was in use before the arrival of the Fathers, now it has taken on an almost religious character, I would say, the way it is practiced. A day when one of these Indian feasts was taking place, two or three of the tribe came to me and said: "Blackrobe, you, too, come and eat with us.["] I took advantage of the opportunity and the invitation to see how things were done. I remained very satisfied with it all. Imagine two or three lodges joined in the shape of a big tent or cabin formed by hide. The men were sitting on the ground in a circle under the tent and behind them were the boys. Behind were the women and the girls in a circle, and finally the dogs which formed a third circle far back, and they, too, were waiting for something, only a little hungrier than their masters. When I arrived the chief had me sit down on a buffalo hide. They were all in silence and the chief said: Come Blackrobe and see all your children. As customary the silence wasn't broken by any other voice: two or three stepped into the middle to cut into pieces the quarters of the ox which were already more or less cooked. During this ceremony which lasted a long time, two or three of the chiefs made their speeches. They eulogized the deceased. Then some of them took their blankets off their backs and, to honor me, spread them in front of me. They did the same with the chiefs. Then they took the pieces of meat and put them in little piles on the blankets. When I saw that everything was ready and all that was left was to reach for the food and eat, I said: Children, let us make the sign of the cross and pray. You shouldn't think that if I hadn't said anything the Indians wouldn't have done so. It doesn't happen that the Indians start to eat without saying a prayer. Then they laid hands on their work, still in silence. Only the chiefs could talk, standing up to make their speeches. For me it was a real pleasure to listen to them, they were saying beautiful things, and you know, they always do that, and they were not things said because I was there. One said: "Men and women, we grieve when someone dies, but find consolation thinking of Heaven, where we will all be called."

And another chief said, even more eloquently: "My people, you are now feasting because Susanna has died, but you don't know when the others will feast for you. Perhaps in a few days another ox will be butchered for the death of one of us. Maybe we will die at home, maybe hunting: we don't know. So forsake sin and prepare yourselves." Then at the end they gave the condolences to the relatives of the deceased, and after another prayer, the Chief lit the long pipe which was passed around to everyone. Custom requires everyone to take two or three puffs and pass it to his neighbor as a sign of friendship. Then before the crowd dispersed the Chief said in a loud voice: "We thank Blackrobe Pilip who came to us." And everybody replied approvingly, *a*, which means *yes*. I shook hands with the chiefs, said a few words of sympathy to the husband and children of Susanna, and came back. . . .

We have heard with great pleasure that another father (Father [Alexander] Diomedi} has requested to be assigned to these missions, and has already left Tronchiennes, they tell me, and is on his way. *Deo gratis*. [Thanks be to God.]

By the way I left out the best; do you know that the Indians ask me about you? An old man who belongs to the tribe of the Coeur d'Alenes (who speak the same language as the Flathead Indians), a few days ago asked me: "Blackrobe, is your father still alive? Is your mother alive? How many brothers do you have? Are they also *Blackrobes?*["] I wonder about all that solicitousness and warmth: finally when the old Indian deemed it the right moment, he added: I don't have any more tobacco for my pipe! I wouldn't have believed that the communication skills of an Indian could be so artful. I gave him the tobacco and asked him to pray for my father, my mother, siblings, and relatives. With all his heart he answered *a*.

I end with greetings for everyone, embracing each of you warmly. Many wishes to the fathers and brothers scattered everywhere etc. etc.

Goodbye, goodbye, goodbye,\
All yours\
Philip S.J., Apostolic Missionary.

Document 80

Complaints from Pend d'Oreille Chief Michel

May 2, 1874

Source: "Statement of Michel one of the chief the Flat Head nation," May 2, 1874, enclosure in T. J. De Mers, Frenchtown, to M. Maginnis, May 2, 1874, Martin Maginnis Papers, MC 50, box 1, folder 22, Montana Historical Society Archives, Helena.

Editors' note: The signatures to this statement were witnessed by a local Justice of the Peace, but the handwriting is that of T. J. DeMers, a Frenchtown merchant who was married to a Pend d'Oreille woman. DeMers also operated stores on the reservation. Agent Daniel Shanahan was involved in a conflict at this time with the priests at the mission over the treaty funding for a school on the reservation. Some of the complaints in the statement were probably from DeMers as well as Michel.

Statement of Michel one of the chief the Flat Head nation

On This 2nd day of May A.D. 1874 Michel one of the Chief of the Flat Head Nation, personally appeared before me, Al Pichette, a Justice of the Peace for Missoula County, Montana Territory, — and under oath made the following declaration. —

That him and his Tribe has been ill used by the United States Indian agent Major Daniel Shanahan present agent at the Flat Head agency on the Jocko Valley in Montana Territory. That the said Major D. Shanahan is trying to create a disturbance among his people by trying to have a part of the Indians on the reservation work against the other part. — so as to create disatisfaction — and that the said Major D. Shanahan is not giving them all of their annuity goods, — but Robbing them of a good part of their annuities. — and that he can prove that said Major D. Shanahan has already sold goods that was sent by government for the Indians, as annuities. —

And that by the Treaty made with the United States in the year 1855 that any white man who wishes to live among the Indians on the reservation, can do so providing the chief and the agent are willing to let them stay on said reservation. — And that according to that part of the Treaty. — he the said Michel one of the Chief of said Flat Head nation, and with the consent of the

U.S. agent he has given permission to Five (5) white men who are married to Idian [sic] woman and have famillies of Half breed children. — to locate and settle on the reservation and that they them white men have taken up farm and made improvements on the lands which are expensive, and never have been troubled by any body to leave the reservation. — and now this present United States agent has ordered them to leave the reservation, and has given them only 30 days. —

Now the said Michel, one of the Chief of the Flat Heads, and also his tribe do not want these white men removed, — that they have given them permission to settle and locate there and that they consider that they have a perfect right to allow a few white men if they Think it is to their interest to have them there to obtain knowledge of Civivilization. Said Michel says that him and his tribe do not wish to have any difficulty with the White men but wishes to remain friendly with them, — but that he said Michel feels it his duty to inform the government that unless there is a change in the present way of conducting affairs at this Flat Head Agency, — he really believes that there will be trouble before long and that he wishes to avoid it. — And that he does propose to the government the following changes to secure permanent peace and satisfaction among the Indians. —

1st. That an Inspector be sent immediately by the U.S. government to inquire into the management of affairs. —

2nd. the Removal of Major D. Shanahan.

3rd. That the choice of an agent for them be left to the Indians themselves and that they by Election or otherwise with the approval of the reverend fathers of the mission — shall name who shall be agent for them. —

Said Michel wishes further to state that Said Major D. Shanahan is trying to create disturbance between his people of the Reverend Fathers of the mission, — and that said Shanahan has stopt the pay of the Sisters for teaching schools to their orphans — and that at present they have no schools, no black smith, no tin smith, no gun smith, no hospital, no Farmers. — only one miller, and that according to treaty they are entitled to all these things. And said Chief Michel wishes the Peace commissioners or whoever are the proper authorities to take immidiate steps to settle the present state of affairs. and that he would be thankful if there was an answer send to him immidiately. — to know whether there will be anything done for them soon.

Address. — the answer, at French Town as he does not wish to trust the
Postal department at the Agency —
Michel Michel his x mark, one of the Chief of Flathead nation
Indian Chief of the Flat Head. —
French Town

Missoula Co
Montana

Subscribed & sworn before me this 2nd day of May A.D. 1874 — Al. Pichette
Witness to the above, Louis Brown
Ignace his x mark (Indians), witness of Ignace mark, T. J. De Mers
Thimothy his x mark (Indian).

Pend d'Oreille Chief Michelle
Drawing by Gustavus Sohon, NAA INV 08501400, National
Anthropological Archives, Smithsonian Institution, Washington, D.C.

Document 81

Chief Arlee Complains About Not Receiving the Garfield Agreement Payments November 1, 1874

Source: Alley Quill-quill-squa, Flathead Chief, to U. S. Grant, President of the U.S., Nov. 1, 1874, U.S. Office of Indian Affairs, "Letters Received by the Office of Indian Affairs, 1824-1880," National Archives Microfilm Publication M234, reel 500, fr.191-195.

Editors' note: This letter of complaint from Salish Chief Arlee was written by Duncan McDonald. McDonald was a mixed blood trader and businessman on the reservation, and there is no way to tell how much of the letter reflects his complaints rather than Chief Arlee's. Some periods have been added to the transcript to separate sentences.

Flathead Indian Agency
Nobr 1st 1874

U.S. Grant
President of the U.S.
Washington D.C.
Sir

I write you to let you know how this Department has been carrying on & how they are treating us. I want to Know where is the money that is coming to us in the treaty of 1872 with General [James] Garfield this is $5000.00 five thousand dollars that we ought to get yearly since Agt 27th 1872. we did not get a cent yet & we must have it. Further more Peter Whaley our new Agent is not fit to hold this office. he is lead by the Jesuite priests by the nose. Such Agent that is governed by priests we do not wish to have him around here whatever. The Priests has taken enough money say to the amount of $22000.00 twenty two thousand dollars for schooling from this agency. And where is our Students. we have not got one that can read or write. is it possible that we could not get one of our natives that could not read or write after the government spending $22000.00 twenty two thousand dollars. It is a shame for the priests & most of the Agent except Maj. [Daniel] Shanahan to use us in This manner after getting so much money from us. We could send 5 Indian boys to West point or other colleges five or six years ago & spend as much as the above amount. we could be have those boys by this time fit for the Senators but we have not one fit for any thing.

About Peter Whaley did you send him here as a prize fighter or for the Interests of the Indians. He wanted to whip one of my chiefs on account of our threashing machain. Whaley he wanted some of our employees to take the meachian to the Mission & threash for the priests & Michael one of my chiefs would not allow it. he wanted his Indians wheat threashed first. Now you can see that the Agent is working for priests & not for us. The priests & agent are a band of speculators.

We believe in the Holy Catholic Church but not in this firm that are around here.

I'll will State you another affair. we had a good man here that was honest & true man by the name of FK Daker an Engineer. he was discharged by Whaley because he was honest & hired a man that can cheat us & harm us & Steal. we would like to have your answer in this question if we the six Chiefs select a good man that we Know is honest if you will appoint as Agent. Then if he does not suit you you may turn him off. if your answer is yes we will send you his name. There is a boy 12 or 14 years old hired as a laborer getting $60.00 dollars pr month doing nothing only eating. his name is David Whaley son of the agent. 4 or more driving cattle for the agent & drawing governments money. those men ought to be working for us. What Kind of a government is this. No Doctor Interpreter No Miller no Wagon maker &c. I could post you more but it is to long a complaint if I was to tell you all. I wish to get the money for the Flatheads due for last two years.

This letter is written by a half blood. he is one of my own tribe a native of this Reservation.

I remain
Your Affct Svt
Alley x Quill-Quill-squa
Flathead Chief

pr Duncan McDonald

Address
Alley Quill-quill-squa
Care of Frank Daker
Flat Head Indian Agency
Montana Territory.

Document 82

Friendly Relations Between the Bitterroot Salish and One Settler Family 1874-1890

Source: Carrie May Warren, Reminiscences, MSS 269, Toole Archives, Mansfield Library, University of Montana, Missoula.

Editors' note: Warren's memories of relations between the Stevensville whites and the Bitterroot Salish include a reference to the 1877 Nez Perce War. The other memories would have been after 1874 when her family moved to Victor and before 1891 when the Salish left the Bitterroot. Warren described a relationship between the races that was friendly and respectful, even though the white settlers had only a limited understanding of Salish customs and values.

Flathead Indians & a few of their beleifes & custums

Some of us remember the time when a portion of victor town site was the camping grounds of this tribe.

the milky way is the Flatheads road to heaven. all good Indians go to this heaven. All Indians have a totem, a sacred animal which was selected for some quality which They admire. the bever was the totem of the flatheads, flatheads say that bevers used to be Indians but that They wer very bad & as punishment the Grate Spirit changed them into animals, but because they work so hard some day they will be made Indians again.

this tribe was allways friendly to the White People. some of can remember a kindly act of a flathead brave when we wer gatherd in fort Owan at the time of the nesperse out brake. one man a black smith in stevensville refused to leave His home & move into the fort.

the Nesperse camp being Just across the river west of stevensville. some of the Wariors wer in town every day.

this day some generous hearted white man had sold or given an Indian whiskey. When He was full of the fire watter He went on the war path. took it into His evil head to kill this mans wife. in this act of murder. a flathead man steped in betwean the woman & drunken Indian saying no killem white woman killem me. the white People surly owed that oald flathead man a lot, had that woman ben killed war would have started right then. one can easily guess what would have happened to the little hanfull of whit People in the vally at that time.

the flatheads wer very good neighbours attending to Their own buisness.

in those days People never thot of locking the doors of their chicken & smokehouses. what would be left inside unlocked doors these days? the Indians wer very fond of watter mellans but never would they go into the mellan patches untill after the fall frosts. then Mr Indian would go help Himself a plenty & I doant mean maby. one of their friendly custums wer on the new year day to go into the homes of the White People & shake hands with Them. that would mean weel be friends all year. I well remember one perticular new year day we wer living in Stevensville, all day the Indians had ben coming in shaking hands with father & mother then going on Their way. in the evening an oald fellow came in. He was quite a friend of fathers. this evening He had a few drinks of something stronger than watter. He came in went up to my fathe putting his arms around His neck & kept kissing Him & repeating my good friend my good friend, father dident seam to apresiate it yet He couldent resent it for fear of making the oald fellow angrey. so He Just sat & took all that loving without a murmer, we youngsters thot it a grate Joke on Dad to be kissed by a Buck Indian. those are days we like to think of many experiences we fondly remember as Children.

C. M. W.

Index